# AKEE TREE

**A Descendant's Search for his Ancestors
on the Eskridge Plantations**

# AKEE TREE

### A Descendant's Search for his Ancestors
### on the Eskridge Plantations

## Stephen Hanks

**PepperBird Books**
**Portland**

PepperBird Books
PO Box 8241
Portland, OR 97207

First printing February 2005
ISBN 0-976-58660-6

Printed in the United States of America.

Photograph of Colonel George Eskridge and Rebecca
Bonum, from *Daughters of the American Revolution
Magazine*. Copyright © 1917 by R.R. Bowker. Used
with permission.

Dedicated to my parents,

And to the memory of
Aunt Doris, Bill and Gladys, the Sheltons
Hugh and Marcella, and Uncle Billy

# ACKNOWLEDGEMENTS

I would like to thank the following people for their input towards the Mississippi part of my story: Betty Wiltshire for her genealogy research when I first began, local historian Norman Ezell for connecting me to the Swanson family, Carleen McBride, Anderson Elliot, Emma Mae Elliot, the late Leon Crockett Sr., Adean Brown, Dorothy Bellmer, Judy Mitchell Stanford, and Kathleen Mason. Special thanks to C Swanson and her family, Robert & Billie Rigdon, the late Tommy Hanks Jr., the late Madie Jones, and to the staff at the Mississippi Dept. of Archives & History. I'm grateful also to Mrs. Elizabeth B. Stegall for her Alabama research.

For helping me get the complete picture in Kansas I thank genealogist Katy Matthews, all my Hanks cousins formerly and presently in Manhattan & Wichita, especially to Patty Sue Glenn, Barbara Hanks, Helen Kanion, the late Mrytle Foster, the late Harry & Madaline Sullinger, and the late Edward Hanks. Thanks to the staffs at the Lyndon County Courthouse, Kansas State Historical Society, Osage County Historical Society, and the Crable Funeral Home.

For help on the Tennessee research I truly thank W.B. Howerton of the Roane County Genealogical Society, genealogist Gale W. Bamman, staffs at the Roane County Courthouse, Tennessee State Archives & History, and the Roane County Register of Deeds. Special thanks to Mr. & Mrs. Rue Eskridge, Jerry Eskridge who referred me to them, and to Terri Likens and the *Roane County News* for permission to quote from the *Rockwood Times* Newspaper. Now turning to South Carolina, thanks to the staffs at the Abbeville County Courthouse, Edgefield County Register of Deeds, and the Old Edgefield Archives, especially to Elzie L. Turner and Elizabeth Holtzlander. Also, thanks goes to the Hancock County Courthouse in Georgia.

I'm indebted to the staff at the Library of Virginia. Special thanks to Darlene Tallent of the Westmoreland County Museum. Thank you Samuel Gaskins, caretaker of Yeocomico Church Cemetary, for showing me the tomb of Colonel George Eskridge. Special thanks to Mrs. Ruth Brumley for allowing my camera on Sandy Point House, to Preston Haney for providing his records on indentured servants who were sentenced in Westmoreland County, to Betty M. McDade for her tithable lists of Fairfax County, and to Nelson Langford of the Virginia Historical Society. Thank you Olga Lewnes and R.R. Bowker Co. for permission to reprint the photos of George and Rebecca Eskridge in the *Daughters of the American Revolution Magazine*, and appreciative gratitude goes to the staff at the National Archives branch in Seattle. A load of thanks to the New York City employee who finally found Uncle Billy's medical

# ACKNOWLEDGEMENTS

autopsy record after we figured out Billy had been listed under his father's name instead of his own.

To author Ann E. Eskridge, thanks for your early support. This is about your family too. I'm looking forward to your next book. Thank you Velma Harris and to your children (now growing old like me) who were a second family to me while growing up. A special thanks of appreciation to all in my spiritual family, especially to Larry Brown, thanks for not giving up on me. Cheers to all who shared my experience of growing up in North Portland, particularly Alphonso and Dickey. Buddy and Randy where are they? Hope their fellowship comes back. Gratitude to longtime family friends, Marvin Welt for his suggestions on writing, and Bobbie Dore Foster, Executive Editor of the *Skanner* newspaper, for getting my feet wet in writing articles to an audience. Appreciation goes also to Portland reporters Nancy McCarthy of the *Skanner*, Lisa Loving, Fred Leeson of the *Oregonian*, and Ray Summers of KOIN-TV. Thank you Shirley Hancock, I haven't forgotten. I'm grateful also to editors Charles H. Washington and Joy Ramos of the *Portland Observer*, who published my first creative writing short story for their Black History Month issue. I cherish the support of my co-workers and supervisors at U.S. Bank, especially to Kathy Legg for allowing me all that "towop" to fly to West Africa and later to go down South to research. I value the critique of the book's early drafts by my wife Lynn and also by Mona Mellenberg and Allison King. A great, big thanks to everyone at the Genealogical Forum of Oregon. There's no way I can name all of you who gave support during workshops, seminars, writing contests, and in many other ways.

Special note of thanks to Yvonne Eskridge, widow of attorney Chauncey Eskridge Jr.; I highly esteem the contributions from Velma Burrell, Roy and Kathy Hanks, Len and Lillian Hanks, Ruby Jones Burroughs, Harry Williams, Alberta Boston, Eleanor B. Gibson, Dedeer & Nancy Amani for being wonderful hosts during our stay in Abidjan, Cuyou Anderson for putting us up at his hotel in Cocody, Djessou Solange, Begou Eugenie, Jochebed Essien, Atteby, Barou Winde-Laurent, and Djibom Justin who escorted us to the airport.

Last but not least, a ton of thanks to the late Jack Grantham Jr. for all of the many contributions he made in researching the vast Eskridge family history, but especially for his contributions to my story. Also, I would be amiss without sending loads of love to my McCoy cousins and to Aunt Sue Carolyn! Finally, thanks to my parents, Zane & Fern, to my brothers Laurence & Michael, and to my wife Lynn for her continued support during this long, long, project.

# AKEE TREE

**A Descendant's Search for his Ancestors
on the Eskridge Plantations**

# CHAPTER ONE
## Beginning the Search

The newspapers carried meaningful stories that year. Things such as Apartheid, Tiananmen Square, Liberia, and Hurricane Hugo.

But one headline impacted me personally, and would continue so for the next ten years.

Dad and I sat in the living room watching the baseball game that Saturday. "By the way, here's something I want to show you," Dad said, as he handed me a letter recently received in the mail. Opening the envelope, I noticed inside a newspaper clipping and a funeral announcement. Dad's close cousin, Murt Hanks Jr., the first black mayor of Manhattan, Kansas, had died of a heart attack. My brothers and I had never personally met Cousin Murt. In fact, we had never met any of our relatives on the Hanks side in Kansas or anywhere else for that matter, except for two of my father's aunts. My family were the only ones of the Hanks clan out on the West Coast, out in Portland, Oregon where the weatherman's forecast of liquid sunshine keeps everything a lush green.

I remembered seeing pictures of Murt in Dad's high school yearbook and also in the family albums. That's all I knew of him while growing up, his picture. I never was told hardly anything about the history of the Hanks family. I never knew my father's father, Hugh Hanks, a retired appliance repairman in Manhattan. Hugh Hanks never saw Portland. He had died in 1960 when I was one year old. And I never heard the story of how Cousin Murt when he was eight years old lost his father in a tragic accident in 1941. Murt was elected mayor in 1972. He won a second term in 1975. I heard he had personally met Vice-President Hubert Humphrey and author Alex Haley, who signed his copy of *Roots* at a book-signing. Haley knew his family history. I didn't know mine. Suddenly for the first time I realized what little I knew about who my relatives were on my father's side of the family. I started to read the obituary on the funeral card:

"Murt Hanks Jr. departed this life on July 8 in the year of our Lord of 1989...former mayor of Manhattan, KS...the son of Murt and Monette Cavens Hanks...surviving him is his wife...two sons...two daughters...one brother, Robert Edward, four sisters...and three grandchildren..."

Who were all these relatives that I had never met? I realized for the first time also that this cousin's father was also named Murt. Who was Murt Hanks Sr.? Who were his parents? Wait a minute. I needed to take a step back. Who were *my* father's parents? What did I know about them? Honestly, I could not answer those questions. The only relatives I had met from Dad's family were his two aunts who were his mother's sisters. One of them, Aunt Peggy Flowers of Manhattan, Kansas, had sent the letter, a letter holding a tiny headline.

The narrative I proceed to share is both an investigative search for identity and a saga about four women. Four women who kept the family bloodline alive during 140 years under slavery. Each of them--Akey, Jenny, Rose, Eliza--bore the successive generation leading to the next until the eventual birth of my great-grandfather, who grew up a slave on the Eskridge plantation in Mississippi. This fact brings up yet another story that flows down the middle of the aforementioned two. Besides researching my family from public records, I also conducted numerous interviews. And if I was going to fulfill my dream as a genealogist and trace my family tree, then I would, ultimately, have to interview members of a once slaveholding family--the Eskridges--and also see if there existed any of their family slave records. Could the silence about race and slavery in both our families be broken? Could a trusting dialogue be established between us, so that whatever information they possessed about their family slaves--my ancestors--would be shared with me?

If I had not assembled the courage to initiate contacting descendants of the slavemasters who bought and sold my ancestors, then this book probably could not have been written. They were white and lived in the South. I was black and lived in the Northwest. I was born at the end of the 1950's, when segregation was beginning to crumble. They were born at the beginning of the 1920's, when it was firmly entrenched. We were complete strangers. Both our families were bound by one common thread--slavery. Yet, their help was invaluable.

During the next occasion to visit my parents, Zane and Fern Hanks, natives of Kansas and Missouri, I went straight to the picture albums and the family file cabinet. Inside was one big, bulging folder entitled "Our Roots" that Mom had been collecting together. How glad I was that she had. I started my family search that day. Newspaper clippings, funeral & birth announcements, photographs--I carefully studied each item, writing down everything pertaining to names, dates, and places. I finally had to quit after a few hours because there was just too much to go through. But by the time I had finished that day, I had found information on my mother's father, my father's parents, his brother (who died when I was one month old), and some old photographs including one of Dad's grandmother Rosetta Hanks, a former slave.

Before going home, I reviewed my main notes:

William McCoy(mom's father) born July 25, 1897 at Port Gibson, MS; died at St. Louis, MO May 10, 1971; the son of Henry & Louise Turner McCoy

Billy Don Hanks(dad's brother) died in New York City June 1959; attended Kansas State University

Marcella Hanks(dad's mother) born Dec. 25, 1898 in Ogden, KS; daughter of Benjamin & Gertrude Barnett; died Nov. 11, 1952 in

Manhattan, KS

Hugh Hanks(dad's father) born May 1896 Osage City, KS; died June 1960 in Manhattan, KS

Murt & Monette Hanks(dad's uncle & aunt) born? died?

Rosetta Hanks(dad's grandmother) born?  died?

Now I was starting to get excited. How far back could I trace my ancestry?  If I had found these precious wrinkled and yellow-stained fragments of history by just going through family records, imagine what I might find by searching other files?  And since each person born in this world starts off with four ancestral lines:  paternal  grandfather/grandmother,  and  maternal grandfather/grandmother, which ancestral line would I concentrate on first?  Another question I pondered was whether to include extended family into my genealogical line, since my mother's mother had later remarried, marrying an Arkansas man, James Shelton.  Should I include his family line and trace it too?

After a few weeks of planning this family project, I decided to start tracing my mother's side first and include Grandpapa Shelton's family line too.  Why not? Although James Shelton wasn't my grandfather by blood, he had put in just as much time in shaping my life since I was born as anyone else.  Grandmother Shelton's first husband, my biological maternal grandfather, William McCoy, I had met only once, I was told.  I surely didn't remember.  On the other hand, my brother, Laurence, distinctly recalled how Grandfather McCoy came to Portland, Oregon to visit us when we were young.  But I still couldn't remember.  Now I was quickly learning the importance of *asking each family member* of what they might recall.  To begin the search, I headed to the public library and started looking up books on how to trace one's lineage.  I learned about how to search marriage records, wills, probate estate records, court minutes, land deeds, tax records, military records, and funeral and cemetary records.  Another valuable source of family genealogy I learned about were the federal and state censuses. And last but not least, there were hundreds of records specifically dealing with Afro-American genealogy. For Black Americans, besides searching the records already mentioned, there also were slave records, and ex-slave interviews and biographies. Of course, the most important interviews would be those with one's own family members who may likely be able to recite the family history and provide one with a detail or two that might prove to be an invaluable clue down the road. One other rule of thumb I took with me: Always work your way to tracing the past by starting with what you *ALREADY KNOW*; never try to start from the past with what you don't know and start assuming it will lead you accurately to your present family.

James and Lucy Shelton, my mother's stepfather and mother, had moved to Portland with my mother in 1945 from St. Louis. James Shelton's uncle, who was already living in Portland, told James about job opportunities at Portland's shipyards due to the raging of World War II. When the war ended, Grandpapa James took a job as a presser at a downtown cleaners-alterations shop. Grandmother didn't work outside the home, but helped "Grandpopper" ( that was the way I thought I had heard everyone call Grandpapa when I was a child) by keeping house. When the owner of the cleaners shop retired, he liked Grandpapa so much that he decided to give him the business for nothing. But instead of letting the owner do that, Grandpapa raised $1,000 and bought the owner out. For the next 26 years until retiring in 1974, Grandpapa Shelton would work six days a week from eight in the morning until 10:30 at night, and sometimes five or six hours on Sundays.

I jumped in the car along with my tape recorder and drove over to Hodge Street in North Portland where the Sheltons' modest white-colored, 1950-built two bedroom home was located, including seven apple trees and their vegetable garden in the backyard. A large housing project called Columbia Villa was just a block away, the same ghetto that my mother's brother Bill McCoy and his wife Gladys and their family lived in before they bought their first house. Uncle Bill went on to become an Oregon

State Senator, and Aunt Gladys went on to serve on the Portland School Board, then later became the Commissioner Chairman for Multnomah County, the county that contains Portland.

I knocked on the Sheltons' front door. Grandpapa answered. "Why hello there; Come on in." Grandpapa Shelton had the baseball game on, too. He loved baseball, having played in the Negro Leagues for a team in his hometown of Arkansas. He had kept all his memorabilia from the Negro League golden days. But I never saw them. According to what he told me, Grandmother Shelton thought they were household junk collecting dust and threw all of it out.

As we all sat down, I explained  my idea of wanting to trace the family's ancestral line. After a little probing and coaching, Grandpapa Shelton dove in. "My grandfather on my mother's side was Lee Butler, and my grandfather on my dad's side was Richard Shelton, he was from Chattanooga...passed before I was born," said Grandpa. "I was born about 1904 or 1905 in Arkansas...John Wesley Shelton was my dad...born in Tennessee somewhere close to Dyersburg...died in 1925 when he was 46...my mother was Elter Butler...had some Indian in her...she was born in Dewitt, Arkansas and died when she was only 22...Grandfather Lee Butler, he was named Butler after the man that owned him...Ole' Grandpa Lee was a foreman...my father John worked for a lumber company...and Richard Shelton was a smooth operator, he was a ladies man...my great-grandfather, they called him Clayton Wilson, he was married to Great-grandmother Minerva Butler...got my great-grandmother's picture in the room there...Minerva Butler...she was born in South Carolina...was around 100 years old when she died...I heard my grandmother Jennie Shelton say they slipped off from the Massa and went over to the Yankee side."

Grandmother Shelton then went next, reciting her Mississippi history belonging to the Lipscomb family, her maiden name. Her parents, my mother and her siblings Doris and Bill McCoy's maternal grandparents, were Julius and Nora Fuller Lipscomb of Indianola, Mississippi. Julius was named after his father Julius who was born a slave around 1834 in Alabama. He in turn was the son of a slave couple named Kit and Leah. Grandmother Shelton's stories and lineage dating back into slavery days would fill a book of its own. Soon my grandparents were describing their customs and culture, such as their fish fry gatherings down by the river, the Arkansas boys' love for making moonshine, and their love for the "ole ragtime music." I listened to them tweak their memories, their tired, stiff frames suddenly becoming limber, straighting up in their chairs, their wrinkled faces and chins lifting, as they recalled nearly-forgotten events and dates, the low pitch in their almost extinguished voices now rising, becoming loud, with clarity and certainty, and a twinkle showing in their eyes. They were enjoying their narratives and so was I. The pride that trickled from their lips due to being asked by a younger generation to talk about their forebears, that someone cared to know, could be felt in the room.

As we ended the evening and I turned off the tape recorder, Grandpapa Shelton fired up one of his filterless tobacco camels. While he coughed and gagged while puffing, my hair wanted to stand on end, as Grandpapa already had two strokes. But at eighty-five he wasn't about to quit his old habits then even though he should have. About four months later one day in November, Grandpapa Shelton had a heart attack. He passed away two days later. After the funeral, I kind of put down my family genealogy for awhile. It wouldn't be until the spring of 1990 that I would get all my family notes out again.

Between working in retail banking and running a genealogy research business out of my home, a strong desire to learn *the past* through documentary evidence had ignited me to launch this journey. It felt like a daunting task was before me, and seemed virtually impossible that I could ever excavate my buried over and long lost lineage. But over the next ten years I would learn of fascinating connections to families who share the namesake Eskridge and Hanks today, yet who once shared the same plantation yesterday. I would discover the colonial Virginia attorney who bought my African ancestor, and a Chicago attorney who was with Martin Luther King Jr. on that day in Memphis. I would find a link between a civil war President and a famous actor.

I would stare into the face of the slave overseer who changed our family name.  I would stumble upon many other strange connections, but also profoundly important ones.  Tree branches grow in different directions yet each follows back to its original start, the root.  I am grateful to the people who were willing to help me back to my original tree root.  Help even from unexpected persons, the descendants of the very master whose lineage I also had to unearth.  But years needed to pass before their worlds would cross mine.  Everything has an appointed time.  For the time being, I still needed to learn more about my family clan in Kansas, then try to find out who came before them, and from where.

# CHAPTER TWO

## Somewhere from Mississippi

In the spring of 1990 I decided it was time to resume my goal of tracing back into my family's unknown past, focusing this time on what I might find out about my father's side of the family, the side of the family which was a complete mystery. Although today's world entered a new millenium, a millenium that appeared promising yet now seems full of growing racism and intolerance, war talk and looming destruction, what actually fueled my undertaking this quest of learning about my family heritage was in seeing the unfolding events and breaking out of peace in Eastern Europe in 1989 and 1990, coupled with the death of Dad's cousin. Seeing a historical era quickly passing away in Eastern Europe caused me to realize just how quickly memorable dates and events of my family could pass away by death to the family historian--the household griot. Now I just hoped that I hadn't waited too long, that someone was still alive who could answer my many questions that were growing by the day.

Looking at my notes, Dad's brother Billy Don Hanks passed away in June 1959 at the young age of 31 in New York City. I later learned it was on a Sunday, and one month after I was born. No one mentioned how he died, except that Uncle Billy was mainly a drifter, no wife or children, at least as far as the family knew, and shifting from one city to the next. He had moved to New York by 1958 and lived in an apartment in Harlem at 751 St.

Nicholas Avenue.    Billy was buried at Potter's Field on Long Island, as the family could no way afford the heavy expense of bringing his remains back to Kansas for a funeral.  Mom said they found out about Billy's passing when a Portland policeman pulled up at our house to notify the next-of-kin.

The Chief Medical Examiner of New York City reported that Billy had been drinking all Saturday night at Battery Park, located on the south end of Manhattan's waterfront along the Hudson River and six blocks from where the twin towers of the World Trade Center once stood.  Sometime Sunday morning Billy started feeling terribly sick and rushed himself to Beekman Hospital.  He died of a heart attack right in the doctor's hands.  Two of Billy's friends, an older man named Ioway Parris and a young woman named Goldie Reid, were called in to make an identification at the mortuary.  (I tried to contact these persons, but Ioway Parris was deceased, and Goldie Reid I've never located to this day).  The medical report went on to say that Goldie had last seen Billy on May 25, Memorial Day, when he came by her apartment to visit.  Apparently Goldie lived in apartment nine of the same building at 751 St. Nicholas Avenue.

Prior to New York, Uncle Billy Don worked as a cook at a Chicago restaurant, the Alamo Cafe, after serving his Navy duty.  I remember distinctly that serious look on Billy's face, as if he were taking on the world, shown on his 1945 Navy training unit photograph in San Diego, California, the only black in his training company.  Billy Don came out to Portland to visit my parents in November 1957 a few months after they were married, and stayed with them for a week.  I always wondered if Billy heard the news of my being born in the last remaining weeks of his life.  I knew I could easily get the answer to that if I just asked Dad, but for some reason I didn't.  Out of respect, I was afraid to bring up something that I still sensed was a painful memory.

Dad's father, Hugh Hanks, was born  in Osage City, Kansas, and died on June 17, 1960 a year after I was born, and ironically, exactly one year after Billy Don's death.  Although Dad's father Hugh this time knew not only about my birth and also that Mom was carrying my brother Laurence, the realization that

Dad had lost both his father and only brother within a one year span was a painful tragedy to me, a sorrowful wound that would fester in my spirit.  I had internalized Dad's twelve-month woe as my hurt, finding myself at times imagining what his pain would have been like, then afterward imagining the strength it took him to move on and raise three sons.  But on the journey on which I was about to embark, delving into the closet bones of my family's ancestral past, I would soon learn the need to copy his strength, to move past obstacles and finish this journey on a high note.  At this point, though, I had no idea how long this odyssey would take.

There was an old funeral program of Grandfather Hugh still at the house, inside it listing the relatives who attended,  relatives I had never heard of:  "Granison Pitts;  Ernest Hanks;  Eliza Miller;  Mrytle Williams;   Monette Hanks and family: Murt, Edward, Richard, Patty, and Phyllis;  Valjean Jeeter;   Harry Sullinger.  Contributions of carnations sent from Mr. and Mrs. John Q. Hanks of Richmond,California; Madaline Sullinger."

I asked myself, "Where were Grandfather Hugh's  parents born?  What was the name of his father?"   I honestly didn't know a thing.   Asking Dad these questions, the only thing he remembered was that his grandmother's first name was Rosetta, a former slave, who died around 80 years of age when Dad was only ten.   At least I had that much, since Dad didn't know his grandfather's name or heard anything about him.  I began to sense this search wasn't going to be easy.  Nothing was laid out.  And any genealogist, even Haley himself, would tell you there's no such thing as logging onto the internet and simply download your entire family tree. It's never been that easy. As my Grandmother Shelton would often say, this would take alot of "elbow grease." My father also recalled that Cousin Murt, whose funeral program had sparked in me this desire to unearth my family history, was named after his father Murt, but everyone called him "Moon."  Dad then related a few things about his parents, how his father Hugh had a habit of chewing cigars, and how his mother Marcella and her sister, Valjean Jeeter,  would play their home piano, Valjean being a popular local singer & "boogie woogie" piano player in the jukebox night clubs of Manhattan, Kansas.  Dad's mother Marcella

Barnett died in 1952 before I was born.   Valjean passed away in 1978, so Dad's Aunt Peggy was the only one left on his mother's side.  My question was:  Who was left on *the Hanks side?*

When asking if we had any relatives still in Osage City, Dad said he wasn't sure.       One day I picked up the phone and asked the operator to give me the telephone number to the main library in Osage City.  The closest one was in the town of Lyndon.  I called and explained to the librarian my grandfather was born in Osage City and that I was trying to find out anything about his family.  "You say the last name was Hanks? Let me check;  We just completed a book on the history and families of Osage County," the librarian said.  After a minute or two, she came back to the phone and said, "There is an article that was written by a Mrytle Hanks Foster on a family named Hanks," then she started to read a couple of the paragraphs:

"Many years ago the Crockett and the William (Billy) Hanks families came to Osage City from Mississippi.  I can not remember what part.  The Crocketts were the parents of Rosetta Hanks. She was the wife of Billy Hanks...I can remember Grandma Hanks telling me she and Grandpa Hanks were the parents of thirteen children, Sue, James, Clifford, Granison, Eliza, John, Murt, Ernest (Teat), Margaret and Hugh, the others passed at birth..."

As she read, I couldn't believe my ears!  "Well," the librarian said, "these people are probably your family.  I can make a copy of it and send it to you."   Before we hung up, I asked if she could read the names of the children again so I could write them down, so I could recite them in my head.  Names from my family's past. *Names I had never heard about.*

I just couldn't believe I had found this much information in just one phone call.  I decided to try one more call, this time to the Osage City Cemetary,  asking if they held information about Grandfather Hugh's family, a black family that had migrated from Mississippi.  I wondered why they had migrated.  The cemetary office suggested I contact the Crable Funeral Chapel.  After dialing the number, I asked them if they could check their register for a few persons named Hanks. I was afraid to give them all ten names for fear they might say they were too busy to check. "Just wait a moment and let me check, it might take a little while," the receptionist said. About five minutes later she returned and said, "I have...

James Hanks, died Dec. 17th, 1899; Sue Orendorf, born Dec. 22nd, 1873, died May 20th, 1950; Margaret Hanks, died May 4th, 1914; Clifford Hanks, killed by a train, May 5th, 1900; infant Crockett, died 2-11-1902; ordered by Dave Crockett, infant 12-9-1906, infant 1-12-1908; D.D. Crockett, born North Carolina, died Jan. 17th, 1911, 92 years old...

"That's all I can see here." Their files contained more family history. And I had made only three phone calls. But why hadn't I been told about these past generations? Why didn't someone collect and record the entire family story from it's first beginning so it could be handed down? What hurt me more was the haunting thought of what would have become of these cemetary and funeral pieces of office paper, pieces to the past, in a few more years. Left unprotected, old records eventually become unreadable or destroyed.

The following week after calling Osage City, I received in the mail the article from the Lyndon library, "The Crockett and Hanks Families," by someone named Myrtle Hanks Foster. It was a one page, four column writeup with an overhead photograph. Since the librarian had already read me the first two paragraphs, I picked up where she left off:

".....They lived at 1419 E. Laing St. The Crocketts lived on the corner of the same block. The Crocketts had three boys, Drew, James, and C.C. Drew was a coal miner, James and C.C. left Osage and became ministers. Grandma Crockett...I do not remember her at all. Grandpa Crockett passed when I was very young. He was about 95.

"I am the daughter and only child of James and Lillian

Queenry Hanks.   James passed in 1899 during the small pox epidemic.   I was just nine months old.   My uncle, William Queenry, also of Osage City told me my father was buried at night as they did during the epidemic.   He said he watched out their window as the lumber wagon went by with several bodies.   My mother had to go to work after my father's death so she moved to Topeka and I lived with my grandparents until I was five years old and came to Topeka.

"...I do have pleasant memories of Osage as I would go back to visit Grandpa and Grandma Hanks before they moved to Manhattan.   I would then go to visit my Aunt Sue Orendorf...We had to walk everywhere we went as my uncles said the horse had to take them to the coal mines, so it had to rest.   We walked Laing St. from 9th out to 14th St. on a dirt road.   We went around the railroad tracks if it was muddy.   It was a lot of fun.   I looked forward to going to visit my relatives in Osage City."

There was no question about it, this was my family, and Mrytle was Grandfather Hugh's niece, which made her and Dad first cousins.   It was amazing how much she could recall at ninety years of age.   I had no idea I had a cousin who was that old, born in 1899, and still living.

A few days later I showed my parents the article I received. They were elated.   Mom wanted me to make copies to put in the family files, another addition to her bulging "Our Roots" binder. "So cousin Mrytle wrote this?" Dad asked.   "I haven't seen her in years, she lives out there in Topeka, Kansas...got a picture of her in the albums."   I pulled down the photo album books stacked high up in the hallway closet.   After going through a few, there she was, an old black & white photograph of Mrytle taken probably in her late 40's or early 50's.   "Dad, you should go back to Kansas and visit Aunt Peggy," I mentioned.   "I haven't been back to Kansas since my father died, that's been about 30 years ago;  besides, it gets too hot back there for me," Dad responded, referring to his asthma.

I recalled the last time Aunt Peggy came to Portland to visit us.   It was in the summer of 1979.   I had just turned twenty, shared an apartment with a roommate, and owned a gas-guzzling 1969 blue Dodge Polara that I wished I had never bought, except for the fact it had an 8-track tapedeck blasting out the jazz fusion sounds of the 70's. Dad and Mom had opened a downtown night club the year before, "The Jazz Nest," offering food and beverages, a juke box full of jazz and blues selections, and live performance bands on certain occasions, and Aunt Peggy had come out to celebrate their first year in business. Mom and Grandmother Shelton would run the club during the day, then Dad would operate it at night after his regular job at Bonneville Power. During her visit, Aunt Peggy asked me to drive her to a fresh meat market. What did I know about fresh meat markets? If I was hungry for meat, I went to the hamburger drive-thru. But Aunt Peggy thrived on fresh-cut roast beef. And don't forget to stick in the hickory ham. So I drove her from our house on North Alaska street to the only meat market I knew, clear on the other side of town, on 65th & Killingsworth. I was barely out of gas, nervously looking at my low gas gauge, and worrying here I'd run out of gas with ole' Aunt Peggy stranded on the road.

But from the day of that call to the Osage City library, my thoughts had become totally immersed as to how soon I could take off to go meet my relatives in Kansas. I finally decided to call Aunt Peggy and Cousin Mrytle and let them know of my desire to come visit. Aunt Peggy was thrilled.

"I'd be glad to have you out here...you haven't ever been out this way before have you?"

"No, that's why I want to come out there and see what's it's like, see where Dad grew up."

"Well, you're welcome any time; you just let me know when you're coming."

Next, I called Mrytle. "Hello...you're a Hanks? From Portland, Oregon? Well, I'm a Hanks too! Your father is Zane, the son of Hugh Hanks? Isn't that something! I remember Hugh very well." I mentioned about her article, my plans of coming out to Kansas sometime soon, and my looking forward to our meeting as I had about a thousand questions to ask. Mrytle responded enthusiastically to a visit and so I promised her I would come that year--1990. We then exchanged addresses.

How excited I was!  Not a  day went by without my thinking of when I could leave for Kansas.  However, in May of that year I received a devastating letter from Mrytle.  Aunt Peggy had died.  Dad was actually arranging for her to come out to Portland again for another summer visit.  No one had notified my father of Peggy's death, due to a non-relative in Kansas who made all the arrangements and wasn't aware of Peggy's nephew in Oregon.  It was a sad evening at my parents' house the night I brought the bad news in Mrytle's letter.  Death is truly an unrelenting enemy.  And here I was notifying my parents rather than the other way around.  My chances of visiting Aunt Peggy in Kansas was now gone.  How I had hoped to see her, but, it was not going to be, at least not in this world.  From my Bible I knew there was a better one to come.  Mrytle was still looking forward to my visit and so I felt even more determined to go.

Around the time of Cousin Mrytle's letter, I also received a copy of the death certificate on  my great-grandfather, William Hanks, another new name I had now learned through Cousin Mrytle.  I had requested it from the Vital Statistics of Kansas, asking them if they could do a search since I didn't know what year he had died.  The certificate stated he died  August 5, 1918 in Manhattan at the age of 74.  No wonder my father Zane M. Hanks had never met his grandfather, since Dad wasn't yet born until 1930.  William Hanks' residence was 826 Riley Street, which I now realized was next door to Dad's parents at 822 Riley, across the street from  his Uncle Murt's family at 917 Riley, and a block from another uncle, Ernest Hanks at 922 Riley.  Then I came to that familiar section on a death certificate that I hoped would help me in my genealogy chart: the names of his parents.  But in that section I found only three words written across: "*Born in Slavery.*" Not even his parents' birthplaces were listed.  I was feeling down and out.  I thought for sure that Great-grandmother Rosetta would have known something about her husband's parents, she being the informant on the death certificate.  But maybe she did know and just didn't think to put it down, or maybe she might have forgotten.  Anyhow, at least the certificate told me my great-grandfather was not *born free.*  William Hanks' birthplace was mentioned as being in Tennessee.

Next I sent a letter with a check to the Mississippi Department of Archives & History in Jackson, Mississippi to inquire if William and Rosetta Hanks were listed on the 1870 federal census, the census which listed all African Americans *by name* for the first time. All African Americans were listed down as free persons, which was also a first. Hopefully I would find out where in Mississippi William and Rosetta lived before they had left for Osage City.

Sure enough, about two weeks later they wrote back saying, "We have located a Wm Hanks in the Carroll County 1870 Census and wife, Rosalie." Enclosed inside was a copy of page 599 of the census, taken five years after the Confederacy surrendered, showing William and "Rosalie" Hanks living in Carroll County, Mississippi, in the village of Duck Hill, William's age listed as 23 and birthplace Tennessee, while Rosetta's age was listed as 19 and birthplace Mississippi. Calculating back, William would have been born around 1847 and Rosetta about 1851. Just seeing their names on this 120 year old census gave me a wonderful feeling of belonging, that I had a beginning, a history. Now I needed to find out what that history was.

I called the U.S. National Archives in Washington, D.C, the agency that maintains all the holdings of the federal censuses starting as far back as 1790, and asked them how I could order the entire 1870 census roll for Carroll County, Mississippi so I could see if there were other family members I could find. They recommended the best way would be to come to any of their regional archives across the country and search the census for myself. The closest archive to Portland was in Seattle, Washington, just three hours away.

In August I drove up and spent two days at the Pacific Northwest Regional Archives in Seattle. Housed here were the entire microfilm roll collection of the federal census from 1790 to 1920 (the 1930 census is now available), a privacy restriction being on census years that were less than 70 years old. The 1890 census also was not available, it being destroyed by fire in 1921. To help make research easier, indexes were made available for each census year and state.  I was amazed at seeing so many other researchers who came to search their families too.  I located the 1870 census roll for Carroll County, Mississipi.  There on page 599 was listed not only my great-grandparents but also all their neighbors they lived next to in 1870.  But strangely, I didn't find anyone named Crockett as Cousin Mrytle had said were Great-grandmother Rosetta's parents.

William and Rosetta Hanks lived next door to a black couple, Armstead and Maria Campbell.  Next, I looked up the 1880 Mississippi "Soundex", an index based upon the sound of the last name, which is assigned a "Soundex Code."  The 1880 Soundex only indexed families with children ten years old or younger.  I figured that by 1880 some of the Hanks children had to have been born.  But I couldn't find their names anywhere.  "Maybe they moved to Kansas by now," I thought to myself,  so I went over and pulled out the 1880 Kansas Soundex and placed it on the reader.  I kept turning the film hoping I would find something this morning after driving all the way up here.  Finally, there they were:

Hanks, Wm 36, Rosetta 29, Susie 9, James 6, Clifford 5, Maria 1

The 1880 census also listed the birthplace of each person's parents.  William listed his mother's birthplace as Tennessee, but for his father the section was blank.  Rosetta listed her father's birthplace as "Old Virginia" and her mother's birthplace as North Carolina.  But there was something else I discovered.  Living next door to the Hanks were:

Crockett Armstead 60, Maria 54, Armstead 16, John 14, Dudley 11, James 6

Now I knew the names of Grandfather Hugh's *maternal* grandparents.  Armstead Crockett listed not only his birthplace but that of his parents as "Old Virginia," whereas Maria listed herself and that of her parents' birthplace as North Carolina.

Then it dawned on me: "The Crockett names look very similiar to the Campbell family that lived next door to William and

Rosetta in Duck Hill." So again was placed back on the 1870 Carroll County census roll. Sure enough, the Crocketts were living next door but instead were going by a different surname:

Campbell Grannison 21, Charlotte 20, Malinda 5, Sarah 3, Robinson 1
Campbell Armstead 44, Maria 36, Harris 16, Camilia 12, Armstead 6, John 4, Infant 1

So they had changed their surname from that of "Campbell" to "Crockett" by the time they came to Kansas. Why? Was the former a slave surname, whereas the latter was their real family name of origin ? According to history, many blacks after Emancipation faced the decision of choosing surnames for themselves and their families. Some chose the name of their former owners, while others chose a name that they identified with as the beginning of their genealogical line, such as the name a grandparent or great-grandparent chose generations ago. Others just chose names because they liked the sound of it, having nothing to do with a former owner. Several families had different names within the same family, such as a remarried mother taking the name of her new husband, whereas her children choosing instead the name of their blood father or of a former owner. I soon realized there were no hard fast rules on name selection during that era. I searched to see if there were any other black persons or families with the surname Hanks living next door or in the same town. Although there were two families with the same surname living in two towns within Carroll County, there were none listed in Duck Hill. How would I ever be able to find out anything about my great-grandfather's parents and family? Now, staring at all those hundreds of names on the microfilm census roll began weighing my eyes down. Suddenly I then realized the enormity of reaching my goal. "This is going to be impossible," I said to myself in resignation. But then I reasoned, "If Great-grandmother Rosetta's family were listed under a different surname while in Mississippi, perhaps Great-grandfather William's parents were listed likewise." Since he had reported his mother as having been born in Tennessee, I looked to see if there were any black persons born there who were living nearby William and Rosetta in Duck Hill. There was, just eight cabin houses away, and the name flew off the page. This name put a funny feeling in my gut:

Eskridge, Jeff 45  Kentucky , **Eliza 41 Tennessee,** Tom 11 Mississippi , Bettie 8, R.J.  6, L.J.  2

They in turn were next door to a freed family named Binford. I remember asking myself, and I'll never forget it:
"Could Eliza Eskridge be my *paternal* great-great-grandmother?"
The answer would not come that day.

I made sure to note down all families who lived in close proximity to mine, not worrying at that point if they were related or not. Two particular freed families that I took special notice of from the 1880 Osage City census was Andrew & Matilda Binford, born in Virginia and North Carolina, respectively, and Richard & Martha Eskridge, from Alabama, and their son Burdett, who was born in Mississippi, curiously wondering why those surnames would appear again, this time in the same Kansas town that my family had come to settle in.

After spending a hot summer evening sleeping overnight in a blue B210 Datsun, I woke up about 6 a.m. and drove over to a nearby Mcdonald's to get myself together. The archives opened at 8 a.m. and I wanted to be on time as a large line could grow very quickly. Once the doors opened I picked up where I left off the day before, this time pulling out the 1900 Kansas Soundex and Osage County census roll. I learned that on the 1900 census each person's birthmonth was listed:

Crockett Armstead Feb. 1818, Maria Sept. about
Hanks William slave about, Rosie Aug. 1851, Grannison Feb. 1881, Eliza Mar. 1884, John Feb. 1886, Murt Jun. 1888, Ernest Jun. 1890, Margaret Sept. 1892, Hugh May 1896, Lillian Aug. 1879, Mrytle Feb. 1899

Now I recognized the names of Murt, Grandfather Hugh, and Cousin Mrytle.  After copying down as much as I could from the 1870, 1880, and 1900 census, I was curious to see what I could learn about my family from one of slavery's mirrors--the 1860 Mississippi census.

I knew my families would not be listed by name because in 1860 they would have still been under the system of slavery.  Of course, blacks who were free would be listed on each census.  I checked the 1860 Mississippi index and saw a person named Hanks listed in Duck Hill.  There on page 61 was: "Marion Hanks 33, overseer, Alabama."  I wondered if he was the person whom our last name had come from.  Living next to him was Benjamin Campbell of North Carolina, Richard Eskridge, and Taliaferro "Tollivar" Eskridge, both from South Carolina.

Also taken every census year up through 1860 was a "slave schedule," listing the name of each slave owner, their number of slaves, and each slave's age and sex.  However, the name of each slave was not listed.  The slave schedule of Carroll County taken on Tuesday October 9, 1860 listed Benjamin Campbell with 59 slaves and eight slave houses, Richard Eskridge with 48 slaves and nine slave houses, Taliaferro Eskridge, 14 slaves, four slave houses, and Marion Hanks, one slave, one slave house.  What next caught my eye was the slave that Marion Hanks held: 1 male, 13 years old.  That is how old Great-Grandfather William would have been in 1860!    There wasn't any doubt in my mind that I had found a record of my great-grandfather in slavery and also the name of his owner.   Could there perhaps exist also a slave deed record that would show where Marion Hanks purchased my great-grandfather William?  The 1850 slave schedule, on the other hand, did not list Marion Hanks as a slave owner that year, but Benjamin Campbell and Richard Eskridge were.   I finished my research at the Archives and prepared myself for the three hour drive back home.  As I closed my datsun door and turned on the radio, a special news report came on.  Iraq had just invaded Kuwait.

After getting back from Seattle, that week I wrote a letter to the Carroll County Courthouse in Mississippi, asking for any information on deed records for Marion Hanks and also for Benjamin Campbell. About a week later I received a letter from a professional genealogist in Carrollton. The courthouse clerk had forwarded my letter to her, who was happy to try and help me. What a relief. I sat down to write, explaining what I had found from the census records and slave schedule:

"Dear Betty:

"...I would like your help in finding the birthplace of my great-grandfather William Hanks (also went by the name of Billy) who lived in Carroll County in 1870. He was 23 yrs old , born in Tennessee. I am interested in finding any bills of sales/purchases of slaves from Tennessee, the county or town where he was born, and any names of his parents or brothers or sisters. In 1860 there were several slaveholders who lived in Carroll Co.: Marion Hanks-1 male 13 yr old slave( Did he purchase him from one of his neighbors? This slave would have been 23 in 1870, same age William was in 1870); David Washam-2 slaves; Hardy Bennett-5 slaves; Richard Eskridge-48 slaves; Benjamin Campbell-59 slaves. The name of the area was called "Police District no #1... Look forward to hearing from you soon."

On August 21, 1990 Betty wrote back:
    "There were two Hanks brothers, Marion and Tolliver or Taliaferro, that came to Carroll Co. in the 1840's, both born in Alabama. They were here by Nov. 1846...I agree with you that the slave owned by Marion Hanks in 1860 was probably your William.
    I searched deed records for both Hanks brothers because slave sales and purchases were recorded in deed books. I didn't find the purchase of any slave by either brother during 1850 to 1866...It's possible that the sale wasn't recorded, or someone may have given the slave to Marion Hanks...Since Marion Hanks was listed as an overseer in 1860, and he lived next to Richard Eskridge, a large landowner, he probably worked for him, and may have been related to him because Richard Eskridge also had a brother named Taliaferro. I searched deeds for Richard Eskridge

to see if he may have bought William and given him to Marion, but there wasn't any purchase of slaves before 1860, and only one after that time, which was a woman...I've done several slave genealogies before, usually with some luck, but this one has me stumped and I don't know where to go from here...If I run across anything that may help you in the future, I'll let you know."

So Marion Hanks may have been an overseer on Richard Eskridge's forty-eight slave plantation, and may have purchased my great-grandfather William from there.
*Purchased him.* My wonderful family heritage.

**"Part of Guiney called the Grain Coast...as soon as
his ship arriv'd...and the Captain went on shore in the boat,
several of the Natives surrounded them...Just arrived in James
River, from Africa, The Ship Bassa...with a cargo of fine
healthy Windward
and Gold Coast SLAVES."
Excerpt from the Virginia *Gazette*.**

## CHAPTER THREE

### The Kru

Everyone huddled together on the Oregon beach warming their toes in the sand. A relative with his family and mine were here enjoying ourselves for three days. As I peered across the churning and crashing waves, I was reminded of how my family would never have even existed if one of my members had not survived another restless body of water--Middle Passage. As firewood was being gathered for the evening's planned bonfire, I asked my relative's daughter if she had ever heard the story about the family stretching back to Africa.

The young girl and I sat on the beach with our backs against a massive fallen timber, as I painted with words a rural village setting from which my African family heritage was born. I imagined myself embarking to another remote coastal range where life in the village dakos can be seen and heard, the scent in the air is the stench of fish, and seaworthy vessels small and large, near or afar, plow their preferable choice cargo. My vista of the beach coastline reminded me of the books I had read about Liberia, and of the names to some of Monrovia's town elders: Botswain. Korwolo. Sensobo. Men who were no doubt named after a family patriarch. In turn, their names would pass onto other male infants who also would grow to maturity. I began to connect to the world and culture that my great-great-great-great-great-grandmother had come from. As my words of imagery passed from my lips to the child's ears, I caught sight of what looked like black faces just over the jetty, and voices in the Ocean waves' roar:

"In the year 1692, anno domini, in the first month, in the tenth year of the headship of Korwolo, Chief Elder of the southeastern dako, there was a woman in the village Zwedru near the river Cavella, who was heavy with child.  Her name was Akee, and her husband, the father of her child, was Sensobo.

In the first month, on the fourth day of the month, the woman Akee gave birth to a son and named him Mennah.  So the sons of Sensobo now were Prero, Bodebe, who called himself Botswain, and Mennah.  Prero was the husbandly owner of Mimba, and Bodebe the family head of Couba.

That warm exhausted night, while Akee nursed her gentle newborn separately in her oblong clay hut with the aid of her midwife and a female servant, Sensobo and his sons and their wives and children ate together, feasting on fish and sweet potatoes,  along with a concoction of red pepper soup.  Sensobo then began explaining to the family his plans of working another foreign ship starting in the morning, and his desire to take Bodebe with him.   Sensobo knew full well he now would not be allowed to see his wife or newborn for the next eighteen months until the child was fully weaned.  He also now knew that he and Akee's love-making pulsations upon their guinea fowl feathered-mat and under their sheep blankets had finally brought reward.  This was now Akee's third son, and he was just as lively as on the morning she had Bodebe, and Prero under a full moon.

"It is now time for me to go to the Great Ocean to find a voyage to take again, and bring home wealth for my son;  I will have Bodebe, my boatman, come with me;  Prero, my fisherman, will remain here and watch our wives and our children," Sensobo said.  "We will leave tomorrow before sunrise."

"Another voyage?  Oh, yes! I will bring back many riches for all of you, and especially for my beautiful Couba!" Bodebe said excitably.

"Prero will be the family head while I am gone. He will protect, he will provide, in the name of the Great Nyeswa," Sensobo concluded.

Prero knew already what to do. Prero was a skilled fisherman, having learned his trade nine years ago when he was eight and sent to live with his teacher for his training. His duties starting that next morning were all too familiar to him. He had been trained to do this the last four years, as was the family custom. A good son would always humbly obey his patriarchal "Bieju" and will forever protect his "Di matriarch."

Bodebe still in an excited mood jumped up from his eating mat and began stomping and gyrating, jubilantly uttering, "Bi dyadye namu, nedye omrane kani! (father has a dream, to bring his son gold and wealth), Bi dyadye namu, nedye omrane kani!" This he repeated over and over while in dance. Soon Prero got up and repeated the words with him. Then Sensobo, Couba, and Mimba joined in. Next, Bodebe began another rhythm, "Botswain dyadye namu, nedye mwe kani! Botswain...(has a dream, to bring *everyone* gold!") Everyone was now repeating the new chorus line. Finally after some twenty chants of their melodic interchange they all broke out in cheer and laughter.

"Yes, you are Botswain; Now go!  Show the Nye-puru (man of white skin) why they named you thus!" Sensobo said. It was in fact the Europeans who gave Bodebe his nickname "Botswain," a result of seeing his superior skills as a seaman, and also because of their inability to pronounce the names of the Kru.

Sensobo and his son Bodebe were sailors, who sold their skills of seafaring to the European merchant ships that came up and down the West African coast. Ships would stop often along the Grain Coast to purchase the rare and invaluable commodity-- Ethiopian pepper. Sensobo and his son had gone on several voyages together, Sensobo having taken Bodebe with him the last four years now since he had reached his sixteenth year. They had even gone all the way to a place the Europeans called "Liverpool" twice, as well as Portugal and Spain, and returned bringing with them their earnings as well as articles of clothing, fabrics, jewelry, and other goods that were still being distributed among their community panton. The accumulative wealth Sensobo brought home represented well his reached destinations: gold doubloons from Spain, pistoles from Portugal, guineas and shillings from England, silver pesos from the New World, as well as local African currencies in shekels, talents, stones, and pebbles in every description.  All this he would entrust to the management of Akee upon his returns, a woman skilled in shaking her money-maker and dealing out wages to her female servants or obligated income support to blood relatives not only but also to in-laws and kin by marriage.

Prero then turned to his father and brother, hugging both of them and urging "May you both return swiftly, and in peace." Bodebe turned to Prero. "Dieju (brother), I will see you soon. May *you* be safe and in peace.  What can go wrong?"

Early the next morning while still dark, Sensobo and Bodebe rose from their sleep to begin their journey, gathering the supplies and food that had been prepared.  As they headed to the door of the hut, the family said their final goodbyes until their unpredictable return.  They began their walk towards the outskirts of the village, using the morning stars as their compass to lead them to the river Cavella, the river they called "Niwa Duyu." From there they would then paddle their canoe south until reaching the mouth of the river at the ocean cape.  As Sensobo and Bodebe headed through the thick forests while carefully balancing the canoe on their shoulders with one hand, their other hand stayed close to their knives, ready to use if confronted by the leopard, the python, or the sharp-tusked hog.  For some reason they also dreaded the harmless skink lizard, believing it to be poisonous. Their worst fear, however, was to be captured by a warring tribe and sold into slavery.  They believed the blue stripe running down the forehead to their nose would protect them.  Besides, the Kru strongly believed they would never be enslaved, that their mark had always protected them.  The proverbial saying among them was: "Alligator know the war canoe from the peace canoe."  And they would never negotiate a slave sale involving their own.  A Kru would never sell another Kru.  Carefullly they noted landmarks on the way, as these would aid them on their return. After a twenty kilometer trek, they finally reached the river.

As a gold yellow sunrise began its bright ascent over the distant Nimba mountains, the women in the village  Zwedru headed out to work their plantations.  While Prero went to check on his mother and the newborn, Couba and Mimba and their women servants prepared themselves to resume work in their crop fields.  They had been earnestly preparing a new field for yams and guinea peppers all that month while the ground was still dry.  In two more months the rainy season would begin and the ground would soon become too muddy to work.  The women felt relieved that the field finally had now been cleared.  The bush and trees had been cut down and left by the women to dry, Couba and Mimba burning them, then hoeing the soil, mixing with it the ashes of the burnt brush and vegetables.  Soon the ground was  ready for sowing.

Sensobo and Bodebe in a day's time reached the coastline.  A Portuguese ship had anchored off sea and it's captain was promptly securing a crew of Krumen.  Sensobo and Bodebe hurried down to take their place in line.  As the captain and his trading translator went down the line followed by a Kru interpreter, they were met by some who already spoke Portuguese, and still a few others who spoke a mixed jargon of Portuguese and English.  Soon Sensobo and "Botswain" were given their assignments:  load 5000 lbs. of the melaguetta pepper, known by the Europeans as "Ethiopian pepper" and "guinea pepper," then ride the merchant vessel to the Gold Coast Country and load ivory, gold, and 360 heads of cargo, afterward unloading the ship in Brazil.  In time the two men would see the 360 heads of cargo:  three hundred & sixty slaves.  But seeing enslaved Africans was not alarming.  Many tribes purchased slaves for use in their villages.  These servants were well treated, well fed.  Many of them became part of families, could marry, had rights, and could even buy their freedom.  Some, upon purchasing their release, married into families of royalty and thus rose to the status of princes.  So when Sensobo and Bodebe saw their African brothers being put upon foreign vessels, it did not even enter their minds that they would not  be treated by the Europeans any differently than the way the Africans treated them.  Of course, to personally be caught and made a slave would be a totally different matter.  No African welcomed being made a servant.

Sensobo and "Botswain" soon began their work loading the

guinea pepper into the sturdy carved canoes. With powerful strokes and rhythmic timing, the heavy loaded boats swiftly cut through the water to the Portuguese ship anchored off the coast of Cape Palmas. Every trading ship, frigate, and men-of-war heading to Cape Palmas on the Grain Coast had to also anchor offshore likewise, since there was not a single dock built along its entire beachhead, due to the dangerous jagged rocks hidden underneath the water surface. Captains not heeding this local knowledge paid the price for ignoring provincial wisdom and being ill-advised, as some ships were dashed to pieces. That was why the traders of the Portuguese, Spanish, Dutch, and English understood very well the value of hiring the Krumen to ferry trading goods to their vessels. The threat of contracting malaria was also constant. Hiring the Krumen, then, kept all the European traders in business, competing among themselves, each one against the other.

The next day the Portuguese ship arrived at the Gold Coast port of Accra, after a brief stopover at the French slave port Sao Andrea. Most of the Krumen recruited from Cape Palmas rode along to continue their assignment, but those who did not wish to continue the trip stayed behind, either tired from previous assigments and eager to return home to their loved ones, or holding out for a bigger paying assignment from another merchant vessel. The Portuguese captain promptly replaced these with Kru who were working the ports of Ghana. Sensobo and Bodebe now began loading at Accra the items of trade onto larger canoes. Next, they turned their attention to the three hundred sixty chained "servants" comprised mostly of men but some women and children, who seemed to resemble those from the ethnic Ashanti and Ibo.

They were ferried by canoe through the shark infested waters to the waiting ship in gangs of about eighty each, requiring about twenty paddlers, taking the large canoe five trips back and forth. In exchange for the African prisoners the tribal village chief received items of cloth, beads, and raw iron and copper for his village. Ironically, some among the prisoners were skilled craftsmen, artisans, and welders. Sensobo noticed this due to the flesh marks and scars on some of them and wondered why their skills and knowledge were being given to the Nye-puru instead of being used among their peoples.  Sensobo remembered a time long ago, told to him as a boy by his grandfather Krahn, when this would not be done.  No, Grandfather Krahn would many times orally relate the stories of when the Fanti first came, how they shared their knowledge of deep sea fishing using the long sharp jlode;  Or how the Mandingo and Mali traders would pass thru, sharing their trade and smelting skills with the Kru and other coastal villages along the Grain Coast, such as the Bassa, Grebo, and Dey peoples.  Apparently this village chief was not from his dako, Sensobo reasoned.

Each time the canoe was fully loaded and packed with bodies, the Portuguese priest who was brought along for this voyage would sprinkle his "holy water" on them, "baptizing" them in the name of his God, and in the name of his king.  Some of the priest's demonic water would spray upon Sensobo and Bodebe, as they sat unemotional during the ridiculous ritual.  While awaiting the signal to resume their paddle  through the "terrible surf," Sensobo and Bodebe stared oddly at the black African chief and the pale white priest, and both of their strange customs.  They now began paddling, coached by the drum beat of a Kru captain who sat at the front of the canoe.  Upon boarding the "loose packed" slaver, the Portuguese captain headed to Angola for more trading goods, and slaves, then up anchor again and embark to Brazil, then return to Portugal.  From there Sensobo, Bodebe, and their other African crew partners would hitch a ride to a vessel heading to "Guinea Coast" and thus secure a return trip to Kwa-speaking country.

The Portuguese ship weighed anchor at high tide that night and began to make her nautical bearings toward the Guinea current.  The ship captain was relieved when he finally felt the swaying movement of the vessel, inching away each minute from the port of Luanda.  As the deck officers informed the captain that their launch proved timely from their readings of a red sky, Sensobo and Bodebe with several of their countrymen took to the galley below to receive a portion of rice, peas, and beef,  and crouched on the wooden floor, huddled together with fingers fast in the food bowls to replenish what energy they had emptied from their strenuous work.

The sixth day, the purser prepared his accounts for the payment of their wages. Each shipmate received two doubloons daily which, by the time of the ship's entrance into Brazil's haven, would increase to a total of eight. The hired Krumen would only receive a lower boodle rate of one pistole increased to four doubloons at the final unloading. These were cutthroat wages, but this was a cutthroat practice. Who was complaining? Bodebe-- who started a clamor among his countrymen in Krutalk.

"Why we get no good pay? Nye-puru better workman than us? We want same pay!"

Sensobo reasoned with a stern warning.

"Keep quiet! You no complain, lest Nye-puru drop us for good and the Kru at Cape Mount, Bushrod Island, and Liverpool will snatch our duties as quickly as the wind! You remember last time one from our dako complained on the men-of-war; He never saw home again!"

Bodebe respectfully listened to his father, but at the same time was seething with protest, causing his next remark he was unable to hold in.

"Our brother never saw home again, that is true; But *we* may not see home again, not to mention the war captives down in the hold; Where are we taking them? To a better home? A better life? Why do the Nye-puru recruit us?"

"They cannot hire themselves."

"They use us with "little money;" Maybe we should let all the prisoners free! Then the Nye-puru will pay us deep from their pockets!!"

"Do not worry, my son; We can rest assured that the prisoners will be taken care of in their new land; They will make excellent servants, and some day many of them will rise again above a low status and spread Africa's wealth and knowledge far and wide! Is this not a much better wage?"

"One that a price cannot be put, my father."

"Just as speedily as the day turns into night, these servants will soon be princes just as in our village Zwedru; Why would you even *think* they would be treated less?"

So confident was the ship captain in the well-known abilities of the Kru in ensuring a vessel's cruise, he allowed them, without reservation, to check that the riggings to the sails and jumbo were secure, as his own sailors were known to, at times, be haphazardly negligent in climbing the spars and mast for inspection.  But, as is always true of any dangerous endeavour, the potential for injury always lie in wait, as was shown to be the case when the bucket of lard-oil was kicked over by a clumsy fourth-mate, causing Bodebe to lose footing and plummet over the railings into the deep, bottomless sea.  But this proud African, a sailor, a Kru, would not think of calling for help.

The Kru countrymen exploded in emotional alarm as they watched Bodebe hit.  "Man-man niwa down go!  Man-man niwa down go!" Sensobo yelled out in broken English mixed with his native tongue, trying in vain to capture the attention of the Portuguese men that a man had gone overboard, Sensobo and the others jumping wildly and pointing consistently over the ship's side, down to the bubbling circular ripples which spotted Bodebe's smashing impact.

Finally the Portuguese on duty caught on to the emergency alert, but not after much valuable time had been lost, as the freezing ocean temperatures could spell death within minutes.

Plunging at least twenty-feet down, from the sheer speed of descent, into the gloomy dark abyss of the vast ocean, Bodebe regained his equilibrium and popped his head back above water, but the seas were icy, suffocating the life from his muscles and lungs.  Suddenly, one from Sensobo's gang began to notice a moving streak rising above the surface, a white fin in the distance cutting through the surf and heading in Bodebe's direction.  "Zumi yeno! Zumi yeno!" the African mate cried out.

Bodebe soon reached the hull, but a *zumi yeno* had now fixed it's attention to his underwater treading.  "Hurry!  Throw down rope!  Throw down rope!" Sensobo and his gang frantically shouted to the seemingly indifferent Europeans, moving ever so slow, due perhaps to bored entertainment thus far on this long voyage of many dull days, and now being tweaked to excitement by this pressing grotesque scene.  The callous slave traders knew full well that in a few more minutes the scene would soon turn into a freak show.  But Sensobo and his men wasted no more time, hurling the ropes down and pulling Bodebe up to the coxswain's chair and ladder just as the great white *zumi* brushed the side of the hull,  then landing him back onboard through the lower gun room deck.

Finally in the fifth week, the pilot-officer reduced his knots and began his navigational performance into the harbor of Rio de Janeiro just by five o'clock p.m.  After unloading half of the four hundred twenty-eight slaves, the ship tacked further down to within reach of Sao Paulo and dropped anchor.  Sensobo, Bodebe, and their crew lowered their boats filled with wretched inhumanity loaded with festering sores and lice.  The chained company began instantly, hurling every description of desperate cries, wails, and moanings, in numerous foreign-dialects, at the oarsmen.  Tight-lipped as the Pharoah, the drum-captain, sitting at the front facing all, seemed not even to lose a beat in his drumming amid the clamor, keeping the Kru in perfect unison.  The boatsmen were reserved, perhaps thinking that their perceived mission was, in delivering servants, glorious, in that of expanding some African king's empire to the New World.

Now with an empty hold, the Portuguese ship headed for Liverpool to be refitted.  With doubloons in hand now exchanged for gold guineas, Sensobo, "Botswain," and their countrymen stormed the town buying up goods to later be distributed to their village panton and to their wives.  After several days shopping along the waterfronts, they happened upon a ship, *York Merchant,* heading for the Gold Coast.  The ship captain allowed all of them aboard with their crates of purchased goods.  Bodebe sat down tired as he watched from sea the ports of Liverpool become further and further away.  He felt his facial blue mark had protected him and would allow him to bring home *kani* for his wife.

One evening seventeen months later in the village, Prero, still serving as the temporary family head until his father's reappearance, returned home bringing his catch of soa for the day.  After handing it to his wife to prepare, Prero went to fill a calabash bag with hot water then went to bathe, pouring the water over his long arms, shoulders, and short legs, using a soap made from a sapindacee tree and then afterward, lubricated his muscular build with palm oil.

But inside Akee's hut, soon brought to her horrible notice was the sickness of her son, eating the food given him, but the food does not stay in him. Quickly, Akee summoned her servant to find the fruit of a certain tree, have it boiled, and brought back. This tree was known to cure many ailments. When Akee was herself being carried in the womb with difficulty, this tree had been used to help her mother give birth to her, after which, in thankfulness mother named her baby thus. But now would her baby live? It appeared that the child would not. Akee feared her husband would soon arrive home from sea and then learn his son might be dead. The earnings Sensobo would at that time hand over to her, a portion which she would turn in to her father's clan while the rest she would manage for her household, would mean nothing if Sensobo was being met by a funeral ceremony. Desperately, she continued to feed her child the tree's fruit, afraid to close her eyes at night for fear of what she might discover upon waking. The child already was refusing to feed from her breast. Seven moons later, the child now began to show signs of strength. The baby would survive. As the young male infant Mennah began to once again eagerly suck from his mother's nyitie, Akee chose to give him the nickname Dju teat, "the sucking child."

The young boy Mennah continued to grow strong. Having reached his eighth year, he was sent away to learn the ways of the fishing Krumen under the tutorship of the village teacher. On the day of Mennah's return, a wandering village storyteller came to Zwedru to recite the ancient folk tales to the young and old who came to listen. Mennah would listen intently, so to learn and understand the meaning of each story, ready to respond in case the old man should pose a question to him. On this occasion the storyteller related:

*"There was a man very happy and satisfied with what animals he had, a goat, bokro, that yielded milk and gave him*

drink;  an ox, bli, that plowed the field and produced food;  a lamb, blabe, that grew wool with which to clothe;  and a chimpanzee, tuawe, to help him scare away yewa, the birds from the field, and bring in firewood for him to keep warm.  One night a Puff Adder snuck onto the farm, crawled over to the goat and bit it. Next, the serpent made its way over to the ox and did likewise.  It then quietly slivered over to the lamb.  Finally before leaving, the adder cornered the chimpanzee.

The next morning the man rose to milk his goat, but the goat would not give any.  He went to plow the field but the ox refused to move.  He decided to shear his lamb but the lamb kept running away.  After toiling all day without any success, he finally retired to his hut that night to build a fire to eat.  But the chimpanzee had not brought wood.  This continued every day with the man's prized animals, who had been his cherished family for many years.  Soon the man had hunger pangs, due to the birds swooping into his field and eating his food, and was dying of thirst. He became cold at night from no firewood and his clothing was wearing out.  After many days the man cried:  "I am no longer happy now;  all that is left for me now is to lay down and die." When the animals saw that the man who had cared for them had died, they became sad.  Then the bokro spoke up saying, "This is my fault, for I thought he loved me less than you three, so I refused to give him milk."  But the bli quickly jumped in, "No, I am at fault. I believed that I was the one appreciated less than you three, so I did not plow his field to produce food."  "You are both wrong," said the blabe,  "It was me that he did not love, so to teach him a lesson I swore that I would never again give him my wool."  Now, the tuawe was crying and   beating himself saying, "Why are the three of you blaming yourselves?  While you spent time with him, all I did was make him laugh at night and scare the yewa while gathering firewood by day."

Just then, the puff adder appeared in the yard and began to laugh at them, saying, "Now who will take care of you?"

The old storyteller now finished his fable and asked the young minds a question.  "Tell me if you know;  What was the snake's name?"  The old ones were silent, all in deep thought.

Mennah and the other young thinkers strained to answer, but were stumped.  The storyteller held the audience in suspense for he knew he had them.  Then he revealed the key.  "The serpent's name was "Jealousy!"  The old man then drove home the point further: "No one is greater than another, but all in the family contribute to its happiness."

Mennah took this moral saying serious to heart because he knew the time was fast approaching for Mennah to choose a "nyeno" among the girls of the village.  Mennah had been developing a fondness for a young girl also present before the storyteller named Bina, whose father was Kru and her mother Grebo.  Upon notifying his father and mother of his selection, they soon would approach the parents of the girl to ask permission to purchase their son's future wife.  When he becomes of age will he then bring her home.  One day Mennah approached Bina and placed a flower in her hair to signify his interest.  Sensobo and Akee soon visited the parents of Bina to ask their permission, which was granted.  Then, Sensobo negotiated the dowry price: two bli, a cow bri-de, and one bokro.

Ten years later, finally Mennah became of age and brought Bina home as his bride.  Joyously she entered the rectangular hut made of palm fronds that would become her home.  Sensobo had purchased two oxen and two cows for them from the wealth he had earned on his voyages, and even gave them a jackassi and a few sheep from his own herd.  Father Sensobo also didn't fail to pass along a word of wisdom to his son on how to treat his new wife: "You cannot harvest a farm in one day."

One morning months later,  Mennah and his two brothers, Bodebe and Prero, departed  to the fishing grounds,  returning with snapper, catfish, mudskipper, and turtle.  But upon their return, Mennah soon learned of a surprise awaiting him.  As Mennah turned over his catch to a village panton servant to ready the cooking meal he then entered his hut and greeted his wife Bina.  "It is so good to be home again, the catch lasted long today," Mennah said as he delivered Bina an arousing kiss to her neck.  "I am glad you are home," Bina said as she let out a faint moan caused by where Mennah's warm lips landed next, below the neck.  Already excited by her groan, Mennah asked, "Come help bathe me," as he playfully hinted his intentions while preparing his bath water. As Mennah climbed into the washing trough while Bina began slowly pouring the first water bucket over his shoulders, Mennah reached around Bina's back and began caressly patting her. "Look what I caught here! I better cook this fish," Mennah said teasingly as his hand now had worked its way from Bina's back to her tummy. "Hold still, or I'll miss all your filthy spots," Bina said, knowing his signals all too well. "Step in and join me before dinner is served," Mennah said this time while stroking his hand over Bina's waist string then up across the side of her face and into her hair, then palming the back of her head, nudging it softly toward him.

Bina well knew this routine, and as usual would begin her climb into the trough on such subtle command. But not this time. "Come here my little fish," Mennah came, while hooking his hand around her back and gently pulling in repeat fashion. "Eager fisherman, twenty-seven moons won't be long at all," Bina said as she grabbed Mennah's hand from her back and brought it to her tummy, placing it right over her brown-skinned navel. "After twenty-seven moons I will gladly swim after your active bait," Bina said while patting Mennah's resting hand upon her belly. "Dear, are you...?" Mennah now asked in surprise. "Yes, I am," came her answer. Mennah realized Bina was carrying a child.

During the evening meal of fish, okra, tomatoes, fruit, and turtle meat, everyone in the family clan who were present talked about Mennah and Bina's future child.

"If a boy, he will grow up to be an excellent hunter, like the leopard," said one of the men relatives, which was enthusiastically echoed by Sensobo and the other men, wearing ornamental finger rings made of gold, silver, and horn.

"I say he will jump good, like the gazelle! Just make sure to cover his legs each night," proclaimed another male relative, who chose this saying because his own male child at six months had been accidently dropped by his wife's servant.

But Akee and the womenfolk present, wearing wickerwork bundles of string around their loins, bead necklaces, and wrist bracelets of silver and brass, now made their preferences known, as they together in unison wildly cheered out, "Our little daughter will become a Queen!  Her bride-price will be so high that none of the boys can buy her!  The marriage of our little sister will be a strong tree branch, and her owner will praise her at the village gates!"

Throughout the evening the family clan pampered Bina with food and attention.  They also made sure that Bina not eat any of the turtle, as they believed that when the child was born it would crawl on its belly just like a turtle.  (In time Bina gave birth to her child, a son, whom they named Nadi, after Bina's father.)

Seven days later,  the women arose to labor in  the pepper gardens.  They plucked the ripe berries, soaking them in water for several days, then laid them out to dry under the hot tropical sun. As Akee was busy gathering her peppercorns, she suddenly  fell sick.  The women brought her inside to her hut and laid her down while the servants fanned her with palm reeds to cool her.  Couba fed her a drug made from banana skins, kola nuts, and pineapple leaf, while Mimba had her drink limejuice.  When Sensobo and the young men returned home, they then learned of Akee's condition.

Akee was burning with fever and becoming more weaker. Couba and Mimba stayed up throughout the night nursing Akee, feeding her a concoction of rice and corn soup, and junumo wine to help ease her pain.  Sensobo came over to Akee's bed, kneeled down, and began to whisper in her ear while holding her hand. What he said to her the women could not hear.

The next morning Sensobo and the women came out of the hut.  Sensobo then instructed his servant to go and dig a hole.  For the next three days following the burial, no work in the fields was to be done in the village  Zwedru.

In the year 1715, in the fifth month, in the thirty-third year of the headship of Korwolo, Chief Elder of the southeastern dako, there was a woman in the village of Zwedru, near the river Cavella, who was heavy in child.  Her name was Bina, and her husband, the father of her child, was Mennah, the son of Sensobo.

In the fifth month, on the ninth day of the month, the woman Bina gave birth to a daughter.  They named the girl Akey, in honor of Mennah's deceased mother.  The son of Mennah was

Nadi, and Mennah's  brothers were Prero, whose wife was Mimba, and Bodebe, who called himself Botswain, whose wife was Couba.

"See, a girl!" the female slave said to Bina while holding up the slippery-wet newborn then placing her in Bina's arms.  The child was crying her head off.  Mennah now let out all his pent-up nervous laughter as he finally could hear the whining and whimpering coming from Bina's specially-built weaning hut while he stood outside with Bodebe and Prero, all three men not allowed inside.

"Shhhh, my beautiful little black Akey, shhhh; you have announced your arrival very well," Bina said.  The child hollered two more times, then relaxed.  "Quiet, my dear little Akey;  I can tell the strength in your voice;  With Great Nyeswa's blessing, you too some day will watch your own sprouts grow."  The baby finally drifted to sleep while Bina hummed an old folk song.

Mennah's son Nadi reached his eighth year and was sent away to live with the village teacher to learn the skills of fishing.  There he would learn to canoe, make a fishing line, the use of weights, and how to use the jlode.  He also would be taught geography, metreology, and astronomy, so to learn how the winds, clouds, landmarks, and position of the stars all aid a skilled fisherman.  Nadi's father, uncles, and grandfather had all gone through their training during their respective time.  They were thankful for the knowledge they gained, such as knowing the fishing grounds of the rock fish, the snapper, and the cavella.  And all Kru fishermen would always relate with great pride their stories of bringing home to the feast the prized shark or crocodile.

When Nadi returned home from his training, he was very eager to show his father, uncles and grandfather the seafaring skills he had acquired.  It was a happy occasion as Nadi greeted the first person he met when entering the family yard, Sensobo, sitting on a stool and wearing a felt hat to protect his head from the afternoon heat.  Nadi then proceeded on to greet his father Mennah, working out in the pepper field with Bina, nine year old Akey, along with the families of Bodebe and Prero.

"My son!  Everyone, stop the work!  We will prepare a meal for this man!  Mennah said proudly.

As soon as the afternoon meal was prepared outside their hut, little Akey jumped into her father's lap as Mennah began listening to Nadi.

"Father, I will become a sailor in the tradition of you and Grandfather," Nadi said honorably. "I will not squander the reason as to why I was sent forth."

"Are you prepared to catch a crocodile?"

"Yes! I believe I am."

"And how do you kill a crocodile?  With both hands holding down his neck, or both hands holding down the tip of his jaws?" Mennah said cleverly.

"To *kill* him one must strike him thru the center of his skull with the long jlode, my father;  The hands are used only for *capture*, at the tip of his mouth."

"You have been taught well;  I can still recount the time when Grandfather, your uncles, and I went out to catch *Zumi Masake*, "The Great Reptile.""

"Bieju, please tell us," little Akey pleaded.

"We took three boats early evening to Lake Cestos;  There was a great reptile no one could catch, a powerful crocodile with a huge tail and jaws, which killed several villagers and livestock; The people who lived by the lake named it *Zumi*. We volunteered to go on the hunt and had went out, when it started to storm. The rain was very great and the heavens thundered with flashes of fire. Grandfather decided we should go back for safety, but while oaring we felt something under all three of our boats. We were hitting the back of the reptile!"

"Go on Bieju!  What happened?" little Akey asked while trying to sit patiently on Mennah's knees.

"We threw some dead chickens into the water to see if there were more than one *Zumi,* then as the giant head of the creature came to the surface to devour its meal we encircled it and threw out the last chicken tied to a string, leading the reptile closer and closer to within striking reach of our long sharpened jlodes."

"And then?"

"And then we *THRUST* into the center of the crocodile's head three of our jlodes one after the other!"

Akey nearly fell off of Mennah.  Then Bodebe began to demonstrate how he pushed his spear through the armorlike skin and cartilage of the "crocodylus."

"I lifted my arms high over my head, and with all my muscle might *BURROWED* the harpoon into *Zumi Masake's* skull!"

Little Akey was now at Mennah's feet.  Now Sensobo stood up to finish the story.

"The "Great Reptile" screamed and jerked violently from our attacks as it brushed our boats hard and threw us into the waters with it.  The heavy downpour was still falling and the sky turned dark.  A village elder saw our plight and sent his sons to rescue us as we swam toward their boats.  But as we swam, the creature started to come after us.  We were at the mercy of *Zumi*."

"So what saved all of you?" Nadi asked.

"The monster was upon us.  Then, as the thunder kept roaring, fire from heaven came down at that second and struck the three jlodes stuck in the monster's skull, killing the life of the sea creature."

Mennah now turned to Nadi and pulled Akey back to his lap.  "Yes my son, I believe you will become a great sailor."

After the meal, Akey watched as her brother and grandfather began their ancient art of canoe crafting.  After cutting the tree down, they then proceeded to measure it to the proper depth and degree, using a combination of knives for lengthening and fire to square it up.  Soon they began chopping and hewing away at the insides of the log, burning and chiseling away the burnt sections, until their knife implements had produced a round bottom, hollowed dug out.

Thousands of miles away, in a different land, another boat-building project was underway.  A sixth-rate English naval dispatch ship was being constructed.  There, the team of builders laid out the ship's wooden hull, planking its ribs, deck beams, and cross supports which would frame the hold.  Next, the orlop was carefully overlaid according to the draft, then the measurements and wood blocks to the gun room deck.  Following this, were the planks and beams joining to the officers' cabins, upper gun deck, and galley. Finally, the railings and timbers were laid and fitted to form the upper deck and gallery, leading to the forming shape of the prow, forecastle, and stern. The vertical spars were then mounted, supported by the railings for securing the rigging and sails. When the ship was finally assembled it was named *Providence*, and soon thereafter received its registry number and insurance bond. The hold of the ship was huge, built to hold large amounts of goods and potential trade. The man who had invested in this vessel, owner Dudley Digges of the House of Burgesses, evidently had something in mind.

Knowing that Nadi wanted very much to show his skills as a fisherman and boatsman, his uncle Prero brought him along on a trek to visit their kinsfolk across the Cavella and over to the fishing villages of Tabou and Berebe. Prero observed with great impressiveness as Nadi carefully made landmarks on the way, using his knife to carve markings in certain trees along the trails, or breaking certain tree limbs to be left hanging by its bark.

In time, Akey began accompanying her brother Nadi to the fishing grounds at the river Cavella. Occasionally the women of the village went with the men to assist with the catch. Couba, Mimba, Bina, and Akey would build traps to catch the fish in. They also would take the bark from certain trees, beat it on the rocks, then take the chaff of the bark and throw it into the water to stupify the fish.

One day the women had gone with their men to fish for mackerel along the Cavella. Sensobo and his sons and their wives prepared to depart for their desired spots along the banks of the river. The young children were commanded to stay behind in the village under the care of the family servant. But Akey was now in her tenth year. Fearing that her spirited movements this day would be relegated and confined only to the quietness of the village, Akey quickly approached her mother. "Am I to come, too, mother, since I have now reached my tenth year and am capable of assisting the men just as the women are, or am I to stay here with the little ones?," Akey asked defensively. Mother Bina answered, "No, my daughter, if you are old enough to have caught the fish for your father and brother at the fishing holes of the catfish and the snapper, then you are old enough to help them catch the mackerell at the big river; and when we return, YOU will show me how old you are and clean and cook them." Overhearing, Nadi chuckled at his young sister's surprised look.

The fishing on this day proved good for the Kru, as many men and several families toiled for hours amidst the hot heat, while the river's waters sought to cool them. Stopping briefly at the sixth hour since the sunrise for nourishment, Sensobo's clan soon resumed the catch during the seventh hour.

By the eighth hour the heat was intense. The black muscles of the men--Sensobo, Prero, Bodebe, and Mennah--glistened as they pulled in their fishing nets. Even the sweat of the women poured off their bodies as they busied themselves picking out the bouncing mackerell from the tangled nets. As Akey began to tire she soon stole away to sit in the shade underneath a silk cotton tree off in the distance. Akey knew this was not the time to quit and be idle. It was a time to work. But Akey reasoned she was still a girl--a worker, yes--but still a girl. And a Kru girl in her tenth year still needed some time to play. As she sat in her shade, Akey observed the capableness of her mother Bina, in harmonious step, laboring with Mennah. Akey could tell that their love for each other was a happy love. Akey noticed the joyful laughter of Couba and Mimba, and the seeming gleefulness expressed in their tasks which proved doublefold: 'Honoring thy husbands' while maintaining their feminine force as contributors to the family booty. Yes, Akey knew some day she would take her place among the village women, soon to be given away in marriage, and then become an astute trader like her mother Bina, the family accountant. But this will all come in time. Akey then broke her gaze as a ground squirrel caught her attention.

"Where is Akey?" Bina asked. "Go find her," Mennah said. "She didn't want to stay home and play, and she didn't come here to play." Bina asked Nadi where his little sister had gone to hide, but Nadi hadn't a clue.

Bina approached Bodebe, who had been busying himself stringing a new fishing line. "Did you see where Akey went?" Bina asked. "She went to sit under the silk cotton trees over there," Bodebe said as he pointed toward that direction.  But when Bodebe looked over to the tree area Akey was no longer there. With concern, he walked over to the spot where she had sat to find out if she had fallen sick.  Suddenly several Sedibo, "young soldiers," who were not of the Zwedru village dako, with wooden clubs and spears, rushed upon Bodebe. He ran faster than they and yelled at the top of his lungs "MU! KWE-KWE, MU !!!" the warning cry to flee.  "Akey!  Come here!  Akey!  Come here now!!" Mennah shouted.  But it was too late.  Akey had been snatched by the Sedibo. Sensobo, his sons, and the women fled into the forests, but the Sedibo were still pursuing Bodebe. Spotting an opening, he ran along a trail they were not familiar with.  Bodebe decided to run back towards the river and retrieve his canoe for escape, but that proved to be  unwise, as two of the soldiers were standing guard over the canoes. Bodebe stayed still where he was and hid among the bush.  He could hear the soldiers were near  again, and he began to fear that he would soon be discovered.  Grabbing some small rocks in one hand, he threw them into the brush.

Thinking it was their prey, the two standing by the canoes converged upon the sound of the rocks.  Immediately Bodebe swiftly ran towards the closest canoe, grabbed it, and jumped into the river.  The paddles were still inside.  But the time he had bought himself proved shortlived as the soldiers spotted him and came again.  Two jumped in one canoe with ropes, and two more in another.

# CHAPTER FOUR
## Village Life in Portland


I paddled as hard and as fast as I could. Two foreigners in the vessel just behind me flipped over their canoe into the cold river. In the corner of my eye I caught a white man jumping into the river to save them. But I kept oaring. I wasn't going to make the same mistake. I knew the power of the river, the strength of its might, the force of its currents. I respected the river's heart, that it beated in the depths below me, and that no man can kill it. On the contrary, the river could kill me, for I knew the rock hazards that lay ahead. And at this moment, I didn't care if the foreigners behind me knew about the smashing rocks up ahead. All of my concentration was totally centered on controlling my canoe. As I entered another forward-moving rapid that ran alongside the bank for several yards, I quickly turned my head back momentarily to measure the drive and progress of the parties behind me. As I turned my head forward again, a low tree branch caught me in the face, cutting my forehead. The stark fear which was boiling in my blood and through my body, tempered the pain from the tree. Soon my face became pulled through a string of twigs and twisted limbs. While passing through them, my whole body could feel the exhilarating sensation of the speed of my canoe, swiftly shooting down one section, then zig-zaging and descending down another. Then my craft hit the rocks. My waist and legs became numb from the chilly water splashing into my canoe that the rapids had invited. The white man and the two foreigner canoe were getting closer. I lashed out at the rock boulders with my oar to release me, jabbing, pushing, digging, panicking. My kicking, coupled with the force of the rapids against my pinned canoe upon the rocks, had now turned the canoe totally around, so that now the back was toward the front and I was pointing to the rear, facing the canoes that were now upon me.  One white hand reached out and grabbed the side of my canoe, while another hand took my oar.

The soldiers overtook his canoe, and  binding him with ropes brought him back ashore.  He then was taken  to their camp, and there he saw young Akey along with several others who had been captured, though not recognizing any others  as his clan except Akey.  Akey cried out,  "Dear Nyeswa (God the Creator), please bring down your fire on the Mumawi, these devils!"  Bodebe now  implored their captors to let them go.  Not understanding their dialect, but seeing that Akey was greatly distressed,  the Sedibo allowed them to sit together through the night while under guard.

The next day Akey, Bodebe, and the others were all roped together by the neck and marched to the coast, where they were then sold to the Nye-puru  and put aboard a large ship.

At Bence Island, Sierra Leone on September 18, 1721, an invoice pertaining to the shipping goods onboard a peculiar ship registered as *Providence* was sent to the Royal African Company in London.  Accompanying the invoice was a report, giving an apology as to why the ship laid so long undispatched, along with a comment about the ship's goods: "231 slaves...Consigned to Jamaica."  Referring again to *Documents Illustrative of the History of the Slave Trade*, the ship *Providence* made her travel route back to West Africa where this time she lay landed on October 24, 1723 at Bassam, Ivory Coast, a narrow strip of land between the ocean and a lagoon 45 kilometers from Abidjan.  The commanding officer of *Providence*, a Captain Pariss, voiced frustration at being outbid by other traders coming there to avoid the high prices at the slave market of Cape Coast.  Why were the price of slaves higher there?  The African armies of Asante by the beginning of the 18th century began its empire with the defeat of their tribal neighbors, and control to dictate the prices of slaves at Cape Coast and Elmina.  An earlier document sent to the Royal African Company on March 3, 1708 confirmed this state of affairs:  "Captain Bonham...from London...slaved here before the battles were fought, and they gave 14 pieces current for men, and nine pieces for women, when the battle was fought we expected slaves to be cheap, but...kept the prices up."

The Atlantic slave trade was obviously wrong and immoral no matter which side. What is also sad is how firearms began to be sold from the European slave traders to the African tribes. Power begets more power. Greed and riches beget more greed and riches. Pretty soon it corrupts you and destroys you. That's what happened to Africa when she was taught the slave monopoly, and what also contributed to the colonization of Africa, the effects of which you can still see today in the form of civil war and a growing minority power-grabbing elite. The million dollar question I wished could be answered is: Would the village chief lords and all other Africans who added their complicity to the Atlantic slave trade have continued doing so if they could have *seen* the constitutional slavery system structure in America?

The only thing I knew about Africa while growing up was from what I saw on TV and movies. Besides learning about the animal world and beautiful scenery, the only thing I came away with about Africans were that they were just a group of tribespeople, the "Natives," who loved to dance or go hunting. These shows never really told me about the people themselves, their customs, their family life. Africans were always portrayed as one big group. So as a young person growing up, there was no connection in my mind that they were my ancestors.

I was born in 1959 in Portland, Oregon to Zane and Fern McCoy Hanks. My two brothers, Laurence and Michael, came later to the world of 1960 and 1964. Portland, the largest city in the state with a population of some 500,000 and nicknamed the "City of Roses," had its city name determined by a coin flip in 1851 between two businessmen. So the other name choice "Boston" lost out.

Portland's populace and other cities and towns in then "Oregon Territory" came together in June 1857 for a Constitutional Convention. As the Oregon constitution was in time adopted, the question of allowing slavery was raised and answered--it was rejected. Although the majority of Oregonians were Southerners they were not of the slave-holding class, and those who did settle with slaves did not hold them in bondage. So when President Buchanan admitted Oregon as a state in February 1859 it was clear that the new state would be anti-slavery. There was, however, one hitch. Exclusion laws. Anti-slavery didn't mean pro-negro. In other words, slaves were free, but blacks could not stay. Whipping was the penalty for staying, and signs around eastern and southern Oregon carried signs to remind one of that fact: "Do Not Let The Sun Set On You."

Blacks who were able to somehow remain found themselves mostly in Portland. By the 1920's, during the peak of the Ku Klux Klan in Oregon, Portland's black populace was about 2,000. Black businesses thrived--barber shops, grocery stores, shoe makers, billard parlours, saloons--mostly down Broadway Street near downtown Union Station. The Golden West Hotel on Broadway & Everett served as the community center for Portland's black community on Sundays. Sunday was a day one could see their friends and socialize at the popular ice cream parlour next door.

By 1926, Article One, Section 35 of Oregon's Constitution exclusionary clause was repelled. But even though blacks in Oregon could share the same restrooms, the same water fountains, the same classrooms, and could vote, they still were not allowed in white restaurants, pools, hospitals, unless an emergency, and reduced to balcony seating only in theatres. Things were worse when the Depression hit, destroying black businesses. Before the Depression, whites would not touch certain jobs--elevator operators, cooks, porters, waiters. But during the Depression, blacks were being pushed out of those very jobs. Then came World War ll.

Mother was from Caruthersville, Missouri, attending college at Lincoln University in Jefferson, Missouri before moving with her parents to Portland, and settled in the Albina community district south of Vanport City. Bill McCoy, my mother's older brother, was born in 1921 in Indianola, Mississippi but grew up in Caruthersville and St. Louis, later moving to Portland and becoming a senator for the state of Oregon for twenty years.

Healthcare and housing became two of his main concerns.  I wondered if that was a result of his memories working the passenger train routes as a porter between St. Louis and Utah, because it was then that he got his firsthand look at Japanese Americans on his trains who had their civil rights stripped from them and were being deported to American detention camps during World War II.

By the time my mother arrived in town with thousands of other African Americans, Vanport went up almost overnight, becoming then the second largest city in Oregon, a city literally built in 1945 along the Columbia River between Portland and Vancouver, Washington, hence, the name "Vanport."  In 1805 the famous explorers Lewis and Clark passed through the area as they came down the Columbia River in search for the Pacific Ocean. But one hundred forty years later the area had become a segregated public housing community.  Many  blacks lived there at the time as a large number came to Oregon during World War ll to find jobs at the shipyards.  Now Portland's black population grew from 2,000 to 25,000.

This was the reason that brought my mother and her parents to Portland in 1945 as well.  But about three years after moving here, something happened that would affect the face of Portland forever.  That was on Sunday, May 30, 1948.  Mom was standing out at the bus stop that early afternoon waiting to catch the city bus.  But on this day the bus would not be coming.  At about 1:30pm a dike broke on the Columbia river and headed toward Vanport, washing out homes, cars, and anything else in the surging waters' path.  18,500 people were now homeless.  14 people lost their lives, and eight were never accounted for.  The number of deaths no doubt would have been higher had not the disaster happened on Memorial Day, when most of the residents were away visiting relatives or friends.  The threat of another broken dike was averted near Portland's Airport with the help of "Negro Troops" from Fort Lewis and citizen volunteers.  Even President Truman was flown out to see the $21 million dollar devastation.

The city of Vanport never was fully rebuilt after that flood. As a result, numerous black residents moved to Portland, where communities began to sprout, fusing with Portland's already present small African-American community.

My father was from Manhattan, Kansas.   After graduating from high school Dad enlisted in the Navy in 1948 just before the Korean War, working as a storekeeper on a refrigerator ship.

After being stationed at the Naval Operating Base in Guam and playing the outfield unit for the "NOB Blue Jackets" baseball team, finishing one season as "Diamond League Champions" with a 31-8 record,  and two years of touring Guam and the Pacific islands, Dad wound up stationed on the coast of Astoria, Oregon instead of being transferred to Oakland, California as originally scheduled.   This reassignment was due to being laid up in a Chicago naval hospital with a broken hand, resulting from a car accident while on leave.   So this explains why I wasn't born in Oakland.   So after my parents' wedding day in 1957, Mom worked as a secretary, for such organizations as the Housing & Urban Development and the Urban League of Portland, while Dad took up computer training and was later hired as a computer engineer programmer with the federal government's Department of Energy at the Bonneville Power Administration.

The fact that I felt no connection between myself and African people was understandable.   It was my parents who brought me here. The only genealogy in my immediate mind was "from my parents to me."   Africans, in my mind, were merely headhunters, engaging in festive dancing, or trained fierce warriors. And as far as my knowledge on American Slavery, there was none, at least not until seventh grade.   In seventh grade we were taught how the first African servants, not slaves, came to Jamestown in 1619 but that there were also white "indentured servants."   We were told how Crispus Attucks, a former slave, was the first person killed at the Boston Massacre.   And, of course, everyone knew that it was Abraham Lincoln who "freed the slaves" during the civil war. This was the extent of my American slavery knowledge.

Yet, at home it wasn't about being educated on the history of slavery that mattered.   Instead, what mattered was being educated about the racial strife that was going on during the

1960's.  My parents, and also my grandparents, did a wonderful job as best they could in teaching us how to survive in the face of racial prejudice and discrimination.  They did it by showing us by example how to get along with all types of people and walks of life.  We did things as a family with other families who were of different cultures than our own, and were encouraged to explore and develop whatever skills we had.    Laurence developed an interest in music and played guitar.  Michael was athletic in sports, receiving letters in baseball and football, as well as being handy with cars.  I had a love for reading books and an interest in the stage.  Like most kids growing up, we joined the boy scouts, little league, and enrolled in swimming lessons at the local Y.  We had our newspaper routes, sometimes inviting on occasion our neighborhood friends to accompany us, until customers started complaining their delivery milk jugs were turning up missing.  Kids today wouldn't know, but back then empty milk jugs were as valuable as pop cans.  A record language course in Japanese also found its way into our home, obtained by our parents from another African American family in the neighborhood.  Although Mom and Dad possibly knew mine and my brothers' attention span probably wouldn't translate into an acquired taste of foreign languages, their main motive was no doubt that it would keep our minds open to the fast-changing world around us.  And we had homework to do, too. Mom kept a well-stocked library of English, science, and history books near the fireplace and encouraged us to read them   during the summer.  Dad would be right there,too, giving us math problems to tax our brains.

All these things helped keep our minds off of the explosive events that were happening in the nation.  So when Mom and Dad turned on the T.V. on Sunday mornings and we watched black children being blown up in church, or young people being sprayed with water hoses, we knew something was wrong even though my brothers and I didn't fully understand it.

I remember watching on T.V. the funeral of President John F. Kennedy when I was four.  I didn't understand what that was about either.  All I remember was sitting on the sofa with Mom and Dad as they were glued watching the television set, watching these horses and soldiers marching down the street. And everyone was so quiet. I didn't know what it all meant, but I knew it was something serious. Something had happened. My parents may have told me what had occurred, but it wasn't until years later that I understood the phrase "Kennedy was assassinated." Now when I look back on it, although I still remember with fondness the close friendships I developed through sixth grade at a local catholic school, I understand now why in second grade a white kid at recess time hit me square in the face with a rubber kickball as he shouted out to his friends "let's play hit the nigger"! Or why one white kid in my class would set on my chair an open switchblade that I almost sat down on if I hadn't noticed at the last second; Why another would joke: "What's yellow on the outside, black on the inside, and going off a cliff? 'A school bus with niggers in it!!" Or even by fourth grade why kids were throwing rocks at us on the last day of school. After walking home from school one day, I turned on the television set to watch a Tarzan movie. Not more than ten minutes into it, Tarzan was interrupted by a newsflash:

"Dr. Martin Luther King has just been shot at a hotel in Memphis, Tennessee...he is being taken to a nearby hospital...again, Dr. King has just been shot...Please stay tuned for further news..."

Immediately I got up and ran from the living room into my bedroom closet and closed the door. I was in shock! "Why would someone want to shoot him?" I asked. Then after about ten seconds I sadly became realistic, saying "what can anyone do now?" I then walked back to the living room to watch Tarzan. Surely it could be argued that the so-called "fierce warrior tribes" shown on Tarzan were nothing compared to the "fierce tribes" that were right in this country. I realized that on Thursday, April 4, 1968.

Dr. King, who was born in Birmingham, Alabama, had visited Portland in November 1961 as principal speaker at the Urban League of Portland's "Equal Opportunity Day Program," and also guest speaker at Portland State University's program commemoration of the civil war.  The next day following Dr. King's assassination, classes at Portland's Thomas Jefferson High School, a school with the highest black student enrollment in Oregon at thirty-seven per cent out of their 1,700 student body, were dismissed early after several students refused to attend. Incidents of fighting broke out, including one girl who ended up in the hospital after being pushed down a flight of stairs, and five fires were started inside.  After the dismissed students left the school grounds, there were reports of automobile windows broken, store windows smashed, and other acts of civil disobdience.  The University of Oregon in Eugene also dismissed classes. Except for a few, the majority of schools in Portland and Multnomah County opened late the following Tuesday in honor of Dr. King's funeral, and many black businesses closed that day.  Several silent marches and memorials could also be seen taking place around the city.

I remember the first time I thought I had learned the name of an actual African tribe.  It was at my grandparents house while watching a tv movie about what I thought at the time was a tribe called the "Mau Mau's," but actually was the name of a secret organization made up of members from the "Kikuyu tribe" fighting for independence against the British in Kenya.  This movie really struck me that here this African tribe "even have their own name." As a ten year old I asked myself "why are the Mau Mau's fighting for independence within their own country?"  I later learned that what partly sparked the fightings in the 1950's in Kenya was that about a million Kikuyu were crowded into two thousand square miles of unfertile land, while less than four thousand whites occupied 16 thousand square miles of spacious land.  By fifth grade, the black militant movement had begun spreading throughout the United States. It reached the "City of Roses" with the opening of the Portland headquarters of the Black Panthers, being organized in a store front near Union and Fremont street.

But before those defining times came to Portland, we lived in the close-knit neighborhood of North Portland in 1960 at 9021 North Bayard.  Later we bought property to build our very own home over on North Alaska street, one of several streets where new homes were starting to spring up.  We moved into the new house in 1964, shortly before brother Michael was born.    It was beautiful, four bedrooms, three bathrooms, fireplace, a huge basement, and a large back yard surrounded by several locust and cottonwood trees that dotted the area.  We were surrounded by the "sticks," which gave a nice country feel even though in the city.

Up the street was the Portland Sports Arena, where night people would come from miles around to attend televised wrestling matches.  Cars would be lined up and down the street on both sides every Friday and Saturday night.  I never could understand why people would pay to see something that they could stay at home and see on T.V. for free.  These weren't just normal wrestling matches.  It was like a circus, and hyped to the hilt.  When we would see wrestlers getting thrown over the ring, and "blood" coming from head cuts with a little stage acting added, then we knew why people came from miles to buy a seat.

I remember when school let out in the summer of 1968. Around noontime one day in June I strolled over to our next-door neighbors, the Dorseys, for a visit.  Suddenly one of the girls came rushing out of their sliding glass patio door screaming, "They shot him...they shot him!!"    I tried to gather from the others what it was she meant and heard the name Kennedy.  Right away I said to them, "Of course President Kennedy got shot, that was a long time ago, didn't you know that?"  They finally got it through my head that they meant Senator Robert Kennedy.  I ran inside and there we watched the afternoon news.   Two assassinations within nine weeks apart.  Why?  It didn't make any sense.

So as far as genealogy went, I knew as a child that my mother was from Missouri and my father was born in Kansas City, Missouri but grew up in Manhattan, Kansas.  I remembered Dad telling us as kids he had a brother named Billy Don, a fluent Spanish speaker and the president and program chairman of "La Organizacion de Espanol", the high school's Spanish club, and would show us pictures of him from Dad's old high school yearbooks.  I also recalled being fascinated with Dad's scrapebook, containing old newspaper clippings in the late 1940's and early 1950's of jazz musicians, recordings, and concerts of the day. People I never heard of before, like Louis Jordan, Lionel Hampton, or Dizzy Gillespie.  When it came to jazz, I didn't know anything about it except that it was what we expected to be woken up by on Saturday morning. Every Saturday morning.

But after Dad was finished with the turntable to his huge 1964 Packard Bell stereo, then it was our turn.  First it was Jimi Hendrix, The Beatles, Santana, Chicago, and The Jackson Five. Then later it was Earth,Wind, & Fire, Funkadelic, Kool and the Gang, Ohio Players, The Isley Brothers.

The summer of 1969 saw Portland glued to television sets with the landing of the Apollo astronauts on the moon, and high school seniors being drafted to Vietnam. Thank goodness the U.S. troop involvement ended in 1973, as certainly more young men would have been drafted and sent, including myself.  One of Dad's high school friends re-enlisted during the 1960's and came out to Portland to see Dad before he was shipped out, although I was too young at the time to remember the visit.  The schoolmate did survive the war and ended up meeting his future wife who was a native of Thailand before both coming back to the States.  They eventually had a son who later grew up and became the youngest African American pro golf player to win the Masters tournament.

The ending of the decade known as the 60's also found free breakfasts being served by the Black Panthers each morning to children at the Highland Community center off  Ninth & Going street, while either being harassed, beaten, or arrested each month. Foodstuffs were being donated by the Kienows store at Union and Monroe streets.  But by February 1970 things turned ugly for Portland.

On February 18, 1970 a 19 year old black panther allegedly wanted for petty larceny noticed he was spotted by police as he headed to the panthers' headquarters.  A local radio station, monitoring police radio and learning of the planned police action, placed a telephone call to the Black Panther headquarters asking if any police action had taken place.  Minutes later the police pulled up to serve the warrant, an officer kicked the door opened, and allegedly the youth aimed a rifle at the officer.  Shots were fired and the wounded youth was rushed to the hospital.  The next day at City Hall while the City Council was convened, a march protesting the shooting was heading on its way. Carrying signs, the march stormed into council chambers as session was under way, filling the lobby and chanting with clenched fists. A Grand Jury was called to investigate the officers actions. Ten days later the policeman who shot the youth was cleared by the Grand Jury.

By the end of 1970, the panthers had been invited to speak at two all-white high schools despite angry parents trying to block entry, picketed the McDonald's store across from their headquarters for poor hiring practices of blacks and an alleged non-participant of community programs sponsored by panthers, and were featured in an editorial in the city's *Oregonian* paper. The editorial was meant as an eye-opener to the positive side of the group's often misunderstood viewpoint: renting store fronts in black neighborhoods and asking doctors, nurses, and pharmacies to donate supplies, time, and knowledge, providing services free regardless of color, calling pimps "lackeys," protecting black women, and opening rehabilitation centers for addicts. Years later, declassified files of the F.B.I. revealed that in 1970 the bureau had anonymously mailed material to Portland doctors and dentists to dissuade them from donating services to free clinics run by the panthers. This counterintelligence operation, called Cointelpro, also involved contacting Portland Jewish leaders and established black community leaders with inflamatory articles. The "City of Roses" in 1970 did indeed record a hot summer.

In 1974 the National Urban League held their annual conference in San Francisco on July 27-28. So that summer we got to see the streets of San Francisco. The speakers scheduled to appear were such ones as Vernon Jordan, Jesse Jackson, and Vice-President Gerald Ford, among others. Some felt then that Vice-President Ford's appearance, the first time in President Nixon's five years in office that one of his top leaders had addressed a major Black organization, was just a way to win Black support should a run toward the White House arise in 1976. Apparently he didn't have to wait long. Eleven days later on August 8, President Nixon resigned as the 37th President of the United States. The next day Gerald Ford succeeded him. So while my parents attended the convention, my brothers and I along with friends favored instead a

Bruce Lee movie.

I started to take a personal interest in religion during my sophmore year in high school.    Our next door neighbors, the Dorseys, had accepted a free six-month home Bible study course by Jehovah's Witnesses.  At the time, Jehovah's Witnesses were banned in about ten countries, one of them being the East African country called Malawi.  The Dorseys would describe to me the reports heard coming out of Malawi, how 18,000 members were being violently persecuted just for refusing to participate in political activities on any level.  How pregnant women, because of refusing to buy a 25 cents political party card due to their religious conscience, were kicked and struck.  Or how itching beans, called *chitedze*, would be rubbed into the wounds of the men and women, who received vicious blows for being neutral.  How six-inch nails were driven through men's feet and then forced to walk.  Women and young girls being raped.  Men's genitals being tied to heavy bricks, then beaten.

Many of these reports I read about in their published journal *Awake!* magazine.  As a young teenager I couldn't understand why so much hatred was being placed upon peaceful religious people just because of their beliefs.   The subjects discussed in the Dorseys' living room were so interesting that I soon joined in, always each week looking out my bedroom window to see if the elderly white woman teacher in the white cadillac, Ms. Hendricks, and her partner Larry, had arrived next door for another question and answer Bible session, her constant emphasis on why "1914" was an important year, and her memories as a young girl seeing people dropping dead from the Spanish Influenza.

I attended four years at Woodrow Wilson High School, a student body of over 1600 and about sixty African-American students.  Although I highly enjoyed joining the high school track & field team, my main love without question was a school course in TV broadcasting during my junior and senior year.  Cable TV was still in its early development during the 1970's, and so it was exciting when Portland high schools were being given access to a local cable channel and the chance for some to produce their own educational shows.

When it was our school class turn to broadcast each week I had to make sure my "student profile" segments were taped, edited, and ready to air.  But then one day Mrs. Barrett, an English teacher and one of the few African-American faculty members, approached me in February 1976 to see if I could broadcast something for Black History Month.  I never even knew what Black History Month was.  She provided me with a deck of history cards featuring the lives of prominent black persons, and so that night all the homes that were tuned-in got to hear about Harriet Tubman.  The next two weeks were about someone else, I can't remember now just who they were.  But what bothered me was why I felt embarrassed, or maybe a better word--inadequate--in sharing that history.  Why?  I felt comfortable in profiling my classmates, but not that of my own people.  If I could see Mrs. Barrett today I would thank her, for she taught me an invaluable lesson:  Make sure you have an understanding about your own culture and history, or you will eventually even deny yourself.  Yes, the psychological scars I had acquired in first and second grades were still playing tricks on me.

My first real encounter which made me realize my yearning for identity was on October 15, 1976.  That was when I met an African man for the first time.  I was working an after school job as a parking attendant at Portland's Memorial Coliseum, which was hosting an exhibition basketball game between the Portland Trailblazers and the Los Angeles Lakers.  The Coliseum was across the street from a commercial shipping port.  Earlier that week a ship named *Spetsai* from Japan arrived at port.  One of the ship's crew came up to my parking booth that evening to ask for directions, an African named Jack Abul.  A friendly conversation started, followed by an invitation to come tour his ship.  A couple days later, I along with two friends went aboard Jack's ship as he gave us a tour and introduced us to his crewmates.  We then asked Jack if we could bring him to my friend's place for a meal.  He gladly accepted.  It was a wonderful evening.  Something was jumping up and down inside me, a feeling I couldn't describe nor define, a touching experience of human brotherhood.  Days later, on October 19, Jack's ship departed for India and I never saw him again. However, several months later I received a letter. Although the grammar was lacking, the spirit behind the words were felt:

My Dear Brother Steve Hanks
I hope you are in good health and your work is going well, if so thanks to god, we are all well in my ship tow, no trouble , Steve I thank you for all what you do to me when I am in portland may god be with you and may god help you in your work Amin
everybody in my ship say that I should greet you. that is my  co workers in my ship.
plesc do not be anoyed that I dont write you in time, it is becuse my ship was too sloy on the road, and we keep long on ankor in India, that is why. plese...try to send one of my picture to me when you are replying me. and greet all the people that we all take the picture to gether in portland...both the wife and the husband, that I greet them tow
May god be with them, and help them Amin.
I stop here, I am yours black brother Africa. Mr. Jack Abul.  good bye, we shall see again, by the name of god. Amin.  good bye.

That was the last time I heard from my African friend, Mr. Jack Abul.  I hope he's well and doing okay.  Maybe I'd just have to go to Africa myself and see him.

# CHAPTER FIVE

## A Generation Born Free

It was now time to take that trip to Kansas and meet Cousin Mrytle. I waited until October when it would be less chance of running into a twister, or so my city mind thought. I caught a greyhound bus scheduled to arrive in Topeka two days later. Needing something to read, I bought a newspaper along the way and read the headline news about Germany being reunited with jubilation after 45 years due to the recent fall of the Berlin Wall. Meeting Cousin Mrytle would soon be a reuniting also, between the two branches of our family. My only hope were that the old crumbled walls of slavery had not blocked the ancient generations of my family from sharing its history to descendants of the new. After transferring buses in Salt Lake City and covering 1700 miles of pavement, I finally arrived in Topeka at 10:30 p.m. Being a little short on money, I had planned on just sleeping in the bus terminal since they usually stayed open 24 hours a day. But the one in Topeka was not. I ended up sleeping outside on the front steps.

By sunrise, I freshened up, then warmed up with fresh coffee and breakfast. Before calling Mrytle, though, I wanted to spend some time at the Kansas State Historical Society and research their records on the "Exodus of 1879." The "Exodus of 1879" was when thousands of freed Afro-Americans left the South and migrated to Kansas to escape the oppression and bigotry that still existed towards blacks after Reconstruction.  Even during the Reconstruction years of 1865-1877 atrocities were just as severe, causing several public figures, such as Frederick Douglass, to speak out and draw attention to the dangerous instabilities still present in the South.   I remembered reading about the events which finally led up to this massive migration at the library in Portland.   The Kansas State Historical Society held a large manuscript collection regarding the exodus.   One collection I looked at was called the "Singleton Scrapbook," named after one of the organizers of the exodus, Benjamin "Pap" Singleton of Edgefield, Tennessee, a cabinet and coffinmaker.   Other records described the mistreatment Afro-Americans received leading up to the exodus.  Henry Adams, of Caddo Parish, Louisiana, a political organizer and one of the leaders of a "Back to Africa" underground emigration movement to Liberia, West Africa in connection with the American Colonization Society, possessed a paper documenting 683 violent attacks upon blacks.   One incident involved a man named Hiram Smith, who gave an affidavit:

"De Soto Parish,

State of Louisiana:

My name is Hiram Smith.  I lived on Joe Williams place, about two miles southeast of Keachie.  I asked Mr. Williams to pay what he owed me on my cotton;  also seventy-five dollars he had taken away from me, what another man had paid me.  He jumped on me and beat me so badly I fear I cannot live.  He made me crawl on my knees and call them my God, my master, the God of all power.   They then drew revolvers on me; all because I had asked for a settlement.  This was done on the 16th of March, 1876

Hiram Smith"


Benjamin "Pap" Singleton also recalled two incidents:


"Julia Haven; I made the outside box and her coffin, in Smith County, Tennessee.  And another young, colored lady I know, about my color, they committed an outrage on her and then shot her, and I helped myself to make the outside box."

The Freedmens Bureau, a bureau created by the U.S. Congress soon after the civil war to assist newly freed blacks, also kept a register of complaints made by blacks whose rights and freedoms were being violated. In Carroll County, Mississippi an affidavit was made by Mary Eskridge, whose apparent former owner, William Chiles Eskridge, had taken her child:

Jan. 30th 1867

Mary Eskridge Colored makes an affidavit that her child Wesley Ann aged 8 years was apprenticed to Wm. Eskridge of Carroll Co. Miss. without her consent and that she has made repeated efforts to get possesion of the child but that Eskridge threatens to injure her if she comes on his place   that she is fully able to support said child and prays that the custody be given her

Feb 19th 1867
Mary Eskridge
            makes complaint on oath that her child Wesley Ann aged 8 years or there about was apprenticed to Wm Eskridge without her consent   that she never deserted the child voluntarily but left to avoid a whipping and has not dared to go back or he has threatened her with violence.  States that she is fully able to support her child and asks for the custody of it

her<br>
Mary   X   Eskridge<br>
mark

Another complaint was filed against William Eskridge by freedman Buck Bladock:

April 20th, 1867
            Buck Bladock(Col) complains that Mr. Wm. Eskridge near Duck Hill Carroll Co. pulled his ears then acted to whip him, drew his pistol and shook it in his face and told him he "would put me

where the buzzards wouldn't find me"

As the exodus picked up momentum, threats and intimidation sprang up from Southeners to try to halt the movement. In September 1879, freedman Joseph Starks of Grenada, Mississippi mentioned in a letter  sent to the Kansas governor: "We want to come out, and have no money hardly. We have to be in secret or be shot, and not allowed to meet...We have about fifty widows in our band that are workmen and farmers also. The white men here take our wives and daughters and do them as they please, and we are shot if we say anything about it...We are sure to have to leave or to be killed."  Some blacks were killed for attempting to leave; others had their property or money taken away from them.  But these tactics did little to stop the flow of blacks from the spring of 1879 to 1881.  The "Great Exodus" came from Kentucky, Tennessee, Alabama, Mississippi, Louisiana, and Texas. They left by train, steamboat, or wagon.  Some walked by foot till they crossed their state line, then took other means of travel. Others were stranded for weeks on the Mississippi river because of steamboats refusing to pick them up, leaving families with barely enough food to survive.  One observer stated:

"The encampments all had hailing-signals up for the north-bound steamboats, and when these wildly, frantically waved signals were cruelly ignored while the boat proceeded complacently on its way, I saw colored men and women cast themselves to the ground in despair, and heard them groan and shout their lamentations.

What is to become of these wretched people God only knows.  Here were nearly half a thousand, refused , scattered along the banks of the mighty Mississippi, without shelter, without food, with no hope of escaping from their present surrounding, and hardly a chance of returning whence they came."

Chicago Daily  Inter-Ocean, April 25, 1879.

Even the *Osage City Free Press* of  Friday, April 25, 1879 reported on the condition of the refugees once they arrived in Kansas:

## THE REFUGEES AT LAWRENCE
[Lawrence Journal, 20]

Some four carloads of the colored refugees came up last night, arriving at the Kansas Pacific depot at half past nine o'clock. Their coming was an entire surprise to our citizens, who knew nothing of it until yesterday afternoon when it was rumored that a hundred families, numbering some five or six hundred persons, were to be shipped...We hope the farmers of this vicinity who can use farm laborers, or can let them have land to work on shares, will give these needy people assistance....Just as fast as possible they should be shipped into the country, where they can work and earn their living. The farmers of Douglas county, we are confident, will sustain their old-time [reputation] as friends of the oppressed by giving these people, not charity, but a chance to work.

## LOCAL NEWS

The colored exodus reached Osage City last week. The new arrivals seems to be very energetic. Some of them have already erected small dwellings and settled down to business in a way that merits commendation.

Based upon the 1880 census, I determined my family must have arrived in Kansas sometime between June 1879 and June 1880, since a child named Maria Hanks, who apparently later died in childhood, was listed by the family as being one year old and born in Mississippi. Other freedmen families that fled Duck Hill and went to Osage City were the Bradleys, Lotts, Crowders, Eskridges, Purnells, and Binfords.

Although some blacks returned to the South for various reasons, the majority remained. Several towns and communities were created in Kansas due to the migration such as Morton City, David City, Tennessee Town, and Nicodemus, settled by blacks from Lexington, Kentucky. Poems and songs were inspired and penned:

Nicodemus

Nicodemus was a slave of African birth,
And was bought for a bag full of gold;
He was reckoned a part of the salt of the earth
But he died years ago, very old.
Nicodemus was a prophet, at least he was as wise
For he told of the battles to come;
How we trembled with fear, when he rolled up his eyes
And we heeded the shake of his thumb


Chorus:
"Good time coming, good time coming,
Long, long time on the way;
Run and tell Eliza to hurry up Pomp;
To meet us under the cotton tree,
In the Great Solomon Valley
At the first break of day"

"Them Golden Slippers"
Let de old back log give out its light
An let us all feel good tonight
An hab a good time for de last time heah
Fore we start for de land of Kansas

   It was time now to visit Cousin Mrytle. I called to tell her I had arrived and would be over shortly. Since it was such a nice day, I decided to walk to her house from downtown, the heart of Topeka and one of the battlegrounds of desegregation when in 1954 the critical case of Brown vs. Topeka Board of Education was first fought, before later won in the Supreme Court and establishing that "separate but equal" school classrooms for blacks was unconstitutional. After about a half hour walk, there I was, 1022 West Boswell.
   As I knocked, Mrytle came to the door and two generations

collided. After getting acquainted, I then told Cousin Mrytle that I had many questions about the family, but didn't know where to begin. Mrytle started by reading aloud the article she had written up for the Osage County Historical Society. Next, she gave me an inside glimpse of generations I had not known about, including the first one born free:

"...My husband was Clarence Foster, he was a fireman; When he retired he did carpentry work; His family came from Murfreesboro, Tennessee...settled in an area of Topeka known as Tennessee Town, it's called that today, just not too far from here; Why they called it Tennessee Town is because nearly everybody who lived out there had come from Tennessee right after slavery times; My husband he passed in 1970...Grandpa Hanks down in Osage City, it was nothing to see Grandpa and I going down the road together going up to get rabbits...I think he was a coal miner...Armstead, that was Grandpa Crockett's name...He made Hugh and I gather his apples and he didn't allow us to eat a one, he stood under the tree, he had very little hair, Hugh & I were in the tree and I found an apple that was just barely hanging, it was so rotten...when Hugh shook the tree I threw the apple...it splattered all over his head and when he went to wash his head we ate apples...he told Grandma Hanks the apple fell when we "shook the tree," so we didn't tell her I threw the apple so didn't get a whipping..."

Osage City in 1880 was a population of 3000. 1419 East Laing Street, where William and Rosetta Hanks moved to, was situated on property owned by the Osage Land and Mining Company. So if men were looking for work, coal mining was the answer. The daily wage for a coal miner then was 5 to 8 cents a bushel, bringing home $2.00-$3.20 if a miner pulled his expected standard of 40 bushels. But the new black arrivals soon had a rude awakening. The question of white and "colored" men working in the same shafts was agitated to a degree when white miners, although not opposed to black men working in the same mines, felt that they should have separate shafts to work in. So much for free Kansas. A day's wage for other common jobs of that time were $1.48 for a laborer, $2.30 as a blacksmith, $2.48 as a painter, $2.50 as a tailor, and $2.98 for a stonemason. Other sources of income included selling one's country produce at the local Alliance Exchange on Sixth & Main. Apples could earn $1 to $2 dollars per bushel. Perhaps that explained why Great-great-grandfather Armstead was so concerned about having his apple tree picked. Who wouldn't feel uneasy with having a financial investment loss come down splattering all over the crown of your head? Cousin Mrytle continued:

"...It took an hour to get to Osage City from Topeka and my mother had put me on the train, and she paid the porter, I don't know if she paid the porter fifty cents, but not over fifty cents I'm sure, to make sure that I got off at Osage City; See, she was afraid I'd go to sleep and they wouldn't see if I'd got off; When I got on I saw somebody setting across the aisle from me having lunch; Now, I don't know how long they'd been on the train but I got on the train half past nine and was goin' be on there an hour, but I needed to have a lunch! In that 35 miles it had to be fried chicken and apple pie! My mother wouldn't fix it...Grandma Hanks WOULD fix it; 'Cause I saw these other people having it, so I thought that's what you supposed to have;...One night on the way home from an ice cream social, 1909, Hugh, Teat, and I, it got so cold that we started running to keep warm; It was a long narrow road; back then you didn't have to worry about crime like you do today; well, I couldn't keep up so by the time I reached the house they were already in bed...another night the boys ran home and left me again; this lady in a horse & buggy carriage came up to me and said "I'm gonna get after those naughty boys."

The Hanks and Crocketts soon settled into their house lots along Laing street, while the Bradleys, Binfords, and Eskridges lived in the three lots next door. The Lotts, Crowders, and Purnell families took up lots in another part of the city. After work, there was plenty of time to socialize. Every few months blacks in Osage would hold a large festival ball at city hall, attracting persons from throughout the city and from other surrounding towns nearby. Young couples engaged to get married came to the ball to exchange their wedding vows. After supper, the floor was cleared close to midnight and the dancing would begin to the sounds of the Williams Bros. String Band, lasting till five or sometimes seven in the morning.

In February 1881 Rosetta gave birth to her fourth child, and named the son Granison, after her brother Granison Crockett who, along with her other brother Harrison Crockett, had decided to stay in Duck Hill.  Four months later a huge cyclone touched down on Osage County, destroying  homes mostly in towns along the Marais des Cygnes River, thus averting disaster on the families in Osage City.  Unfortunately two months later on August 22, 1881 the home of the Bradleys, four houses down from William Hanks and next door to George C. Eskridge, caught fire on a Monday evening and was destroyed.  A white woman was moved to collect fifty dollars for their relief.

On August 26, 1882 arrived a special day, for on this day Armstead Crockett officially received the deed to his property lot that he had purchased for $60.  No doubt it was a joyous occasion that surely had to have been celebrated by the family.  And the yearly tax that Armstead came now to be assessed was, in his mind, not an annual inconvenience, but rather a constant reminder that he indeed was the owner of his land.

By 1892 it had now become William Hanks' turn to experience the feeling of laying claim to his land plot, sold to him from his wife Rosetta's brother-in-law, William Campbell, whom the Hanks previously were paying rent to.  It didn't matter to William Hanks that his plot was somewhat smaller than his mutual neighbors' on Laing street.  Just waking up and observing through his front door the beautiful sunrise each day rising up over the neighboring farmlands across the road, the town's local meat market owner's ranch, and the five cows grazing between his and Armstead's section, gave William a peace of mind and a satisfaction of days.

"...Grandpa Hanks was a mighty good grandpa...he was tall, slender & slim, and Grandma was a little chubby...my uncle said Grandpa and Grandma lived here, and we lived about a half mile here, and then Aunt Sue lived about a half mile here this way...and there was someone at each place that had smallpox, and there was one at Grandma's here that was going to our house and Aunt Sue's house trying to take care of all of us;  Well, we had run out of coal, and my father went out, got up early out of bed and went outside to bring some more coal in the house until someone from Grandpa and Grandma's got there...and he had a chill, and never got over it, he had small pox..."

By 1896 William and Rosetta's tenth child was born in Rosetta's forty-fifth year on May 26 and named Hugh. Rosetta would attempt three more children while in her fifties between 1902-1908 but all three were stillborn. William and Rosetta's firstborn child, Sue Hanks, married a miner named Albert Orendorf who came from Tennessee. Armstead Crockett was now working as a miner. Two years later the eldest son and second-born, James Hanks, became engaged to a girl, Lillian Queenry, of Mississippi. They had their first child, Mrytle, in February 1899. The day she was born, James' brother Ernest was asked what he thought of his new baby niece. Everyone was amused when eight year old Ernest responded, "She ain't pretty, but she ain't ugly; She's just right." Starting that February, James entered the responsibilty of raising a family. Kerosine oil was 13 cents per gallon. Flour was $2.50, salt went for $1.25, sugar was 7 cents, and soap was 5 cents. James was a hard working provider. But sadly, the smallpox outbreak nine months later would claim that provider.

"...We really had good times together, we had very little to go on but we were all happy...I can remember Grandpa Hanks, he had this coal stove in the dining room, and with everyone around it at night Grandpa would make the fire go down to little coals and then he'd pop corn for us; We had a smokehouse and had apples out there, Grandpa would go and bring apples in from the smokehouse...he would crack black walnuts and we would pick out the walnuts...If someone close in your family had died, you wore a crape on your arm for six months...Cliff was killed by a railroad train..."

In 1900, Clifford Hanks, the third-born, employed himself as a shoe shiner. When not working, he would engage himself in the dangerous pastime of "train-hopping." Tragically one saturday while walking on top of the freight cars, Clifford slipped and fell to his death in between the cars. The *Osage City Free Press* of May

10, 1900 reported:

## Cars Claim Another Victim

"Last Saturday afternoon at about 3 o'clock Clift
Hanks, commonly known as "Jumbo," the colored boy who
has blacked shoes in Ohrn Bros. barber shop for several
months past, fell between two box cars in the Missouri Pacific
yards and was crushed to death...he lived for nearly an hour
and was able to tell how the accident occured. He was walking
on top of the train, while it was being switched in the yards,
and went to step from one box to another when he slipped and
fell between the cars.

He was about twenty-two years old, of a very happy,
cheerful disposition and had many friends. His death, of
course was purely accidental and clearly the fault of no one but
himself. He had no right on the train and his death should be a
warning to others who are in the habit of thus climbing onto
the moving trains as they are run through the yards here. The
train men and officers do all they can to stop this practice yet
the boys [persist] in doing it."

After hearing about Clifford's fate, I was sick to my
stomach. And to think that he had lived for nearly an hour while
lying severed in half. That was too much. The sorrow of William
and Rosetta finally reached clear up to me nine decades later.
They hadn't even healed yet from the death of their son James only
five months earlier. Here I had viewed my loss of Uncle Billy Don
as a festering emotional wound that still would prick open on any
given moody day. But this account of Clifford took the cake. I
finally felt relief temporarily when Cousin Mrytle turned to
another subject.

"...I think Grandma Crockett's name was Mariah...the boys
said one would get Grandpa Crockett to come over here and talk to
him, while the other one over here was getting apples, filling his
pockets with apples, then he went up the road and would whistle;
that was to notify this one that was talkin' to Grandpa that he had
his pockets filled up; then the conversation would end; he would
leave to go eat ! Grandpa and Grandma Hanks couldn't read or

write...we thought we were being smart one day, we wanted to get some ice cream, so I spelled it on the board, but Grandma knew what I was writing down because as soon as she walked in the room she said "ice cream"...We had, I'm sure, more clean fun than the kids do nowadays;  we didn't have T.V, didn't have a radio...we had a horse but the boys was leaving early at 6 o'clock in the morning driving to the coal mines, so us kids didn't get the benefit of the horse...there was one coal mine not too awful far from us, and I got to go down in it, was I glad to get out of it!  My uncle said "You haven't been in any coal mine yet, that one was just 90 feet deep, now, where we were it's 150 feet deep;"  They had to lay on the ground to dig...one uncle was crippled up, Uncle Drew;  as far back as I can remember Uncle Drew walked on two canes...I don't remember Grandpa Hanks having a cane, the only one I remember having a cane was Uncle Drew cause he was injured in the coal mine..."

When Granison, the fourth born child and nicknamed "Gub," was old enough, he headed to the coalmines with his older cousin Drew Crockett.  Since  James and Clifford had both died at the ages of 25 in their prime--James from the smallpox outbreak, and Clifford from a train accident--Granison  was now the oldest son, while Eliza, John, Murt, Ernest , Margaret, and Hugh were attending school.  Mrytle and her widowed mother Lillian now lived with William and Rosetta's family.    Finding herself having to work to help support herself and her daughter, Lillian worked as a cook at one of the eight restaurants in town.

William Hanks, also known as Billy in the family, worked as a farm laborer finding work on neighboring farms as well as doing odd yard jobs, while Rosetta would stay busy keeping house and baking her homemade bread, making up to twelve loaves at a time, it had been said.  And whenever William got the chance, he would go hunting with his buddies for rabbit, coon, and opossum, including at times his own boys and their cousins, ready for the hunt and wearing their fashionable sporting caps.  Live pigeons brought home $1 dollar per dozen.  Often at times there would be wolf hunts, too.  And in no way would he pass up taking Rosetta to the dance balls, William wearing his suit and ready-tied black soldier's knot now being called the "four-in-hand," or instead fronting his mailcoat neckcloth French cravat which he preferred wearing since 1870;  And Rosetta wearing her 1895 ruffled shoulder and ballooned-sleeve blue skirt with her huge bustled petticoat.

By now Armstead was still working as a miner, even though the feel of getting old was slowly creeping up on him. But certainly he didn't mind; that was nothing compared to all the hard work and toil he had sweated as a slave for most of his natural life. For he and his wife Mariah to  have made that crucial decision to escape the South--leave family behind and endure the long exodus that crossed hundreds of miles--to smell and taste freedom in the North was well worth it. Besides, Armstead would pick running off his rascal grandchildren out of his apple tree any time over the rascals who came dressed in white robes. Even the pain of losing his wife Mariah during the  Kansas spring of 1901 would not kill the pride and meaning of his name. Ten years later, his 1911 obituary read:

"Ninety-Three Years, A. Crockett Dies at an Advanced Age.  Armstead Crockett who would have been 93 years February 28, died at 1407 East La[ing] street Tuesday night.  Since Mrs. Crockett died he has lived with his son Drew Crockett where death occured.  The surviving children are:  Grannison and Harris Crockett, Duck Hill, Miss;  Charles, Topeka;  Drew and Mrs. Rosetta Hanks Osage City;  and James of Decatur, Ill.  Mr. Crockett was a native of North Carolina and was a slave in that state. He came here in 1880. He was a negro of the old school and had many friends among his own race and among the white people as well."

To his dying day, Armstead Crockett said he was born on February 28 and, according to the 1880 Federal census,  said it occurred in "*Old* Virginia."  Where was that?  His master, Benjamin Campbell and the Campbell family had lived for many years in Northampton County, North Carolina before Benjamin later moved to Halifax and then later on to Mississippi.

Northampton County meets up with the Virginia border. Interestingly, the name of the Virginia county across that border is Southampton. I began to believe that by Armstead stating he was born in *Old* Virginia, he was qualifying his birthplace to that specific region. North Carolina was once part of Virginia.

I somehow doubted, however, that Armstead would have turned ninety-three if he had lived another month, since he had stated his age on the 1870 census as being forty-four. At best, Armstead was probably around seventy-three at his death. If true, then one could estimate his birth to have been around February 28, 1826 or thereabout. Something else made me wonder about Rosetta's father Armstead Crockett. Had he heard about the slave uprising of Nat Turner? That revolt began on August 21, 1831 in which Turner and his followers took 57 lives. Nat Turner didn't escape slavery. He was captured on November 11 and was hanged. I wondered if Armstead as a child had recorded the mention of this event in his memory, an event that spread chilling fear throughout the countryside. Nat Turner's revolt took place in Southampton County, Virginia.

Cousin Mrytle told me another story I hadn't heard: "We didn't have money, but we did have happiness...I can remember one Sunday morning at Grandpa & Grandma Hanks, we always had fried chicken for Sunday breakfast, and this one morning, there was one gizzard on the platter, and Hugh and I both wanted that gizzard; everytime I'd go to get it, he'd jab it; Murt saw what time we was having, so he said "You all has got to quit that fightin' over just one chicken gizzard, what I'm gow'n do is cut it in half"; "When Murt came to Topeka to work, he lived with us, and every Sunday he'd give me a spanking then give me a quarter..."

About this time, Lillian Hanks and her daughter Mrytle were now living in Topeka, and Granison went to Manhattan to become a tailor, and later got "hitched," marrying a Manhattan, Kansas girl named Matta, the daughter of a Riley County family by the name of Pitts. By now Murt and Ernest, the seventh and eighth-born and whose nicknames were "Moon" and "Teat", had decided to try their "lot" and become coalminers. After daughter Margaret, the ninth-born, had died suddenly at home from an illness at the age of twenty-one in 1914, Billy and Rosetta Hanks decided to leave Osage City and move to Manhattan, Kansas about the time of World War I. As the war raged on in Europe, soon American men were being drafted for military service including Murt on July 15, 1918, and Hugh the next day on July 16. Murt was sent to Camp Dodge, Iowa with the "Casual Detatchment Demobilization Group," while Hugh was stationed at Camp Funston, Kansas with "Detatchment Company "D" Reserve Labor."

Three weeks later their father, Billy Hanks, passed away. His obituary, appearing in both the newspaper of Osage City and Manhattan, read: "Death of William Hanks, Colored Man, Aged 74 Years, Died at Midnight. A former resident of this city, died Aug. 5, 1918 at his home in Manhattan, Kansas at the age of 74 years; He was born in Nashville, Tenn; and came to Kansas at an early age, making Osage City his home for 38 years. Three years ago he moved to Manhattan...We wish to thank our friends for their kindness during the illness and after the death of our beloved husband and father, William Hanks." Yes, Billy Hanks had sought freedom too, by he and Rosetta coming to the North to raise a family. But he also had to suffer the pain of watching three of his own blood be plucked like baby chicks. Now he too would go to his grave not knowing if two more from Rosetta's bosom would be taken again in their fresh youth. But both boys were spared being sent overseas, and were discharged at the end of the war, Hugh on April 4, 1919, and Murt three months later on July 26.

By 1920, five years since leaving Osage City and two years since the death of their father, it seemed that the remaining children of five sons and two daughters were now establishing their own separate lives, yet staying close and keeping track of each other's whereabouts. That same year Rosetta decided in May to sell the old family homestead property that was still left in her husband's name down in Osage City. For some unexplained reason, the deed purchase had not been recorded in the register of deeds office, despite William Hanks' name clearly listed on the city surveyor's land plat map. Thus, in order for Rosetta to sell the land, the children and their spouses had to all sign over a "quit claim", as one-by-one they were notified: Granison and his wife at their home in Manhattan; Murt and the wife he married on New Year's Eve 1912, even though now separated and going through a divorce; Hugh and Ernest, still living at home although Ernest was now preparing for his wedding; Susan, now a widow and living in Emporia, Kansas; John and his wife, sending their signatures from Washington, D.C. via a notary public; and Eliza and her husband, sending their signatures via a notary public from their mission residence in Oklahoma.

I listened as Cousin Mrytle went on and on, relating how Rosetta's daughter Eliza, the fifth-born, had earlier married an Adventist preacher in 1914, Henry Miller, and how John Quintin Hanks, the sixth-born, moved to Denver, Colorado to work as a butler and later to Oakland, California where he used his savings to become a real estate investor. Ernest, the shortest of the family, married a single mother, Geraldine Taylor of Kentucky in August 1920, worked as a porter, raised four children, and later became an expert in the art of candy making while employed at a local candy store. Hugh, a little bit taller than brothers Murt and Ernest, used his skills as a maintenance repairman working for a Jewish businessman who owned a music and appliance store.

On February 21, 1922 Hugh Hanks and a girl from Ogden, Kansas, Marcella Barnett, were united in marriage. Their first son, Billy Don, was born in 1927, and on February 18, 1930 in Kansas City, Missouri, their second son was born, Zane Milton. Hugh and his family remained in Manhattan, raising his two sons just as the Depression hit.

Sadly, about this same time toward the close of the 1920's, Sue Orendorf's daughter back in Osage City, Ina, and her husband, Charlie Witt, were going through hard times, too, but of a domestic nature, not to mention also financially trying to raise seven children. It didn't get any better when Ina gave birth to twins in December 1926. But for Ina, just as important as feeding her children was an equally important task that spelled life or death-- surviving spousal abuse. Ina's husband Charlie, to put it mildly, was not treating her right. Physically and verbally, Charlie was not living up to his "marriage vows." The cause of his rage was not made clear to me, although, aside from the usual imagined slights and low self-esteem mood swings that characterise this brute breed of men, a clue might have been found in the alleged "family secret"--that Ina had had previous twins from an affair with her husband's brother, he raising the twin boys as "cousins" to Ina's other children. Whether there was truth to this or not, whether an affair or "rape", one thing was made clear to me: Ina had had enough of the spousal abuse. She separated from him and moved in with her mother Sue, leaving the children with Charlie. By 1930 Ina wanted a divorce. Eventually Ina and Charlie mutually made plans to meet at the Osage County Courthouse in Lyndon on a designated day and sign the papers. As I was told, the designated day was a Monday. It turned out to be a fateful day. Ina, not having seen her children for quite some time, thought she saw them over at a neighbor's house and so proceeded over to greet them before heading to the courthouse. Unaware, Ina didn't know that Charlie was following her. Cutting into her pathway, he pulled out a rifle and shot her to death. Charlie was tried, convicted, and spent the next fifteen years in prison. I was later told that one of Ina's children was still alive and heard to be last living in Denver.

I shook my head as I wondered how many woes could Great-grandmother Rosetta take. Here she had tragically lost three of her children and husband William. Now I learn she had the news broke to her that her granddaughter was gunned down! How long could Rosetta's heart hold out? How long could mine? Mrytle wasn't about to let up. I had come into her home to hear about the generations before me, and Mrytle wasn't about to tell me only the pleasant times while leaving out painful ones.

In July 1937 Murt Hanks married a widow named Monette Cavens, and raised eight children. Employing himself as a stone mason, Murt even built his own home, and was in excellent shape physically. Murt's army medical examination reported him as 150 lbs, 5 feet 4, and perfect 20/20 vision. The family legend was that Murt's vision was so good that he didn't use a measure when building, such as when he built a swimming pool for a Mexican family that lived next door to Hugh and Marcella. Tragically four years later, Murt and a workmate were fatally struck by a train as they were inside the workmate's car.

Another sorrow added to Rosetta's bag of tears. Now I had come full circle. Murt was the father of the first black mayor of Manhattan, Kansas. He was the father who left a widow and six children. And the father of my dad's cousin who had started me down this path in the first place.

Granison "Gub" Dumas Hanks passed on in December 1940 due to chronic alcoholism after twenty-five years as a tailor. Mama Rosetta went on to live a full life, always liking to sit out on the porch of her Manhattan home and say a friendly hello to people passing by. She finally expired on May 6, 1941 while living in Kentucky at the age of 89, carrying a heart full of memories.

"...I don't remember Grandpa or Grandma Hanks talk about slavery... I don't remember anything being mentioned about his family...I was visiting Aunt Eliza and Uncle Henry in Louisville, Kentucky, they lived about a mile from the Ohio river, and we were going to Nashville for three or four days, and had gotten someone to stay with Grandma. Well, Grandma was mad at us because we wasn't takin' her with us. Uncle Henry before we got ready to go said "Let's have a word of prayer, that mother will be alright while we're gone and that we'll have a safe trip." Me and Aunt Eliza knelt together which we never should have done (because they would almost cause each other to laugh during the prayer)...then Grandma gave a prayer, "Now Lord, I'm gonna tell you all about it, I'm gonna tell ya jus' how it is...they're all goin' away, and leaving poor ole' me here by myself!" When she got through, Uncle Henry says "goodbye mother", and I and Aunt Eliza says "goodbye mother", (acting like they were crying)...after we got out the door Uncle Henry says "I'm ashamed of ya, ashamed of both of ya, making fun of mother's prayer, and especially you Mrytle, as long as I've been in the Hanks family, this is the first time I've been ashamed of you." I said, "Thank you Uncle Henry, because you sure have been in the Hanks family a long time!"

Soon it was getting close to evening. Another cousin, Madeline Sullinger, the daughter of Ernest "Teat" Hanks, and her son Harry Jr., were on their way over to meet me.  We all ended up going out to dinner, after which I ended up spending the night in Manhattan and spent the next day visiting there.  From there I headed to St. Louis to visit my  mother's half sister.  It was interesting to learn that Mom's half-sister, Aunt Sue, had begun searching her roots, too, on the McCoy family--Mom's side of the family, Aunt Sue having mentioned her intentions of getting started on it at the McCoy Family Reunion that was hosted in Portland that summer.

Inspired by Cousin Mrytle,  I was now more determined than ever to dig as deep as I could to learn more about where our family had come from.  Grandfather Shelton would always say "history is my favorite subject," and  I was exactly like him on that score.  As I reviewed my notes and interviews, I was struck by some of the family customs that Mrytle recalled, such as wearing a crape on one's arm for six months when someone in the family died;  Always having fried chicken for Sunday breakfast;  Murt's custom of spanking Mrytle before giving her a quarter.  I also began  wondering about the family nicknames "Jumbo, Gub, Moon, Teat."

I wondered where those nicknames came from.  Since I had a fascination for looking up words in dictionaries and in etymology,  curiously I went looking up those nicknames for any possible meanings behind them.  I stopped at a book store located on Jantzen Beach, situated on the Columbia River where the former city of Vanport once existed.  Starting first with the name Jumbo--besides having the meaning "large"--it also had two other significant meanings.  For one, the word derived partly from the African Congo language word "Zumbie" which in African religion referred to an evil spirit.  The English phrase "mumbo-jumbo" came from this word.  The second meaning of the word Jumbo had reference to a triangular sail set in place of the foresail on a schooner vessel.  This maritime sea term of a triangular forestaysail was also known as a "jib," developed by the Dutch between the 14th & 15th centuries, in which its edge was attached to a ring called a "jib hank."

Next, I looked up the name Gub.  It was a short word for

"Goobers" which meant peanuts, deriving from both the African Kimbundu word for the Angolian Goober Pea, and the African Congo language word "Nguba," also meaning peanuts. During the slave trade, goobers were brought on board slaving vessels to serve as food for African slaves. For the nickname "Moon" I found dozens of definitions, far too many to arrive at any one particular meaning. But for what reason was Great- uncle Murt given that nickname? Why did Great-uncles Clifford and Granison receive their respective names? Were they handed down from slavery? And did their other siblings have nicknames? I later asked Dad if his father Hugh was given a family nickname, but Dad didn't recall him having one, only remembering his uncle Murt being referred to as "Moon." Cousin Mrytle only recalled her uncle Ernest's nickname "Teat." When contacting Murt's son Edward Hanks of Wichita, Kansas, whose nickname was "Doc," his memory brought to mind that his father Murt was called "Moonie" and his uncle Granison, who he added, loved to drink a little too much, was called Gub; but whether the other eight children of his grandparents William and Rosetta Hanks had nicknames, his memory failed him.

A subsequent telephone conversation with a cousin in Kansas City, Missouri, Cousin Helen, the daughter of Eliza Hanks Miller, turned out to be an eye opener, not about nicknames, but rather, something I never realized about Great-uncle John Quintin Hanks.

Cousin Helen was born in 1915, making her the second oldest living cousin on my father's paternal side, after Cousin Mrytle. Out of all ten children to William and Rosetta, Helen's mother Eliza lived the longest until her death in 1971 at the age of eighty-seven. Helen spoke about alot of things the day we talked, such as when she and my great-aunt Eliza had driven to Oregon from Great-uncle John's Oakland home in 1962 to witness spectacular Crater Lake, how Uncle Billy, Dad's brother, would often come to visit her family when he was in town, and how Helen remembered it being mentioned that Grandfather William Hanks was treated more like a slave as a child in slavery times than Grandmother Rosetta.

Soon we got to talking about Great-uncle John.   When Cousin Mrytle had mentioned that John had once worked for the governor of Colorado, I had called the Colorado Capitol archives building in Denver for his dates of employment, but was told his name was nowhere listed.  I soon learned from Cousin Helen that John never worked for the governor.  Instead, she said:

"He worked for a senator...Uncle John's hobby was going fishing for trout, one time he sent mother some trout in a box with ice; When we lived in Denver I remember we went to visit him at the senator's house, a large mansion;  I think Uncle John was a butler, but I'm not sure, he had a cap on, but I don't think he was a driver...we went there when I was about eighteen or maybe twenty, and he took us inside the senator's house...there was a cook, baker, housemaid, and many rooms, all kinds of fancy silverware and valuables...showed us the offices, even saw the cars in the garages; But Uncle John didn't live there, he and his wife had their own home...then they later moved to Oakland, California with their son."

After calling a Denver public library, it was confirmed that Great-uncle John was indeed listed as a butler in the city directory from 1916 to 1945, and employed at 3400 Belcaro, that address being to Lawrence Coyle Phipps, the industrialist, millioniare, and senator of Colorado who served from 1918-1931 in the United States Senate.   Senator Phipps, who at thirty-eight was a top executive for Andrew Carnegie's steel company when it merged into the United States Steel Company in 1900, received his 1924 reelection support from the backing of the Grand Dragon of the Ku Klux Klan in Colorado, though the senator was not a klan member. Another detail about Great-uncle John was furnished by his son Roy, whom I spent quite some time locating, who divulged that his father John was the head butler, responsible for the hiring and firing of servant staff, and, Roy added, who never failed to lock up the senator's silverware  and liquor cabinet.

Indeed, my chat with Cousin Helen was most certainly an eye opener.  Now back to my nicknames.

Pouring over my many family documents failed to show if the other children had nicknames, although the 1965 death certificate of Great-uncle John Quintin Hanks stated his race as "Haitian." John was born February 5, 1886 in Osage City, not in the West Indies. But did he possess some knowledge of the family's origin? Did one of our family ancestors come from the West Indies? Other relatives could not shed any further light either.

While at the public library, I used the encyclopedia for help on the possible meaning for Great-uncle Murt's nickname. But all I found was just a section discussing the literal word "moon." However, on the next page after that section appeared the word "Moonstone," a traditional birthstone characteristic of health and customarily ascribed to the month of June. Then it hit me. Murt was born on Wednesday, *June* 6, 1888. Was he nicknamed to mark the time of his birth, a custom that was practiced by West Africans in naming their newborn?

When I returned home from Kansas, I contacted the Mississippi  Department of Archives & History, this time to request any tax records and possible military records of the overseer Marion Hanks. In November 1990 I received a military record from 1863 and tax records on file for the years 1855-59. The military record were discharge papers from Company E, Culbertson's Battery, Artillery, of the Confederate Army:

Headquarters
Culbertson's Battery
Near Canton, Miss.
Nov. 1st, 1863
To All Whom It May Concern
Marion Hanks a Prvt Co "E" Culbertson's Battery was enlisted by Capt. Atkins in Grenada, Miss. on 12th of August 1863 to serve two years of the war  is 6 ft high  Dark Complexion  Black eyes & Grey hair  aged 40 years  & at the time of Enlistment was by occupation a farmer.  born in Pickens County State of Alabama.  is now entitled to a discharge by reason of deafness  Said M Hanks has not performed one day's duty during

the time that he has been in the Service.  He has recd no pay
I have known Prvt. M Hanks since March 1860 & during this time
he has been subjected to the Treatment of several [illegible]
Physicians for deafness with out any beneficial results & I must
earnestly request that he be discharged from the Service

Jas T. Smith Capt

I certify that I have examined Private M Hanks and find him in my
opinion unfit for the duties of a Soldier by reason of Deafness,
which he says he has suffered from for the past eight years  I
would therefore respectfully recommend his discharge from
Service in the field

Charles C Thunton<br>Asst Surgeon

The tax records showed the overseer owned a horse, a
pleasure carriage, a pocket pistol, and a watch;  but no owning or
selling of slaves were reported.  This meant Marion Hanks must
have purchased William in the year 1860 and sometime before
October 9,  the date the overseer's name was recorded on the slave
census for Duck Hill owning a thirteen year old black male slave.
But purchased a thirteen year old black male slave from whom?
Hanks and a blacksmith from Georgia named Chesley Holloway
co-owned together a plot of land in Duck Hill.  Some of the
Holloways in the county had intermarried into the family of
matriarch Elizabeth Hanks Best, a South Carolinian born at the
turn-of-the-19th-century, who finally settled in Carroll County
with her family by 1841 after her husband Kencheon picked up
their stakes from Georgia and Pickens County, Alabama.
Elizabeth Hanks Best, whose old tombstone today rests inside
Bethsaida Cemetary, was said to have claimed to be a cousin of
Nancy Hanks, Abraham Lincoln's mother. Chesley Holloway, who
was dead for some unknown reason by the age of thirty-seven in
1859, was a slaveowner.  Might Overseer Hanks have gotten his
male slave from blacksmith Holloway?  On September 14, 1859,
Chesley Holloway's estate inventory listed, besides his blacksmith
tools and his double-buck shotgun, three slaves:  a boy named

Tom, a girl named Louisa, and a woman named Emily. No slave named William. I was beginning to reason then, that Marion Hanks purchased William possibly from off the Eskridge plantation since he was likely the overseer there based on the census taker's visitation notes, and possibly may have been related to Richard Eskridge, the plantation owner. Hired slave manager Marion Hanks had a brother in Carroll County named Taliaferro Hanks. At that same time, a widower named Taliaferro Eskridge, who I later learned was Richard Eskridge's recently widowed son, had moved back home to his dying father's big house in 1859. But as the genealogist in Carrollton had said, there had not been found any *recorded* slave purchases between the Eskridges and the overseer. Was Great-grandfather William given to Marion Hanks as a gift bequest?

I was amazed to discover also, I had to admit, that Richard Eskridge, a widower himself since losing his wife in 1821, was living next door to a free mulatto woman, Polly Waters, who was born 1797 in South Carolina, while at the same time in 1850 Taliaferro Eskridge and his wife Sophia were living together in their home with a free black woman, Jane Waters, 24 and born in Alabama, and her three year old son Moses, born in Mississippi. Two free women of color in the state of Mississippi, both under their own vine and fig tree near the plantation yard. Was I missing something? What was the connection? That partial answer wouldn't be forthcoming until several years yet in the making, when I would one day contact a Texas man who was a descendant of Richard Eskridge.

By 1860 Richard Eskridge had turned eighty-five years old. By 1870 his name no longer appeared on the census rolls. Soon I learned why--he had died in December 1860. Seven years before his death, he had written his will in 1853 mentioning, "three negroes, Rich, Martha and her son Jim. These slaves are given as a separate estate free from any debts or liabilities...Luke and Amanda his wife, Nelson their child, and Elias and Abram." This was followed by a codicil in 1854, and a final will on Friday March 9, 1860, which was presented to the Carroll County Probate Court on December 19, 1860:

I Richard Eskridge do make this and publish this further codicil to my Last Will and Testament
...and hereby give and bequeath the slaves...viz Moses Jr, Bill, Mitch,...Jim aged about 22 years...Luke, Amanda, Nelson, Elias, and Abram together with all the children and descendants of said slave Amanda in my possession at the time of my death to my grand son Burditt  Eskridge son of Taliafero Eskridge...Richard, Martha, and her son Jim...to my said grandson Burditt Eskridge...

In faith whereof I have hereunto set my hand and seal this 9th day of March A.D.  1860

R. Eskridge

Who were these slaves?  One of them was named Bill.  Did my family descend from them?  I wondered too, were "Richard" and "Martha"  the same persons as freed family Richard and Martha Eskridge and their son Burdett who went to Osage City about the same time my family did?  Three executors were appointed in the will, John A. Binford, Robert Neal Sr., and Burdett Eskridge, Taliaferro's son.

The next several months of research took me to constant dead ends.  The Mississippi Archives could not find the estate inventory record of Richard Eskridge.  I contacted a genealogist in Alabama and other record sources in that state but could not locate any slave purchases for Marion Hanks or Richard Eskridge.  I did, though, learn about a court case involving Richard's cousin in Marengo County, Alabama, *Eskridge vs. State*, June 25, 1854 in which Richard M. Eskridge "was indicted" for disabling the leg of Maria, a slave belonging to his wife.  The court stated:

"The principal evidence...consisted of his own confessions, as testified to by the physicians who amputated the limb...it is said, the defendant was much intoxicated...when the master attempted to chastise the slave, she seized an axe and told him not to come near her, else she would kill him...defendant called to her to stop, which she refused to do, and thereupon he shot her."

The judgement against him later was reversed. Nor could I find any recorded slave records in the name of Marion Hanks or Richard Eskridge at the Tennessee State Archives in Nashville. A genealogist in Osage City could not find anything nor could the Crable Funeral Chapel locate anyone by the name of Eskridge in their burial records. Cousin Mrytle did not know anything about them either, nor was she aware that the Crocketts had changed their surname from Campbell.

I did learn, however, that President James K. Polk owned a plantation in Grenada, Mississippi, about ten miles from Duck Hill. James K. Polk served as Governor of Tennessee from 1839 to 1841, then served as the 11th President of the United States from 1845 to 1849. When he died on June 15, 1849, his wife Mrs. Sarah Polk took over the management of the plantation along with her brother-in-law William Polk. Mrs. Polk personally visited the plantation herself in early 1850. Ten years later she sold the estate. "Albert F. McNeal," a lawyer, merchant trader, and first cousin to James K. Polk, was contacted often by Polk regarding business affairs with the plantation. Within James K. Polk's estate papers were preserved a collection of correspondence between him and others who helped run the plantation during its years of operation:

[Wednesday] Jan. 15th, 1840

Dear Sir:

"...few men have money and those who have it, will be disposed to hold on with the expectation of buying negroes low for cash at sheriffs sales before and at the spring term of the approaching circuit courts...All are well at the plantation, Addison however in the woods...Your crop of cotton (136 bales) is at Troy, ready for the first rise in the river. Carroll County lies immediately south of this county and I practice law there. The first time I visit that county I will see Mr. Hamon and get his note with security as desired. Mr. Hamon ought to give you about $400 a year for Harry. If Harry be the same blacksmith who worked at the Caldwell place 5 miles from Columbia, then owned by Uncle Sam

Polk, I remember him well(tall & muscular) though some 18 years have elapsed since I saw him..."

A.F. McNeal

Harry the blacksmith, hired out to an employer in Carroll County named Kimbrough, also wrote to Polk:

[Tuesday] May 10th, 1842

Dear Master

"As a servant I want to subscribe my friendship to you and famley as I am still in Carrollton yet and doing good labour for my imploieer...Dear Master I looked for you of Febuarrary but you never come up to Carollton.  Dear Master I have eleven children I have been faitheful over the anvill Block evr cen 1811 and is still old Harry  my childrens names 1 Daniel 2 Morcel 3 Ben 4 Elis 5 Carrell 6 Charles 7 Elushers 8 David 9 Moonrey 10 Carline 11 Opheeler  Som Request from you please to send me a Letter How all of the people are doing in your country.  Dirrect your letter to Mr. Edward P. Davidson, Carrollton, Miss."

Harry your Servent

James K. Polk frequently had runaways occuring among his 56 slaves, "repeat offenders" such as Jack, Ben, Harbert, Charles, Addison, and Gilbert, whom Polk's overseers were assigned the unwelcome headache of capturing  on more than one occasion.  In November 1833 Jack fled to Memphis where he met the unfortunate irony of being kidnapped by two slave-stealers heading for Texas.  Polk's hired men eventually caught and arrested the men in St. Helena, Arkansas.  Jack escaped again in September 1834, taking refuge in a runaway settlement called Shawnee Town.  In March 1836 Harbert stole a stagecoach and tried to take off to Nashville before being captured.  Three years later Charles was presumed to have run away to be with his wife in Tennessee. James K. Polk wrote to his brother William H. Polk to make inquiries as to where Charles may have gone. William H. Polk replied back:

Dear Brother:

"I have been delayed in answering your Letter, by not being able to see Mr. John L. Smith and obtain the information which you requested in your letter, relative to your negro Boy Charles. I this day, saw Mr. Smith, and he informed me that your Boy, the year you bought him was hired to Mr. Hatch Esq and would refer you to a Mr. Dickerson the son-in-law of Capt. Jones as a person who is well acquainted with the Negro...That the Mother and family connexion of Charles belong to the family of Cox's near Cornersville. I will in the course of ten days, ride up to that Neighbourhood, and endeavour to catch him, if he is there, though Smith is of opinion, that he is still in or about Somerville..."

Even as Polk became President-elect, he continued to receive briefings about his cotton operations, sometimes directly from his commission merchant cotton factors based in New Orleans: [Monday] February 3rd, 1845

Dear sir:

"We hand you annexed acct sales of 101 Bales Cotton, nett proceeds to your credit $2,127.44. This cotton we placed upon the market some days ago under an active demand and improvement in prices, consequent upon the reception of favorable news from abroad, and having obtained an offer, full a 1/4 ct. above the current rates(in honor of the mark) we did not think it proper to decline it. We did not intend for some time to have troubled you with the acct. sales of your cotton, as we presume you have your hands full, about this period, with more important concerns, but our Mr. Walker (now in this city) prefers that you should be advised of the sale at once...We are furnishing the necessary supplies for your plantation upon the orders of Col. Campbell and J. T. Leigh"

Very respectfully, Your obt. servts.

After the death of Polk in 1849, Mrs. Sarah Polk began receiving the continual updates on the plantation accounts. Her commission merchant W.S. Pickett had to inform her of an investment loss on March 7, 1855:

Dear Madam:

"...When I heard of the fire at Troy, I feared that some of your cotton might be there "in transitu", and I deeply regret now to learn that my fears have been realized, and to the extent reported by Mr. Mairs. I have no doubt it is a total loss to you, unless your instructions and customs heretofore has been to have your cotton insured against fire at Troy previous to shipment. This is so rarely done, indeed the chances of loss are considered so remote, that not one planter in a hundred thinks it necessary to adopt this precaution, and I presume you did not..."

By the summer of 1857 W.S. Pickett left the New Orleans cotton market and joined a firm of cotton brokers in Memphis, Tennessee and wrote Mrs. Polk on July 7, 1857 of the growing profit potential in that market:

"I trust however this severance of our business connexion, will be of short duration. The cotton business of Yalobusha is fast concentrating at Memphis. Already there is a great deal of cotton from that county, hauled to within reach of the Mississippi and Tennessee Rail Road and thence to Memphis. In another year the Rail Road will perhaps penetrate as far as Grenada (its destined point) and it may be within a very short distance from your plantation. In that event, you will find it to your interest to send your cotton here, like everybody else, and order your supplies from this point. Memphis is the best market for cotton planters, who are in reach of it by Rail Road Communication, as it is accessible at all times, and the charges are much less than in New Orleans."

Mrs. Polk also received letters from the overseer John A. Mairs. When Harbert again ran away along with another slave named

Wilson, the poor spelling overseer wrote:
[Saturday] February 23rd, 1856
Marim

"i nough write you a few lins  your servants are all well
Wilson is not at home  he left about 2 weeks ago and i have not
heerd of im sense  i surpose he has taken the same Rout that
harbard tuck  iexspect harbard got him of  ihave this day got Mr.
James Leigh to write to Mr. Harris of Memphis to nough whether
he is thar  I lurn that some negro give Harbard a pass and he went a
part of the way on the ral cars and exspected to git on a bote at
Memphis..."

Mrs. Polk also wrote to the overseer Mairs as to how much money
was being paid her slaves for their labors.  The overseer replied:
[Sunday] June 17th, 1855
Mairm:

"...You wanted to know [how] much you had to pay
your [negroes] you... pay them about 200 hundred dollars at a time
I have not collected much of the blacksmith [accounts] the most of
them got [their cotton] burnt Harry [does] not [get] much work to
[do] the most of the planters has a [blacksmith] and makes out with
them..."

When I read about Harry the blacksmith, now old and no longer
needed for his faithful service over the anvil block, I recalled an
1867 entry found in the Freedmen's Bureau Register of Complaints
concerning Polk's former slave Addison:

April 17th        Addison Wilson (Cold) 78 years of age,
Formerly Servant of James K. Polk late President of the United
States  for whom he worked 35 years, has now in his old age been
driven off.  being of no further use, is destitute and unable to
support himself and wife  Applied for medical aid and assistance.

Soon the genealogist in Mississippi had sent me three slave
deeds that I had requested.  One was the deed of sale of James K.

Polk's plantation in 1860, the other two deeds involved "A.F. McNeil" and members of the Eskridge family. This "Albert F. McNeil" was the husband of Richard Eskridge's granddaughter Mary Tabitha. The deed of sale from the Polk plantation was dated January 25, 1860 from Mrs. Sarah Polk to James M. Avant of Rutherford County, Tennessee. The transaction included the names of 56 human souls. As I read the names of each person, I came across the names *"...Mariah, Rosetta,..."* I then said to myself, "Could this be...?" But quickly I dismissed it as just coincidence. That just couldn't have been Mariah Crockett and her daughter Rosetta. Or could it? It shocked me that both names were recorded next to each other out of all those fifty-six names.

Next I came to the other two slave deeds. One was dated February 14, 1854 from Albert F. McNeil, his wife Mary, and her brother William C. Eskridge, to their mother Julia A. Eskridge, the widow of landowner Richard Eskridge's deceased son Thomas, for a twenty-five year woman named Mary Jane, her six year son Dick, four year Joanna, two year Rosa, and three month Jane. Then on September 30, 1862 Albert F. McNeil sold his "one third interest" in the woman Mary Jane and her children to Julia Eskridge's other son, Richard E. Eskridge. As I read these deeds I felt the anguish inside me for the bold audacity to "barter" this innocent woman's life away. What bothered me even more was the haunting thought that perhaps this was the same person as the woman named Mary who complained to the Freedmen's Bureau, after finally freed from slavery, for having suffered the cruel mistreatment of having her child taken from her by "Wm. Eskridge."

I wondered if James K. Polk ever came to Duck Hill. I imagined seeing my great-great-grandfather Armstead running into President Polk on the old road from Duck Hill to Grenada; or Mr. Polk coming to Richard Eskridge's home by way of invitation through Albert McNeil, Richard Eskridge giving a tour of the grounds, then in the evening, entertaining themselves to the music of Stephen Foster or Mendelssohn, while the Eskridge and Campbell slaves next door got together and held a little entertainment of their own.

As 1991 arrived, I was no closer to discovering the origins of my family tree.  Seventeen months into my hunt I began to realize how naive I was in thinking this would be a pure "quick and easy," simply scroll down a couple census rolls, order a few death certificates, and locate a slave bill-of-sale listing all my ancestors.  As the tiring trips and hours at the library, countless query letters to the archives of Kansas, Mississippi, and Tennessee, and impatiently checking the mailbox almost every other week counted up, I began hearing the stories of people who had been studying their families for years and years and found nothing.  Found nothing.

One Saturday morning a cousin from Wichita, Kansas called me whom I had never met, a nephew of Murt Hanks Jr., who was passing through on his way to see relatives in Tacoma, Washington and decided to stop in Portland and spend the day.  We ended up having a backyard barbeque at my parents' home and had a great afternoon.  Even found out we had a cousin just drafted that year into the National Football League, number 36 defensive safety for the San Francisco 49er's.

During the 1930's and 40's the Federal Works Progress Administration conducted a series of interviews with ex-slaves.  Volumes of autobiographies were compiled of ex-slaves from many states and counties giving detailed narratives of themselves and their families.  Several interviews were with those from Carroll County and two other counties that were formed from Carroll and Yalobusha County: Grenada  in  1870, and Montgomery in 1871:

Austin P. Parnell, Little Rock, Arkansas
"I was born April Fifteenth, 1865, the day Lincoln was assassinated, in Carroll County, Mississippi, about ten miles from Grenada...When I got older, I moved to Grenada and I come from there here.  I was about thirty-five years old when I moved to Grenada.  About 160 acres of Land in Grenada was mine.  I bought it, but heirs claimed the place and I had to leave...My mother and father lived in a two-room house hewed out of big logs-great big logs...I laid in bed many a night and looked up through the cracks

in the roof. Snow would come through there when it snowed and cover the bed covers..."

William Hunter, Brinkley, Arkansas

"John Mcbride was my mother's last owner. His wife died in slavery. I never heard her name called. My mother come from Abbeville, South Carolina, a negro trading point. When she was put on the block my father went to Mcbride and asked him to buy that woman for him a wife...I don't know how they got to Carroll County, Mississippi but that is where I was born..."

Smith Simmons, Montgomery County, MS

"...Any could visit around if they had a pass. When we do the visiting, we tell all the news we knew and received news in the same way. Saturday at 12:00 we were left off from work...Saturday night we most always had a dance using the banjo and pat of the hands. Sunday was rest and play day...On a place about a mile away from us they held big corn shuckings. We would hear about it but never did get to go. One day while war was going on two black soldiers rode up who were said to be yankees came to get all our horses. The fighting of the war wasn't near enough to even hear it..."

But no interviews found in the Mississippi counties for anyone named Hanks, Eskridge, Crockett, or Campbell.

On the other hand, there was an interview with Melissa Munson, a former slave of the Binford slaveholding family of antebellum Carroll County, at the age of 101 years of age. Melissa, a slave of Colonel J.R. Binford, in her own words recalled the time when the Yankee soldiers came to Duck Hill:

"It was endurin' the war and Mr. Thomas Purnell, that lived about two miles from Old Marster, come to give warnin' that the Yankees wuz comin.' He said dey would be here next mawnin.' Ole Marster warn't hardly got at home when he come, so he went on; but he hadn't hardly got out o' sight when Ole Marster rode up. He got down and hitched his hoss. an' 'bout that time he saw the Yankees. Well, I can see him right now jump dat fence and run right tru de yard to de back an' on into de field back of de barn.

"De Yankees come on, an' Ole Marster's cousin, from New Awleens,dat was keepin' house for him, come to de do'. " 'Who wuz dat doin' de runnin' ?' asks one of de men. " 'Dats de overseer,' says Old Miss.

" 'You's jus' a lie, dats ole man Binford.'

"Well, de Yankees come on in de house an' went thu ever drawer an' took all de valuables..."Jus befo' de Yankees got ready to go, one of de mens struck a match an' throwed it in de bed, an' just went on an let it burn; den when dey all come down de stairs one of de fellers brought down Marster's white sheepskin apron...when de Kuh'nel of de Yankees saw dat apron he made dem go upstairs and put out de fire, an' dey lef' right den an' didn't bother us no more."

I went back to the National Archives in Seattle to recheck my notes compiled over the last year, and to verify Melissa Munson's interviewed recollections, especially upon learning she was once owned by the Binford family and also since John A. Binford was one of the three persons Richard Eskridge appointed in his last will to be executors of his estate. I recalled too, that in my first earlier notations I had noted a freed family named Binford living next door to the Crockett and Hanks families in both Duck Hill in 1870 and in Osage City in 1880.

As I finished verifying my old notes from the Kansas census rolls, I turned my attention back again to the rolls of the "Magnolia State." Suddenly I came across something that literally startled me:

STATE: MISSISSIPPI
COUNTY: MONTGOMERY                16 DAY OF JUNE 1900

|              | Date of Birth | Birthplace of Father...Mother |        |
|--------------|---------------|-------------------------------|--------|
| Dave Binford | Feb. 1820     | **AFRICA**                    | AFRICA |
| Eliza  wife  | Mar. 1830     | **AFRICA**                    | AFRICA |

This couple, Dave and Eliza Binford, both listed their parents as being born in AFRICA.

**"Negroes...Akey, Rose, Jenny...Botswain...Frank."**

**George Eskridge's estate inventory, Feb. 3, 1736.**

# CHAPTER SIX

## Captured and Brought to Virginia

During the course of many days and months retrieving service requests for pieces of family history as well as for myself, a printed invitation reached me announcing a gathering for family and friends. Everyone came together that Saturday evening for food, sounds, and a talent show. Bringing with me a few notes, I waited my turn and soon was called up to the stage to share pieces of my family history. I described to the large gathering how Akey and was brought to Virginia on a slave ship and later sold to a tobacco plantation along with others. The audience went from silence, to gasps, to applause:

"Akey and two women were then fastened with irons on the deck of the ship, while Bodebe and the other men, twenty of them, were taken below in the hold. As Akey saw them being marched down into the hold, she kept screaming for her uncle, "*sla bi* (kinship father)! *sla bi!! sla...*"

The ship *Providence*, a ten gun English brig built in 1721 at Elizabeth River, Virginia, owned by Sir Dudley Digges of the House of Burgesses, prepared to depart the "Windward Coast" carrying young black African men, women, and children. Some were princes, teachers, doctors, artisans, weavers. Some were welders, fishermen, miners, smelters, mathematicians, farmers. They were fathers, mothers, husbands, wives. They were sons and daughters. The voyage would take many days to reach its destination across the choppy Atlantic.

That was only one of many dark days in history when the brig *Providence* stole away from Africa and headed to America. I could feel that frozen moment in time when Bodebe's head began to clear, and he came to the horrible realization that he was going down in that notorious part of a ship which would warehouse and transport the many Africans Bodebe used to help ferry for the Portuguese and Spanish traders, to be used by them as servants in their faraway villages. Bodebe knew he had never actually climbed below when hired for those jobs, since his only duty was to ferry, then the Portuguese or Spanish crews would take over.

Bodebe cleared the last three steps then immediately felt the pain shoot up his arms as he was yanked to a certain spot towards the front of the hold on the wood-splintered and boot-scuffed plank surface. Bodebe wished it better to be laid down in the back of the container by the store room where there was plenty of space to move about, than to be parallel stretched undignified touching someone else's body, and having someone's buttocks touching his. The hold had a faint smell of Quicklime. Flies persisted.

As Bodebe was pulled down and locked into place, he noticed that some of the men had messed inside themselves, as there was not even a squating hole privy. Trying to stay calm, Bodebe watched as a Nye-puru quickly began pacing away back towards the stair ladder.

"Do you know where they are taking us!" Bodebe rapidly asked the man pinned next to him whose musk was tolerable for the moment. Bodebe watched as the man turned his head left facing him, yet straining to understand Bodebe's words. In return, Bodebe couldn't understand what the man was now shouting to him with a look of fear and desperation in his eyes. Suddenly Bodebe couldn't see anything, as a pitch blackness engulfed them when the last Nye-puru mounted the ladder and dropped the hatch, leaving slits of light rays. Bodebe started yelling.

"Where are we going! Someone here speak and tell me if you know!" There was silence.

"I am Bodebe, son of Sensobo from the village Zwedru; Is

anyone from the dako of Settra Kru?  Grand Kru?  Sasstown?"

Bodebe listened as his appeal echoed lonely throughout the container, followed by a flood of groans, cries, and questionings. But Bodebe hadn't realized the questions now bouncing around from several of the men scattered from one row after another were being directed at him and the twenty new captives, asking of them the same begging question as Bodebe, the search for that answer having been exhausted among them and hoping Bodebe and the other newly caught victims were found to be of each one's respected tribal language.  But no one understood.

Bodebe now began to feel the big ship's movements, the sensations running up his back and head from his floored position. "Where are they taking me?"  Bodebe asked himself in the darkness.  "If headed the Leeward route, then perhaps the ports at Cape Mount or Bunce Island;  But if heading the Windward route, I may land anywhere from Sao Andrea to Angola."  Then something else clicked in his mind.  "What will become of my brother's daughter, Akey?  Where do they plan to take her?" Again, Bodebe tried to remain calm and optimistic.  The dried sweat and odors Bodebe carried on his body felt twice removed.  A hot bath in the village trough back home would be in order.

Having been a sailor on past vessels of this size, Bodebe felt certain, after watching for a good part of the day the direction of the light from the sun through the slits in the ceiling and upper walls, that the ship was heading east, perhaps toward Gold *Kani* Coast country.  He also discerned it was not yet evening.  Soon Bodebe heard above him the accelerated tempo of boots over to one side of the deck, as though the Nye-puru were readying themselves for some anticipated activity.

"Everyone listen!  I do not know if anyone understands the language of the Kru, but I think we may be docking!  I believe we might be near the Kani Coast!"  Bodebe yelled out to keep the men's spirits high, as well as his own, although his dialect wasn't understood by a single man.  Sure enough, as if Bodebe himself were at the helm, the ship was preparing to stop, and Bodebe felt certain the anchor had now dropped, as the ship slightly keeled and shook on one side.  Now everyone could tell the big canoe had landed, and each man now waited. Bodebe noticed the hatch to the container now opening. Many gave sighs of relief, as fresh air blew in. Bodebe turned to his chained neighbor, a man of the Vai tribe.

"Praise God that we may now arise from this death camp! If I discover that indeed we are at Kani Coast country, I will work my way back home! I can find work for you, too, my brother!" Bodebe kept his eyes fixed as he carefully read each step two Nye-puru took as they climbed down the stairs with rods in their hands, then separate, as Bodebe soon began sipping the drinking water from a cup held out for him, while intruding knats swarmed in his face and pesky flies clung to the round tin, studying the droolings from previous mouths. The other Nye-puru stood at the ladder base while looking at the remaining open space in the container. Bodebe's eyes stayed upon this Nye-puru. But Bodebe's face now started turning grim as he observed that instant about 55 shackled African men being marched down and led to the opened area far in the back, then lowered to the ground floor and locked down. After them, Bodebe watched as maybe 60 more men were forced led and pinned down in the same manner.

"O God! Noooooooooo! Pleaseeeeeeee! O Great One, pleaseeeeeee spare me! Please release me from the evil Mumawi devils!!" Bodebe shouted out in anguish.

As Bodebe continued his pleadings, yet another string of about 100 more men were pulled and yanked down, some fighting, which the Nye-puru hit with their rods.

With the sunset having long ago ended, the hold had now become tightly packed. Now another man was literally pressed against the opposite side of Bodebe's perspiring body. Bodebe tried to reach out and catch each one of the seven Nye-puru that quickly rushed past his head and darted up the stair ladder. Bodebe now knew darkness would follow.

As the ship headed out to sea that night, Bodebe, barely able to turn himself, now gave way with breathing trouble as the air became unfit due to the perspiration and contagion bacilli, while great numbers were cramping with diarrhea, fever, and dehydration. It was obvious some would not survive the night, poor souls who would never produce a generation of sons and daughters in their father and mother's line. Bodebe listened as he heard female screams from on deck. Suddenly, he felt cramps to his stomach as he tried in vain to control his bowels but lost the contest as human mush discolored his girded dress. Humiliated and feeling abashed, Bodebe now surrendered inside the belly of the big fish.

On the eighth day--March 1725--Bodebe layed flat on his back in his chained and pressed compartment, trying to keep his head tilted to the left from the frothing warm vomit coming from the mouth of the Mandingo laying next to him who was trying not to choke. Bodebe couldn't even move his shackled hands in order to help the man, and Bodebe's neck was already sore due to tilting it to the right, caused by a previous episode from the Vai man crammed to his left, but the contents that gushed from his stomach had dried up two nights before, providing a meal fit for the vermin. The air was rank.

As Bodebe kept his head tilted while feeling a stinging hot sensation running down his shoulder and ribs, he suddenly noticed overhead the light pouring into the hold caused by the removal of the door hatch leading to the deck. Bodebe watched as three Nye-puru climbed down the steps and led between twenty and twenty-five chained men up the stairs as he could count, some of them still showing notable signs of physical strength but some walking sickly, then watched as the hatch was closed tight. Bodebe later observed those same number of men return to the hold and then twenty or more different men would climb out. Bodebe began noticing this procedure being repeated over and over in intervals of about the same time it would usually take him to walk from Zwedru to Tappita, until after the fifth interval now came Bodebe's turn to see for himself what was happening on deck.

As Bodebe climbed out and lined up with the other men, he noted a drummer beating a sound foreign to Bodebe's ears, and at the same time a whip continually being flayed near his feet. While he began jumping in unorganized spurts as some of the Nye-puru clapped their hands, Bodebe was bewildered as to the purpose of this absurd exercise, yet it having a redeeming merit in that of breathing fresh air, being rinsed with a water bucket, and seeing daylight for the first time since leaving the Grain Coast off Cape Palmas.

It was then that Bodebe noticed the women prisoners fettered around the entire main and upper decks. But by the time it took Bodebe to focus his blurry eyes in search of Akey, the musical escapade stopped, the door hatch to the hold was lifted up, and Bodebe found himself being pulled down the stairs by the chain weight and movement of the man in front of him.

The following week the men down in the hold were brought up again for fresh air and exercise, as the bottom was so foul not even a dirty dog would lay its head. Indeed, the hold's floor was covered and caked with feces, resembling an animal kennel. When it became Bodebe's turn to be pulled up to deck from the foul-smelling chamber of darkness, he looked up at the stars to try and pinpoint his position and how far he was from the river Cavella, but his bearings were totally thrown off in his weak state. The direction of the poporo, the wind, as it hit the main sails and jumbo, made Bodebe think the ship was heading west, but he wasn't sure. Examining his hands, Bodebe, straining to find a finger not tainted with dried potty lodged underneath his fingernails, finally found one finger to lick then raised it in the air. North? His eyes made every effort to pinpoint Akey's exact location among the females chained to the railings, but failed to locate her by the time the three Nye-puru began directing them back down to the hold with whips. Akey was pinned right across on the opposite side of the deck, squinting her eyesight to see if she could notice Bodebe among the crowded deck and noises. Bodebe passed right by Akey because of being blocked from her view by the other African men, and so didn't even realize she was there, nor Akey of him. Soon he was back below.

Akey was at least given a blanket past the third night to be put around her when the winds proved too cold for her shivering body to absorb. But when she woke up that next morning she never saw the blanket again.

Lined up together on one side of the ship from the front of the railings clear to the back, pressed and shackled, Akey squatted with the nearly one hundred other women, legs outstretched and ankles padlocked, hands outstretched and chained above her, yet her ten year old spirit giving her an advantage when reserved strength was needed to manuever for fresh position. On the eighth night Akey began drifting back and forth into semi-consciousness, thinking herself on the banks of the Cavella, then realizing she was merely dreaming. Akey recognized the sphere hanging upon nothing in the night sky, watching it each night as it would sometimes change color, from white, to gray, then reddish-yellow, reliving in her memory the moments when her brother would purport how the constellations meant survival for an experienced Kruboy returning safely to the village from the forest, which, upon mental recall, rallied her spirits each evening that by morning, pray, she would be back in Zwedru.

Akey, still not knowing if Bodebe was even alive, finally caught on that hundreds of men were coming out in different sections on certain days from the square door hatch that the Nye-puru kept opening and closing. On this day--the twenty-fourth--Akey glued her eyes to the square hole where the village assembly of the men would parade out, and focused more closely as the first group, not the size of a large dako, Akey noticed, but more the size of a small village panton, rose to the deck from the stair ladder. Akey observed carefully each masculine body emerge with each unique posture, height, facial expression, and color tone, hoping to see again the male member from her dako.

After noticing at least three panton assemblies, Akey's eyes began to tire as the heat of the sun starting taking toll and the frequent pushing of the bigger Fulani woman tied next to her had practically worn Akey's smaller body out. But a huge ocean wave shot up the side of *Providence* at that moment and sprayed across Akey, causing her to wake up and resume her concentrated watch. But after watching the fifth panton, Akey now began fearing the worst. As she finished observing the sixth parading panton in front of her, Akey still found no sight of Bodebe. By now Akey's peering guard had turned into almost a trance as she sat whispering Bodebe's name over and over when each lifeless body below was pulled out of the square hole by rope and chain. Shovel-scooped buckets full of excrement were also hauled up to expel, while vinegar and lye were carried down to cleanse. Giving up hope, Akey collapsed into a deep slumber.

"Wake up young sister! Tell all your female companions to awake! Pray for our deliverance from the oppresors!" shouted the voice toward Akey, who immediately woke up and faced that direction. Akey soon realized that another village assembly was now taking place in front of her, and that one of the African men was addressing her as he danced to the musical drum. But Akey didn't recognize the man nor his dialect in the Yoruba tongue. Akey observed that other men now began joining the war cries of the Yoruba man, some in Ashanti, some in Mende, others in Mandinka, while even the women began adding their interluding voices in corresponding tongues of their countries. The ship captain, his sailor crew, and the assigned slave traders looked on confused yet amused, they not understanding the words or meanings.

"Dju! Stay strong! The Great Nyeswa will protect us!" shouted another African to Akey as the Englishmen stood right by him listening in ignorance while other Nye-puru routinely kept walking right past tending to their duties. Akey, when catching the repeated sound of words from this voice, jolted immediately to attention and quickly began glancing at every angle view to catch sight of who was making these familiar tonal utterances.

"Do not lose your spirit! Remain strong! You will have water to drink soon, be like the antelope; Do not forget why you were named: The tree that saved your father when but a baby, and helped give birth to your mother's mother!" shouted again the chained voice from out of nowhere. Akey's spirit soared. "I hear your words my antelope, my dear antelope I am listening!" Akey shouted back. Finally finding an angle opening, Akey now saw and recognized who the voice belonged to, the one whose name for antelope is "Bodebe" in Kru. As Bodebe shouted these sayings to Akey their English captors did not wish to pay any attention due to the many cries and wails that were being made by all. Casava, gub--also called goobers, meleguetta pepper, palm oil, along with yams, corn, rice and other plantains had been brought on board to serve as food during the long passage.  Slips of the Akee had been carried on board, not only to be sent to grow in the West Indies, the ship's first scheduled dock, but also because the English crew had learned how valuable the fruit had proven to be in preventing their rashes of bowel sickness, who, pitiably, due to confined mobility and reduced radius while shackled upon the upper deck, the negresses had the unfortune of smelling and seeing the offensive matter, including young Akey, before it was tended to.

On the seventeenth day, May 1725, a breakfast ration bowl of goobers and mushy rice was placed in Akey's dirt-infested hands.  Her wrist-irons were slackened and Akey brought the bowl to her mouth.  But on this particular day the officers on deck wore concern as they looked at the horizon, a hazy fog and blood-red sky as if painted with blood, causing murmurings of "Red sky at night, sailors delight;  Red sky at morning, sailors take warning." The Africans' numbers had been reduced to two-hundred thirty down in the hot hold.  They were now pried apart and, in sections, were pulled up for air.  The hold was then emptied of its stiffened corpses which were tossed overboard.  "Botswain," now fully living this unthinkable misery, stretched his cramped muscles and, with powerful inner calm, inhaled and exhaled repeatably.  The sea breeze refreshed him as an icy bucket of water was splashed into his ashy face, bare chest, and lower region.

But as his section was ordered back down into death's hold, several of the chained warriors attempted to overpower the guards-mates and, in hand-to-hand combat, wrestled some of the sailors to the ground before their vain strike was subdued and quelled, the guilty parties separated out and severely scourged, although four of the nine mutineers managed to jump overboard to their symbolical freedom.  Akey witnessed the entire unfortunate episode and outcome from beginning to end, noticing how great the women cheered and chanted when they saw the men jump over, many of the women on the railings in a frenzied state, begging for the men to come back up from under the waters and take them off ship, too.

That night the English captain soon came to learn in what manner they would pass the night.  A heavy thunderstorm with great flashes of lightning descended on the ship.  Gusts of seventy knots began batting the brig.  Waking up and looking out their cabin port-holes, the sailors climbed the stairs from the galley up to the forecastle and prow, and began cutting the reefs and clipping the cables, before the sails were reduced to mere rags.  The mate on duty in the mast quickly came down through the riggings, praying that a bolt would not strike him.

The now eighty-odd negresses still alive were pelted with rain as lightning danced around them.  Thunder louder than the ship's cannon guns almost made them deaf.  The captain hoped his ship would be spared damage.  Dropping anchor, the ship hunkered down to ride out the storm.  Akey and the other women watched the universe at war.

Bodebe and the brothers in the hold were yanked from one side to the other as the waves buffeted the slaver itself.  Even the rats retreated because of the storm and hid deep down in the remotest parts of the hull.  A brother chained on the end row from Bodebe's, tightly packed right next to the timber walls, had managed to smash one rat with his leg irons, pinning his tail then crushing him with ankle blows.  Others were not as fortunate, as the rats would sniff out fresh blood from oozing ankle and wrist sores rubbing against the shackles or lying in leaking seawater.  The storm was causing water to spray in through the hatch above them.  Bodebe gave a silent prayer.  "O Great Nyeswa, please protect me, not only me but my dear brother's daughter from the anger of the heavens;  O Great One, only you know what my fate will be, please give unto me faith and endurance;  I have tried to be good all my life, dear God Nyeswa;  Please forgive me for all my errors and transgressions, for I know the great issue that exists, the great struggle between you, the pure one, and your enemy the evil devil;  If it be your will, let me use my life again to bless your name;  But if not, please forgive and remember me;  Remember my family, and remember any on this big canoe who seek your truth."  As Bodebe finished his plea in the dark hold, loud thunder roared as if in answer.

By four o'clock a.m. the sea calmed.  The slaver soon resumed its course, positioning her latitudes so to converge into the Canaries current, disembark in West Indies to exchange for rum, then make toward its final landing.

Finally, the *Providence*, registered in 1724, bonded at London, England, and mastered by Captain Egerton Cutler, entered the waters of the English colonies with only 174 enslaved human souls left spared. As they entered the bay, Akey became confused when seeing all kinds of giant canoes and many Nye-puru along several banks of the River Cavella. The palm trees now looked strangely different, yet the tropical heat felt normal. Akey also noticed that for some reason the pepperbirds looked odd, their singing completely off its beautiful rhythm. Akey observed likewise the reaction of the Fulani woman, who had been fettered to Akey this entire crossing, as the woman's depressed state of mind fled and her spirit revived when seeing she was back home on the River Sherboro near Freetown. Suddenly, her countenance turned to revulsion when the ship started entering the port and she realized only the Nye-puru were standing at the landing dock.

Akey became frightened as the Fulani woman's knees began shaking uncontrollably while all of a sudden Akey soon felt pungy warm water saturating her thigh. As the vessel kept charting closer and closer to the land, Akey noted a banner that the ship passed by with funny scribble lines making no sense, that to Akey's eyes looked like this:

YORKTOWN

Finally the slaver came to a stop. The date was June 7, 1725.

Within days of its arrival, the ship's "cargo" had been advertised in the town paper, with an auction already scheduled to take place. Now Akey was gestured to stand up, which was quite laborious since Akey's legs were weak from insane periods of being squat, but also because the Fulani woman appeared limp even though her eyes were wide open, and so had to be removed from the links and left there on her back. After the deck was secure, the door hatch to the hold was raised and then the men streamed out. Akey and Bodebe were put together according to the owner's initials branded on their cuffs and sent with about fifty to a pen, where they would be kept until auction day. The rest of the cargo was divided into other groups of fifty to sixty and led to their pens. That night the African brothers in each pen took turns forming an instinctive survival watch throughout the night while the women and children slept. Bodebe did likewise as young Akey lay completely exhausted, clutching tightly in her small hand one of the akee slips.

As consignment day now arrived, people came from miles around: planters, merchants, lawyers, judges, councilmen, slave traders, even clergymen. The buying would prove fierce, each one trying to choose what they considered the "best pick of the lot." The African men and women were comprised of many tribes: Ashanti, Yoruba, Gola, Bassa, Fulani, Vai, Mandingo. With strength, dignity, and faith, they gathered themselves with all the courage they had left to try and comprehend where they were and why. Akey huddled with Bodebe as she payed special attention to the strange hut with wooden floors and iron bars they had sat inside during two full moons.

Two women followed Akey as she followed Bodebe out of the wood floor hut. Bodebe, in turn, was following two men who were following a Nye-puru.

Akey began looking peevish and feeling a growing anger as to why chains were constantly upon her, causing her to wonder if she had done something punishable. She tensed up as a village bucket of water was poured over her head and body, but gradually eased when she felt the pleasant softness of a cloth drying and wiping her. Akey let out a groan when an unexpected oily ointment began being brushed onto her, similiar to the village palm oil, and reminded Akey how her mother helped prepare the village brides. But Akey didn't think she was being given in marriage. With a new cloth wrapped around her waist, Akey now followed Bodebe again. Her eyes became blinded by the sunlight. Continuing to follow Bodebe, Akey soon found herself stepping up on a platform which faced many Nye-puru.

"Who will start this bidding?...I have 30 pounds!..do I hear 40?...two fine breeding wenches!"

Akey stared in fright as the head Nye-puru kept shouting loud gibberish while certain Nye-puru would perform some strange ritual of raising their arms and shouting back.

"SOLD!"

Akey watched as the two women standing next to her were removed from their links and suddenly taken away.  Akey glanced again at the head Nye-puru, who was now pointing his finger at her while chattering more gibberish.

"Look at this choice, healthy, fine little wench...in a few more years will be a prime breeder!..six months credit will be allowed with bond and security...who will start this opening bid?"

Akey felt the tight grip of both her shoulders by a servant Nye-puru, who seemed to obey the headman's commands, then Akey became dizzy when turned around in a circle by him, then tasted the sweaty-salt tips of his yellowish-stained fingers, which smelled like burnt smoking leaves, running the sides of her mouth and chafing across her teeth.

"SOLD!"

Akey watched as Bodebe was next turned around, and soon noted the head Nye-puru shouting out that same gibberish word to the same Nye-puru in the assembly performing the peculiar arm-raising ritual.

As the auction appeared to die down and lose steam, the Africans who were still left were taken back to the pens.  Soon they would be shipped to the next towns along the rivers until each and every last one of them were taken.  On June 11, *Providence* cleared for Maryland, carrying fifty-three human beings less than when it arrived.

"Burgess, see to it that my two "new-country" slaves are sent under guard to my estate immediately, as I must return to session," said the satisfied purchaser of human flesh cargo to his black carriage driver.  Akey and "Botswain" were to be transported into the northern neck of the Virginia colony to a tobacco plantation in Westmoreland County, owned by their auction buyer, Colonel George Eskridge of Sandy Point, a prominent attorney and member of the House of Burgesses, which honor called upon him to frequent the House sessions at Williamsburg.

Akey began noticing she was being led to a village wagon, tied to two strange-looking animals Akey had never seen before.  They resembled village mules but larger, and much faster Akey discovered as she and Botswain were jolted backward in the wagon by the takeoff of the snorting beasts.  Botswain refused to squat down, but his chains yanked him into place and spared him from serious injury.

The driver Burgess drove down the streets of Yorktown unhindered by the constables, his face and appearance readily identifiable from previous Yorktown auctions with his master.  A sterling English-made sword resting nearby on the driver's seat. Akey didn't know what to think when she spotted several Africans, poorly dressed compared to the Nye-puru's garb, and seeming to walk gloomy with no spirit of freeness in their step.  Akey noticed practically all of them, as the wagon carted past, in subservient roles involving some sort of labor--lifting, carrying, bending, hoeing--except, that is, for the wagon driver.  He was dressed just as fine as the Nye-puru, making Akey and Botswain imagining him to be of importance in the community dako, perhaps a prince, which Botswain concluded to Akey in Kru talk was perhaps the reason the two of them were entrusted in his care.

As the wagon driver made the final turn out of the town and onto the country road heading to Westmoreland County, Botswain attempted to ask the driver as to their whereabouts and destination.

"My brother--where are you taking us?  To your village?"

Akey watched as the driver, Burgess, gave no response.

"Please, my dear African brother--I say you are a prince! Where is your village?  What is the name of your chief?  How far is your village from Zwedru?"

Burgess turned around, held up his sword menacingly, then turned back to the road.  Botswain now became alarmed as he yanked at his shackles for attention.

"Where are you taking us!  Have we landed in the New World?  If you are a prince, show your honor and answer me!"

This time the black driver immediately brought the horses to a yielding halt and brandished his sword.

"If you two Africans plan on trying to escape, you got another thing coming!" Burgess said nervously.  "You best better keep quiet and stay put!  Understand?"

Fearing the waving sword, Botswain pushed Akey behind

him, then crouched down with her and remained silent the rest of the way, his silence making the wagon driver even more nervous. Finally, after traveling most of the day, the wagon crossed the county line into Westmoreland, and, a few hours later, arrived at the plantation.

Soon the carriage carrying Colonel Eskridge could now be seen approaching, coming home from its weary Williamsburg travel, the House Sessions having recessed until its next court term. The carriage proceeded past tobacco fields through the aggresive horde of horse flys and up to the estate courtyard porch. The Colonel climbed down and was met by his wife Lady Elizabeth, daughter Little Elizabeth, adopted daughter Mary Ball, and male house servant Beck, who brought the Colonel a silver tray holding a glass and bottle of the finest Spanish Castle Rum. A special dinner in the Colonel's honor was to be held that evening.

The Colonel sat in his leather chair, caught his breath from his long travel, and sipped the delightful glass of rum. Unquestionably, an evening of entertainment among friends and family brought a breath of relief to him, a short but welcomed reprieve from the attorney matters that surely would now demand his attention as soon as word got around to the townfolk that the "King's Attorney" had now returned to Westmoreland County. Colonel Eskridge picked himself up and headed down the hallway past the Backgammon table and into the study room which held his business ledgers and housed his distinctive eighty-one book library collection. Those of the county who called upon Colonel Eskridge for legal advice or to conduct matters of the court at his home knew exactly the particular belief, persuasion, and knowledge he held just by some of the titles of his books: "History of the Primitive Church," "French and English Grammar," "The Way to Get Wealth," "The Lives of the Popes," "Aristotle's Speculative Philosophy."

Meantime, Botswain and young Akey were handed over to a black overseer, a Virginian-born slave named Jack King. There they were led away to the slave quarters to receive their first "breaking in" session. "They call's me Jack King, but I ain't no king 'round here...where ya'all from?...West Indies?...or you from dat place they calls Afrika...ya'all speak any English?...I know you done picked up some English somewhere...I don't know where ya'all from, but this here's tobacco leaf...better get used to seein' it, too, 'cause this the reason why massa done brung you here...now watch me, this here how you pick it...watch me now..."

Akey and Botswain watched in confusion, not understanding a word this old man had spoken. Soon ole' Jack King got frustrated and tired. Frustrated of not being understood by these newcomers, and tired of having to do these "sessions" in the first place, tired of having to do this just to not have to work as hard in the fields. For his obedience he received extra helpings of food that the other field hands didn't get. Off to the side another slave observed, an African named Quamino, an Ashanti from Ghana, who was bought two years ago and since then had been made to assist Jack King as interpreter whenever "Gold Coast Negroes" were brought onto the plantation, Colonel Eskridge having a preference in purchasing them. But Botswain and Akey were not "Gold Coast Negroes." Although they were labeled and listed on the slaver's manifest as such, their tribal identity was much, much further down the Gulf of Guinea. Their ethnic origin lay embedded deep within the forest regions all across the Grain and Ivory Coasts. Quamino stood and listened to the language of Akey and Botswain, which all day hadn't been much, just a scant few whispers and murmurings, being cautious and afraid to open their mouths to these strange black devils standing in front of them. Suddenly Quamino's eyes widened as he heard a word from Botswain that sounded familiar to him when overseer Jack King finally got around to his repetitious demonstration about how to use a plantation hoe, as if they didn't already know. He approached them and began to speak. Unexpectedly, Akey and Botswain quickly became animated, speaking sounds in the Akan tongue with Quamino, a dialect many West Africans shared together from different tribes. The three of them were now totally caught up and entertaining themselves to a rapid word exchange. Quamino would speak first, followed by Botswain and Akey:

"Pre." "Pree," as their fingers felt the *iron* of the hoe.

"Nyimeyu." "Nyime," as they pointed at the *man* Jack

King.

"Poro." "Nye-puru," as they angrily pointed to the house of the *white man* who had bought them.

"Niwa." "Nywa," as they gestured toward the *river* that had brought them.

"Nyame, Okra Nyan Kopon." "Nyeswa," while pointing to the sky at *God* who had spared them.

Right at that same moment, two good, plump chickens wandered over. "*Ciroki...nedide ciroki*!" Botswain said excitably, licking his lips as he eyed the delicacy he hoped to get his hands on to kill and eat that evening. Jack had a big smile on his face. "Ole Massa fixin' to have a big celebration tonite. His whole family gettin' ready for one grand party," Jack King proclaimed. Quamino interpreted Jack King's words to Botswain in the Akan tongue. Suddenly, they all heard the sounds of footsteps coming from the main house. "Shhhh," Jack warned, "Someone coming." It was one of the white servants passing by and heading over to the smoke house, the Sandy Point plantation being run by over sixty blacks and three white indentured servants. Jack King then took Akey and Botswain and showed them their sand and dirt floor cabin, with a garden in back of it. As old Jack began to leave the garden he turned to look back. There was Akey down on the ground covering in the soil her akee slip, the only thing she had left to remind her of her home.

Guests from Westmoreland County continued to stream to the party. Inside the main house they tipped their glasses to the keg of cider brandy, and being danced by the musicians' concerto of Handel and Purcell. The Africans celebrated their own homecoming. Back away from the main house and into the yards of the ten to twelve small house cabins dotted along the fields entered Akey and Botswain, escorted by Quamino, as they were introduced to each family. Those who were on hand to greet their new extended family members included Mingo, Quamino's wife Taffy, Charles and Sarah, Joseph, Nan, and "Congo" Judy. There also were George and Bettie, Hannah, Auntie Rose, Cumey, Black Jenny, and young Frank.

The cabin families sat huddled together in their eating yard, some upon old shipping crates, some upon cut logs made into stools, yet others sprawled out on the grass, while fish, potatoes, and oysters were served out, a course specialty the prized hands would receive once a week as well as during special occasions when the Colonel's family was in a celebrating mood. "Eat up child," Auntie Rose said to the dejected face of Akey. "We don't get this everyday; What wrong? Hath not you eaten oysters before?" Akey didn't care for the look or smell of them, consuming instead the tender cooked fish and baked potatoes like a famished fawn in the forest when fed by its mother. Akey stayed close by Botswain's side, her eyes roving at even the slightest movement by these strange faces around her. "Child, you hath nothing to be fearful about, we all family here; Bound we are to take good care of you now that you here," Auntie Rose said, the sound of her voice sounding sincere and reassuring to Akey. Auntie Rose, a half-century old native-born of His Majesty's colony, had been brought to Sandy Point by way of the Colonel's marriage to his first wife, Lady Bonum, and being a family slave was presented as a marriage gift along with her mother, Congo Judy, who was purchased at Elmina Castle by Lady Bonum's father, Squire Samuel Bonham. Auntie Rose had seen families come and go at Sandy Point. Often she would be heard composing the mournful cry:

> "Hark! I hath seen those who was purchased,
> those who was sold,
> those who was sick, runaway, whipped,
> and those who died old."

Black Jenny, when hearing Auntie Rose's rhyme, just laughed, a result of hearing her say that repeated verse every time slaves were brought in or taken out of Sandy Point.

"You always sayin' that old raggedy rhyme, Rosie! I 'member you sayin' that even when I first come here. And I been seeing 'em come and go, too. Nows' that I think about it--this here the first time we had a child this young come straight here from Guinea country!"

"This young child is sho' 'nuff something special, we can be certain," Auntie Rose replied, "and shall God be my witness, I am committed unto her that this child grow up and survives. We know not where her people is, 'cept this here African man she keep clutching, but know I a thing or two, as a humble soul giveth birth to wisdom, if the child made it all the way here, of this we are well aware, then there must be a reason why she still alive!"

Botswain, not certain about the meal being served him either, then turned to Quamino and uttered in Akan: *"What is this? Do you eat?"* Quamino replied: *"This is oyster; NEDIDE! EAT! Same as the village."* As Botswain began cracking open the cooked shells and swallowed the slimy-muscled flesh, his eyes lit up when the familiar taste finally registered, and began telling Akey in Kru talk that the oysters were safe to eat, that it was the "food of the pearl."

Still sensing the rare privilege of having an African child at such a tender age in her midst, as well as never having had children of her own, Auntie Rose turned to Quamino: "Speak that African talk and tell the child I'm "Auntie Rosie." Tell her the only one been here the longest tis I, except Mama, and know I well the child is scared to death. Understand, Massa treats his negras fairly well, but this child will have to fix her way to survives. Tell her Auntie Rose be right here 'case she coming crying for help." Quamino then translated in the Akan talk to both Akey and Botswain: *woman say this place she old mother Di   her name mean 'flower' possess knowledge to give, how not to be eaten up like the fish."*

The next day the Africans at Sandy Point and their Virginian-born cabin mates arose from their coveted and prized deep sleep to begin another muscle-aching day out in the tobacco fields. As Quamino and Jack King directed the fully eaten laborers away from the mush breakfast pot and to the field rows, a group of slavecatchers on horseback rode onto the plantation, pulling behind them with a rope a black man in shackles. The shrieks and cries of the field hands could be heard as they glanced up and recognized who the black man was. Colonel Eskridge hurried out to meet the strangers.

"Excuse us, my Lord, we found this here negra 'bout ten miles from here, near Northumberland, and we compassed every plantation from there to here to ascertain who the slave belongs to, and why he was discovered exposed to naked freedom, but if no one can produce the necessary proof of ownership then he will surely be sold off at the very next auction;  Here he is, take a look! What say you?" said one of them.

"Why, this slave belongs to me, his name is Ralph, and is my property-in-trust for one of my daughters!" quickly replied the Colonel. "And if proof is what you need, proof is what you shall have, as well as two Spanish pistoles to each of you for your troubles;  Just put him in my irons over there!" as George Eskridge pointed to the horse stable.

The horror in the field hands' faces was visibly seen as one and all knew what was about to come next upon the unfortunate Ralph, who had apparently run off during the time of the evening celebration the night before, this being now his third attempt. "The last time you did this to me, boy, I gave you only twenty lashes; This time I'm going to teach you a lesson you'll never forget for shamest thee before thy neighbors that I can't keep my negras under control...!," as the Colonel jeered, both gripping the handle of the whip and gritting his teeth with uncontrollable emotion. Next, the whip was flayed thirty times less none.

As the Colonel and the three slavecatchers went inside to settle matters between them, the man named Ralph lay slumped, dangling from his wrist shackles hung upon the hook on the stable wall, his feet in irons and his body twitching, convulsing. His back was indescribable. "Go quickly and fetch a bucket of water!" Jack King commanded to the young slave named Frank. That was the first time young Frank had saw such rage from Massa Eskridge. Young Frank was no longer young from that day on. Frank was about the same age as Akey, about one or perhaps two years older, and had been born in the West Indies to a Jamaican mother and an African father who was of the Akan tribe. Frank's father, Quashie, later joined a band of runaway slaves who had banded to fight against King George's soldiers, who held control of the island. Fearing for their lives, the runaways took refuge deep in the forests to avoid capture. Frank never saw his father again. During the "Maroon Wars" his father was later killed by His Majesty's soldiers. The last time Frank saw his mother was when he was led away from her out of the sugar cane field one day, put on a ship, and sold with nine others to be imported into the Colony of Virginia.

As is true of all young men who in nature come to seek a mate, soon Frank became fond of Akey, this young beautiful black skinned girl. He did not know where she was from, or why she wouldn't speak, but he knew something terrible had robbed her smile. But at least her name had not been robbed from her. Although twelve months had now gone by since being purchased at Yorktown, Akey remained determined to keep her African birth name, refusing to adopt the Anglo "Molly" that had been picked for her and which the hired English-lady tutor had tried to impose on her during their daily learning sessions. Surprisingly, the colonel's wife, Lady Elizabeth, had requested that Akey be trained a house servant, in spite of the fact that Lady Elizabeth knew full well it was not common practice to employ a newly arrived African into a private home. But Lady Elizabeth felt Akey was not a threat at her young age. Either that, or Lady Elizabeth was naive. But not quite naive so as to allow Akey to be assigned sleeping quarters inside the main house.

"This is "chair.""
"Shair."
"This is "cup.""
"Kupa."
"My name is Miss Payne."
"Mssss....Payna."
"Your name is Molly."
"No! Akey!"
"Repeat after me--Molly, "Mol-ly.""
"No Mollee...Akey!...Akey!"

As Akey returned to her cabin after each day of word session, Auntie Rose and Black Jenny would be sitting on their cabin porch, observing the tired and resentful look on Akey's face. "Here come that poor child again," Black Jenny said. "Massa sho' tryin' to break her in fast. Why, he ain't never brung in the house any fresh Africans this soon, not even been one year yet, I don't think. Wondering why he so driven to having that child be serving?" Auntie Rose looked at Black Jenny and gave her a 'you-don't-know-by-now?' look.

"You haven't spun to a reason yet? Lookie here--who be lookin' after Madam 'Lizabeth's daughter Little 'Lizabeth and that other little missy named Mary, the one who they calls daughter, but really not her daughter by nature, mind you; Who be pickin' up after them?"

"I see's now what you driving at," said Black Jenny as the look on her face started her to viewing the matter at a total different angle. "Old man Beck and old woman Nanny can't keep up with them younguns as old as they keep gettin'. Madam 'Lizabeth wants a child servant! And don't even know what that little guinea girl got sealed up inside her, before she come bringing her right past them kitchen knives! That a poor shame."

"Say not that! I don't even want to think what would happen to that poor child if she was to go into a fit up in that house--she would never see the sunrise."

Auntie Rose didn't want to be reminded of what did happen one time back, one time when a family on another plantation at Sandy Point hamlet was attacked in the middle of their sleep by two slaves and one indentured servant armed with striking instruments, robbing the family of what currency they had and then left them for dead. According to her mother Congo Judy who told her the story, Congo Judy could remember hearing screams at night coming from that plantation, as slaves were being whipped and beaten by a surviving member so a coerced confession could be extracted as to which ones had aided in the conspiracy. She remembered, too, how Squire Bonham even went for months, after that incident, keeping a loaded musket beside him at all times, keeping it even next to his bed. Colonel Eskridge was capable of doing whatever it took to protect his own, too. He had already demonstrated what he could do in a fit of rage, during that very next day after Akey and Botswain arrived.

As Akey, escorted by Quamino, walked past the two women on the porch, Auntie Rose called out: "Quamino! Quamino! Bring that child over here!" As eleven year old Akey approached the porch, Auntie Rose asked her, "How's my young lady princess doin' today?  Alas!  Why the look on your face?  You don't take a liking to what they doin' to you up at the big house?  I know;  I seen that look on many befo' you, don't matter if they was African, West Indie, or plain ole' country negra, don't nobody marches to be made into somethin' they isn't.  Tell her Quamino! Know you her season is not yet to understand my words!"

Quamino began translating as best he could, though certain expressions lacking, as Auntie Rose continued.

"What is your name again, child?  Your name--what is your name?!"

"Akey!"

"Ah, Akey!  So I count they hath not fashioned your name as yet;  Either that, or you struggle to give not it up."

"Namea, no...Akey, yesa!"

"Um-um-um;  You hear that Jenn?  She goin' come to blows over her name.  KEEP your name Akey, KEEP IT!  'Cause I can tell that's what goin' keep you alive.  Did you tell her, Quamino?"

"I tell her;  Now, she must go;  Horses need clean."

The next day's sessions would produce the same predictable result.  And Jack King's similiar efforts with Botswain also left the black overseer frustrated and exasperated.  No wonder Colonel George Eskridge had a rarely mentioned standing policy at Sandy Point:  "I will grant any negro mother to name their newborn, and any African slave whose will is entreating to retain his or her birthname is obliged, provided his work is complete, no nature of insurrection abideth in him, and conspires not to run away."  This he would proudly maintain to visiting guests who would ask, viewing his custom as unorthodox yet admiring his uniqueness.  Actually, what else could he say if certain "new country negras" refused to have their identities totally stripped and replaced?  Soon the lady tutor avoided the subject of name altogether.  And the day after that.  And the day after that.

As "a true friend loveth all the time, and is a brother born when thou is in distress," Frank settled to ease Akey's bruised heart and spirit.  Whether it was hoeing in the tobacco fields, picking in the apple orchards, or hanging meat in the smoke house, young

Frank would work next to Akey. She still wouldn't smile with her mouth, but each time he walked by her, their eyes would meet. The day Akey finally opened up to laugh was when Frank slipped and fell into the water while Botswain was trying to show him how to fish along the Potomac. A Kru, Frank was not. And when Akey would grab a catch but Frank didn't, she wondered what had robbed Frank of his smile, if only for a moment. Yes, Botswain was now satisfied that his brother's daughter, Akey, had found a future mate that would take care of her.

As the year 1727 began rearing its head, Colonel Eskridge found himself re-elected to his seat in the House of Burgesses on March 5, after a nasty campaign marred by accusations of election fraud conducted by one named Augustine Washington. Sheriff Washington of Westmoreland County, took the task of lobbying votes for the Colonel and later was cleared of any impropriety in the so-called scandal, which affair seemed to have been totally unnecessary in the first place had not it been for the poisonous wine of sour grapes that was served by the three losing candidates.

On May 31, Sheriff Washington and his wife met in council with the Colonel to have a deed of trust drawn conveying their home at Popes Creek and nine slaves, to their two minor sons in the event the sheriff and his wife met an untimely death before the sons had reached their maturity. On previous house visits to the Colonel's home at Sandy Point, Sheriff Augustine Washington had become convinced of the Colonel's capableness in overseeing deeds of this nature as he observed the blossoming growth of the orphan girl Mary Ball, whom Colonel Eskridge had brought under his roof and guardianship.

While the ship *Margaret* owned by Squire Samuel Bonham and mastered by Mr. Edward Weedon entered the ports of Yorktown carrying 244 African slaves from Angola on June 20, 1727, Sheriff Washington galloped on his horse to Montross town to have his deed trust recorded in the county courthouse. There sat that same day on the banks of the Potomac, Frank, with a fishing line in hand, and above him the warm rays of sun which invited him to frolic about this late afternoon Friday, since by this time of week plantation work, such as the transplanting of tobacco seed, was winding down.

. The shoreline beach of Sandy Point rested right behind the plantation. Accompanying Frank, with their fishing lines were Botswain and Akey who never missed the opportunity Massa Eskridge gave them for leisure time when the end of a work week had arrived. Botswain and Akey would sometimes sit for hours simply staring while Frank would just have a ball seeing how many fish he could catch. It became apparent the river was keeping memories of home alive. Either that, or Botswain was perhaps trying to measure the distance of the river to the Grain Coast, especially if he had caught sight of the brigitines which passed them carrying Angolians, Gambians, and Coromantees heading to Tappahannock or Annapolis.

"Lookie here! I done caught another one!" exclaimed Frank as he hauled in another biting trophy. "They bitin' real good today! Look how many I got Botswain! How many these here fish? How many Botswain? Let me count 'em: 1-2-3...huh...1-2-3...1-2..."

Frank had about twelve fish lying in his pile but kept counting them over and over. Frank knew he couldn't count past three, those being the only numbers he memorized from listening to one of the plantation's indentured servants.

Botswain picked up his fishing stick that so far had laid beside him dormant and cast the long thread into the river. Honest to God, within one minute he had snagged a fresh catch and yanked it onto the shore, working the fish loose from a sharp crude-made hook. Botswain then threw his first catch of the day into Frank's pile. Frank protested. "That's my pile of fish! Put your fish over there!" Frank pointed away from his. Botswain, though not understanding Frank's words, UNDERSTOOD. He left his single catch just where it was and calmly proceeded to count all of the trout in Kru numbers: "due, so, ta, nye, mu, munyendue, mnyeso..."

A Kru would never worry about whose catch was whose. In the Kru villages everyone shared in the spoil. As Botswain kept counting and soon reached the number eight he seemed to have trouble recalling the next numerical sequence.  Akey quickly jumped in to assist, after which Botswain repeated after her: "munyeta, sopadue, pue, puenyadue, puenyaso."  After Akey finished their count at twelve, out of the blue Frank pulled out of his recall one last numeral he had memorized.  "There must be 'bout *twenty* of 'em altogether!"

Suddenly there appeared a black man in tattered clothing and with a full beard, seeming to look lost, like a runaway, approaching them on the shoreline.

"What business you got being on this here plantation!" shouted Frank to the stranger.

"Do it look like I got business up here?  I thought A MAN could walk down these beaches without no kinda business in mind; You out here paddyrolling 'dese beaches?" the man asked as he carefully examined Frank, Botswain, and Akey.

"Noooooo!  I ain't no paddyroller;  You a runaway?" Frank asked as his voice tuned down to almost a whisper and developing a small grin.  "You needs some help?"

"I sho' do needs some help, but I ain't no runaway;  Let's me introduce myself--my name's Tom Tate, from way back at Cople Parish;  Back's there the white folks call me "Mulatto Tom.""

"You sure you ain't no runaway?  If your massa lookin' for you and they catch us out here standing with you, then we all jus' might as well be good as dead!"

"You ain't got to worry 'bout that , at least not yet."

"What you mean 'not yet'; Whose your massa!"

"You mean who *was* my massa;  My massa was Marse Alexander Spence, that is, until he died;  You see, my mama was a white servant bound to Marse Spence for seven years and my papa was a black man on marse' plantation;  My mama and papa wanted to get married, but papa being a slave there wasn't no chance of that happening;  When marse found out about the two of 'em he was as mad as a hot bull, then when I come out mama's belly, marse was even more hot, hotter than the white fire of a blacksmith!  He was so upset he bound me for 30 years even though I supposed to be free when mama became free, that's the law!"

"So what happened when your massa dead?"

"Let me tell ya; 'Bout 20 years later after I born and Marse Spence got sick and frail, he wrote down in his will that I become a freeman after he leave this here world."

"You free?!  You freeman?!  You hear that Bo'sn, he a freeman!!  Free like a bird!"

"Freeman?" asked Botswain, still trying to understand odd English grammar.

"Freeman;  *Bird*--Yewa!"  said Akey as she confidently confirmed her understanding.

"But I just heard from the sheriff of Cople Parish, told me a new law just passed that freemen have 30 days to leave the county! That's why I made my way up here, 'cause the new law say whomever the man who helped free me must pay my way out of the county;  I showed my freedom papers to the last farmer next to here--he told me I need to find Sandy Point Plantation."

"Why, this is ......", Frank couldn't finish his sentence, a lump formed in his throat.  With disbelief in his eyes, Frank tried to mask his emotion, and went on to asking "Mulatto Tom" who was the man he was looking for.

"The sheriff said I need to find Colonel George Eskridge."

As bewildered Frank pointed to the direction of the veranda to the Colonel's big house, the freedom papers that Mulatto Tom carried on him for the last seven years read in the following words: "The Bearer hereof, Tom Tate, a mulatto man, five feet nine inches high, about twenty one years of age, a scar on the back of his right palm near the wrist, is a free man of color, Manumitted by the last will of Alexander Spence decd; and confirmed under oath by executor George Eskridge upon his motion before the County court of Westmoreland this 28th day of January seventeen hundred and thirteen."

As house servant Beck was polishing Lady Elizabeth's silverware set, he heard a knock at the back door.  Servant Beck headed down the hallway to the east wing and opened the door. Young Frank and Akey had long since abandoned their spots at the river bank and were watching from afar as Tom knocked on the big house.

"Excuse me, sir, my name's Tom Tate from Cople Parish, and with your permission I needs to speak with your massa Eskridge, it's powerfully important!"

"You want to speak to who?!  Why, you saucy fool!  Hurry up and get away from this door before someone else causes you more harm than me!!"

"These are my freedom papers!!  I'm no slave!  Massa Eskridge the one done freed me, so you go tell him Tom from the plantation of the late Massa Spence has been sent here from the sheriff of Cople Parish!"

"Wait here," said the house servant with a stunned look on his face and heart.  Beck closed the doors, collected himself, and then strode slowly to the Colonel's study, trying to think how he was going to word this with each deliberate step.

"Pardon me, my lord, but there is someone here to see you, who says he's a free man of color by the name of Tom Tate formerly the servant of a late honorable Mr. Spence, and that the sheriff of Cople Parish sent him here, my lord."

"Mulatto Tom?  From Alexander Spence's estate?  What on earth bringeth him here?  Ha!  Show him in to my study, dear Beck;  Please guideth him in!"

"Yes, my lord."

Tom Tate was directed in by Servant Beck.  The playing of a violin could be heard as Tom strode over hand-loomed French rugs and led down a hallway to the study.  Lowering the violin from his chin, the Colonel turned around.

"Why, Mulatto Tom!  Good day!  Good day!  You doth desire to see me after such a long time;  What say you, dear Tom fellow?"

"Long live the King, and peace be unto you, dear Massa Eskridge, for I am forever grateful for what you did for me many a year ago.  And God knows I doth made the best of my time on this earth.  My hands have not been idle or asleep in the cookie jar; I've worked at..."

"Tom, Tom, say no more;  I can see my departed friend Lord Spence has nurtured you well, and even after his passing I have heard of your industriousness;  But something has caused you to travel such a long distance.  Hide not your troubles!  Confess your grievance openly."

"My Lord, the sheriff of Cople Parish has given me notice that in 30 days all freemen must leave the county!"

"I see;  Alas!  There, in fact, was a revised bill in the house which was approved last year by the governor requiring the removal of all free persons of color and Indians from that year forward.  But this law is far from being made clear on this point, it being loosely interpreted from county to county.  I wouldn't worry dear Tom, there have been similiar laws passed before your time and even since then."

"Pardon me, dear massa, but the sheriff gave me notice himself just five days ago!"

"Nay, be not troubled;  I gave my oath to my dying friend that I would have you manumitted, and a travesty it would be if I were to sit by and watch thee good gifts stolen away from Westmoreland County!"

"Thanks you, dear massa, may God bless you, and long live the ..."

"Enough said, thy freeman Tom;  I envision that you are more a freeman here in the colony than in England itself!  Let me have my overseer make room for you here at least for now."

"BOOM-BOOM-BOOM!  BOOM-BOOM-BOOM!"  At that moment, a wild commotion could be heard at the front entrance.

"Open quickly!  Hurry!  Open up!  Let me in, quick!" shouted a man from the other side of the heavy cedar doors.  The Colonel turned and looked at Tom.  "Beck!  Take this man and stealeth him away to the wine cellar;  Hurry and go!  This may mean trouble;  Quick!"

As servant Beck whisked away Tom to the protectiveness of the underground cellar, house servant Nanny charged to the banging front door.  It was Massa Eskridge's cousin Samuel Rust, who immediately rushed in.

"Cousin George!  Did you get word?  The King is dead! King George of England is dead!" as Samuel Rust held the special edition of the Virginia *Gazette*, waving it wildly in his cousin's face.

"When did this occur?"

"Just last week in Osnabruck, June the 12th;  Lords Townshend and Walpole are now in emergency session;  What will this mean for England do you suppose?"

"What will it mean for the Virginia Colony?  I'm sure Parliament will now have their hands full with the Puritans."

"I'm certain.  Perhaps even the Puritans here in the Colony will now want to make everyone a "Roundhead."  Looks like a special session will be called in Williamsburg for all burgesses to be present. Need me to take you?"

"That's kind of you, dear Cousin;  Yes, let me gather my things."

"We've much to talk about on the way, Cousin George! This may be the golden opportunity to lower the tariffs on slave imports. Ha! Long live the King!  Long live the Triple Alliance! Long live the Royal African Company!  Say, let's go down to the wine cellar and pick out a fine bottle for the journey, shall we?"

For a moment the Colonel hesitated to answer, not knowing what a trip to the cellar at that moment might entail.

"Dear Cousin Rust, I think not this be a time for merry-making;  Let us depart!  We will have plenty time later for such occasion."

As Akey stood outside and watched the clamor about some dead king, she wondered what this might mean for her own future? Could she become a *bird* like Mulatto Tom?  Perhaps Massa Eskridge could do the same and pronounce her liberty before he left the world.

Eight years later, realizing that his time on earth was nearing its end, Colonel Eskridge sat down at his estoirte and began drawing up his last will and testament. By November 1735 Colonel George Eskridge, the King's Attorney, member of the House of Burgesses, tobacco agent for Westmoreland and Northumberland County, and slaveowner of Sandy Point Plantation, was dead.  His estate would now be divided among his five children heirs.  After the funeral, the colonel's family gathered at the main house to welcome relatives and friends.  The colonel's adopted daughter Mary, now married to the county sheriff Captain Augustine Washington, soon arrived by carriage with her husband and their three year old son.  Quamino opened the gate to let them in.

There was no work to be done in the fields on this day.  The sixty men and women servants stayed close to their small cabins, while the friends and family of Colonel George Eskridge paid their respects and comfort his widow Lady Elizabeth.  Akey trotted half-awake to her chores in the livery stable under the command of Jack King.  As Akey was bent down watering the horses, she noted two small feet standing before her.  It was adopted daughter Mary's three year old boy, who had slipped away from his mother's attention.  The harmless tot came over to Akey and spoke:

"My grandfather died."

"Yes, I know," Akey replied, who now had learned to speak a crude form of English.

"Why did he die?"

"Everyone die," Akey said in her African accent.

"Did your grandfather die?" boldly persisted the vigorous youth.

This was the first time Akey had ever been asked such a question since she came to this strange country.

"I not know," Akey answered as she stood up. "It be long time since I see him."

"Where is he?" continued the boy.

At first Akey hesitated to answer, but on the boy's insistence she looked around, and not seeing anyone watching, bent down eye level with the child and pointed toward the visible Potomac.

"My grandfather live out there, across the water, far, far away from here."  Then Akey began picking up grains of sand by the child's feet. "Do you know what is "pepper?" People come to my grandfather to buy his pepper, the guinea pepper."

Picking up the sand also, the lively child was now repeating after her. "Pepper...pepper...the guinea pepper...the guinea..." Someone now walked in upon them.

"Wench! What are you doing with my son!" It was Mary.

"Nothing, Ms'um Mary!" Akey said as she quickly emptied her fistful of sand.

"How did my child get in here!" The horses were becoming startled, as was the boy, who stepped back right behind one of the mares.

"The boy lost; I here watering the horses; He walk away from big house and come in here."

"Well then, go back to your work," Mary said, as she calmed herself down. "Come over here child. Let's go back inside. There will be changes made soon." Akey, rubbing down the horses to keep them tranquil, watched as the mother and her pride and joy left the stable. The three year old pupil kept turning back to look at Akey.

The late colonel's son Samuel Eskridge began dividing up his father's sixty-seven slaves with the assistance of the inventory appraisers. Quamino, Botswain, and Akey's fate were now in the hands of their former master's son. Quamino and his wife Taffy were allotted with others to the colonel's widow Lady Elizabeth. Botswain, his new wife Black Jenny, Frank, and fifteen others were allotted to another of the colonel's sons, Dr. Robert Eskridge, a medical surgeon. The surgeon's five hundred acre property adjoined his late father's land. Akey, along with Auntie Rose, a coach driver named George, and several others, ended up the profit inheritance of Massa Samuel Eskridge, a justice of the peace and Burgess member of the House. As it turned out both Akey and Botswain had the rare privilege of not being sold off but instead able to carve out an existence side by side despite different owners--two brothers. This blessing stayed intact even when one of the brothers, surgeon Robert, later sold out his five hundred acres to a man named Captain Richard Jackson.

In 1744 Lady Elizabeth Eskridge  sought counsel to devise her final parting wishes. "I Elizabeth Eskridge, living of sound and perfect mind and memory give my spirit to God that gave it and my soul to the earth from whence it came, to be buried in such decent manner as my executor shall see convenient, trusting the merits of my Saviour to find pardon for all my sins."   By November of that year Elizabeth Eskridge entrusted her soul and spirit to her Creator, leaving her son Samuel with the inheritance of the main house and plantation according to his late father's wishes. The family heirs came together again to make their final arrangements and pay their respects, including adopted daughter Mrs. Mary Washington, again accompanied by her young son, now twelve.  Akey, who was now twenty-nine, had eventually mated with Frank and had a daughter which they named Rachel.  Frank and Akey had formed their union six years ago, just before Dr. Eskridge had left for England after selling away his inheritance deed to his land and slaves, so Frank had now become Massa Samuel's property.  Yet Botswain and his family remained on the neighboring estate.

As Akey was sitting and holding her baby daughter outside the smoke house one day, the adolescent  who was now twelve came over to her.

"You 'member when you the size of my little Rachel, and Massa Eskridge died?" Akey asked him.

"Barely can I recall," admitted the boy. "I just recall many people coming and going, and the horse coffinwagon slowly going down the road with everyone following behind it."  But then the boy added something else. "I also recollect seeing you in the horse stable, and you were showing me the sand."

"Do you know why I show you the sand?  It because you ask me if my grandfather die.  You even ask me where he was."

"What did you tell me?"

"I tell you I not know if he dead or alive, but he live a far away place, across the many rivers.  I picked up the sand to show you my grandfather grow pepper, and many come to his farm to purchase this pepper, the berries when crushed look like the sand."

"What was the name of this place?"

Akey proudly told him. "My home called Zwedru, near the river Cavella."  Akey went on to tell him that her grandfather, Sensobo, was a sailor and had travelled on ships, returning home with much wealth. But these things were new to the ears of the boy, not knowing whether to believe them or dismiss it as poppycock. But Akey continued to speak proudly, telling him that her uncle Bodebe, a sailor too, was given the name Botswain by the Englishmen on the merchant ships. "And my name was given me by my father...he named me after his mother. I never see her, she die before I born. The name come from a certain fruit tree. Look! I show you."

There in the garden behind the cabin, she showed the boy the fruit tree she had planted nineteen years ago, although its few surviving woody red berries were much smaller and the tree much shorter than in Akey's Kru country, its potential height stunted by its unnatural climate. With that, the young boy cordially said his gentleman-like goodbye as he was called away by Mother Washington. That was the last time the young boy, whose name was George Washington, and Akey would ever speak to each other.

While Mary Washington and her son George departed for Mount Vernon, Akey was in a few days time giving out goodbyes again. This time to Frank, as Massa Samuel was preparing to bring several male slaves along with him to his other manor "Flatlick Quarter" in Fairfax County. Massa Samuel needed some good strong muscles for repair work to be done on a public county road which intersected with the road leading to his private Fairfax residence. Massa Samuel, at his appearances before the House Council in Williamsburg, vigoursly lobbied for the repair of such county roads, his own wife, Lady Jane the daughter of Lord Ashton, having started him on this crusade using persuasion, a result of constant reminder as to how terribly needed for repair was the very road leading to their Sandy Point plantation. Even more pleasing to Massa Samuel was when it was voted the public road intersecting his Fairfax estate would be annexed with Fairfax County rather than the former Prince William, and his expenses for the repairs would be defrayed one half out of His Majesties Revenue and the other half to be paid by the Honorable Lord Fairfax. If Massa Samuel was going to use his negro slaves for county work, it wasn't going to be for free.

"Come hither, Jack King; Have thou a suitable number of servants ready to leave for Flatlick? If so, saddle thee my horse and set my bondsmen on their way, as my clock ticketh while morning is still young," Massa Samuel commanded.

"Yessah! They are most ready, sah, except 'fore one of 'em, Frank, worried he won't be back to see his wife or babychild."

"Tell Frank to quit that frettin', he always seems a bit fearful when leaving to Flatlick as though he's never coming back again! I don't know what gets into him; Tell him he'll be coming back just the same as he has been; My goodness! Can't he stay away from his mate for just a short time? Pretty soon I'll have to start taking all my wenches along!"

"Yessah! I'll set him right, sah."

Then after caressing his wife with a goodbye kiss and admonishing his growing children of Charles, Richard, Burdett, John, and Rebecca to behave themselves during his absence, Massa Samuel mounted Toby his horse.

"I shall see thee soon my dear, just as speedily as the light of dawn which shineth brighter and brighter unto the perfect day, I promise thee; I'll be back in two weeks time and no more; I'm certain the matters before the Council this term will not drag on, my dear, even the debate on prohibiting export of the Indian corn, mind you, think I will be nipped in the bud this time around! Au revoir, a bientot!"

Jack King now stormed off to face Frank's feisty concerns, hoping firm reasoning would motivate Frank to cease his resistance.

"You ain't goin' be sold off Frank," said Jack King with a plea in his voice. "Massa jus' takin' some of you good strong bucks to help fix the King's road over in Prince William County. You wasn't sold las' time you got brought down there, now was ya?"

"Las time I wasn't worried 'bout no slave auctions either, 'cause Ms'um Lady 'Lizabeth was alive then, and my Akey wasn't carryin' my baby Rachel. Now--Prince William County--ain't that up there near Maryland, where they be havin' them big slave auctions?!"

"That may be.  But like I jus' done told you, Massa plan on keepin' all you darkies, and 'specially now that his mother dead.  Now--you see what I got in my hand?  Don't make me have to use it, and don't make Massa Samuel late for his meetings.  You see George the coachman sitting up there on the coach waiting to go?  Don't make him late neither, or else Massa Samuel might tell George to jus' keep right on going to Maryland, ya hear me!?"

As Frank begrudgingly climbed aboard, his father Quashie's 'aversion to Tyranny' blood still running in him, Akey, with child in her arms, stood watching the whole affair from her cabin porch.  Frank had voiced his concerns to her about this trip.  Now Akey was worried.  But should she be?  Had not Botswain explained to her the ways of the Kru that it was customary for the husband to leave home for long periods of time and for the wife to stay busy while awaiting his return?  But it was not supposed to be like this.

Akey looked out over the yard at the cabin across from her, Auntie Rose's, and noticed her sitting on her porch.  Akey wondered if she ever left that porch.  Quickly Akey carried her child Rachel and walked across the yard to Auntie Rose.

"You wear worry in your face, my child;  What bothers thee?" Auntie Rose asked.

"Where they take my Frank?  Why they take him today?  Massa sell him?"  Akey asked in despair.

"Why child, what did your husband himself say?"

"He say Massa want him fix the road near Massa's other house, but Frank don't believe him, he thinks Massa lie so he can take Frank and sell him now that Massa's mother dead.  That true Rose?  That true?"

"You hear me sitting here singing lamentation?"

"La-men-tay-shun?  What that?"

"That mean sad song;  Your ears do not hear me singing, do they?"

"No."

"If Massa Samuel say he take Frank to mend the roads, then that is all he will do, you can be sure, for Massa Samuel say what he means, and means what he say, for a man to speaketh deception he is not, for if he were to sell Frank and the whole lot of 'em, he would have made clear the matter to your husband straight, nay, even to King the overseer before yet the wheels on the cart turned even once, before yet the horses Toby, Sparke, and Ranter should lift hoof and heels to the cobblestone pavement. Restez calme, restez calme, ne desespe'rez pas my child, rest easy, for you will have your man back, tis no question."

"Thanks you, Auntie Rose, thanks you. I trust your word."

"And understand I your words, child, for a frightening thing it is indeed to lose a loved one, to be severed from the one baptized with affection. Tell me, what was the name of your mother, your father, your sisters or brothers, do you still remember?"

"My mother's name Bina;  My father, Mennah;  My brother, Nadi."

"I perceive their names still burn fresh in your memory. 'Tis a good thing to know one's rootstock, to know the beginning of one's sprout, just as the brickmason can point to the cornerstone, or a gardener to his orchard the first tender branch. Just as the birth of the butterfly giveth thanks to the caterpillar worm, and the legs of the jumping frog to the eggs of the tadpole, even the possum, the rat, and the wolf all know their rightful den even in the darkness. While the creeks, springs, and rivers know their mother is the ocean, the raindrops their father, and the sun their grandfather. Nay, to all living things render thanks to the sun, even whose immortal father is the Eternal Creator of heaven and earth. Yay, tis a good thing to know whence one came, just as one follows the path of footsteps on the sand, or a traveller sailing abroad, knowing his chartered course bringeth him home again on an unchangeable current. On a ship laden with treasures of every kind, talents of gold and ivory teeth, spices and delicate stones, fruits and fowl, horses and peacocks, apes and baboons--and no-- even thine own mother! Yay, thine own mother, ripped from her own mother's arms, just as a lion a breeding deer his prey, or a midwife lacking natural affection her own daughter's child tradeth away. Alas! My dear mother, born in the Congo but raised an orphan, her rootstock cut out of her and chopped down. The names of her wounded family she remembered not, but peculiar the name "Congo" stayed branded in her mind, just as fixed as the trader's seal branded in her callous skin.  Tis a queer thing indeed the memory of a child.  But as I convey you this, feel not sorrow for thy mother nor shed a tear, feel not melancholy nor gloom of spirit, nor your heart give birth to rash ill-temperedness, for an oath I have kept since leaving the womb, that shall I never pity the one who nourished and protected me when crawled I like a puppy in nature.  For verily I say unto you, be resolved to her story only to pride and gladness as I am, for despite her facing dishonor due to the evil company lying in her bed--them sickly pack of ravens and lustful crows,  vile trash!!--she still held in her hand the courage to live, whose product of her courage has the credit of standing before you now!"

Akey wondered if Rose was talking to her or, instead, to the garden trees, maybe even to the actual crows that were circling overhead.  "Let me go bring you some *good* tea."  Akey thought offering Rose her special made brewed tea made of  Whig plant, ginger root, and leaves from her akee tree would calm and wake Rose from her transfixed gaze.

By the middle of the following week, Frank and all the others in his gang had returned to Sandy Point.  Massa Samuel returned from session the week after.  And there was heard no lamentations coming from Auntie Rose's cabin, nor disturbance on the plantation for a period of three years.

After three years time Massa Samuel Eskridge now breathed his last.  That same year Frank and Akey had another daughter born to them, Jane, who was also called Jenny.  But sadly, families would now be separated, as was soon discovered as the seal on Massa Samuel's last will was broken open and read to his surviving family by his appointed executor:  "I Samuel Eskridge, being well in health and of perfect mind and memory thanks be to Almighty God, but knowing it is appointed for all men once to die, I Bequeath my spirit to God and my body to be buried in a descent manner...to my son Charles I bequeath the slaves Joseph the carpenter, Jane and her child Whitley, and four other slaves to be picked by him or his heirs...to my son Richard in Caswell County, North Carolina I bequeath Adam, William, Tom, and Hannah...to my son John I give unto him Benjamin, Nan and her child Beck...to my son Burdett and his heirs I give negro slaves George, his wife Bett, Frank, his wife Akey and her child Jenny...to my daughter Rebecca I bequeath negro man Charles, his wife Sarah and her child Judith, Mulatto Peg, Black Peg, and four other slaves to be picked by her or her heirs...to my beloved wife Jane I give to her negro girl Rachel and all the rest of my slaves including those she brought me in marriage, as well as my plantation for as long as she lives and residue of my estate in every description...I hereunto set my hand and seal, this Twentieth day of May, Seventeen hundred forty-seven."

"Who you think our new massa is now?," George asked Frank.

"I don't know and I don't care, so long's they don't sell off my family;  I been thru too many massas' to not know by now there ain't no use in frettin' 'bout it--they be 'round to let us know when they good and ready;  sometime you jus' DON'T want to know," underscored Frank.

Little did Frank realize that his own daughter Rachel had been already assigned out to Massa Samuel Eskridge's widow. Eventually, Rachel came to bear a son whom she named Prero, after Bodebe's brother the fisherman, who  later came to be known by the nickname "Prue" on the plantation, since no one seemed able to pronounce his African name.

Botswain continued to live on the land adjacent to Sandy Point Plantation.  Since his arrival to this large tobacco-growing region, his sea-faring skills, of course, were inevitably recruited by the Majesty's tobacco agents in order to paddle the tobacco hogsheads by sloop to the awaiting ships on the Potomac anchored off of Sandy Point.

As Botswain rowed back to the docks one day to pick up more hogsheads to place in his bugeye in order to complete the consignments being loaded onto the ships *Olive* and *Success*, Botswain noticed a great commotion occuring as he approached the docks.

"It was burned!...Burned to the ground!!...the ship *Black Princess* was burned up last night at Hampton by some twenty pirates!!," shouted a merchant trader just arriving off of the King's Road.

"The ship was plundered of all of its fresh choicest Gambian slaves!...the pirates took all of them and were heading last toward St. Augustine!" shouted another.  Soon the naval officers on port were notified by the customs collector of the turn of events in Hampton and were put on immediate alert in case any of the "Gambians" had made it to shore and were roaming the countryside.

"What happened?," asked Botswain to the ship captain of *Success*, as he hoisted himself out of the bugeye, "What they sayin' 'bout Hampton?"

The ship captain, a man named Jeremiah Cranston answered him. "Some pirates got ahold of the ship *Black Princess* last night--burned it to the ground and plundered all of the ship's goods; You had better hurry up and finish this loading before they decide to send you home early today, 'cause looks like they goin' be watching my ship all night."

"Marse Cranston, nobody ever since I can recall been able to bring harm to that there ship.  Aye 'member way back when the ship come to my country a time ago--they asked me if aye want to work the ship so I got on and worked it.  Then it brought me to "Lib-er-pool.""

"You a livid lie," replied a merchant trader overhearing Botswain. "You ain't been on no ship!  And you sho' ain't been to no Liverpool--unless you were shackled in chains!"

"No sar, aye no lie, I work *Success* when I a boy all the way to "Lib-er-pool," then I go back to my country, an' later aye work *African Galley*, an' *Vine*, an'..."

"Shut up boy!  You talkin' out yo' head;  You think I'm a fool, huh, guinea boy?"  The man was now ready to explode, thinking:  'This Virginian slave has the nerve to make up wild stories as these?'  Although furious to the point of striking Botswain, the man held back out of fear of Botswain's employer Cranston, standing right next to him.

Since the merchant trader couldn't teach this "uppity" slave a lesson with a whipping, he chose instead to humiliate him in front of his employer. This he chose to do, since knowing a substantial amount of maritime history, by asking Botswain:

"What were the names of the ship captains if you truly worked onboard their vessels when they arrived in Guinea, huh boy?"

"Aye worked with many of 'em, shipmates, too. There was Jack Yarn...Jim Jumbo...let's see...Elias Whisky-jug...Captain Bonham...Captain Seacom on the *Vine*...there was Marse Cassills on the *Margaret*, and when I worked this ship here, *Success*, Captain Fothergill hire me..."

When the man heard Botswain say the latter name, his eyes opened wide. Quickly he tried to hide his look of surprise by struting off in disgust, "I ain't got time for yo' stories, guineaboy." But later, once he walked over to the other side of the port, he whispered to a naval officer, "keep yo' eye on that negra over there of Captain Cranston's; he been acting a little strange since he heard of the incident at Hampton. I think he's planning to jump onboard the ships." A boldface lie. In reality, Botswain had unwittingly called the man's bluff when he spit out the names of shipmates and captains he had encountered during the early dark days of the slave trade in his country. Although most of the names the merchant trader hadn't heard of anyway, there was one name he knew that couldn't be refuted--Captain Fothergill. Little did Botswain realize that the name of this captain several years ago, after having plowed the waters of the Windward Coast, hit big news in the columns of the Virginia *Gazette*, for sometime during early 1737 off the Grain Coast of Africa as the captain's ship arrived on the banks of the River Sherboro and he went ashore, several of the tribes people surrounded him and cut off his head with a hatchet.

Each year that went by after harvest season, Botswain, his wife Black Jenny, and their small daughter Dina would then turn their attention to harvesting their own personal gardens. Many of the slaves on the plantations at that time of year would now have time to glean their own family plots, the gardens which they had faithfully tended to during their days off on Sundays. The crops that Botswain and Black Jenny dried and stored had been their survival each winter. Young daughter Dina and her playmate girl companion Uwayma, a child of slave parents born in the Congo, would always look forward to Sunday to help work in the gardens. Frank and Akey's family continued to station themselves next door at Sandy Point plantation, tending to their gardens, chores, and the duties of family life. Nearly two decades now came to pass, and everyone remained a family. Nearly two decades.

Then one evening in the winter snow of 1765 Botswain began shivering inside his cabin despite the two worn out blankets covering him and Black Jenny. The cutting-cold wind slid through their cracked-wood walls without letup. Although Black Jenny could tolerate the annual winter seasons, Botswain never did grow accustom to the harshness of that time of year, let alone a snowstorm.

"I hate this weather, it is no good...jus' no good," Botswain muttered bitterly while trying to keep the top fringe of their sleeping blanket nestled around his neck.

"But this breeze not usually be this cold," Black Jenny said. "This here feel like a powerful storm is brewing."

"Well, I no lay here and freeze to death, I go build a fire!" Botswain said as he threw the blanket off him and rose to get up from the pallet. However, there was not enough wood. Botswain peeked his head out the cabin door.

"You can't go out there to get wood, old man!" Black Jenny protested. "It too windy! You be blown away! Jus' wait 'till morningtime come; You know Quamino be 'round first thing."

"I no wait for Quamino--I be dead by then! Wait here--I go get some wood for the stove."

"Honey, please don't go out there! I's telling you it too stormy!" Black Jenny repeated. But Botswain stormed out the cabin.

As he did, he noticed it had begun snowing again, but this time much harder. His fourscore year body, slowed by the beatings of time, limped over to the woodpile shed, and, grabbing four or five cut logs into his arms, began to make his way back to the cabin as the snow fell even harder.  But in doing so, Botswain lost his balance and fell backward into the deep snow, too weak with age to pull himself up without help.  But this proud African, a sailor, a Kru, would not think of calling for help.  He was a man, and it was a man's job to provide for his family, even if it meant rising up to gather firewood during one of the worst snow storms ever to hit Virginia.

But each time Botswain tried to raise himself, his strength would fail him.  His hands were now bitterly cold, and his legs began to stiffen.  Suddenly Botswain's mind flashed back to a different time.  He could see his life as a child roaming the forests of Africa.  He looked up at the stars and calculated his distance from the River Cavella.  A warmness soon came over his entire body.  Now he was a young man, sailing on a merchant ship, travelling up and down the coastline.  He could feel the hot sun warming his tropic-born skin.

Across the property-line from Massa Jackson's plantation, Akey, Frank, and daughter Jenny huddled together under the warm protectiveness of three quilt-knitted blankets.  The winter-snow chill could be felt through the cracks of their planked walls.  After nearly an hour of tossing and turning underneath their covers from the increasing blasts of invading snow filling the cabin, Frank finally rose to start a stove fire with their few remaining sticks of wood.

Suddenly a frantic knocking was heard on Akey and Frank's cabin door.  Everyone was surprised to see a troubled-looking Jack King standing in knee-deep snow.

"Is Botswain, from Massa Jackson's in here?" Jack King asked urgently.

"Why, no suh," Akey answered.  "What wrong?"

"Someone heard his wife calling out his name, said he went out to get some firewood and never returned;  Quamino come asking me if he wandered over here."

Frank immediately rushed out to join Jack King and Quamino.

Frank, Jack King, and Quamino finally found Botswain just

before midnight. He was barely alive. They brought him to Frank and Akey's cabin and tried to warm him next to the fire. He passed on sometime later the next morning.


By the early part of 1770, Massa Burdett Eskridge, and his wife, maiden Nancy Grigsby, decided to strike out West with nearly fifty other families, mostly relatives, and head to the lands of South Carolina. On this five hundred mile wagon migration would be oxen, mules, horses, milking cows, and Akey's family. There also would be Massa Burdett's two young sons, Samuel and Austin. Akey's daughter Jenny was already assigned by Lady Nancy to look after them.

Massa Burdett's family made ready to depart Sandy Point and make way to the meeting point of the wagon train, which would hopefully reach its halfway point by June. As the wagons and horses began to head down Sandy Point road, Akey sat, in her fifty-fifth year, in the back of the wagon, observing the faces of Quamino, Black Jenny, Auntie Rose, and all those who had been family all those years she had lived here, and those who always would be, such as her daughter and grandson, Rachel and Prero, bound to the hands of Massa Burdett's mother.

While a servant gardener lay knelt working in the yard below them, ninety-four year old Auntie Rose and Black Jenny sat on the porch. Auntie Rose looked out over the procession, then began her observant dirge.

"I seen those who was purchased,
those who was sold,
those be sick, runaway, well-whipped,
and those who died old.
I hath seen 'em come and go...I hath seen 'em come...and go."


In time, Massa Burdett and the slaves he inherited from his father eventually settled on four hundred seventy acres of virgin Carolina land in an area called "Ninety-Six District"--ninety-six miles away from the Cherokees. Included in the deed was a wagon road leading from Charleston to Augusta.    In 1773, Frank and Akey's daughter Jenny married William, a slave   born at Sandy Point who had been brought along to South Carolina.  Later that same year, Jenny gave birth to a child, a daughter named Ruth. Three years later she gave birth to another daughter and gave her a French name, Barbe.  And yet again, in 1779 a third daughter came forth.  "I's goin' name her Rose, named after Auntie Rose who befriended you when you first arrive in Virginia," said Jenny to her mother Akey.  "Besides, she born in late Spring and pretty as a rose anyhow," Jenny maintained, who seemed to be producing issue just about every three years.  Yet she wasn't the only woman on the new Carolina plantation doing so, as Massa Burdett's wife Nancy was bringing forth fruitage from her belly as well, demonstrated three years back with the birth of her third son, Richard.  Now she was carrying her fourth.

Times and seasons in the English colonies were quickly changing.  War was in the air and a desire to break free from England's yoke was growing.  In 1775 the colonies claimed independence from England, and men were called to bear arms. Massa Burdett, a Whig, stepped forward for service, and his brother John in Virginia responded as well.  Lady Nancy later gave Massa Burdett two daughters before her sudden death, leaving behind a husband and five children.  The mourning of Massa Burdett was great, so great that he fretted all afternoon the day of her burial as to how the children would be nurtured.

That night a replacement was found.  Massa Burdett's mother-in-law was nearly worn down and emotionally drained since the morning ceremony laid her daughter Nancy to rest, as the children kept their grandmother at a steady pace tending to their natural needs of affection, fueled now by confused fear.  *I want my mommy.*  Jenny stood beside the grandmother, lending a hand in keeping the children under emotional control, holding safe the ends of both rocking horses as little Richard and little Elizabeth bucked and bounced inexhaustively.  The two lads Samuel and Austin, tiring from their game of marbles, begged to go back outside to the barn and mingle with the horses and livestock they had earlier helped their father to feed.  Then the babygirl, craddled in the grandmother's arms, began screaming. Holding up the tired, hungry, tiny adult, the little one's eyes widened as she became the center of attention and a new fresh set of arms secured the blanket around her. The child was whisked away. In the nursing room the woman unbuttoned and stretched low the right shoulder of her blouse as the baby took the signal and parted it's lips in glee. Acting like the mother of all mothers, the resourceful attendant softly held the back of the baby's head and nudged it forward while gently guiding the infant's white mouth next to her brown breast. Excited, the baby quickly took over from there, raising it's mouth over Jenny's protruding black nipple and cried no more. Jenny was the one chosen to replenish the lost milk and bosom of the children's mother. As cruel as life can be, from that day on Jenny's loyalty was forever assigned to them first. Only after satisfying them with suck would then her own children.

Around 1781 the widower Massa Burdett married again, to Mistress Hannah Belle-Watson of Edgefield District, although originally from Petersburg, Virginia. But when Massa Burdett was killed in November 1781 along with other soldiers during a night raid massacre carried out by bloodthirsty British Tories, the unity of Frank and Akey's family was brought into jeopardy. Frank lamented, "Is our family to be torn apart and sold again?"

## CHAPTER SEVEN

## Whose Name Did You Take on Jubilee Day?

What first just started out as a simple itch of curiousity, now had turned into a full-blown outbreak of *"genealogy-itis."* Suddenly I was completely absorbed in my journey to the past. After a year, so totally absorbed I was in the search for my family's past that one of my close friends complained, "this is no longer a hobby with you--it's an obsession! All you're doing is just studying dead people!" That person was actually right. I just couldn't stop my research. Yet at times I felt like I was spinning my wheels. As a kid, I recalled when a friend and I decided to jump on our bikes one wet afternoon and ride to the end of the rainbow, where we believed a pot of gold would be found. But after riding a couple of miles, we soon realized the end of the rainbow was out of our grasp. Decades later now as an adult, I wondered if I was chasing the rainbow again.

One day in March 1992 while I was restudying the will of Richard Eskridge, something dawned on me as I read the codicil dated September 24, 1854:

"I Richard Eskridge...desiring that this codicil shall be taken as part of my said will.
**The last will of my brother Saml. B. Eskridge having been sustained by the Judgement of the Courts of Tennessee** by which will my grandson Saml. B. Eskridge is made the devisor &

legatee of his Estate after the death of his wife Sophia Eskridge and my said grandson being now sufficiently provided for by said bequest by my Brother  I do now revoke all the bequest and devises that I made to said Saml. B. Eskridge..."

  Richard Eskridge had a brother in Tennessee, and who left a will!  His name was Samuel B. Eskridge.  Checking the 1850 Tennessee census index, I found two persons named Samuel Eskridge:   one in Rutherford County, about 30 miles from Nashville, the other in Roane County, located in East Tennessee between Nashville and Knoxville.   According to the census, Samuel Eskridge of Rutherford County arrived there by 1810, and had four female slaves by 1840.   However, after 1850 he and his slaves had disappeared, causing me to wonder if he had died.  I now needed to know if he had a will or an estate inventory, especially since Great-grandfather William was born around 1847 reportably in "Nashville" according to his obituary, although that and anything else orally cited was far from conclusive.

  Soon I learned why Samuel Eskridge's name no longer appeared on the Rutherford County census: he had moved to Davidson County, the county that held the state's capitol at Nashville.   On the 1860 Davidson County census there he was listed at the age of 84, birthplace North Carolina.  What was more interesting were two slave deeds that were found.

  Both deeds were dated November 30, 1854:

"For the love and affection I entertain for my son William Eskridge I do hereby give transfer and convey to him my negroes named as follows, Lynce, aged about 20 years of age and Mandy aged about 18 years of age and her child Mary Ann aged about 10 months of age.  I warrant the title to the said slaves to the said William...for life..."

"For the love and affection I entertain for my son John R. Eskridge I do hereby give transfer and convey to him my negro woman Jane aged about 26 years of age and her three children Leathy aged 7 last April and William Franklin aged 5 years last April and Caroline aged about 14 months. I warrant the title to the said slaves to the said John R. Eskridge his heirs and assigns forever against the claims of all persons and I also warrant them to be sound healthy sensible and slaves for life this 30 day of November 1854"

Was "William Franklin" my great-grandfather? According to the deed, this William was born around April 1849, very close to the year 1847 that I had calculated my great-grandfather had been born. However, the 1860 slave schedule for Rutherford County showed the slave grantee son, John R. Eskridge, having twelve slaves, one being the eleven year mulatto male slave "William Franklin." This was the same year that the overseer Marion Hanks reported a thirteen year old black male on the slave schedule for Carroll County, Mississippi. So John R. Eskridge's male slave could not have been my great-grandfather. Nonetheless I was still amazed at how close "William Franklin" matched my great-grandfather in description. At least I had found *someone else's* great-grandfather.

I received material from a researcher in Kingston. Amazing. He was a member of the Roane County Genealogical Society, but as I read his letter I was moved when I realized after he had checked their library files and finding no data on any black families in the county, took it upon himself to not quit there but, instead, continued his search at the Roane County courthouse. I'm truly thankful he did. The material he found contained copies to the estate of the other Samuel Eskridge. As I read it, I couldn't believe what I had found:

"I Samuel Eskridge of the County of Roane and State of Tennessee being of sound mind and disposing memory do make and ordain this to be my last Will and Testament...

...The rest and residue of my property both real and personal at the death of my wife I give and bequeath to Samuel Butler Eskridge  the son of my nephew Taliaferro Eskridge **of the State of Mississippi** to him and his heirs forever...it is my will and desire that said Thomas N. Clark take the control and management of the entire property left by this my will to the said Samuel B. Eskridge until he shall attain the age of twentyone years..."

...In testimony hereof I Samuel Eskridge the testator have hereunto set my hand and seal this 29th day of March A.D. 1852

Saml. Eskridge

This was Richard Eskridge's brother.   Here Samuel Eskridge had bequeathed his entire estate to his great-nephew Samuel Butler Eskridge, the grandson of  Richard Eskridge whom he had mentioned in the codicil to his will.  Now I understood how my great-grandfather ended up in Mississippi from Tennessee.  Of course I didn't know exactly when.  He may have arrived in Duck Hill before Samuel Eskridge died in 1852.  In any case, here I had found a direct link from Tennessee to Duck Hill, his parents and siblings possibly brought to Duck Hill also.  The will also named "Thomas N. Clark" as guardian of Taliaferro Eskridge's minor son Samuel B. Eskridge in Duck Hill, as well as manager of the estate until the minor reached the age of twenty-one.  I had come across the name Thomas Clark among one of James K. Polk's letters written right at the time of Polk's Presidential Election victory:

STATE OF MISS  CARROLLTON  CARROLL COUNTY

Dear Sir              I now take the opportunity of writing you a few lines to let you know of a friend and where I am.  I have _____all  I hold for you in all your affections.  I moved from Brownsville Tenn,  I am well aquainted with all the people there and I have seen you there several times.  I wish to be remembered to you as a friend and do hope that you may please the people of the United States as a president and that these lines may find you encouraged and in great health.  I wish you to right me if you please and I am also your servant with pleasure_____

Thomas Clark.

Thomas Clark then concluded with a few lines from a familiar servant:

"I have become aquainted here with your servant.  Harry has a wife at  O.L. Kimbroughs, says that he belongs to J.K. Polk and that he wanted me to write you some word of him and how his circumstance was at this time and that the man that he lived with now would not use him well and that he wishes to be remembered to you as a servant one time more. The old man seems to be greatly rejoiced to think that his master is going to be president. tell master how much I won on him this hunt...I win about forty dollars; master send me a letter how all is, tell them that I am getting old and some afflicted with the rumytism master write me a letter in Mr. Thomas Clark's name then send them...Mr. Kimbrough will not let me hear from you and he is a Whig too and I do not want to live with him he done all he could against you master. Write to Mr. Bobbit, tell him that I do not want to live with Mr. Kimbrough any longer master please write soon I am your humble servant until death

      Harry

                              Clark."

     Samuel Eskridge's estate inventory included a list of 75 slaves. The name of the overseer was a man named John Casey. Other estate papers grouped most of the slaves by families and listed some of their ages. I also received copies of federal censuses which followed most of these same families five years after Emancipation all the way to the turn of the century in 1900. Comparing the Tennessee census records to the estate inventory, I began writing down the confirmed ages of the slaves and their families next to their names in the order in which they were listed:

**Slave Inventory, Taken on Eskridge Plantation lying near Clinch River February 1853**

**Lucy 49, Aaron 31, Major 28, Thomas 21, Hampton 17, George 11, Sally, Esther 13, Sophia 7, Trousdale 1, Amy, Tom(Alias Long Tom), Hiram 18, Lewis, Will, Selia 12, Cynthia, Israel 18, Nelson 27, Armistead 11, Polk 13, Martha 13, Cass, Butler 6, Charles, Ralph 67, Viney, Lucy 5, Julia, Matilda, Neety, Julia Ann 23, Wiley 6, Delialah, Jim Suddath 34, Jesse, Carpenter 28, Jackson, Dick 13, Albert 10, Mary 8, Aggy 18, Manda 17, Savannah 4, Matildah, Mary Jane, Clayra, Edmond, Aleck 49,**

Jenny, Joshua 34, Pirely 24, Isaac 12, Wash 9, Letha 5, Nancy 2, Davis 1, Brisborn 43, Margaret 45, Mariah 18, Solomon 18, Fed 17, Elizabeth, Eliza, Fanny 6, Clementine, Rosa Ann, Eliza, Fanny, Catherine 16, Governor 14, Jordan, Jackson 45, Haywood 16, Henry 28

The following farming implements & stock viz, 1 Harrow, 7 two-horse plows, 28 other plows, 2 Cultivators, 1 imperfect set Blacksmith Tools, 1 Wood work of Waggon, 2 Carts, 1 on wagon, 3 four-horse wagons, 1 Carriage, 21 stacks of oats, 8 hay Stacks, a quantity of wheat about 300 bushels, About 500 bushels old corn, 75 head of sheep, 80 head of cattle, 85 hogs, 75 stock hogs, 20 mules, 3 cutting bones, a lot of plaster, 6 mares, 4 young horses, 3 small colts, 2 yoke of oxen

The following Household furniture, viz, 1 Cupboard, 19 beds & bedstands & beddings, 3 Falling-leaf Tables, 2 Half-round Tables, 3 Common Tables, 1 Book case, 1 Set & part of set Windsor chairs, 2 sets-14 Common Chairs, 1 small sideboard common, 2 Guns, 2 pairs shovels & tongs, 9 pair Andirons

The following Kitchen furniture viz, 4 Ovens, 2 Frying Pans, 3 Kettles, 3 Pots, 1 Skillet, four or five hundred feet of Walnut plank and about 10 cherry plank.
Sworn in open Court   7th Feb. 1853

Just reading the inventory that was taken on the plantation made me truly realize just how much hard work, how much responsibilty, rested upon these 75 people entrusted with keeping this plantation running. And not only did they have to see to the caring of the many numbers of stock and cattle, they also had to see to their own survival in living--men, women, & children. *I noted too, that there was a female named Elizabeth, two females named Eliza, and a male named Will.* It was obvious the estate appraisers took certain care to list the names in the order written, as if they were grouped by families.

Now I knew where I was going to take my next trip: Tennessee and Mississippi. About this same time, the genealogist

I had first contacted in Carrollton, Betty, sent me a letter saying that while doing research for someone else, she came across court minutes revealing that Marion Hanks died in 1864. I began telephoning several funeral homes and cemeteries in Carroll, Montgomery, and Grenada counties, asking for names of predominantly black funeral homes whose records possibly went back to the late 1800's and early 1900's. The caretaker of one cemetary referred me to a local historian of Carroll County, who later supplied me with locations where I might find black cemetaries in the county. Although I had no idea at the time, this county historian would eventually lead me to something that silently stood in the back of my mind: Could I contact a living descendant of slaveowner Richard Eskridge? And if so, could this person possess information about his or her ancestors' slaves--my family?

August 1992 was now time for the "McCoy Family Reunion" which was decided again to be held in Portland. Must have been something about all the fresh air out here. Several families were coming from Los Angeles. Perhaps some good ole' country air was in order, since the smoke signals from the riots that swept South-Central Los Angeles in April still were thick with anger, the simmering heat of burnt-down buildings and burnt-out lives, ignited by the spark of a jury acquiting four policemen on all but one count in the videotaped 1991 beating of a motorist. The unlawful riot took 52 lives.

Some relatives arrived a few days early. One night we all went out to eat at a Chinese restaurant in Portland's Chinatown. While enjoying our meal, I shared with them the progress I had made regarding Great-grandfather William Hanks. As I passed around my indexed note cards, my father made a comment that struck me as he read the index card showing that the slave overseer, Marion Hanks, had one thirteen year male. "He probably had his mother too," Dad said.

By October of 1993 I was ready to take my research trip south. Along the way I decided to include a stop in Kansas to meet more cousins for the first time, the children of former Kansas mayor Murt Hanks Jr., along with his widow. As several of us sat visiting in the kitchen, I was told by Murt's wife that she and Murt had bought Grandfather Hugh's old house after his death in 1960. As they were cleaning out the house they stumbled upon two old unknown family photographs. (Later they were identified as William and Rosetta Hanks and his mother Eliza Eskridge). Last but not least during my stay in Manhattan, I took the occasion to visit the family graveyard "Sunset Cemetary," and after spending quite awhile searching the grounds, I finally spotted the family names. There was Granison. Two of his daughters were next to him: Mattie, born stillborn Jan. 17, 1924, and Margaret, who died on November 20, 1926 only seven days young. There was Ernest. There also was Murt's son Richard Hanks, "born Oct. 22, 1940, died Oct. 25, 1969." There was Hugh and Marcella, the grandparents I did not get a chance to meet. Finally, there was the family patriarch, William Hanks.

I then headed by to see Cousin Mrytle in Topeka. Mrytle was happy to hear that I was still pressing on in the search of our family roots. I reminded her that the information she had provided was what had greatly oriented my direction.

Now it was on to the Tennessee State Archives in Nashville. After Samuel Eskridge settled in Roane County, on November 10, 1802 he purchased 200 acres at "Buckeye Creek" which included a certain public road. This public road became the most important road in the state, becoming a stage route in 1822. The stage coach would pass both ways twice a week on this road, and would travel from Virginia to Nashville. The *Rockwood Times* newspaper of Nov. 29, 1906 mentioned the Eskridge property as being "on the pike between this city and Kingston, owned hundreds of acres of river and ridge land, had a large negro quarters, kept a stage stand, had a magnificent residence for that day when the mail and passengers traveling by stage from Nashville to Knoxville." Samuel Eskridge purchased two slaves on May 18, 1803, a twenty-four year old woman named Fanny, and her three year old child Winston for one hundred twenty-seven pounds. Three weeks later he married his bride from Georgia, Sophia Yarborough.

Samuel Eskridge's emergence onto the Tennessee frontier,

however, was upon Indian territory, Native Americans being very much present and still holding lands south of the Tennessee and Clinch rivers.  That is, until 1805.  On October 25, the United States Government sent Indian agent Colonel Return J. Meigs to the Cherokee tribe and negotiated a treaty with the Cherokees to acquire their lands north of the Tennessee River.  Almost a year later, Colonel Meigs advanced $10 to Samuel Eskridge on September 1, 1806 to begin work on surveying the Cherokee treaty line.  But, as anyone holding even a nominal knowledge of American history knows ever so well, the tide of constant pressure to sell or relinquish the lands of their birth came as a sweeping tidal wave upon the Native American that they could no longer fight off.  Too many of the white man's broken treaties, broken documents, broken constitutions, and that was all she wrote.  By 1838, a "Trail of Tears" would sadly be seen marching all across the South and heading to Oklahoma reservations.

Another slave purchase was made again by Eskridge on March 24, 1806, acquiring a twenty-one year old man named Ralph for $250.  Samuel Eskridge also found himself that year being appointed with four others by the Tennessee Legislature to serve on the board of trustees for a new educational school, the legislature having passed an act establishing a school of higher learning called Rittenhouse Academy.  Rules were soon adopted governing curriculum and student duties.  Besides paying their three-month sessions, students were also required to contribute one dollar annually for firewood and to attend public worship.  Besides the basic given of the "three R's", teachers were brought in to smack down geography, astronomy, trigonometry, geometry, philosophy, Latin and Greek.  And if that wasn't enough, the students in Roane County no doubt braced themselves for what the board of trustees laid on them next: no fighting, use of profane language, getting drunk, gambling, frequent taverns, associate with base abandoned characters, use of tobacco, wearing hats while in session, and being tardy or absent without an excuse.  The academy lasted until January 1862 due to the outbreak of the "War of the Rebellion."  I wondered what was going through those students' minds when if, in their geography class, they perhaps had to draw a pencil line down the middle of a United States map.

Twenty years before that fatal conflict would erupt from political chaos, Samuel Eskridge seemed busy politicking in the meddlings of his day.  On August 23, 1841, eighteen days after his reelection defeat, Tennessee Governor James K. Polk received a letter from Samuel Eskridge to contemplate a run for the Federal Senate:  "I have had several conversations with Major Thomas Brown since the election.  I know he was your personal friend, and I find he is much inclined to be your political friend and if so he can do more to promote your election for the Senate than any one man in East Tennessee.  My object in naming this to you is he told me a few days ago that he should be in Nashville Thursday.  If you see him you will now have to approach him."  In another letter on September 4, 1841 Samuel Eskridge wrote Polk again: "Dear Sir, I am informed by Mr. Thomas A. Brown himself that he is a candidate for Engrossing Clerk to the House of Representatives...He is a man who I have no doubt if elected...in all probability is the very man thru whom you may be made Senator."  After much thought, Polk eventually made a decision  to remove his name for consideration to the Senate seat.

By September 18, 1845 slaveholder Eskridge opened his coffers again when "Frances K. Suddath" offered to sell him a man named Jim.  Three more slaves, Tom, Kendall, and Matilda, were bought for $1300, Samuel Eskridge being the highest bidder on March 23, 1846.  By 1850, Samuel Eskridge was fully stocked with seventy-five slaves.  But strangely, the Tennessee deed books did not fully account for  his total number of slaves, although women giving birth accounted for some.  Did Samuel Eskridge, then, inherit some of his slaves?  That was the question that needed to be answered.

Two years later, counselor, trustee, landowner, and slaveholder Samuel Eskridge was dead, his will entering probate on May 5, 1852.   His wife Sophia, upon learning that the entire estate had been bequeathed solely to her husband's great-nephew, contested the will and on Monday, March 6, 1854 the case finally went to court, Sophia Eskridge vs. Thomas N. Clark, the executor. Judgement was made in favor of Thomas N. Clark.  A decision then was made of Sophia's dower on May 5, 1854, in which she was to be alloted one third of land from the estate, and one third of the slaves, twenty-eight, comprising six families. There was Sally the seamstress, with her three children Esther, Sophia, and two-year old Trousdale; The next family allotted were the couple James and Matilda and their children Neety, Henrietta, and three month Tom; Next in line was the fifty year old matriarch Lucy, born in 1804, and her first born Aaron, who was borne when Lucy had turned eighteen, and her other children Major, Tom, Hampton, and George; They were followed by the couple Joshua and Pirely, with children Issac, whom Pirely bore at the age of barely twelve, Washington, born 1844, Letha, Nancy, David, and Elbert; The fifth family picked was Fanny, her daughter Catherine, who was carrying in the womb her soon-to-be daughter Eugenia, and sons Governor and Doctor; The sixth and final family distributed was fifty-year old Alexander and his wife Jenny. Also thrown in to round out the widow's dowry were three other slaves, Richard, Haywood, and Selia.

Samuel Eskridge's great-nephew, Samuel Butler Eskridge, would be alloted the remaining forty-seven slaves. Another petition came before the court on March 27, 1855, this time Richard Eskridge's name now being added to the party of his deceased brother's widow, to present further questions to the court on the matters of property possession, distribution, and the use of the slaves during the widow's lifetime. On July 3, 1855 the court chose to take one of the families first given to Samuel Butler Eskridge and make an exchange with a family that Sophia Eskridge had--Matilda and her three children--"to avoid the separation of families." Strangely, Matilda's husband James was not included this time, a "slave father" apparently not considered part of family. A deposition given by the widow Sophia Eskridge also mentioned that the slaves on the plantation were made up of fourteen men, ten women, "and three that are men at the present time...they were I think ploughboys...the remainder were children." Sophia Eskridge later died in 1857. Just before her death, she had deeded her portion of slaves to her husband's nephew, Frederick G. Thomas Jr., of Hancock County, Georgia, who as estate administrator returned an inventory of slaves on December 7, 1857 before the Court: "Alex 53, James 38, Lucy 53, Aaron 35, Major 32, Thomas 25, Hampton 21, George 15, Joshua 38, Ferrely 28, Isaac 16, Washington 13, Letha 9, Nancy 6, Davis 5, Elbert 4, James 24, Sarah 35, Ester 18, Sophia 11, Trousdale 5, Catherine 20, Eugenia 2, Governor 18, Doctor 15, Richard 17, Haywood 20, Celia 16." But there was something else I was to learn. On September 10, 1810 for $400, Richard Eskridge had originally purchased 230 acres on Buck Creek right alongside his brother's plantation early on.

Finally I arrived in Jackson, Mississippi after another long day of going Greyhound. I was relieved when I learned that the building of the Mississippi Department of Archives & History was only a five minute walk from the bus station. Here were more facts about brothers Richard Edmund Eskridge and Samuel Eskridge, who were raised in South Carolina. Samuel was born around the late 1760's in Virginia, and Richard in Ninety-Six District, Edgefield County, South Carolina around 1775. Richard Eskridge later married Mary Livingston of Edgefield County and had several children before her death around 1821, which by that time the family had already pulled up stakes in Abbeville County and removed to the city of Livingston, Sumter County, Alabama. Despite he and his brother Samuel having to testify inside Tennessee and Alabama courtrooms about their knowledge regarding several fraudulent land deals by speculators during the mid-1830's, Richard Eskridge began purchasing several tracts of land in Carroll County, Mississippi between 1833-36, and with the help of his slaves, a two-story log house was built by 1835, along with several slave cabins.

By 1846 Marion Hanks had arrived from Alabama and soon met his future wife, Elizabeth Miers. They were later married before the Carroll County Justice of the Peace, O.L. Kimbrough, in November of that year. Strangely, the name of the new bride never appeared next to her husband on the census rolls. I suspicioned she had either died in her young life or they had divorced, but there was neither record. Sometime later during the 1850's, Marion Hanks began a business partnership with a local blacksmith,

Chesley Holloway, to operate a plantation together, but after Holloway's death in 1858, he was hired on as an overseer on Richard Eskridge's plantation, Marion likely being  related to Richard Eskridge through his wife Mary. Mary Eskridge had a son who was named Taliaferro, named after Mary's uncle, Taliaferro Livingston of Ninety-Six District, South Carolina.  Marion Hanks had a brother by the same name.  Correspondingly, the book *John C. Calhoun, American Portrait* mentions of a family by the name of Hanks who ran a cross-roads tavern in the area which was once known as Ninety-Six District during the early 1800's.  Born in Abbeville, South Carolina on March 18, 1782, the Statesman John C. Calhoun, when practicing out of his Abbeville law office in 1807, was said to frequent the Hanks' tavern with the other young lawyers of the county for their dinner meals.  The tavern owner, Ann Hanks, and her daughter barmaid, Nancy, who later settled in Alabama, were said to be related to Abraham Lincoln's ancestors.

According to oral family statements found recorded in a few sources at the archives, the family branch of Marion Hanks was related to President Abraham Lincoln through Lincoln's mother Nancy Hanks, the daughter of Lucy Hanks.  On February 4, 1784 at Campbell County, Virginia, Nancy Hanks was born to nineteen year old Lucy Hanks and an unknown father, raising speculation among historians that Nancy was born an illegitimate child.  Historians backed this circumstantial claim with the incident that happened on November 24, 1789, after Lucy and her parents migrated to Kentucky, when a Grand Jury of Mercer County, Kentucky charged Lucy with immoral actions and issued a summons for her arrest by the county sheriff.

Lucy Hanks' parents were Joseph and Nanny Hanks, who migrated later in 1784 to what was then Nelson County in Kentucky Territory, which was at that time still part of Virginia until Kentucky became a state and admitted to the Union in 1792. Lucy's daughter Nancy eventually in time became fond in the eyes of Thomas Lincoln, a carpenter who at one time worked for and was trained by Joseph Hanks.  Thomas Lincoln and Nancy Hanks were soon married at Beechland, Kentucky in June 1806.  By February 1807, their first child, a daughter, was born at

Elizabethtown and named Sarah. A second child followed by February 12, 1809 in Hodgensville, and named Abraham.

By 1817, Thomas and Nancy Lincoln settled near Gentryville in Spencer County, Indiana across the Ohio river from Kentucky. Sadly, tragedy struck on October 5, 1818 when Nancy succumbed to a mysterious epidemic and died. Thomas Lincoln later remarried by December 1819 to a widow, Mrs. Sarah Bush Johnston, who raised Abraham and his sister Sarah.

Another large family that settled in Nelson County, Kentucky about the same time as Joseph Hanks' clan were the family of Nathaniel Grigsby, of Loudon County, Virginia. Nathaniel Grigsby was the maternal grandfather of brothers Samuel and Richard Eskridge. According to the family history, Samuel Eskridge was thought to have lived with his grandfather Nathaniel Grigsby in Nelson County before Samuel moved on to Tennessee. Soon I was to learn an even more stranger connection. Just as Thomas and Nancy Lincoln eventually moved into Spencer County, Indiana, so too, also did several of Nathaniel Grigsby's family members. Growing up together with Abraham Lincoln as children near Gentryville were Nathaniel N. Grigsby and his brother Aaron, the sons of one Reuben Grigsby. It just so happened later that Aaron Grigsby, during the summer August of 1826, married Sarah Lincoln, Abraham's sister.

However, like a recurring nightmare, Sarah Lincoln, like her mother Nancy, would not be blessed with longevity, for by the winter January of 1828, Sarah Lincoln Grigsby died during the birth of her first child, who was born stillborn.

Whether Confederate soldier Marion Hanks knew that the President of the Union just before Hanks' death in 1864 was his family kin, or whether President Lincoln ever knew about his slaveholding cousin in Duck Hill, I'll never know. But the two of them could not have held a more opposing mindset and vision for the future of southern Dixieland.

It would not be until nine years later in 2002 that I learned who else was related to Abraham Lincoln.

"Are you related to Tom Hanks?" people would often sarcastically ask me at places where I'd show my I.D. "He's my cousin," I would jokingly reply in return. I first became familiar with actor Tom Hanks in 1985 while watching *Saturday Night Live*. I didn't really follow his film career until I saw his Oscar-winning performance in *Philadelphia* with Denzel Washington, a story about an attorney fired from his law firm because he has AIDS, and only has six months to live. I didn't see his next film *Forrest Gump* when it was released in 1993, the story about the tender individuality of a man with only a 75 IQ, who shows not his limitations but his strengths, as he takes us moviegoers with him through almost 50 years of his life. The role won Hanks his second-in-a-row Academy Award for Best Actor. When I did finally catch *Forrest Gump* was on TV in 1998. As I watched it, there was something in that movie which made me wonder, who were Tom Hanks' ancestors? I began to wonder, could his family line possibly be connected to Marion Hanks? Not only did they share the same last name, but the hometown of the character Tom portrayed in the movie was in Greensboro, Hale County, Alabama, which, ironically, was only thirty miles from Marion Hanks' birthplace of Pickens County. So it was the *hometown* of "Forrest Gump" that actually caused my curiousity about the *lineage* of Tom Hanks.

In 1784, Lucy Hanks' parents and Nancy Lincoln's grandparents, Joseph and Nanny Hanks, left Campbell County, Virginia and took the wilderness road through the Cumberland Gap on into what is today Hardin County, Kentucky. John Hanks II, Joseph's brother, also brought his family out to Kentucky. John's great-grandson, Captain Thomas Hanks, soon came to be born in 1819 in Gallatin County, Kentucky and upon age married Rachel Cull. In 1851 their son Daniel Boone Hanks was born, the great-grandfather of actor Tom Hanks. Soon after the birth of his daughter in April 1880, Daniel Boone Hanks and his family set out from Missouri to finally settle in Newville, California by June of that year. Two more generations later, Tom Hanks was born July 9, 1956 in Concord, California.

So not only Abraham Lincoln, but also Tom Hanks, was related to the overseer Marion Hanks, the slaveowner whose surname my great-grandfather William chose as his surname. I would later discover that Great-grandfather William had a half-brother named Tom Hanks, who had a white father.

In December 1860 Richard Edmund Eskridge died, and his last will & testament was carried into probate court on December 19.  On that same date, Marion Hanks' first installment payment of $2880 was due to Robert Neal, one of the three named executors of Richard Eskridges' will, for a land lot down by the Duck Hill train depot which Marion had purchased from John A. Binford, the second named executor of Richard's will.  But within the next 24 hours all that wouldn't matter.  By the next day, December 20, South Carolina seceded from the Union.   Three  weeks  later, Mississippi became the second State to secede on January 9, 1861. Other Southern states soon quickly followed.  The approaching clash between North and South were months away.  In the meantime before that forward march became a bloody holocaust, the daily order of business seemed to carry on as usual inside the Carroll County courthouse.  The consequences of secession didn't appear to cancel out the emotional drama being played out inside the Eskridge clan on Duck Hill. On Friday, March 22, 1861 the will of Richard Eskridge was contested in court by his daughter, granddaughter and her husband, and two grandsons, who filed a petition against Burdett Eskridge, another grandson of Richard Eskridge, and the third executor named in the will:

Probate Court
Petition of Rebecca Weed, Albert McNeil, Mary Tabitha McNeil, William C. Eskridge, and Richard Eskridge
exhibited against Burditt Eskridge


...your Honor that at the said December term 1860 of said Court the said Burditt Eskridge obtained letters Testamentary and qualified as the executor of said will   the other executors named to wit   John A. Binford and Robert Neal Sr. failing or refusing to qualify and the said Burditt Eskridge has the entire management and control of the estate and is proceeding with the execution of said will...the said Burditt Eskridge is a young man having little or no experience in the business and is totally unqualified for the judicious and prudent management of a large estate such as that of the said Richard Eskridge...and cannot lawfully pay legacy or perform any act of the nature of distribution pending the contest about the validity of the will, your petitioners show that if the will is set aside they will be largely interested in said estate, that their rights are entirely out of the mercy of the said Burditt Eskridge...

    Landholder Richard Eskridge had changed his last will three times.   The third and final codicil was the one being questioned by the lawsuit, as it had been written during the same time Richard's son Taliaferro and his children, including Burdett, had moved into Richard's home with him after the death of Taliaferro's wife Sophia in 1859.  The contesting family heirs were concerned that undue influence had been exerted on a dying man's deathbed, explaining why Burdett would end up a named executor, who could then divert a fortune in land and slaves to whichever side of the family he chose.

    Burdett Eskridge, through his attorneys, responded to the petition by stating that since there was no evidence presented  to suspect him of fraud in becoming administrator of the estate nor of any  default alleged, the petition was not sufficient in law for the petitioners to have and maintain any relief in the court.  Later the court ordered that Burdett make a crop on the premises and keep the slave property together.   The slave property.   Forty-eight slaves, and perhaps more on the way if one counted expectant mothers.  I wondered what was Burdett's reaction when he heard the court's order to keep the slave property together in 1861 pending the contested will.   What were his beliefs and mental attitudes toward the family slaves?   More important, what were Taliaferro's attitudes and feelings toward his father's slaves?  Was he perhaps sympathetic to their plight and social condition?  It was a valid question I told myself, since it was Taliaferro who allowed a free family of color to reside in his home in 1850, and whom the mother of that family lived next door to Richard Eskridge.

    But the aristocratic Southern way of living up was on its way to changing forever.  On April 12, 1861 shots were fired upon

Fort Sumter.  The Civil War had begun.  Seven months later
Thomas N. Clark would petition the court to be relieved of his
duties of overseeing the Eskridge estate in Roane County,
Tennessee.  As he himself would put it, "...the affairs of the
country are now in a very unsettled state, as war
is...threatening____our own section." Outspoken Black leaders in
the northeastern States began calling for the Union to proclaim
immediate liberation to all persons under American slavery, even
Frederick Douglass writing to President Lincoln.  In his printed
newspaper of *Douglass' Monthly*, the May 1861 issue carried the
article entitled, "How to End the War," in which Frederick
Douglass called upon the Administration to proclaim freedom to
the slaves.  By August 6, 1861, the President signed the
Confiscation Act, which granted freedom to slaves being used by
the Confederate Army.  On August 30, 1861, Union General John
C. Fremont issued a proclamation establishing martial law in
Missouri and declared the slaves in that section free.  President
Lincoln revoked the order, fearing it would alienate the border
states he hoped to regain.  During 1862, Mr. Douglass continued
his tours and lectures calling for emancipation.  On April 16, 1862
the President signed a bill abolishing slavery in the Nation's
capital.

Finally, on January 1, 1863 President Abraham Lincoln
issued the following proclamation:  "On the first day of January, in
the year of our Lord, one thousand eight hundred and sixty-three,
all persons held as slaves within any State, or designated part of a
State, whereof shall then be in rebellion against the United States,
shall be then, thenceforth, and forever free."

Emancipation had come.  By August 1863 Marion Hanks
had enlisted with the Confederacy, but  was discharged in
November due to his deafness.  Six months later he died, his dream
of one day becoming a wealthy slaveowner coming to an end,
leaving his brother Taliaferro Hanks to petition the court to selloff
the land of Marion Hanks:

Petition to sell Real Estate

"...at the time of his death was the surviving partner of Chisley Holoway Deceased  Petitioner shows further that the said Chisley Holoway & Marion Hanks in there lifetime as equal partners owned a certain Lot in the village of Duck Hill. as the ...Hanks and Holloway Lot...appraised at the sum of $14,184.00 on the 20th of May 1864 Together with a small lot of claims amounting to about $1000 some of which claims are worthless & most of them very doubtful & none of them certainly good due said decedent at the time of his death which includes all the effects of said decedent subject to the payments of his debts...the debts of said decedent greatly exceeds the amount the value of said personal estate..."

On January 16, 1866 another petition was brought before the court:

"The Petition of Taliaferro Hanks respectfully shows to your Honor that he is by appointment of this Honorable court administrator of all and singular the goods & chattels  rights and credits where were of Marion Hanks deceased;  That the said Marion Hanks died intestate and seized and possessed among others of the following lands situated in said county...the said land was purchased by his intestate from Robt. Neal Sr. a commisioner appointed by this Honorable Court to sell the same...further shows that his intestate died without any widow or children and no brother or sister surviving him but your petitioner..."

Exhibit A

| | |
|---|---|
| O. L. Kimbrough  act due Feb. 1861 | 30.54 |
| John Lane  Note due June 1st 1863 | 65.00 |
| J. C. Gray  act due        1863 | |
| R. Neal note due Dec. 19th 1860 | $2880 |
| "    "    "    "    "    "    1861 | $2880 |
| Joseph [illegible] Note Jan. 1st 1862 | 43.00 |
| Jane Hanks Note May 26th 1863 | 221.00 |
| T. Hanks  act. 1862 & 1863 | 365.00 |
| R. Pettigrew  Note Jan. 1865 | 220.00 |
| Total amt. of Debts | $6554.54 |

Exhibit B

| | |
|---|---|
| Appraisal value of Estate | $14,184.00 |
| **Subtract appraisal of negroes the same having been emancipated** | **$12,940.00** |
| Add sale two bales of Cotton | $209.58 |
| Add sale corn crop of 1865 | $225.00 |

I noticed the court record's mention of "negroes...having been emancipated." The names of those "negroes," valued at over $12,000, were not given, but I was certain Great-grandfather William was one of them.

In June 1866 Taliaferro Hanks again petitioned the court to sell a gin-stand and horse mill:        "...that said estate is largely in debt and it will be necessary to sell all the personal & real estate to make provisions for paying the debts shows that under orders of this court he has heretofore sold all the personal property except a gin-stand and a horse power corn mill which are on the plantation owned by his intestate in his lifetime.  He prays your Honor to grant an order to sell the same on a credit of nine months & he will only pray..."

Three years later by 1869, William Hanks would marry Rosetta Crockett, and by 1873 Taliaferro Hanks would eventually sell his brother's land to the husband to one of Taliaferro Eskridge's daughters.

As I went through the Mississippi archives that October afternoon in 1993, I came across a catalog card entitled, "Index to Freedmen Marriage Register for Carroll County."  Requesting the catalog number at the stack call desk, I was minutes later handed a roll of film and then took my place at the microfilm reader.  The machine had become my best friend that afternoon.  Turning the film, I gazed upon the names of dozens of brides and grooms who had solemnized their marriage vows in the years following Emancipation, the marriages being in alphabetical order under the groom's surname.  It was thrilling to have followed the lives of many of these persons through census and slave records and now to peer into another aspect of their lives, sensing their great excitement as their long anticipated wedding days now became reality. There was "Welton Binford," who later would go to Osage City, and his bride "Millie McNeil." There was "James Bull," and his bride "Malissa Campbell." I recognized the name "Poldo Eskridge," who was once listed a slave on the 1855 estate of Richard Eskridge's deceased son Samuel, now a freedman with his bride "Eliza Sawyer." There was "Taylor Eskridge" who took "Jane Waters" as his bride. There was even a "Henry Hanks" who married "Francis Eskridge." But strangely, I didn't see Great-grandfather William Hanks' name listed. Instead, there was listed a *"William Wilkins"* who married "Rosetta Campbell." Now I was confused. Why did William list his surname as "Wilkins" immediately after Emancipation?

I rented a car and drove to Duck Hill, the place which hopefully held answers to where my family had originally come from. Duck Hill was a small town of 580 persons. The village began when settlers flocked there after county government was established with the creation of Carroll County by legislative act in December 1833, named after one of the original signers of the Declaration of Independence, Charles G. Carroll of Maryland. Duck Hill, by the time of the civil war, was a growing community of cotton farmers, plantation owners, and slaveholders, adding their share to the business boom of Carroll County along with grocery stores, saloons, trading posts, and courthouse. Slaves were acquired and brought into the county by means of several different routes, such as slave markets in New Orleans, Mobile, and Memphis, or from slave traders marching their dehumanized gangs down the Natchez Trace to French Camp, or by the stage coach route from Kosciusko to auctions in Shongolo.

By 1861 the Mississippi-Tennessee Railroad passed through Duck Hill, built with black and white hand labor. Duck Hill made headline news the following year in a Memphis newspaper when, on Sunday morning October 19, 1862 a train running late and carrying Confederate soldiers heading north-bound at a fast speed slammed head-on into a south-bound train just as they reached the Duck Hill depot. Thirty-three people were killed, twenty-nine being soldiers. Nearly fifty were injured. Four of the dead were blacks, one the brakeman, the other three were body servants of soldiers.  The dead soldiers were buried at the scene in one long pit with only their blankets serving as coffins.

Tragedy struck Duck Hill again in 1878 when an epidemic of Yellow Fever swept through and took the lives of almost four hundred between Duck Hill and the neighboring town of Grenada. The *New York Times* of August 23, 1878 carried headline news from their reporter sent to cover the frightening situation.  The railroad company became alarmed, and train service was halted to Grenada.  The mayor of Grenada called a meeting asking Memphis and New-Orleans for assistance.  The Howard Association of Memphis sent down a body of nurses, black and white, but the fever spread and increased.  The city's sewer drain, containing stagnant and polluted sewage water, was believed to be the cause of the yellow fever.  Those living nearer to the drain became the early victims, as was the mayor.

Although still not yet understood by the scientific and medical world at that time, the real culprit of the plague were mosquitos feeding in the drain.  I wondered how many of my relatives lost their lives as a result.  Perhaps that explained why my great-grandfather's parents were never listed as coming to Kansas.

I drove around and spotted several cemetaries, stopping to see if any gravestones were marked "Hanks" or "Eskridge."  I even started looking at ones marked "Wilkins" just to see if there was something I had missed.  Several of the graveyards were either "all white" or "all black."   Tradition and custom is hard to die. Looking at each tombstone date, I wondered which person's passing was caused by natural death and which by trauma.  I later thought of those who were victims of vicious crimes, black and white.  For example, one local story I heard was of how a black man named Jackson broke into a white home in the 1940's and brutally attacked the wife and her children before setting the house on fire.  The man was caught and executed.  On the other hand, another local story involved two brothers, William and James Winfrey, sons of a former slaveowner from Stone Mountain, Georgia named Absalom Winfrey of Poplar Creek in Montgomery County, who murdered a black woman and her child.  To avoid being tried for murder, the brothers fled to Texas.

Wondering if any of the Crocketts were still living here, I went to a phone booth and perused the local telephone directory. There was a Leon Crockett. I called and introduced myself, and after being certain we were related, let him know I was there doing research on the family. Leon told me--"meet me at the "Binford Cemetary, I live right next door to it." I was there within minutes. A few minutes later Leon Crockett entered over to the cemetary and introduced himself. He was the caretaker of Binford Cemetary and began showing me around the grounds.

Leon was the great-grandson of Granison Crockett, one of the Crockett sons who didn't leave for Kansas. "My grandfather," Leon began relating, "was Robert Crockett and my grandmother was Mary Crockett...my father was Grant Crockett...he said his mother told him he was Black Creek Indian." This was a totally new and unexpected revelation! Apparently an intermarriage between a black slave and a Creek Indian had been introduced somewhere along the Crockett family line.

I recalled the history of Duck Hill in relation to the Native American, how the village was named for a large green hill rising from a plain east of town where Choctaw Chief Duck held his tribal councils. The area was originally part of the hunting grounds of the Choctaw Indians but was later ceded to the United States by the treaty of Dancing Rabbit Creek in 1830. "We're going to have a reunion here next year, the first weekend in August. We have it the same time in August every two years. Give me your address and we'll make sure to send you a letter." He then drove me in his car to Grenada to meet his cousin Harrison Crockett, and, yes, he was the great-grandson of Harris Crockett. After we left Grenada, Leon took me to more cemetaries, including one in the woods a distance off from the main road.

I later learned that Duck Hill shocked the nation on April 13, 1937 when two black men, Roosevelt Townes and Jack McDaniels, were tortured and burned to death by a mob of 200 lynchers, seizing the men from outside a courthouse. Both men had been arrested earlier and accused of murdering a white store merchant in December 1936. They pleaded not guilty and trial was to begin the next day. The *New York Times* newspaper carried lengthy reports of the tragedy just at the same time the U.S. House of Representatives were debating on passage of a federal anti-lynching bill.

As the sheriff and his deputies were leading the prisoners from the rear door of the courthouse, the mob rushed forward, seized the handcuffed prisoners and placed them in a school bus. Taking the two men seven miles east of Duck Hill, the mob chained Roosevelt Townes of Grenada to a tree. "Boot Jack" McDaniels, who lived near Duck Hill, felt the searing blow torch. The torch was next turned on Townes. The lynchers then piled brush, saturated it with gasoline and set a match to it. The mob later reported that both men had confessed.

Officials and citizens demanded punishment for the mob leaders. The Mississippi Governor requested an investigation, and the County Judge called for a grand jury inquiry. In Washington, the House of Representatives passed the Gavagan Anti-Lynching Bill, by a vote of 277 to 118. But by the time the bill reached the Senate, however, it was set aside and hotly debated during the next five years. It was finally buried with the outbreak of World War II. Many blacks, including heavyweight boxing champion Joe Louis, publicly blamed President Roosevelt for not getting the bill through. Twenty-five persons died of lynchings between 1937 and 1941. It would not be until the Civil Rights Act of 1964 that many Afro-Americans felt that they now had guaranteed Federal protection under the Law.

I recalled how Cousin Mrytle spoke about her experiences with racism, for example mentioning how she dealt with second class citizenship when riding on trains and buses--except, that is-- when she finally crossed the state line into Kansas:

*"A girl on the bus started to get off at a stop, and she said "Are you fixin' to get off to eat?" I said, "No, I always bring my lunch with me;" She said, "We'll, I was jus' going to tell ya the only place around here near this bus station would be that cement block hamburger place, and you'll have to stand outside to eat it," you couldn't eat it inside; and I said, "I always bring my lunch with me when I go to Kentucky"....I remember coming on the bus*

*one night coming home and the bus driver says, "To the rear;"*
*Another time I was coming from Denver and we had gotten into*
*Kansas, didn't leave there till late that night, but we had already*
*gotten into Kansas and the bus made  a stop;  Now, I was sitting*
*about midway on the bus and there wasn't any other good seats*
*left, just that long seat across the back;  And this man that got on*
*the bus, I knew he was talking about me, I could tell, 'cus he looked*
*right at me and kinda nodded his head toward me;  The bus driver*
*said very loud and clear:  WE CAN'T DO THAT IN KANSAS."  He*
*[the man boarding the bus] was trying to make me leave that seat*
*and go to that oldie long seat in the back...but the bus driver said,*
*"We can't do that in Kansas."  [So the man] got on that bus, went*
*back there, and just threw his bags down."*

August 5, 1994.   The first day of the Crockett family
reunion had now come.  I arrived in Jackson, Mississippi during
the city's early Friday morning rise.  The cars of the working-class
began whizzing past my bus in different directions.  The city began
coming to life.  I entered the busy Greyhound station on Jefferson
Street while the coach was refueled for the remaining passengers
heading to Alabama and all points east.  But this was the end of my
ticket, and also the end of sustaining myself with soda and coffee,
butter-toffee peanuts, and hamburgers.  I was ready for a real meal.
The reunion was to officially begin at 7p.m. for a "Get Acquainted
Night" at the home of Leon Crockett's son.  Since there was plenty
of free time before then, I made my way back to the Mississippi
State Archives building.   Browsing around inside the archive
library, I came across a microfiche catalogue of Mississippi State
death certificates from 1912 through the 1930's.  I began copying
down all black persons with the surnames of Hanks or Eskridge
who had been born or had died in Carroll, Montgomery, and
Grenada counties.  I payed special attention to any persons who
were born during slavery.

When finished, I had such information as:
*Bettie Eskridge*; Father/Mother: Unknown;  Buried: Port Gibson
Asylum.
*Lewis Eskridge*; Father-George Eskridge; Mother-Phyllis Eskridge.
*Mary  Hanks*;  Father/Mother:  Unknown;  Buried:  Eskridge

Cemetary.

*Nancy Eskridge*; Father-Billy Eskridge-VA; Mother-Mandy-VA.

*William Burgess Eskridge*; Father-Wm. Eskridge; Mother-Unknown.

*Mary Jane Eskridge*; Father-Henry Wright-AL; Mother-Unknown; Buried: Eskridge Cemetary.

*Frank Eskridge*; Father-George Eskridge-SC; Mother-Phyllis Eskridge-VA.

*William Eskridge*; Father-Jennings Eskridge-MS; Mother-Florence Hancks-MS; Buried: Binford Cemetary.

My plan was to compare these names to the names found on the federal census when I returned home. Later on I would realize how important some of these names would be.

I checked into the hotel in Grenada chosen for the reunion. Many relatives from out of state began arriving, including Patty Sue Hanks Glenn, the sister of Murt Hanks Jr., from Gary, Indiana, and Billie Crockett Rigdon of Dallas, Texas with her husband Robert. Robert Rigdon had begun to land screen appearances as a movie/television extra. I found out he was just as heavy into genealogy as I was, doing extensive research on the black roots of the Crocketts, his wife Billie being the granddaughter of Harris and Eliza Crockett. Over the years since meeting Robert, he and I would continue running-up our long-distance phone calls off the hook when we called each other to discuss Genealogy.

A fish fry was scheduled for Friday night. It was truly an experience in Mississippi home cooking. Here we all met, the descendants of Armstead and Mariah Crockett. Saturday an afternoon picnic was held at Grenada Lake where Robert Rigdon shared his research compiled on the Crockett family lines of Armstead's sons, Grant and Harris Crockett.

I then began to fit my genealogical line from Great-grandmother Rosetta to that of her two brothers, explaining how their parents Armstead and Mariah left Duck Hill to go to Kansas, and how the family had changed their surname from Campbell to Crockett. Since Cousin Patty Sue and I were the only ones there representing the Hanks family line, we had occasion to share information about our side of the family, and see pictures she had brought of the family including one of her father Murt Hanks Sr.  I showed her the names found in my research and of the strong possibility that our Hanks family line may  have been originally connected to a family by the name of Eskridge.  "You know what, Stephen," said Patty,  "I think somehow we're all related."   From what I was beginning to find out, I could not have agreed with her more.

That summer of 1994, during one of the most publicized and high-profile murder cases ever in Los Angeles County,  I was finishing up my computer training classes with the Urban League of Portland.  After completing school, I started up my genealogy business and began aiding those needing help in searching their own family histories. Soon phone calls and letters started pouring in, even requests from adopted persons wanting to find their biological birthparents.  Happily, I was able to reunite several of them with their missing families.  The interesting requests I received each month provided much needed breaks from my own family project, the project that I knew full well at the outset would face insurmountable odds at reaching my high goal--finding an African ancestor and tribe.  So far I had traced down to Great-grandfather Hanks on my paternal side, but couldn't proceed past him because I didn't know who his parents were, or siblings if he had any.

I got a chance to spend a couple of days again at the Seattle branch of the National Archives so I could compare the census schedules with the notes taken from the Mississippi death certificates in Jackson.  As I was studying the 1880 Montgomery County, Mississippi census, something caught my eye.  I came across the names, "T. Hanks, 21, mulatto; R. Hanks, 17, mulatto, sister."  Who were they?  The very first thought that came to my mind and gut was--could they be the children of Eliza Eskridge, the woman who was born in Tennessee and in 1870 lived just eight cabin houses from my great-grandparents?  Were two of her children now going by the surname Hanks?  Excitably, I pulled out the old notes taken from the 1870 census:
"Tom Eskridge, 11, mulatto; R.J. Eskridge, 6, mulatto."  I started

to say to myself: "this is them! I bet this is them!"

To make sure, I grabbed the 1900 Montgomery County census to see if I would find them again. There, in enumeration district 78, sheet 5, Duck Hill, dated June 8, 1900 was:

| | | | |
|---|---|---|---|
| Tom Hanks | black | Jan | 1860 |
| Belle, | wife | Feb | 1855 |
| Florence | dau. | May | 1883 |
| Elbert | son | Jun | 1885 |
| Dump | son | May | 1888 |
| Polly | dau. | Mar | 1892 |

This was Tom, the son of Eliza Eskridge! Somehow he had taken on the surname Hanks, gotten married and raised a family. Since Great-grandfather had chosen to keep the surname Hanks after Emancipation, there definitely had to be a connection between him and Eliza Eskridge. She had to have been his mother, who was brought to Mississippi along with William from Richard and Samuel Eskridge's plantation in Tennessee. My gut feeling was that she was in fact his mother, but that William and Tom probably had two different fathers and so were half-brothers. Now I needed to find out what happened to Tom's sisters "R.J.," Bettie, and "L.J." I wondered if the initial "R" stood perhaps for Ruth, or Rebecca, while the initial "L" perhaps for Letha or Lucy, these being some of the slave names I had run across in the Eskridge court records.

There was something else exciting I would come to learn also on this trip, a vital tidbit of information discovered regarding Eliza Binford, the wife of David Binford, who in 1900 listed her father and mother as being born in Africa. Ten years later in Duck Hill she was now listed a widow and living with her fifty-five year old son Willis and his wife and children. But what became so startling was the surname that was listed for Eliza Binford's son Willis.

His family surname was *Eskridge.*

Now as I compared the death certificates to the census rolls, I began noticing that the majority of the black Eskridge families seemed to come from at least three main families: the adult children & grandchildren of William Burgess and Amanda Eskridge, Luke and Amanda Eskridge, and George and Phyliss Eskridge.

William Burgess Eskridge was born   1820 in North Carolina and died in Duck Hill at the age of 99.  According to the 1870 census he could read and write.  Both his parents were listed as being born in Virginia, and his father's name was "Wm. Eskridge." His wife Amanda was born around 1829 in Alabama, and their children were twins Nancy & Eliza, and William Henry. Their daughter Eliza was the one who married Harris Crockett. According to family members, Henry, a short and light-complexioned man, was a preacher and taught school at a one room log cabin out in the woods of Duck Hill called Wilkens Chapel, later called New Fountain. He was said to have later taken a trip to Africa sometime during the 1920's then returned, describing his trip to his school class.  But no one in the family seemed to know anything about where in Africa Henry had gone or other details about his trip.

In 1870 Luke and Amanda and their family were living in a former section of  Yalobusha County now called Grenada County starting that year.   Luke Eskridge was born around 1823 in Alabama, and his wife Amanda was born about 1826 in Tennessee. I previously had come across their names from Richard Eskridge's will.   Their children were Nelson, Elias, Abraham, Stephen, Minnie, and Julia.

George Eskridge reportably was born in South Carolina on an unknown date, according to his childrens' death certificates. His wife Phyllis was born  1825 in Virginia, and  was listed as head of the household in 1870, more than likely having become a widow.  Their children were  Frank, Louis, Doc, and William Harrison.    Recalling again the Freedmen's Bureau complaint register, a dispute involving forty-two year old Phyllis Eskridge was recorded in 1867:

Phillis Eskridge (Cold)
         vs.

Wm. Myers (cold)
Yalobusha Co. Oct 15/67    A case of debt brought into this office For Settlement. both parties gave a full explanation of the matter.    after investigation of the whole debt, it was settled by compromise, paying the said Eskridge $5, and due bill for twenty dollars payable on demand.

Although the officer's report did not provide what was said as "both parties gave a full explanation of the matter," it seemed clear that Phyllis was not the type of woman that was going to allow anyone to take advantage of her, and whatever facts she presented in the case won out in her favor.  Hopefully she received her twenty dollars, "payable on demand."

There also was a 104 year old freedwoman named Hannah Eskridge, born in 1776, who was living in her son Mitch's household in 1880.  Hannah's birthplace was listed as Mississippi, which I felt certain was a recording error on the census enumerator's part, for I hardly doubted she was in Mississippi in 1776, unless, of course, she was referring to the Mississippi Territory, which at that time did stretch all the way to the borders of the Carolinas and Georgia.

Unfortunately, I could not locate Eliza Eskridge or her husband, whose name was Jefferson, anywhere on the federal census rolls past 1870, or from the state death certificates, meaning they must have died by the time Great-grandfather William's family went on the exodus to Kansas.  No records turned up in Osage City, either.  Did they have any siblings, aunts, uncles, or cousins who were living with them in Duck Hill, or in some other nearby town, county, or state?  The furthest record I had found up to this point was Samuel B. Eskridge's 1852 probate.  I felt my search was going to come to a halt there.

# CHAPTER EIGHT

## The Meeting

The question that kept nagging me as I continued to search my family line was: what happened to Eliza Eskridge and her children? I had found her son Tom Hanks, but what about the other three? Could I somehow find out if they had descendants who might still be living and try to contact them? And what about any living descendants of Richard Eskridge? Was there any way I could get in touch with any of them?

I mustered up courage and called the historian in Duck Hill who had helped me before regarding the cemetaries there. The day had now come for me to start asking someone where slaveowner Richard Eskridge's living descendants were. As I dialed the county historian's number, I was as nervous as could be. I didn't quite know how to put this request into words. Of all the books I had read and re-read about genealogy, none of them covered the etiquette on how to contact family members descended from the very slavemaster who owned your great-grandfather. I was on unchartered waters. As the phone began ringing the historian's residence, I suddenly felt that gut fear of rejection, that the man would wonder why on earth a black man would be asking him for a stranger's name, let alone his phone number.

The historian answered, and I started in with my formal introduction, quickly reminding him that we had spoken before by means of the cemetary caretaker's referral. Soon my presentation

had run its course.  Now I needed to get to the heart of the matter.
I don't know how I got the words out.  "Do you happen to know of
any descendants of Richard Eskridge still living in Duck Hill?"  I
then paused and waited for his response, anticipating that he might
likely ask for my phone number instead, and forward the message
on himself, or perhaps just simply tell me he couldn't help, that he
didn't know of anyone.  Instead he might have known the whole
clan of living family members.  To my surprise, he told me there
was in fact a descendant of Richard Edmund Eskridge still living, a
Mr. Swanson.  I couldn't believe it.  I had a name, a living
descendant's name to the person who *knew* my ancestors.  At that
moment it seemed like a heavy weight of anxiety lifted off my
shoulders.  I breathed a sigh of relief, shaking my head why I had
made this more difficult than it turned out.  Then I quickly
reminded myself this was only the first step, for I soon would have
to call Mr. Swanson.  I thanked the historian for his help and then
ended the call.  I didn't even ask him for Mr. Swanson's home
phone number, too nervous I guess.  But I knew Mr. Swanson
lived in Duck Hill.

Directory assistance gave me a possible number for Mr.
Swanson.  I stared at my scribbled number.  Could this person have
information about my family?  Could he possess any family
plantation records of Richard Eskridge and of his slaveholding
sons?  Could Mr. Swanson have heard stories passed down in his
family about Great-grandfather William?  William's father?  His
mother?  His siblings?  In short, did Mr. Swanson hold the key to
my unlocking the mystery of who I came from?

I now began trying to formulate my next intro and
presentation.  My greatest fear now was to end up having the
telephone hang up in my face.  Perhaps this person was as
prejudice as they came, and would curse me up and down for the
nerve to call up his private Southern-Mississippian home about
some old, dusty, confidential, family records pertaining to slavery.

But what did I have to lose?

Or, he might question my motive about this whole
genealogy roots thing.  Maybe he'd think my real motive was to
gather information for a slave reparation lawsuit.  Of course,

legally that wouldn't affect him personally anyway.  But anybody
can fear something they don't fully understand.  That's why there's
an entry in the dictionary with the definition for the word
"prejudice" the last time I checked.  Then too, might he think I was
trying to discover if by chance my family had an inheritance owed
them somehow from Richard Eskridge's estate.  Perhaps an
inheritance *was* owed my family, maybe even stolen from them.
But, if I had wanted to find that out, I could simply visit the Carroll
County courthouse and look up the register of deeds or probate
records.  But that wasn't my purpose.  All the money in the world
couldn't compensate what I was digging after.  Wise King
Solomon put it this way: "A name is better than good oil...wisdom
is O how much better than gold!  And the getting of understanding
is to be chosen more than silver."  I picked up the phone and began
dialing.  What did I have to lose?  Only a long-distance phone
charge.

When Mr. Swanson answered, I launched into the purpose
of my call, letting him know that the county historian had given me
his name, and that my sole desire was to retrieve anything about
my family heritage in Duck Hill.  I told him that Great-grandfather
William Hanks worked for Richard Eskridge, who had employed
an overseer on the plantation named Marion Hanks.  "If it's
possible, I'd like to come out there, and see where my great-
grandfather worked."   Mr. Swanson warmed right up to my
project, and was very friendly and willing to help me.  He
interjected, however, that his mother who lived nearby would
probably be able to answer more of my questions.

I got into Jackson on Thursday morning, September 22,
1994.  After checking into the Holiday Inn downtown,  I called Mr.
Swanson later that afternoon.   His wife answered the phone and
informed me her husband's mother, Ms. C Swanson, would be
happy to meet me the following day and show me around the area.
We made arrangements to meet at the local historian's office.

I reserved a blue pontiac sunbird and began the ninety mile
drive north on Interstate 55.   Questions were now fluttering
through my mind just as fast as the speed of the sunbird.  Would I
really discover something about my family on this trip?   What

would meeting Ms. Swanson be like?  How would she accept me?
She was the great-great-granddaughter of a Southern planter.  I
was the great-grandson of a former family slave who fled to the
North.  Would she share with me her knowledge about her
ancestors past?  Soon we would be meeting face-to-face.

Suddenly, about half way through my 60mph freeway
drive, a car in front of me strangely slowed to a dead stop just as I
momentarily took my eye off the road to glance at my road map.
In the blink of an eye I turned my head up and--for five terrified
seconds--literally knew that I was about to slam straight through
the trunk and backseat of the car in front of me.  I knew hitting my
brakes would not make a bit of difference.  Instinctively, I somehow
swerved to my left at the last second, and drove down a ten foot
embankment into a field separating the north and south lanes.
With my foot still on the accelerator I drove right back onto my
northbound lane.  The driver and her passenger had now pulled
over into the emergency lane after apparently slowing down to
avoid running over something in the freeway.  They were notably
shaken as they asked if I was okay.  "Oh, I'm fine," as I jumped
back into the car for a good head start, the sunbird creating a
measurable distance between us.  "Duck Hill must have something
real good waiting for me," I said to myself while taking a deep
breath.

Finally I approached the exit and soon was passing the old
familiar sign: "Welcome to DUCK HILL."  I parked in front of the
Duck Hill bank office.  Inside I was greeted by the local county
historian, but Ms. Swanson was not present.  I sat and braced
myself for possible bad news that the meeting was off.
Disappointment began to swell up inside me.  "I should have
known better that this was too good to be true;  Why would she
bother wasting her time on me," I said to myself.  But both our
families shared a common history, no matter how unpleasant that
history may have been.  I was only here to learn, to explore, not to
point blame.  A thousand thoughts were going through my mind.
The historian assured me, however, that Ms. Swanson would be
arriving shortly.  Fifteen minutes later,walking with the help of a
sturdy cane, she entered the Duck Hill Bank.

After a warm greeting, seventy-five year old C Swanson became my host for the day. Now a widow, C had worked at hospitals for many years up to her retirement. I pulled out a copy of the 1860 census and showed them how I had traced my family to this spot on the map. "Well, let me show you around," Ms. Swanson exclaimed. I was introduced to her daughter who was waiting outside the bank and had driven her there. "Okay dear, I'll see you later on," as Ms. Swanson signaled her daughter off, then sat down in the front passenger side of the sunbird. I was surprised that she did not feel uneasy in the least bit of going by herself in the car with me--a complete stranger. "My grandmother was Mary Eskridge...she was the daughter of Taliaferro Eskridge...married Drury D. Wilkins, who worked on the railroad and came to Duck Hill around 1861; When he came here he didn't own any *slaves.*"

For a moment there was silence, as the six-letter word resonated off the dash board and caught me square in the face. I had been caught off guard. Sure, I knew that that word would come up eventually, since that's why I was here. I just didn't expect it to come up so soon. But I was okay. That spoken word from my female host didn't carry a sting. I had already gotten over the emotional part quite some time ago. And any African-American even thinking about tracing his or her roots must also work past their emotional hurt about the past. I respectfully listened to her words, listened to the context, and examined each letter and syllable for clues.

Already I was formulating a conclusion on her statement about Drury Wilkins not owning any slaves when he came to Duck Hill. This assured me that I was on the right track. Just because Great-grandfather William listed his surname as "Wilkins" on the Carroll County marriage register when he married Great-grandmother Rosetta, this didn't mean that Drury Wilkins had brought him to Duck Hill as a slave. I turned to C Swanson and listened as she spoke. "Richard Eskridge was my paternal great-great-grandfather...he owned alot of the land here in Duck Hill. I still have his original land plat...we'll drive over to where the old family house used to be. So, you say your family came from Duck Hill?"

I explained what little information I had about my family during the time they had lived here, and also about my hopes of discovering the names of my great-grandfather's parents whom I believed were Jefferson and Eliza, who resided as slaves on C Swansons' great-great-grandfather's plantation.  As we drove down the main street of the town my nervousness disappeared and I began feeling at ease as we conversed past the rows of neighborhood houses, black and white.

We drove to a section of town named Eskridge, in honor of Richard Eskridge, and turned down an old gravel road about one fourth mile from the railroad  tracks of the old Mississippi-Tennessee railway line.  Soon we were walking on the  old site of the  plantation, where the two-story slave built log house and fourteen slave cabins  once stood, slave row, now surrounded by tall trees and bushes since having gone up in flames some years back.  Here I had finally made my pilgrimage  to "ole' Massa Richard's plantation."  I could envision those I had descended from, saw where they once stood, smelled the air they once breathed, touched the soil they once  worked.  And here now both of us stood.  Two representatives of our families.  My great-grandfather and C's great-great-grandfather saw each other here.  Saw the same trees.  Saw the same big house.  Saw the same row cabins.  And saw the same cotton fields.  I turned toward the east and could actually look out over the rolling hills and wooded fields all the way down to the railroad tracks.  "The  house used to sit right over there," as Ms. Swanson pointed to an empty plot of ground.  And "cabin row" used to sit somewhere around there, too.  The overseer Marion Hanks had trudged his way through as well.  He had also made his mark on this tract of land.  Perhaps even on someone's back.  But for some reason, I didn't feel any pain.  I didn't sense any anguish inside.  This piece of land was not haunting me.  It only made me wonder.  My personal pilgrimage to this spot in Eskridge, Mississippi on this day actually felt peaceful.  In my heart I made a silent tribute to all my kin that had existed here, and died here.  There was no reason to show bitterness.  Did not this elderly woman volunteer to bring me out here, and by herself?  She didn't know me from Adam, and yet here she was, all alone out here with me, a total complete stranger.  She didn't know how I would react once I got here.  But she must have sensed in me my yearning for my lost lineage, a desire to reconnect to my past. She was slowly becoming convinced of the serious nature of my mission.  I wasn't just out here on vacation.  I needed to know the truth, the whole truth, and nothing but the truth.  Was she even perhaps herself trying to come to terms with what all occured at this remote family site?  Was this perhaps her own personal way of breaking silence on the topic of slavery and race, and making a statement to her family?  Indeed, was there a reason why C and I came together on this Friday afternoon?  I was starting to wonder, if because of initiating this communicative first-ever meeting, might I be standing on the verge of a turning point.

"Now let me show you the family cemetary."  Going further down the road we entered  Eskridge cemetery where early white settlers and former black slaves were buried.   There were no gravestones marking the black graves.  "Someone took liberty to remove them long ago," C said, with the sound of regret detected in her voice.  The location of the black graves was at the  back of the cemetary.  Dotting the front half of the cemetary were all sizes of tombstones listing the patriarchs of C's family who had strolled the earth.  This time I felt pain, the pain of now knowing that those who sweated and labored wearily for C's great-great-grandfather couldn't even be honored in death.   There were stone-chiseled monuments heralding out her privileged personages. But for those whom I considered great men and women of color, their names and locations were merely shrouded in the darkness of the unknown. The only monuments left standing in their memory were a few tall trees standing in the back.

I walked over to them and observed the clumps of shovelled dirt and blanket cover of leaves that had fallen around its roots.  I noted the softness of the clay ground under my feet.  I asked myself, 'how many of my generations were represented underneath?'  I took my camera out and started snapping.  These images were coming home with me.  The memories of my fallen kin would accompany me back to Portland.  Fearing that these resting places of former slaves might in time fail to be remembered, I vowed that they would never be forgotten.

Ms. C Swanson knew of two people, a couple of Duck Hill's old-time community blacks, who might be able to answer some questions about the family names I was searching. She took me to an old shack of a house, a quaint humble dwelling, looking so old that it, in fact, could have been an original slave cabin. C knocked and knocked, but there was no answer. "He's been mighty sick lately." I wondered if the elderly man would feel like having company. "Looks like he's not home today."

We then stopped at the home of Lindsey and Mary Beck, who were taking care of an old woman named Madie Jones, reportably the oldest person in Duck Hill at the time, holding up at the mighty ripe age of ninety-five. Madie wasn't feeling very well either, but she allowed us into her bedroom where she was resting. Ms. Swanson and Madie were old friends.

"Madie, I brought someone who came here to try and find out about his family," Ms. Swanson explained. I introduced myself. "It's nice to meet you...my great-grandparents lived in Duck Hill before they moved to Kansas...my great-grandfather was William Hanks, and his mother's name was Eliza Eskridge; Do you know anything about the Hanks and Eskridge families?"

Madie began. "Well, my mother's name was *Rosie Hanks*, and she married Labe Jones, who was sold in North Carolina to a man named Labe Jones. But I don't remember too much so I don't think you'll be too interested in what I know." C Swanson and I looked up at each other. Here Madie had just told me her mother's maiden name was Hanks and I wouldn't be interested?

"No, I think he's very much interested in what you have to say," C said.

"Well, okay then, I'll try to tell you what I can," Madie replied. "My mother was Rosie Hanks...her mother died when she was young, so she was raised by a woman named Mollie Burtie. You know who I'm talking about Ms. Swanson, your cousin James Turner's mother. His mother raised my mother...her daughter was Estelle Turner when she about five or six years old. Now, what I was told was that my mother's father was a white man named Hanks in Carroll County, and that's all I know about that. My mother had a brother named Tommy Hanks, and she had a sister named Betty who married George Eskridge...later Betty died in a sanitarium...I have a sister named Maggie, and she's just as old as I am.  She lives with her daughter Burtie in St. Louis.  Tommy had several children too, has a son named Tommy who lives in Chicago."

I then asked Madie what she knew about the Eskridges. "The lady who helped my mother give birth to me was an Eskridge, her name was Mandy Eskridge and she was a midwife; They lived next door to us, and her husband was William Eskridge...he lived a long time before he died."  I was in total amazement.  What I had suspected from the 1880 census that Eliza Eskridge's children changed their surname to Hanks was now confirmed, and I now realized that the initial "R" stood for Rosie. Also, the woman Estelle Turner was the daughter of Burdett Eskridge, the administrator of Richard Eskridge's estate, and Estelle's mother who helped raised Rosie, was Mildred "Mollie" Hill Eskridge, the wife of Burdett Eskridge.

I now understood also why I hadn't found Eliza on the census rolls beyond 1870 because she had died when the children were still young.  And I had no doubt that "the white man named Hanks in Carroll County" was the overseer Marion Hanks.  But, "Was Rosie's mother's name Eliza?" I asked Madie.  She said she couldn't recall;  Rosie was very young when her mother died.  I then asked Madie if she was related to the Eskridge or Crockett families and she said she didn't know.  But apparently she did know the Crocketts.  Madie pointed to the dresser in the room. "Pull that drawer open.  See that Bible in there, take it out and hand it to me."  She pulled out a piece of paper that was tucked inside.  It was a 1982 funeral program in St. Louis, Missouri for Lindsey Crockett, a son of Harris and Eliza Crockett, and grandson of William "Burgess" and Amanda Eskridge.  "I knew Lindsey Crockett real good, he lived next door to us, then he went to live in St. Louis.  Why don't you have this, since he's your family."  I thanked her, and noticing that Madie was starting to tire, decided it was time to take our leave.  I told Madie that I thought there was a good chance that we were cousins.

While driving C to her home, I truly felt grateful for her having thought to visit Madie Jones, a possible relative and potential link to help identify my lineage.  As we drove past the homes of Duck Hill, C Swanson began to apologize to me in behalf of her family for their involvement in slavery and how it affected my family.  She asked me not to be upset with her over what past ancestors had done.  I assured her I was not upset.  "We need to get along with one another today," I said.

We arrived at C's house on Jefferson Davis Street.  I realized I had reached the end of the line when we said our goodbyes.  There were no original plantation slave records that had survived and passed into C's hands.  However, for the present, I was as happy as could be.  What better reproduction text could one get than a living, talking record from the lips of Madie Jones?  I may never have met her if were it not for C Swanson's human hospitality and open kindness.  The next morning before driving back to Jackson, I headed back to Eskridge Cemetary to take one last look at the area where the black graves were, the graves that perhaps included my great-great-grandparents, Jefferson and Eliza.

When  back home I called directory assistance for Chicago to see if I could find Madie's cousin Tommy Hanks.  The operator gave me one number.  Sure enough, Tommy Hanks answered the phone.  He was happy to learn who I was.  I asked him to share his family history.  "My father's name was Tom Hanks, and my mother's maiden name was Mabel Eskridge...they both were born in Duck Hill...had 10 children...my father had three children before he married...one named Elbert, another named Ezra whose nickname was "Dump"...and my mother had a daughter named Jimmie before she married...I can't recall who was my father's mother and father...my mother's father, Grandfather, was Frank Eskridge, and Grandmother's name was Eliza [McDaniel],...I lived with 'em for awhile when I was small.  My father and mother died within six months of each other, my mother passed around September 1919, and my father six months later.  I was born in Wynne, Arkansas in 1914, that's where we lived for awhile...I remember we were in Duck Hill for my mother's funeral, me and my brothers and sisters were living there at the time...my father, he was living somewhere else." After staying with grandparents Frank and Eliza, Tommy and his siblings, Antonia, Lawrence, Elizabeth, and Fredie Belle, moved to Chicago. We exchanged addresses, then Tommy gave me the names and phone numbers of a few other relatives. Tommy also said that some of the Eskridges moved to Wichita, Kansas and that they later changed their name to Livingston. Richard Eskridge's wife's maiden name was Livingston.

With the information that Tommy had given me about his father, who I now felt certain was indeed my great-grandfather's half brother, I obtained a copy of Tom Hanks' death certificate which was recorded on June 3, 1920 in Lonoke County, Arkansas. The cause of death was Dropsey. And there in the section listing his father was the name: Marion Hanks. Here was unmistakable proof linking Tom and his mother Eliza to the Eskridge Plantation in Duck Hill. His mother's name on the certificate was listed as "Lucy Hanks." There was no question that his mother's name as listed on the 1870 census was Eliza, and the name Lucy was a well known pet form of Eliza. Even Harris Crockett's wife Eliza was called "Luisie."

I began calling the phone numbers that Tommy Hanks Jr. had given me. One relative I contacted was Carleen McBride of Grenada, Mississippi, also a grandchild of Frank Eskridge, who remembered being told Frank married her grandmother Eliza McDaniel, who was part African and Indian. She then dropped this on me: "Eliza's mother was one of the cook's for the plantation owner...it was said through the grapevine that the owner was the father." Carleen went on to say Eliza's mother was called Charlotte who married Sam McDaniel. Carleen's words that a plantation slaveowner was the father of Charlotte's daughter Eliza McDaniel kept repeating itself in my mind. Who was this slaveowner? Frank Eskridge, a slave of Richard Eskridge, later formed a union with Eliza a few years before Richard Eskridge's death. Carleen also recalled hearing Grandfather Frank Eskridge say that the family had three names: Eskridge, Campbell, and Livingston.

Next I phoned Alberta Boston, an eighty-six year old former native of West Helena, Arkansas now living in Chicago and another grandchild of Frank Eskridge, who remembered being told that Eliza McDaniel was from "the West Indies." Eliza was born in 1842, according to her death certificate, and in North Carolina, so she couldn't have been born in the West Indies.    It would be another four years before I would read about the origin of her roots. Alberta now  went on to tell me about Frank Eskridge. The next five words she uttered caused me to grip the telephone tight. "Frank Eskridge was from Africa."  My heart started beating fast. "He was from Africa?  Do you know from which part?" I asked. "No, that's all I remember hearing was that Grandpa Eskridge was from Africa," Alberta responded back.

Frank was the son of George and Phyllis Eskridge and was born in Mississippi in 1838 according to my research, so I knew he really wasn't from Africa.  But I thought it very remarkable that Alberta remembered being told this.  Did this come from someone in the family who had knowledge of an ancestor having come from Africa?

By October 1994 I had landed a job with a large bank, while at the same time still operating my genealogy service. After purchasing an old used microfilm reader to continue my research at home,  I ordered the 1900 census to find any information on Madie Jones' mother and Tom Hanks' sister, Rosie Hanks.  There on the 1900 census for Montgomery County was:

**Eskridge Milton**
**Eskridge Eugene**
**Eskridge Wm , Amanda**
**Jones Labe , Rossie,  Newberger, Alma , Charlie, Ethel, Annie, Madie**

William Burgess and Amanda Eskridge lived next door to Rosie. Labe Jones died in 1905 and Rosie remarried. Next, I looked up the 1910 Montgomery Co. census and found:

**Eskridge Harrison, Nancy**

**Eskridge Eugene**
**Eskridge Billy, Amanda**
**Harper Peter, Rossy, Madie, Maggie, Ercile**

Rosie was still living next door to William Burgess and Amanda Eskridge ten years later. Was this an indication that Rosie was related to them? Back then, close relatives customarily lived near each other, especially black families. Since Great-great-grandmother Eliza died when her daughter Rosie was young, it would be reasonable to assume that other family members would have stayed close by.

By applying the science of onomatology to our families' names made my suspicions stronger. There was a Milton Eskridge who was the son of Frank Eskridge, and who, like many other emancipated families, was still living on the toiled soil administered by Burdett R. Eskridge. There was a Eugene Eskridge, who was Milton's cousin, and the grandson of William Burgess Eskridge by his twin daughter Nancy. Eugene was born January 1870, four years after Burdett R. Eskridge's son Eugene Ernest Eskridge on September 1866. William Burgess and Amanda named one of their daughters Eliza, and Rosie's mother Eliza named one of her sons William, my great-grandfather. William, in turn, had a daughter Eliza in Osage City, and Tom Hanks Sr. named one of his daughters Elizabeth. Great-grandfather William also had a son named Ernest. Dad's middle name was Milton.

There also was that other small piece to my puzzle. The Freedmen Marriage Register had listed the marriage of a "Henry Hanks to Francis Eskridge." Who were they? According to the 1870 census, they were listed in the town of Jefferson, five miles from Duck Hill, and living with the family of freedman Jordan Eskridge, born 1823 in Alabama, who appeared to be Francis' father. However, Henry Hanks listed his birthplace as *Virginia*. Why did Henry receive the surname Hanks, and how did he end up in Carroll County from Virginia? I examined the indexes of subsequent census years without success. I finally spotted Henry on a genealogy internet website, listing him on page 34 of the

"Hinds County, City of Jackson" 1880 Mississippi federal census. I was equally thrilled when seeing Henry's name listed among a large group of over 800 people running eighteen pages long, then became excited even more when I noticed on the previous page the listing of a forty-two year old white school principal from Kentucky. It appeared that Henry Hanks became a student at the age of 34. Although his wife and children weren't listed with him, I was beaming inside that Henry was giving attention to his education to better his family's poverty-like condition, who were no doubt waiting patiently at their cabin near the vicinity of Duck Hill. But then, an awful awareness that made me sick to my stomach soon gripped me. I had glanced at the principal's name and Henry's name too quickly. The principal, it turned out, was never connected to those 800 names after all. To my horrifying dread, I had instead come across the enumeration of prisoners inside the Jackson State Penitentiary, 837 blacks, 79 whites. I also saw an entry that said "Henry Hanks, prisoner, laborer."

There was another piece to my family portrait puzzle. On the Freedmen Marriage Register which recorded the marriage of my great-grandparents, Great-grandfather's name was listed as "William Wilkins" but by the time of the 1870 census, his surname had changed to "Hanks." I suspected that at some time William was employed by someone named Wilkins. Since Burdett Eskridge had administered his grandfather Richard Eskridge's estate ten years earlier in 1860, including its slaves, it would not have been a problem for William to have been inherited by Burdett's sister Mary and her husband Drury D. Wilkins, who didn't join the lawsuit filed against Burdett in 1861. William also may have been hired out to Drury D. Wilkins under the forced labor contracts that had gone into effect after the civil war's end. Added to this was the fact that in 1870 Drury and Mary Wilkins were living next door to William Burgess and Amanda Eskridge, and three cabins away from Eliza Eskridge.

And, of course, there was a similiar name to match Henry Hanks' case, too--*Henry Eskridge,* the son of William Burgess Eskridge, who later became a school teacher and reportably took a trip to Africa during the 1920's.

I received a surprise in the mail.  An envelope arrived from C Swanson containing a photograph of the slave-built home of her great-great-grandfather Richard Eskridge,  along with abstracted records about her family's descent from her fifth great-grandfather, Colonel George Eskridge of Westmoreland County, Virginia.  The personal material had been sent to C from a family historian, one of several in the Eskridge clan, a Texas relative named Jack Grantham.

One of the notations, to my surprise, made a comment of a prominent African-American attorney in Chicago whose surname was Eskridge, although failing to mention his first name nor a biography.  I finally found out who he was.  Unfortunately it was from a newspaper obituary dated January 19, 1988 in *The New York Times*.  His name was Chauncey Eskridge Jr.  I contacted members of his family by telephone to learn about his life.  Chauncey Eskridge Jr. was born November 11, 1917 in Pittsburgh, Pennsylvania, giving his parents Chauncey and Julia their first child, who lived at 6 Nimick Street.  Life for Chauncey and later his younger brother John William was difficult.  Their father was an alcoholic who deserted their mother Julia.  Chauncey's parents remained legally married, however.  They couldn't get divorced because they didn't have the money.

Chauncey obtained his formal education in Tuskegee, Alabama at Booker T. Washington's Tuskegee Institute, founded in 1881 for the purpose of providing a curriculum not only in the liberal arts for young blacks in the deep South but equally important an industrial education.  Chauncey graduated in 1939 as an electrical engineer.  Not satisfied with the job opportunities afforded blacks in Pittsburgh at that time, Chauncey moved to Chicago.  He joined the Illinois National Guard by November 1941.  He went back to Pittsburgh to propose marriage to his hometown sweetheart in 1942, then returned to Chicago with his new wife.  Due to the attack on Pearl Harbor, the United States entered World War II and Chauncey's National Guard was mobilized.  Chauncey became a lieutenant-colonel and served as a spotter pilot, flying Piper Cubs during the war's campaign in Italy.

After the war Chauncey became an accountant and an IRS

agent.   Soon he took an interest in law and enrolled at John Marshall Law School in Chicago, graduating in 1949.   By mid-February 1957 in New Orleans a civil rights organization called the Southern Christian Leadership Conference was established, with Martin Luther King Jr. as President and Ralph Abernathy as treasurer.   In time the SCLC would recruit Chauncey Eskridge as part of their legal team.   A deep, personal friendship emerged between Dr. King and Chauncey, and Dr. King would often stay at Chauncey's home when he came to Chicago.   On May 25, 1960 Chauncey took the stand in a Montgomery, Alabama courtroom to testify in defense of King.   The State of Alabama had accused him of filing fraudulent tax returns for 1956 and 1958, which were untrue but designed to discredit King.   Chauncey Eskridge was introduced to Dr. King at this time, Chauncey having been brought along to Montgomery by another Chicago attorney who was one of five lawyers handling King's defense.   According to the book, *Parting The Waters, America In The King Years 1954-63*, King's defense team became worried that Dr. King's financial records covering his gross and net income--including contributions and travel expenditures--might not provide a clear, accountable picture to be presented to a court.   Chauncey learned of this and conferred with King as to how he had prepared his tax returns.   When Chauncey was told by King that he kept a daily record of his expenditures in his diary, a light went off in Chauncey's head, for diaries could be admissible in court.   When later Chauncey got his hands on the diaries, he was beaming to discover detail after detail of daily expenses and receivables on each page.   Chauncey spent the rest of the day pouring over and adding up King's written monetary figures.   Did Dr. King take in more monies than he reported?   The next day, Chauncey produced his findings to the five-lawyer defense team: Dr. King had not hidden any money. After three days a jury of twelve white men returned a verdict of *not guilty*.   Dr. King, fearing a conviction, was stunned, but overjoyed.

In 1964 defense attorney Chauncey Eskridge added another high-profile client to his caseload: Muhammad Ali.  On August 14, Ali married a 24 year old Chicago model in Gary, Indiana.  Soon thereafter at Ali's Miami home, Chauncey placed a telephone call to Dr. King at his Atlanta home, with Ali joining them on an extension.  King wished Ali well on his recent wedding.  Ali invited King to be his guest at his next championship fight, a bout with Sonny Liston.  Little did they know that J Edgar Hoover's FBI had a telephone surveillance on King and the conversation was being recorded.  The 45 minute conversation went on, Ali telling King that he was known worldwide, as far as Nigeria, Egypt, and Ghana, and to watch out for "the whities."  Then Ali's religious activities were discussed, he having converted to the Black Muslim faith that year.

In June 1967 Ali was convicted by a Houston jury for refusing induction into the armed forces during the Vietnam war, sentenced to five years in prison, and fined $10,000, denying his status as a conscientious objector on the basis of religion.  Ali was stripped of his heavyweight championship and  released on $5000 bail, causing Chauncey to become embroiled in a series of legal matters and appeals.  It was then that two years later the FBI illegal wiretaps on Dr. King's telephone surfaced.

On June 4, 1969 a special hearing in a Federal District Court in Houston was ordered by the Supreme Court after the Justice Department revealed the FBI had taped five conversations involving Ali, four of them illegal and one under authorization from then Attorney General Nicholas deB. Katzenbach involving foreign intelligence.  The special hearing was to determine if illegal wiretap evidence had played any part in Ali's 1967 conviction.  Government lawyers urged the court not to allow any of the illegal wiretaped conversations to be made public, saying it would prejudice the national interest.  The court allowed Ali's attorneys to learn the contents of four transcripts.  However, even after hearing testimony from the FBI agent in charge of the wiretappings who said the surveillance continued on past 1965, Chauncey nor the rest of Ali's legal team were successful in arguing that Ali's conscientious objector status had been denied for political reasons rather than a religious one.

But by 1971 the Supreme Court, after Chauncey's appeal reached their chamber, agreed to hear arguments on whether the

Justice Department had erroneously recommended to Ali's local draft board in Louisville to deny Ali's request to be classified a conscientious objector because they interpreted his opposition to war was political and racial rather than religious. Chauncey wasted no time in preparing his legal argument, although months away. As the hearing approached near, he flew to New York and conferred with a lawyer who helped assemble supporting documents and notes to a potentially monumental argument. One night, a month before the scheduled hearing date in April, Chauncey and his New York partner took a break and went out for a bite to eat, leaving their materials in the car. While they ate inside the restaurant a thief broke into the car, stealing material for the hearing. But Chauncey regrouped, flew out to New York again, and the crucial documents were reassembled in time. Then, on Monday, April 19, 1971 Chauncey approached the eight-man black robed Supreme Court, going up against the Solicitor General, who argued the Government's case. Each had only 30 minutes to articulate their case. With his wife accompanying him to the highest court in the land, Chauncey felt confident.

"The petitioner just doesn't want to fight the white man's war, and I can understand that," said the Solicitor General. "But that's not the same as being a pacifist."

"Nowhere on the record has the registrant said that he would fight with weapons for anyone, anywhere," Chauncey declared.

The government's argument conceded the sincerity and religious basis of Ali's position but argued that his views were "so infused and interwined by political and racial implications." But Chauncey maintained that in describing his client's opposition to warfare as "political and racial" the Justice Department was essentially questioning his religious sincerity. Under questioning from Associate Justices Potter Stewart and William Douglas, Chauncey explained that the Black Muslim faith was not identical to Islam in the Middle East and that Ali would not in any way be bound to join a war involving Moslem countries. Associate Justice Thurgood Marshall disqualified himself from the case, citing that he could not take part since he had been Solicitor General during the time Ali was being prosecuted. Ali also was not present. Finally, the one hour time limit had expired. It was now in the hands of the High Court.

As Chauncey and his wife left the Washington courthouse they were met by streams of reporters and a large crowd as they descended the Supreme Court's steps, his wife worried and fearful of what could happen in a large crowd as Ali had his enemies. "The government conceded that he was religious and sincere...the key issue is what the Justice Department told the appeals board," Chauncey told reporters. "We think the government is prejudiced against the Black Muslims...you have to remember alot of young fellows are members of unpopular groups." The Solicitor General also gave his comments to the media. "I have developed my point to the best of my ability," the Solicitor General remarked. On Monday, June 28, the Court voted 8-0, declaring that Ali had been improperly drafted and that the Justice Department had misled Selective Service authorities by advising them Ali's request for conscientious objector status was not sincere based on his religious belief.

"People love money more than their mamas," Chauncey would often say. But his affection for his mother Julia would stay constant. By 1966 Chauncey's marriage had ended.      Three months prior to Chauncey's second marriage on May 5, 1968, black sanitation workers of Memphis Local 1733 of the American Federation of the State, County, and Municipal Employees voted to strike. The mayor warned employees that they would be fired if they failed to return to work. Martin Luther King Jr. was contacted and a march was organized for March 28. King arrived in Memphis while in the midst of outlining a plan for an interracial coalition of the poor, a poor-people's march, set on Washington for April. On the morning of March 28 King and the marchers started out, but by 11a.m. a clash between a small handful of youthful militants in the march and the police caused King and other leaders to halt the demonstration. A sixteen year old boy was fatally shot by the police, fifty persons were injured, and about 120 were arrested. By 9 p.m. three thousand eight hundred National Guardsmen were on the scene and a curfew was imposed. That night President Johnson appeared on national television to condemn the violence in Memphis.

Dr. King returned to Memphis on April 3, and learned that a federal court injunction had been placed barring any demonstrations in the city. Chauncey Eskridge flew to Memphis the following day, a Thursday, to represent King in the 5th U.S. Circuit Court of Appeals in "the City of Memphis v. Martin Luther King," to fight the court order, joining SCLC aide Andrew Young and those on the legal team. The judge conferred with Chauncey in private chambers that he would approve a march and that details would be worked out the next day. The Thursday hearing had run late and King, at the Lorraine Motel with his brother and Abernathy in a room on the first floor, had waited all day for word of the courtroom developments.

Chauncey arrived at the Lorraine and told King news that the march was on for Monday, April 8. Around 6 p.m. King and Abernathy went upstairs to their room 306 to get dressed for a soul food dinner they were invited to attend. While Abernathy was in the room tending to some last second preparations, King stepped out onto the balcony. Jesse Jackson called up to King and introduced him to a music band member. The chauffeur suggested that King ought to wear a topcoat, since it was getting chilly. Dr. King agreed. Then there was a loud shot. Some thought it was the backfiring of a car--others took cover near the driver's limousine. Then everyone realized who had fallen. Chauncey helped place Dr. King on a stretcher and followed him to St. Joseph's Hospital. Some said the shot came from the bathroom of a rooming house. Some said it came from a passing car. Others said it came from the bushes around the Lorraine. One report said it came from where the police were coming from. Another report stated a special forces 8-man Alpha Team was in position on the roof of the Illinois Central Railroad building across from the motel. But whether it was the work of a conspiracy or of a lone assassin, the end result was the same. Chauncey, who had flown in to help settle a labor dispute among the city's black workers, was now settling Dr. King's estate.

Almost six months after Chauncey's 1968 wedding, his

father died.  Chauncey didn't even want to attend his memorial. He had never got along with his father, the father that had left his mother.  But Chauncey finally did go to the funeral.  Soon after Chauncey had a stroke.  1968 was a stressful year for him.  By 1981 he was appointed a Circuit Court Judge for Cook County.  He retired in 1986.  Then another stroke in 1988 swiftly took the vitality of a very prominent man.

I pondered the question of where Chauncey's surname came from.  His widow told me he was interested in learning his roots.  In 1974 he had attended a family reunion somewhere back South, and in 1982 Chauncey had obtained a mail-order book on the history of the Eskridge surname.  I then attemped to see if I could trace back his paternal family tree.  According to census records, his father Chauncey Sr. was born around 1898 in Pennsylvania, and was listed a "mulatto."  Chauncey Sr. also had a sister named Marsaline, born by 1903.  His mother was Annabell Jackson, born about 1880 in Hopkinsville, Kentucky, and the daughter of James and Bettie Jackson, both born in Virginia in 1852 and 1856, who settled in Hopkinsville by 1875, eventually moving to Rankin, Pennsylvania on Fourth street.  Annabell's mother Bettie apparently later died.  Annabell's 42 year old father James Jackson remarried in 1894 to a young woman twenty-one years his junior named Hattie.  Just prior to 1898, Annabell Jackson married a mulatto named Marshall Eskridge, born around 1874 in Tennessee, who worked as a machinist for the railroad then later as a janitor for a steel company.

Marshall Eskridge would have been around six years old when the 1880 federal census was taken, so I checked the Tennessee soundex to see which household he was living in.  This would reveal who were his parents.  But there wasn't a single black household with a son named Marshall.  The lineage of Chauncey Eskridge would remain to me a mystery.  But he did acquire that surname from someone, somewhere.  As far as my research had shown, only two sets of white Eskridge settlers were recorded in Tennessee with slaves.  Both were headed by two cousins with the first name of Samuel.

Another notation C sent related an account which happened

in 1987 about how one of her distant Eskridge relatives went to visit her husband in a Chicago Veterans hospital.  By chance she struck up a conversation with a black patient there at the time named John Eskridge.  Amazed at learning that both shared the same surname, she asked him about his lineage.  John Eskridge told her, "My father, Morris Eskridge, was born in *Jamaica* in 1869, then he came to the USA."  He went on to tell her he had a brother named Hugh Eskridge, who was born 1889 in Duck Hill, Mississippi.  Grandfather Hanks' first name was also Hugh.

On learning this, I wondered if I could locate Morris Eskridge on the Montgomery County census to find more answers about his family.  Eventually I found my answers.  Morris Eskridge was the son of Louis and Mary Jane Eskridge, and Louis was the brother of Frank, Doc, and Wm. Harrison Eskridge.  But Morris was not born in Jamaica.  On the 1870 census there he  was, two years old and living with his parents and his three sisters.  In 1885  Morris married  a woman named Clara who gave him thirteen children including  Hugh, and John who  was born December 1887, making him one hundred years old the year  of that Chicago hospital conversation.  What caused John to say that his father was born in Jamaica?  Louis and his brothers' father, George Eskridge, was born in South Carolina.  Their mother Phyllis was born in Virginia.  According to the death certificates from the Mississippi Department of Archives & History, Morris' father Louis died in 1913 and his uncle Doc the following year.  His mother Mary Jane died in 1919 and was buried at Eskridge Cemetary.  His uncle Frank Eskridge died in 1924, leaving Frank's wife and his uncle William Harrison Eskridge.  I could come up with only two possible explanations for John's answer.  Either he had picked up the story about Frank's wife  as having come from "the West Indies," or an account in the Eskridge family had apparently been handed down.  The West Indies was definitely an important link within the triangle slave trade route that brought sugar, molasses, and tobacco to Europe, which in turn brought rum, cloth, and manufactured goods to Africa, which in turn brought African slaves to the Americas.  Did I have an African ancestor who was taken first to Jamaica as a slave before coming to America?

In 1995 I resumed researching the records of Roane County, Tennessee in hopes of learning more information about the ex-slaves surnamed Eskridge who had lived on Samuel Eskridge's plantation, and comparing this information with the branches of the Eskridge family in  Duck Hill.  According to the court records, Samuel Eskridge bequeathed his entire estate including 75 slaves to a ten year old minor, his great nephew Samuel Butler Eskridge who would inherit them  after the death of elder Samuel's wife Sophia, which was in 1857,  but not until Samuel reached the age of twenty-one, which was in 1863.  Young Samuel did not keep ownership of these slaves for long because two years after turning twenty-one the civil war finally ended and Afro-Americans were emancipated from slavery  due to the 13th Amendment to the Constitution passed by the U.S. Congress in 1865.  The following year they were granted U.S. citizenship due to the passage of the 14th Amendment.

I wonder how that felt, after being bought, brought, branded, bred, beaten, bartered, bequeathed, banned, bludgeoned, bloodied, broken down, and banished for almost 100 years since the signing of the Declaration of Independence, to be told one day that you were now an American citizen?  I wondered, if, after considering their ancestors came here as citizens of African countries, regions, and clans, if any descendants in 1865 were given a choice of citizenship between the two?  I ponder what my own family felt in 1865 when they were told of their elevated status?  Still yet, how did they answer?

As I began digging through pages of census schedules, marriage lists, and cemetary records, a charcoal drawing portrait slowly was being canvassed of close-knit families lead by patriarchal heads, as they emerged from the shackles of slavery and into the turn-of-the-century.  There arose Henry, listed a slave on the 1853 estate inventory of Samuel Eskridge, "officially" registering his marriage to Mary Jane Thornton on June 30, 1866, even though they were already unitedly wedlocked in slavery times by 1855 with the birth of their invalid son Green.  There stood the mulatto Armstead Eskridge in 1866 with his bride Ellen.  There

sprang up Israel, who by 1870 was a steamboat hand, with his mate
Caroline since 1854 and their children. There ascended "James
Polk" Eskridge, sadly a widower by 1880 after losing his faithful
mate Susannah. He then lived on to watch his children grow up
before he himself was buried in 1915. There was Hiram, whose
name also appeared on the special 1890 census schedules
enumerating Union soldiers of Roane County, along with his wife
Louisa and their family of Jennie, William, Hiram, Richard, and
George. Brisborn & Margaret had been raising a family since
1835. Nelson & Amanda didn't allow the year of the civil war
outbreak to prevent the start of their union, and sons Governor,
Carpenter, and George. Then too, there was Brisborn's son
Solomon, a railroad hand, and his wife Aggy, whose Virginian
born father was cited as being George Eskridge on her death
certificate, and son Samuel. Another family I saw in the records
was Marion Eskridge & wife Mary. After Marion died, Mary
continued on raising her sons Tyler, Calvin, Melton and Samuel
right into the new century.

I was amazed that several sons were named Richard,
Samuel, and George. Plantation heir Samuel Butler Eskridge, born
about November 1842 in Duck Hill, also had a son named George,
born in 1872 in Mississippi. Samuel Butler Eskridge married Miss
Mary E. McDaniel in December 1866 and settled in the city of
Rockwood. In the *Rockwood Times* newspaper, its November 29,
1906 issue printed the obituary of a former slave named Fred
Eskridge:

"....who died last week, a notable ante-bellum darkey...the death of
Fred Eskridge in this city last week removes another of the old
time colored men from the worldly walks of life...A.P. Thompson,
of this city, in recounting the death of Eskridge in Saturday's
*Chattanooga News* has the following: The death and funeral of
Fred Eskridge in this city and a good and respected colored man,
calls up some of the early history of Roane county when his master
lived on the pike between this city and Kingston...and much goods,
hauled in wagons with six large horses and "schooner" bodies
passed between the two cities. Eskridge was one of the

weatherwise men of the county, outside of his negro property was not considered a saint, never married, and was peculiar in many respects.  One of his fads was to keep on hand a coffin of walnut lumber for his own use and when he loaded up with corn juice, he would crawl into his coffin and sleep awhile.  He had made several coffins before he had the pleasure of using one permanently.  Some traveler would stop at his stand and die and Eskridge would let him have his coffin.  He was heard to say that every time he got a coffin just to suit him some ___ rascal would turn up there and died and he had, therefore, to give up his coffin."

Many families worked as farm laborers, but some of the Eskridge family heads found occupations as miners, bricklayers, iron workers, and steamboat hands.  Some families experienced tragedy:

"Ollie Eskridge, Daughter of Governor Eskridge, Colored, Burned to Death.  Clothes Caught From Open Grate and Fatal Burns Were Inflicted Before Aid Reached her.  Last Saturday Ollie Eskridge, the nine year old daughter of Governor Eskridge, a colored man living in old Rockwood, was burned to death caused by her clothes catching fire...The girl's father works for the Roane Iron Co. at night and was asleep in the room when the accident occurred...Eskridge is said to be a hard working colored man and much sympathy is expressed for him in the untimely death of his child." (*Rockwood Times*, Nov. 22, 1906)

On the 1880 Roane County census there were eight persons with the surname Eskridge-William, Solomon, Aggy, Frederick, Hiram, Julia Ann, Margaret, Marion--who reported a parent born in *Virginia*.  And there was one person, Brisborn, who himself was born in Virginia in 1810.  Marion's wife Mary reported both her parents were born in *Mississippi*.  I wondered if there were any exchanging or transferring of slaves between the two plantations of Richard Eskridge and his brother Samuel.  Thomas N. Clark, who had been appointed by Samuel to manage his estate after his death, was well known to Richard Eskridge from conferring with Richard regarding the running of the plantation, the contesting of the will, and other matters of the estate. One of Thomas N. Clark's family members had also sold Richard Eskridge 200 acres of land on Buck Creek in 1810. Richard Eskridge surely would have assisted Mr. Clark in the management of his brother's slaves.

The 75 slaves on the 1860 census, now inherited by great-nephew Samuel, included *twenty-three new births* between 1855-1860. It finally dawned on me that although the Buck Creek plantation had around the same number of slaves in 1860 as it did in 1853, they definitely *were not all the same persons.*

After comparing the 1853 slave inventory to the twenty-eight dower slaves given to the widow Sophia Eskridge, and also to the 1870-1900 census schedules, I realized there were    twenty-five persons in 1853 not accounted for by 1870:
"....Amy,Tom(aliasLongTom),...Lewis,Will...Cynthia...Cass...Charles,Ralph,Viney,      Julia,          Delilah,...Jim.Suddath Jesse...Mary...Savannah,    Matilda...Clayra,    Edmond..Elizabeth, Eliza, Fanny, Clementine, Rosa Ann, Eliza...Jordan..."
Those slaves had to have gone somewhere.

As I compared  the increase of slave holdings for the two brothers Samuel & Richard from the census schedules for each decade, I could feel myself being pulled back in time.  It felt as when one pulled the husks off an ear of corn.  Each layer revealed the next generation.  Two years before his death, the 1850 census listed elder Samuel's  75 slaves, mostly children.  The oldest slaves on the Tennessee plantation was a woman born in 1803, a woman born in 1790, and a man born in 1788.  The 1840 census showed 63 persons, with the oldest being two males and one female born before 1785.  Nowhere  could I locate the slave census records for Samuel before 1830 in Tennessee,  nor in Mississippi, Alabama, North & South Carolina, or Virginia.

Just as were Eskridges in Roane County, so also too, those in Duck Hill had ties to Virginia.  William Burgess Eskridge listed his father William as having been born in Virginia.  Phyllis Eskridge  was born there.  Henry Hanks listed Virginia as his 1847 birthplace.   Hannah Eskridge, who was 104 years of age in 1880, was born around the same time as Richard Eskridge. I wondered if Hannah had been owned by an earlier generation of the Eskridge family and Richard Eskridge had inherited her?

The slave census of 1860 listed close to one half of Richard Eskridge's 48 slaves as children, with the oldest adults being a male & female born in 1800, a male born in 1796 and a female born in 1790. On the 1850 schedule he reported 29 slaves, eight of them children, and the oldest adults being two females born in 1805 and two males born in 1790. The 1840 census showed nine slaves for Richard, three slaves for his son Taliaferro, eight slaves for his son Samuel, and fourteen slaves for his daughter-in-law Julia. Richard had the oldest slave, a female born before 1785. I couldn't locate Richard's slave records for 1820 nor 1830, although his son Taliaferro was located on the 1830 census in Dallas County, Alabama listing one male slave born between 1794-1806. Richard Eskridge then appeared again, now in Abbeville, South Carolina with seven slaves in 1800 and with five in 1810, however, their gender and ages were not listed. Where did the two brothers Richard and Samuel obtain their slaves? Were they inherited?

I wrote to the Old Edgefield District Archives in Edgefield, South Carolina, asking for any information on the Eskridge family that lived in Abbeville around 1775. I received two packets of biographical sketches, estate records, and copies of deeds and deed abstracts. As I opened the material, I began to wonder if my search was happily concluding, and that I was now on the verge of finally learning my family's link to Africa.

The estate records were of Captain Burdett Eskridge, a soldier who served in the South Carolina units during the Revolutionary War. He left Virginia and moved to Ninety-Six District, South Carolina--"ninety-six miles" from Keowee, the Cherokee village in the Blue Ridge Mountains of Western Virginia. He later was killed in the "Cloud Creek Massacre." Burdett Eskridge had volunteered on a scouting reconnoitre with a company of soldiers searching for British "Tory" Loyalists. On November 17, 1781 their company was seized upon by about three hundred Tories and after surrendering were then mercilessly executed, under the command of Captain "Bloody Bill"

Cunningham. His written will of 1779 was entered into probate court on August 20, 1782. As I read his will, I realized just who Burdett Eskridge was:

"In the Name of God Amen I Burditt Eskridge of Collenton County Ninety six District in the Province of South Carolina, being Well in Health and of perfect Mind and Memory thanks be to Almighty God for the Same, but knowing it is appointed for all men Once to Die I Bequeath my Soul to God that gave it to me and my Body to be Buried in a descent manner; I do this day being the twenty third day of March Anno Domini one thousand seven hundred and Seventy nine make and ordain this to be my last will and Testament, in manner and to the effect following viz...Item I leave and Bequeath to my Eldest Son **Samuel** that land as lyes on Red Bank...Item at my wifes Decease her thirds of the land I leave to my son **Richard;**
    **Item I desire that my Negroes shall be equally divided at my Son Samuel's coming of age** the child that my wife is now with is to have an equal part of the Negroes and at my wife's Death an equal part of her thirds of the Negroes...

...I have hereunto fixed my hand the day and year above written.
Signed & Sealed in presence of
Jn Davis
Jacob Smith                   Burditt Eskridge
Sarah Smith

Burdett Eskridge was Richard and Samuel's father, and their mother's name was Nancy Grigsby, the daughter of Nathaniel Grigsby and Elizabeth Butler who later settled in Nelson County, Kentucky. Burdett's second wife was Hannah Bell-Watson. Also included in the estate records was an estate inventory. A slave family was listed, comprised of Will the husband, his wife Jane, and their daughters Ruth, Barbe, and Rose.
    Burdett stated the slaves were to be equally divided among his children, upon Samuel's "coming of age." If that meant when

Samuel turned 21, that would have been around the late 1780's. Appearing before the Court of Edgefield County on October 8, 1787 "on application of Samuel Eskridge a youth he being of approved age the guardianship of the said Sam Eskridge was granted to Joseph Thomas." Joseph "Josiah" Thomas would marry Samuel's sister Elizabeth in 1795.

The following day on October 9,1787 Hannah Eskridge, formerly the widow of the late Burdett, appeared before the court with her new husband Daniel Bullock to "Relinquish Renounce and forever quit claim of all and every portion parts parcel or parcels of the Estate of the said Burditt Eskridge from the day before the date of these presents henceforth...all right title and claim to the Dower of her the said Hannah," and thus sold her dower claim to the executors of Burdett's estate, Jacob Smith and Enoch Grigsby, the latter an Uncle of Burdett's first wife Nancy, "for the use benefit and advantage of the heirs of the said Burditt Eskridge."

Since Hannah Bell-Watson was married to Burdett Eskridge for only a brief time before his untimely death in 1781 and had subsequently married Daniel Bullock, the property claims of Burdett's children Samuel, Austin, Richard, Elizabeth, and Rebecca were put into question, as Hannah had dower rights to one third of the estate throughout her lifetime. She also had living children from a previous marriage to whom she might wish to bequeath property. According to other deed records, young Samuel finally "came of age" somewhere between November 1788 and June 1789, his name now being mentioned in deeds of his neighbors whose property acres lay adjacent to his. The court had protected Samuel and his siblings' full inheritance.

While Samuel's sister Elizabeth married Josiah Thomas, his brother Frederick G. Thomas married Samuel's other sister Rebecca. On May 9, 1793 Samuel Eskridge was a witness to the selling of a 47 year old female slave named Jenny, from Josiah Thomas to his father Captain John Thomas of Green County, Georgia, a baptist minister. Hardly did I think this baptist minister's slave purchase was merely to baptize Jenny's soul. I knew full well there were thousands like him who cloaked a Bible at the pulpit in one hand, and gripped a whip in the other. I would deliberate if they also got tax breaks back then, too. (Indeed if so, the slave reparations movement might move to start taxing the churches!) Even though shock went through me upon revelation of the minister's purchase of a slave, I shouldn't have been. The churches of Christendom had kept the Atlantic slave trade alive and well.

Whether Jenny was formerly the property of Josiah's wife Elizabeth Eskridge Thomas, I could not determine. Jenny's age showed her to be born around 1746. Samuel's brother Richard would turn the legal age of twenty-one by 1796, eventually taking his portion of slaves with him to Tennessee and Mississippi. The 1830 census revealed Samuel Eskridge with 58 slaves. The oldest in age being four females and three males born before 1775. I couldn't help to think that those four females were Ruth, Barbe, Rose, and their mother Jane.

The slave Will mentioned in Captain Burdett Eskridge's last testament was born around 1757 in Virginia, since Burdett's son Samuel was born in Virginia before the family's migration to South Carolina. Was "Will" the father of William Burgess Eskridge? Jane's age made her year of birth around 1747. The children Ruth, Barbe, and Rose would have been born in 1773, 1776, and 1779 respectively. The name of Hannah, the freedwoman of Duck Hill who reported being born around 1776, did not appear. It was possible she could have been born after the inventory was taken, or she perhaps grew up on another plantation. I also wondered whether if the three children of Jane had other names, such as "Hannah Rose" or "Ruth Hannah"? The possibility also existed that the woman Jane had borne other children.

The biographical sketches on the Eskridge family showed that Burdett's father was Samuel Eskridge of Westmoreland County, Virginia, a Justice of the Peace and a member of the Virginia House of Burgesses. He first married Hannah Rust, then later married Jane Ashton in 1735. His children, besides Burdett, were three other sons-Charles, Richard, John, and a daughter named Rebecca. In turn, Samuel's father was George Eskridge of Sandy Point, Westmoreland County, an attorney and member of the House of Burgesses.

The four sons of Samuel Eskridge and Jane Ashton eventually moved apart.  Burdett moved to South Carolina, Charles moved to Fauquier County, Virginia,  John remained in Westmoreland County, and Richard moved to Caswell County, North Carolina.  Richard and his wife had thirteen children in North Carolina, one of them being the Samuel Eskridge whom I had learned about earlier  had settled in Davidson County, Tennessee.  To my surprise, I found out through the North Carolina Department of Archives that another of their sons, also named Richard Eskridge, moved to Rutherford County, North Carolina, which bordered the old Ninety-Six District.  According to his will dated November 3, 1831 Richard Eskridge stated, "I give unto my beloved wife Elizabeth my Negro woman *Hannah* to dispose of as she pleases, & her increase also forever...during her life time or widowhood I give unto my beloved wife all the following negroes, to wit Negro man Jeree, Negro woman *Phillis & all her children...*"

Who was "negro woman Hannah" and  "negro woman Phillis?"   And who were their children?   If this was the freedwoman Hannah who was born in 1776 she would have been fifty-five years old.  This woman Phillis I knew was not the Phyllis Eskridge who was born in Virginia in 1825 and married George Eskridge of Duck Hill whose family made up one of the three main Eskridge family branches in Duck Hill.  She would only have been six years old in 1831, hardly able to have had children.  However, was Phyllis Eskridge of Duck Hill possibly the daughter of "Negro woman Phillis?"  There was just too much of a coincidence that the names Hannah and Phillis would appear together.

Throughout my research, I had been constantly amazed at the repetition of names among the slaves owned by the Eskridge family, as if each repetition was like a mark of identification upon one family line, just as the repetition of names in the Eskridge family who were white identified theirs.  Could the slave women Hannah and Phillis have possibly been somehow sold to the Eskridge plantation in Duck Hill from off the Eskridge plantation in North Carolina?  The two branches of the family apparently knew each other, since it was said among the Eskridge family papers that Burdett Eskridge had accompanied his older brother Richard to North Carolina before continuing on to Edgefield County, South Carolina. Even some of the members of the North Carolina branch later migrated to Mississippi in a county very nearby Duck Hill.

Samuel Eskridge of Westmoreland County died in 1747 and his wife Jane died in 1781, a few months before her son Burdett. I came across an index for wills and administrations in Virginia , and a list of tithables in 1776 for Westmoreland County. The index listed an estate inventory recorded in 1747. I then realized something: the year that Samuel Eskridge died in 1747 happened to  be about the same time that the slave Jane was born, listed on Burdett Eskridge's 1782 slave inventory.    Would Samuel's estate inventory  show Jane's name on it?  Just how far back would I be able to go?  Could I find my ancestor who came from Africa?  By January 1997 my inquiry was in the mail and on its way to the Westmoreland County Court Clerk.

Six weeks later in late February the estate inventory had arrived!  Apparently a will had not been written. The inventory was about two and a half pages, everything from the inside furniture to the outside two gray horses named Ranter and Tobey and one black horse named Sparke;

from a Bible & portraits to two gold buttons and a silver watch; from cows, oxen, & a bull to twenty two human souls:

**Estate of Samuel Eskridge gentleman Deceased**
**Negroes viz:  Hery Burk, Lewis Whitly, Joseph Clark, William Clark, Benjamin Clark, Great Nan,**
**Little Nan, Jenney, Charles, Elizabeth Clark, Bess, Prero, Rachel, Giles**
**Mr. Samuel Eskridges Estate In Fairfax County viz:**
**Negroes, Will, Jack, Sarah, George, Tom, Hannah, Jenney, Akey**
**Recorded the 20th day of October 1747**

Here were the names of my ancestors!  They just had to be. The names sounded so familiar because I had run across them many times in the records of Duck Hill.   These names had not been lost through the passage of  time.  They had simply been passed down for other  generations of Eskridge slave families to use.  To have gone back six generations felt like a  dream. But all the evidence I had come across was what now brought me to this point.    Some families were probably separated   and   divided among Samuel's children.   Whatever memories,  stories, customs, beliefs,  joys and sadness  these  families had would then  separate with them.

"Negro man Named Will about 25 or 26 years old
Negro wench Named Jane about 35 years old
Negro child Named Ruth, Daughter of Jane 9 years old
Negro child Named Barbe, Daughter of said Jane 6 years old
Negro child Named Rose, a Daughter of said Jane 3 years old.
Certified this 5th day of September in the seventh year of American
Independence,
Anno Domini 1782." Burdett Eskridge's slave inventory.

## CHAPTER NINE

### "I Think We Fixing to be Sold!"

The Crockett family reunion was held at Memphis, Tennessee, the first weekend of August 2000. I had the chronology of the family tucked inside my travel bag. I was firmly set to share with other kin the tradition of orally transmitting familial heritage from one ear to the other ear. That Saturday night, several families heard about the African ancestor Akey, and how she was purchased by Colonel George Eskridge of Westmoreland County, Virginia, and later bequeathed to the Colonel's son Samuel. They heard how Akey's family later was bequeathed to Samuel's son Captain Burdett Eskridge, who eventually removed Akey's descendants with him to Edgefield County, South Carolina as his slaves, until he was killed by British soldiers. Several of us stayed up 'till midnight sitting on sofas in the hotel lobby, bringing together clusters of old and new memories, old and new faces, and renewing, recharging, family soul. None of us wanted to retire the evening.

My unfinished chronicle was passed around the room to read. The balance of historical events transpiring in Akey's family saga began to emerge and cry out from the tablet:

"In the year 1784, in the twelfth month, in the year of Richard Henry Lee, President of the Confederation, the woman Jenny was heavy with child in the County of Edgefield near the

Savannah River.    In the twelfth month, on the first day of the month, Jenny gave birth to a child, a male, and was named William, after his father.

Frank had longed hoped that the end of the brutal war would have spelled freedom for his growing family.  But as soon as his ears heard news that the war was over, yet could still see his fellow men still being held as slaves on nearby plantations, painfully he realized that the war of "Independence" did not include his own.  But for the sake of his family, he was determined to keep that hope alive within their hearts even though it was slipping quickly from his own.  At supper he would pray "Dear God, Great Jehovah, may Ye please keep us in thine memory and break our chains upon thy necks.  We beseech you to send your faithful servant to set up free.  Come quickly, in the name of your beloved Jesus, AMEN."  This prayer Frank would recite at each and every evening meal.  But the days would go by.  Then the months.  Soon the years.  But as far as Frank was concerned, he continued hoping his prayer was being favorably heard as long as he was alive.  Perhaps a saviour might indeed appear to answer even on this day in 1790.

The blustery afternoon winds blew about the servant coachmen standing outside holding on tight to the individual horsecarriages of each of their mistresses, nearly blowing off the servants' hats.  Akey watched them from inside as the horses' tails frilled horizontally like stretched-out quilting threads and yarns of tassle ribbons with each strong gust.  The Spanish moss hanging from the cypress trees in Akey's view waved and rippled.  She could hear the wind bursts hit the tracery windows of the big house before blowing over its arched vault.  She fixed her gaze as the winds traveled on and hit across the three slave cabins behind the English-Gothic big house, finding its way through inviting holes and cracks in the oak wood planks nailed together in their measured places, then out again to meander toward the meat house, granary house, cow barn, and chickens coop.  Akey observed through the casement window in the kitchen how fast the winds finally reached the fifteen fieldhands, nearly blowing some of them over.  She was glad to be inside the big house at that moment.

Glad that she had finished picking her share of corn for the day. Glad to be called inside by a commanding call to brew her mistress that special tea.  Akey felt the kettle's steam waft over her face, while peering out the window to catch one more glimpse of the cold coachmen standing unhappily at their posts, hoping their respective mistresses would grow tired and ready to return home. As she peered out, an intense gust hit the windowpane in front of her face, violently shaking the four corners of the frame.  Akey jumped back startled, barely catching herself from knocking off the kitchen tray.  Momentarily distracted by the violent winds, Akey quickly filled four of her owner's prized tea cups and carried the serving tray into the living room.  While Akey went about serving her special tea to the guests of Mistress Belle, South Carolina's state convention was the topic of conversation.

"I wonder if President Washington will be attending?" asked one of the women.

"I understand he is in Philadelphia at the present.  But it is very possible he may drop down for such an occasion," said another.

"Oh, what I would do to meet General George...I mean, President George Washington in person if he were truly to visit our state," another voice entered in.  As Akey refilled their teacups she wondered if she had heard that name before.  Later that afternoon the guests began leaving for their homes, agreeing to hold another social luncheon at some other convenient time.  Fifteen year old Richard Eskridge, the son of the late Burdett Eskridge, rushed inside the house from the cornfields and entered the bake pantry hoping to stave off his appetite until supper.  Akey quickly shewed him off.

"And what you think you doing, young Massa Richard?  If you eats up all the bread before mealtime, what be left for your sisters?  Mistress Belle wants to see you at mealtime as hungry as a soldier!"

"Yes Akey, but if I don't eat something soon, I'll die of hunger before the war even gets started,"  young Massa Richard amusingly responded.

Akey suddenly became alarmed.   "What war?  Is there

another war?!  Is the King's men coming again?!"  Akey did not like that word.  It frightened her, having seen the effects of it not only in this country but also in Kru country as a girl.

"I assure you, Mammy Akey, there is no war; President Washington whipped them Redcoats but good.  They won't never be coming back here ever again!"

"Prezdent Washington...who...is he?"  Akey needed to hear more.

"He was a mighty general during the war.  He defeated the redcoats.  Mother said when he was born he was named after my great-granddaddy "Colonel George Eskridge" who raised *his* mother.  So after the war, they made him President of the United States of America!"  The young massa then grabbed the small loaf on the kitchen table and went out just as fast as he came in.

Akey sat down to catch herself, realizing where she had first heard that familiar name.

That night, Akey's family huddled in the cabin before a prepared meal of baked bread, corn stew, rabbit, and turnips.  Frank began giving his usual blessings over the food.  At the end, Akey said "Amen" then shouted "O Hallelujah!"

"Something gotten into you tonite, I can tell;  Come on out with it," Frank said, looking surprised.

"I got some good news to tell all of you!  This here prayer we been praying for is coming true real soon;  Sooner than we think!"  Frank, William, Jenny, the girls Ruth, Barbe,  Rose, and six year old son Billy were all now excited, wondering what Akey was going to say next.

"I just heard from boy Richard that this here man they call "Prezdent Washington" of what they call "Nited State Amerca" is young George, the son of Mrs. Mary in old Virginia!...he..."

"Whoa!   Slow down...you say Prezdent Washington is *who*?" Frank asked, not sure he heard right.

"He's Mrs. Mary's boy!  Little missy Mary of Sandy Point! We been knowing him!...knew him when we was on Colonel Eskridge's plantation!...knew him when he was but a boy!...no more younger than my grandson here!!"  Akey was just warming up.  "Asked me the day his mother's father died, 'Akey, did your grandpa die? Where is he? That's what he asked me, I 'member!! And I told him my grandfather was Sensobo, a Kru, a boatman, from the village Zwedru near the River Cavella, who grew the guinea pepper on his farm!! And...young George asked me years later about my grandfather, and I told him again; Oh, yes, "He" the one gonna free us, FREE OUR PEOPLES!! Oh, Thank God this day have come, Thank God I was in the house when I hear the ladies talking, talking about young George! Oh, my god yes, Hallelujah!!"

After Akey's emotional oratory, Frank had everyone all kneel down and pray. After everyone rose back up to the dinner table, Frank abruptly told them, "Go on and eat. I need to go check on the horses real quick," and rushed out. Frank got outside, but instead of heading to the horse stable, planted himself stationary in the Palmetto grove to wipe away from his eyes a tear or two. Could this really be true? Had their day of deliverance truly arrived? Frank concluded this must be a miracle, since what were the chances that he and Akey had actually known the boy who now had become President? Better yet, that the President was now coming to South Carolina? He then started to think about his mother abandoned on the islands, wondering if freedom could even come her way. At that point, all emotion Frank had tried to wipe away now could not hold sway.

That night they were ready and waiting. The next day they were ready and waiting. Akey swore she heard the tea ladies say "George" may be coming to South Carolina. Maybe she would see him again and could give him a message, a mandate, to abolish the condition of her people. She knew him. Knew him when he was but a boy. Without question he would not have forgotten his visits to Sandy Point. Certainly he could even yet recall the experience of visiting with this African girl as she disclosed the richness and intellect of her black heritage. Yes, Frank and Akey were ready and waiting. That week they spread the news secretly to their neighboring bondservants on some of the surrounding plantations, word getting to the slaves on James Bynum's place first, the news was next conveyed to those on Captain Van Swearingen's land, from there it spread to the bound stricken families on Judge

Russell Wilson's two hundred fifty-five acre estate down by Cedar Creek, from there travelling to Pierce Butler's slave community over between Town Creek and Beech Island. Within three weeks time word had spread even to the plantation fields of the Harrisons, Burtons, John Miller's, and "Old Man Simpkins."

By month's end, all ears were now wide open to any news heard of the President's possible arrival. Already an invention had been crafted to attempt a message from Akey, by means of the underground networks, to the one she remembered only as "young George," first by someone who could skillfully write, and second, by one who would dare deliver it, either in person or if all else failed sent by courier upon it reaching the mail routes at Augusta.

Akey knew already what she wanted penned on paper, but the problem lay in who could be found to carry out the latter? Independence was in haste upon a beat down and weary folk, a dignified folk, who were ready and waiting to be freed.  They waited--they waited--they waited.

One year went by.  By the end of April, Ruth was given in marriage to a man named Daniel who also worked on the plantation, the son of Quamino and Taffy, who had been sold to Massa Burdett from one of his brothers.  After their simple wedding ceremony, a gift necklace Daniel presented made of polished white stones which Ruth before eye witnesses did accept, the wedding feast soon began among the gathered friends on the plantation and from a neighboring one as well.  As the Saturday festivity lingered into late evening, a servant from up the road came rushing into the crowd and, after congratulating the married pair, turned to the bride's grandfather Frank and, catching his breath, whispered in his ear:

"We heard at our marster's place, Marster Butler, we heard him say President Washington in Charleston next week!"

"In Charleston?  Next week?  We need to find someone quick!"

"We already found one, by chance just last Sunday, said he willing to go whenever and wherever!  He can write, and better yet--he a freedman!"

"Who?  Who that?"  Frank cautiously asked under the

boisterous voices of the celebrating throng.

"Snowball"--he finally gave us his answer during prayer time last Sunday when he passed through;  You know we approached him well over six months ago, but he told me, say, "Now the time is right."

"COME ON!  You need to hear what my Akey got to say TONITE so's you can tell him."  Frank grabbed the servant's arm and led him through the midst of the crowd past the corn whisky pot bowl and over to Akey.

Freed man Nan.  Nansmond.  "Snowball" Nansmond, a freed mulatto released from his master for services rendered during the Revolutionary War, and dubbed his nickname due to his distinctive "white afro" despite still a young man.  His complexion was so light he could successfully pass, so long as he kept his Afro hidden with the big straw brim he wore.  Snowball Nansmond had his own horse too, and also a dressed up "gentleman suit" that he kept hung up at his room house, which he could put on for "special occasions."  Only reason why he wasn't present at this special occasion was because he had to wisely pick & choose the times he chose to be seen by the plantation owners mingling with their slave hands.  They considered a freed man being together with slaves a "bad mix."

The next day Snowball Nansmond came strolling by again past the familiar spot where the Butler slaves assembled for prayer. He stopped and nodded his head to them, curiously standing next to one *particular servant* for over ten minutes, then cordially made his departure.  The following day he was seen loading up his horse and riding to Charleston.  Several who saw him ride past said that day he rode as if with purpose, and they took note.  Indeed they should have, for with great purpose he did ride, and with a note that he himself took great care to inscribe:

DEAR HONORABLE SIR,

It has been almost fifty years ago since your friend last seen and spoke to you once upon a time in Virginia at the home of Captain George Eskridge;  I still hold you as a loyal companion Friend and hope it mutually the same;  I and my family are well here in Ninety-Six District, but alas, we are not with Freedom.  If you still remember our talks together and the history of my birth, then in the name of God do not forget the condition of my people. I know as President you can do many powerful things;  My hope and prayer is that you will show this country that we are all EQUAL.   Please come down to my country so I can see you one more time before I die, here at Mistress Eskridge's place on the road heading to Augusta.   Young President George, my friend, please tell your people that we still await the moment to be  FREE, please tell them that we MUST be free

AKEY CRUE

After  nights of riding and sleeping under pines, sycamores and the light of the moon, Nansmond finally made it to Charleston. But sadly, the President's entourage had already departed town. Depressed, Nansmond was too ashamed to return home with the bad news.  The friends back home were anxious to hear if he had gained success.  Little did they know he had hid himself along the back roads.  As the days counted by, Nansmond stopped at an Inn in Richland County to rest his tired mare.  Putting on his straw brim he entered right inside and sat down at a table.  Before he could even yet take the first sip of his liquor malt, his eyes gazed at the  May  17th  headline  of  the  County  town's   gazette: "PRESIDENT'S PARADE IN AUGUSTA TOMORROW;   Will Arrive In Columbia Sunday the 22nd Next."
With lightning speed Snowball Nansmond furiously rode all night.

At one o'clock p.m.  the next day the parade was in full swing.  Crowds were lined up on Broad Street.  The Governor of Georgia and the President made their way down the lines of people shaking hands and kissing the cheeks of mothers' infants, while others were extending flowers, hankerchiefs, jewelry, medallions, and anything else they could extend into his crowded path for attention.  The President's attendants strained to clear the pathway. Finally the President approached a man with a big straw brim and a distinguished dress suit, the color of which was blue silk, and shook his hand, after which a sealed envelope was then handed him.  The President thanked him as he took the envelope.  It was taken by a servant and promptly placed in a bag along with other papers received that day.  Surely in time the President would study his important mail.  In time, surely.

Shortly thereafter, Frank and Akey, William and Jenny, their son, three daughters and son-in-law Daniel were out toiling in the fields with the other workers the following Saturday.  A commotion could be heard coming up on the Augusta-Charleston country wagon road that morning.  They hadn't  seen Snowball since the day he had left, and their worry was now being stirred up. Several men on  horseback with a party carriage rode past the curious onlookers. They slowed down to tour the grounds and observe the working fieldhands, then the driver came to a dead stop.   Frank and Akey looked at the procession.   It was the President's entourage heading on its way to Columbia.

Some who were out in the fields that morning who could visibly see the procession began rumoring that the President was in fact coming to see the old African woman Akey.  Although several yards away from the road, Akey's eyes focused on the President as he stepped out of his carriage to stretch out at this picked spot, then turn in her direction.  For a brief moment both of their eyes met as each acknowledged the other.  Neither one made a gesture or said a word.  Their roles had now been switched.  But  thoughts between them went through the air.  The President's eyes peered sharply at Akey, recognizing a still youthful look in her brow and cheeks. Akey's wide eyes locked in straight ahead at the President, reading, not just his mature-grown face, but his soul.

"Mr. President, if it suits you, there's an Inn just up the way to stop and dine," said the escort carriage driver.  As President George Washington climbed back aboard the carriage he gave an inquiry to the driver.

"Is this place by chance the Eskridge Plantation?"

"Why, yes sir it is!  The planter Burdett Eskridge was once the original owner;  He's taken his place now among the soldier dead in the war of Independence;  But sir, how did you know this was his land?"

"An old friend told me, dear chap."

The next instant the driver snapped the reigns and the President's retinue paced off.

The party rode up the white sand wagon road  which ran

right through Massa Eskridge's plantation. They soon turned off at a log tavern up the road to dine. Akey was dumbstruck. Why had "young George" hurried off rather than spend time in a joyful reunion? Had he received her letter? Had he even read it? Akey was confident that he had. She knew him. Knew him when he was but a boy. Even though "young George" sped off without a greeting, she felt certain he had come to see her in his own way. She wasn't so certain, however, if he had come for the other reason, to act upon her mandate. But why else would he choose to ride the road that passed through Massa Eskridge's Plantation? Akey got to thinking if it was a "sign." She turned to son-in-law William:

"Son, what day is it?"

"Today's Saturday, Mother Akey, and I'm sho' glad, too! You know on Saturdays we only work's till noon, then we's got the rest of the day off, and Sundays too!!"

"So today's Saturday; Frank, what ole' Quamino used to tell us 'bout Saturday?"

"You talkin' 'bout Quamino back in Virginia? That ole' African used to call Saturday "kwamin," said it was the number of the day, or something to that effect," Frank answered.

"It mean "seven" my daddy say," darted in Daniel. "Sometime he would say seven days, sometime he would say seven weeks."

"See now, there was a reason why young George come through here--freed man Snowball got that message to him! He come through here to give us a sign!" Akey exclaimed.

"What sign, mother?" as Jenny and the others all now started inquiring.

Akey stood among them, grappling for an answer to their question. "I reckon it's got something to do with why he choose to ride through here...Saturday...kwamin...seven...We's goin' be free, either seven days more, or seven weeks more! That why he come! Saturday--Kwamin! Jus' like ole' Quamino used to tell us: "Kwamin mean seven." We's goin' get our freedom! Either seven days more, or seven weeks more!"

"Akee! Quit working yuh' self up over them strange

mumbo-jumbo words!" Frank said.  It was hard enough for him to talk English.

"Or seven more *months*," Jenny cautioned.

"Or seven more *years*," Ruth added.

Overhearing, a field hand  pitched in, sarcastically mumbling under his breath, "Or *seventy* years more."

Just then a horse-drawn wagon coming across the fields approached them.  It was Mistress Belle's oldest stepson Massa Samuel, coming to take Akey back to the main house for her last important chore for the day--serving Mistress Belle some of Akey's special-made tea during her scripture reading hour.  "Good morning everyone;  Akey, mother's ready for you now;  Say, you all realize who just passed by on the road?" Massa Samuel asked.

"Why no sir;  You mean those men who just rode by here? Who were they?"  Frank answered as he winked to Akey and Jenny.

"That was President George Washington!  Hurry up Akey! I mean to get up there and get a good look at him before they take off again," Samuel said anxiously.

As Akey later poured her warmed brew into the teacup, there Mistress Belle sat reciting scripture from the book of Jeremiah:  "Behold, I will send and take all the families of the North, saith the LORD...and these Nations shall serve the king of Babylon seventy years.  And it shall come to pass, when seventy years are accomplished, that I will punish the king of Babylon for their iniquity...Babylon hath fallen;  Babylon the Great hath fallen..."


Seven days soon turned into seven weeks.  Then seven months now passed into two years.  On May 9, 1793, Akey and Frank's family busied themselves in the fields preparing the ground, not for tobacco this season, but for a new plant called Cotton.  Massa Samuel was now the sole heir to the plantation since his step-mother Belle had remarried.  He wanted to try a new crop.  Akey didn't mind that one bit--no longer having to fix Belle's tea while sit there and watch Belle get herself all worked up when she read from an old black book, scaring Akey half-to-death with talk about some place called "Babylon" which was going to some day "burn in fire" from some "seven-headed beast."  Akey would listen as Belle would go on and on, especially when the minister, Captain John Thomas of Green County, Georgia, would stop by.  Akey would just shake her head when the minister didn't shed any light either, except to say, "It's a mystery. Only God knows."  But Akey surely didn't mind preparing a daily dose for Samuel and his married sisters, Ladies Elizabeth and Rebecca, who came to visit from time-to-time.

Unbeknown to Akey, however, her daughter Jenny by order of the Probate Court had been bequeathed to Massa Samuel's sister Elizabeth several years back, while the rest of Akey's family and any future increase thereof went to Massa Samuel and his other siblings.  But what mattered to Akey was that her family was together.

Near the end of the field work day, Akey and Jenny noticed the minister, his son, and Lady Elizabeth driving their carriage up to the big house.  Then as the field day ended, a flat-bed horse wagon carrying some type of machinery hauled up off the road.  The drivers then unloaded the wagon over by the barn.  At the same time the county's sheriff showed up.  Soon eighteen year old Massa Richard was now seen driving his wagon across the fields to meet Akey.  Frank approached the wagon.

"The cotton planting real good Massa Richard;   Only got 'bout fo' mo' rows left in this field."

Massa Richard didn't acknowledge a word, seeming oddly aloof.

"Massa, I be there right this minute," Akey said, as she hurried up to the wagon.

"Don't need you today, Akey;  Brother Samuel wants Jenny to come up," Richard said.

"Jenny?  Well, okay then;  She know how to make my tea; Jenny!  Come on a here!"

Jenny scurried up to the wagon, brushing herself off and patting her hair in place.

"Good afternoon Massa Richard," Jenny said.

"Jenny--you climb up here in the back of the wagon;  My

brother Samuel say he need you to do a chore," Richard said.

"Wants *you* to make some of that special tea;  You 'members how to brew it don't you, honey child?"

"Oh I sho' do, Mama;  Can't be nothin' better than to drink some of that strong gumption after a hard day's work, Massa Richard!"

"Well jump on up here then."

"Massa Richard!  When this here cotton get to bustin' open, we sho' 'nuff goin' need one of them new cotton gins that coming out, ain't that right Massa!" William shouted from the field.

Massa Richard's eyes lit up when the word "cotton gin" was mentioned.

"You haven't *seen* one lately, have you William?" Richard asked.

"Why no s..."

"Then keep quiet 'bout it!  We don't need our neighbors all riled up about something we don't yet got;  I here some are *stealing* to get they hands on one!"  Then Massa Richard headed back to the big house while Jenny clung to the wagon.

"I hear this cotton gin can do the work of all us put together;  Could mean us not having to break our backs out here in three more months!" William said.

"That probably mean Massa Samuel ain't gonna buy one," Daniel said.

"The man said to cut that talk about cotton gin or no cotton gin!  We'll find out sure enough;  Now, let's put these tools away and turn in for the day," Frank admonished.

The family now began putting away the buckets, hoes, axes, and wheel-barrow.  As William pulled the harness off the plow-horse, he kept wondering why Massa Richard was so hard on him when mentioning about acquiring a gin.  "What you suppose Massa Richard mean some folks "thieving" to get they hands on a cotton gin?" William whispered to Daniel.

"I ain't got a clue, William;  But his eyes sho' got big when you said it;  But listen here--I seen some men come off the road and headed up here by the barnhouse, carting something mighty heavy in back o' the wagon;  Then they turned around and left."

"Think I'm goin' take a peek and see's if I can find out."

As Frank and Akey reached their cabin door, they heard screams from the side of the big house.  William met them frantically just as they turned the corner.

"They got Jenny!  They got my Jenny!"  William cried out. Akey bolted like a runaway horse past Frank, William, and Daniel, ripping open the back door of the big house so hard she split the wood along the grain.  Her eyes were filled with terror.  Frank was a step behind her, never dreaming that Akey could have outrun him, which all the more impressed upon Frank the grave nature at hand.

"Get out!"  Massa Samuel shouted, as he closed the doors dividing the dining room from the front hall.

"Where my Jenny, Massa?  O' Lawd have mercy please don't hurt my child!"

"Mama!  Help me!  Heeeeeeeelp me!"  Jenny wailed from behind the dividers.

"O my God, what have you done to her Massa!"  Akey cried out, while Frank held tight Akey's shoulders for fear of what she might do.

"I'm afraid Jenny's been sold off;  It was out of my hands."

"You what!!"  Akey lunged, but Frank tightened his grip.

"You just don't understand these things;  Sister Elizabeth had papers on Jenny for a long time;  She and her husband sold Jenny to Minister Thomas;  There's nothing I could have done; Jenny will be taken to Georgia."

"Let me talks to her Massa;  She can sells all of us, not jus' go sell off my baby child and breaks up the family!  Didn't me and Jenny care for you...Massa Richard...and yo' sisters when yo' mama died?  Pleaseeeee Massa...don't I mean something to your daddy's family?  Don't kill me, Massa!  Pleaseeeee, sell us all off!"

"I brought it up, but they only wanted Jenny;  You're too old for them now, Akey.  Minister Thomas gave me his word that Jenny will be in good hands, so stop your fretting and carrying on!"  Samuel said impatiently.  Frank heard that and almost decided to go after Samuel, before reminding himself of the consequences if he struck him.

"Massa, please! please! Tell 'em you jus' can't do it! Tell 'em you jus' don't approve! They'll listen to your word, Massa...spare my child...I'll do anything!...I's your servant 'till death!!" Akey pleaded.

"I'm through talking, woman! Don't make this harder than it is!" Samuel said irritably.

Then a shot rang out.

"Get back, Nigga!" the sheriff yelled holding his smoking pistol in the air. William was trying to block the sheriff from pulling shackled Jenny into his wagon.

Minister Thomas, his son, and Lady Elizabeth all sat in their carriage, a safe distance from the drama.

Massa Samuel, Frank, and Akey reached the scene.

"Mamaaaaaaaa! Pleaseeeeeee come get me! Don't let them take meeeeeeee! I love youuuuuu! I love you Mamaaaaaaa!"

William and Frank were going crazy trying to quickly think of a way to outwit the sheriff. William picked up a stick and slowly began approaching the sheriff on one side. Frank cautiously moved each of his steps toward the sheriff's other side.

"Stay back! Don't make me say it again!" shouted the sheriff as he cocked the trigger and began waving the gun back and forth at them. William and Frank struggled with the command before they painfully backed away. Akey began flaying her arms in abhorrence at Minister Thomas' carriage while sobbing profusely.

"Why? Why?! Where is your God of mercy? I beg you, please spare my daughter, or take all my family kin with you! Don't your God curse this? Don't he?!" Akey shouted scornfully, while on her knees. The sheriff finally locked Jenny into the wagon cart, then snapped the reigns of the horse violently as he knew this was the most dangerous moment of his mission. The minister's carriage was also making a speedy getaway. William seized a stone and ran after the sheriff's wagon, hurling the rock straight into the sheriff's back. William spotted another jagged rock. Dazed and ducking, the sheriff twisted around from his seat and fired a shot at William. He dove and took cover. William attempted to keep up his running pace after Jenny. But in a quick matter of time she had rode out of view.

When Frank and Daniel reached him, William refused help to get back to his feet. He just laid on the ground with his head buried in the dust. Akey was doing the same thing, as Ruth, Barbe, and Rose tried to console her and themselves.

Jenny had given her all, all of her sweat, suck, and soul for her dead massa's family all those faithful years. Massa Samuel, whom Jenny looked after often during the wagon trip from Virginia to Carolina and even when his own mammy died, had in fact signed his name as a witness in approval of the bill of sale. Akey nearly died that night, had not it been for Frank. He once again tried to extend hope to a pierced spirit just as he had done when he first layed eyes on Akey when they were both young back at Sandy Point. But this time it was much harder, for even he had loyally stuck to his notion that the family would soon be free. Now it had come to this.

A year passed. Now Barbe was married, to a man named Charles. Another year. Rose now found a husband. Yet another year. Frank fell ill one morning and could not rise out of bed. Akey made some kind of medicine tea for him from apple tree bark, a substitute for the powerful Akee berries she had left behind in Virginia. She had heard that slaves were growing the fruit tree in the West Indies and down along the coast at some place called "Spanish Florida," but she had no means of getting there, not at her age. Akey also had Frank eat some "African garlic" which the medicine woman supplied her with. It proved effective on Frank for a time. But eventually Frank dropped into a deep sleep and never woke up. Now he was finally freed of his chains.

On the day of his burial the dry autumn wind whistled through the red and gold foilage on the trees surrounding the graveyard back behind the servant cabins. As two servants, Ralph and Solomon, shoveled the piles of dirt onto the oblong oak coffin assembled by a servant called Carpenter, Rose turned to her grandmother Akey and proudly exclaimed, "Grandpapa was from Jamaica, wasn't he," remembering he was born there. But Akey just looked up at the sky and then uttered back: "He from *Africa*...yep...that where he from...from's Africa!"

Six months later brought in 1796.  Akey's body at the age of eighty-one had begun to wear out.  Jenny, who had been sold and sent to a family in Georgia, had begged to be hired out around Ninety-Six District, South Carolina so she could again rekindle what was left of her family.  Upon learning of Akey's condition, Captain Thomas, being both a devout baptist minister of his own church and slaveholder of thirteen of his own slaves, obliged and hired out Jenny to Massa's Samuel and Richard's sister Lady Rebecca.  When Lady Rebecca brought Jenny immediately to Eskridge Plantation, Jenny was embraced by William and their three daughters, who then quickly brought her to Akey's cabin where she lay on her old bed and covered with a quilt.  Jenny probed to get a reading on the possible cause of Akey's condition, which was probably anything by now, as she was soon told by her daughters about days when they were too tired to tend to Grandmother Akey, too tired because of being overworked in the fields.  Jenny quickly got to work, trying all the remedies she had learned from her mother, even combining a tea drink mixture of apple tree bark with the Juniper tree, but nothing could reverse nature's course.

The following week, that dreadful day came.  Akey, in her melodious Afrique accent, made an effort to speak despite her breathing difficulty, requesting Jenny's family to all gather round.  Everyone sensed that Akey was slowly slipping away.  The only question was whether Akey knew it too.

Akey looked confused as she rolled her eyes at the blurry figures standing around her.        "What day is it?    Jenny!  What day is it?" Akey asked.

"It's Sunday, Mama;   Sunday morning," Jenny answered back.

"What's it like outside?  Is it sunny today?" Akey asked, straining to make comprehension of her world that was shrinking smaller each second.  William lifted the board-cover off the window frame and Jenny peered out.  The skies were dark and cloudy. "It's a beautiful sun out Mama," Jenny said.

"Then *git* my shoulder knit," Akey said. "I's going out for a little while...tell your sister Rachel and my grandson Prero I be back 'fore long." Jenny looked at William. Both knew Akey was indeed "leaving." Akey went on in her sickbed monologue, and talking as if she was heading to a family picnic. "Tell Nadi, Bieju Mennah, and Di Bina I will see them on the shore down at the Great River...tell them to bring Grandbieju too, Grandbieju Sensobo...tell 'em to come down the mighty Cavella, it's a mighty powerful river! You'll see it for yourself when you git's there; Now, don't forget to go, and make's sho you bring's yo' children and yo' children's children...I want's them to see where we grew up...how we used to run and play in the forests, used to climb the trees and pick the fruit...that there where my name come from-- "the fruit that saved my father when but a baby and helped give birth to my mother's mother;" Promise you'll go see's them, you and your family."

"Yes, Mama, we'll go, one day we'll go."

Then Akey began to hum an old song she used to recite to her children when they were knee young:
"Someone would like to have you for her child,
But you are my own.
Someone wished she had you to nurse you on a good mat,
But I have you to rear on a sheep blanket.
Dju, dju, leave off crying, poverty!
You have surpassed me in crying.
Even if it is the rain which rains, I put away the tree, I shall call my dju.
And even if it is the Worabanh warrior chief and his sedibo, I put away the tree.
I shall call you, I shall lull to sleep on my arm.
Someone wished you were hers, she would put you on a tiger blanket,
But you are my own, I have you to rear on a torn mat."

Akey concluded, wearing a relaxed smile on her face.

"Mama, take some more tea I'm gonna pour you," as Jenny dipped her ladle into the kettle and tested a sip.

"This tea done got lukewarm! Billy! The fire's almost out! I told you to keep the fire going!"

"But it's hot outside Mama, why we need more fire?," Billy cried.

"What did I tell you?   Boy, if you don't get...," Jenny grabbed her switch.

"I'll help him Mrs. Jenny," Daniel said, not wishing to see young William be disciplined at a time such as this.   But by the time young Billy had gotten his mother's tea warmed up and Jenny had brought it over, Akey was gone.   The relaxed smile still on her face.

In time, George Washington was no longer President.   He may have allowed an African girl to freely speak with him fifty years ago, but his actions as President did not include freeing that African girl's people.     It would be decades before Akey's descendants  would receive their overdue citizenship.

August 3, 1810.   It had been ten years since the oldest son of the late Burdett Eskridge, Samuel, had left Edgefield County and moved to Tennessee, purchasing there a two hundred acre plantation in an area called Buck Creek, near the Clinch River.   On this day, Burdett's other son Richard received a letter in Abbeville from his brother Samuel.    Together they were now operating two plantations, one in Tennessee and the other in South Carolina.   As more land had now become available near Buck Creek, Samuel wanted his brother to have first chance at it:

Dear Brother

Harvest is going fine.   The cotton gin is still working good since we bought it.   Now can use half the negroes we used before. The others are now being used to start new fields.   Some I hired out.    230 acres are now for sale in Buck Creek.   The land looks very fertile and should produce good for next year.   When you come up you can see it for yourself.   The owner is Mr. Clark.    If we want it I think we should make an offer soon.   Bring Ruth &

Barbe and their husbands, Daniel & Charles.

If the harvest here is finished in time, should get a better return this time in Nashville

Samuel E.

Next month Massa Richard arrived in Roane County, Tennessee to inspect the fertility of the land that his brother kept encouraging him to purchase.  Thirty-seven year old Ruth, same year old mate Daniel, thirty-four year old Barbe, and four years younger mate Charles were brought along.  Eventually a deal was struck to acquire the acreage for four-hundred dollars.  Massa Richard returned to Abbeville.  But Ruth, Barbe, and their husbands did not return with him.

By 1820 Massa Eskridge decided to sell off his South Carolina fields and move to the plantation in Tennessee.  Jenny and her remaining family would be uprooted.  Forty-one year old Rose was married to a forty-two year old husband named Jennings.  She bore him a daughter named Lucy some time back and was soon ready to have another.  Thirty-six year old William was now married to a young sixteen year old named Elizabeth who was carrying child, too.  Sadly, Jenny's husband William would not accompany his family.  He too, had been freed of his chains, following the path of Frank and Akey.

Massa Richard now wrote to his brother Samuel:

Brother,

We will leave on July 5th;  should arrive by the end of the month.  I will stop to see our dear cousins in Spartenburg and Shelby for a week or two.  Will give them all your greetings.  The family are all eager to go, although son Taliaferro is planning on remaining here.  He says to tell you he will come see you soon, hopefully with a new bride  Will see Sister before we leave.  The negroes are still loading  Horses and wagons are ready except for one Jennings is repairing.  Grandfather Grigsby & Mr.

Livingston have agreed to buy the chattels on the land.  Negro women Elizabeth & Rose are due with child anytime soon.  If you hear from Uncle John in Virginia ask him about Frederick and esp. China;  boy Brisborn is worried sick about her

Bid you farewell
R. Eskridge

Just as Jenny and her family prepared to leave, Rose went into labor.  Within moments a child was born.  While clutching her infant, a son, everyone departed the plantation and proceeded toward the slave graveyard.  As the wagons passed the graves of William, Frank, and Akey, Jenny recited the words that her mother had many times spoken to her: "Your name is Akey, the fruit tree that saved your father when but a baby, and helped give birth to your mother's mother, your father was Mennah, son of Sensobo of the village Zwedru, and your father's brother was called Botswain, a skilled boatman of the Kru."  Jennings and Rose decided to name their son George Washington Eskridge.

That July of 1820, seventy-three year old Jenny and her family entered Rutherford County, North Carolina and headed to Massa Richard's cousin's home in the town of Shelby.  Upon arriving, two servants escorted Massa Richard's family into his cousin's home.  As for Jenny's family, they were directed by the house servants to the hay loft barn.  Toward the end of the week's stay Elizabeth began clenching her fists in pain.  "Mama!" Elizabeth cried out to mother-in-law Jenny, "My baby's coming!" Quickly two slave women belonging to Massa Richard's cousin, Hannah and Phyllis, rushed to Elizabeth's aid.  Her husband William began to show signs of worry.  "Is my Liz goin' be alright?" he asked the midwives.  The two women just looked at him and stared, not saying a word, then quickly turned their attention back to the young girl as Jennings grabbed William and led him away.  Elizabeth's screams and contractions grew more intense, causing Jenny to ask the women if they had in their possession any wild yams or checkerberries to ease the pain.  The woman Phyllis hurriedly ran to procure the items.  From five o'clock  that afternoon on, Elizabeth wrestled with the life inside her, a life that had no idea what world awaited.

Finally around ten o'clock that evening William and Jennings could hear a baby's cries.  Jenny came out to William saying, "What you standing out here for?  Don't a father want to greet his son?"  William nervously made his way to the barn, not quite knowing what to expect.  The word "Father" had not yet sunk in.  They later settled upon a name for the child, William Burgess, named after Williamsburg, the place where William's father and his father before him, George, had practically been raised while transporting the sons and grandsons of Colonel Eskridge by carriage from Fairfax to the Virginia House sessions.

The clan departed Shelby with their newest addition to the family.  They finally reached the public road at Abingdon, Virginia which would guide their rickety wagons past Knoxville and on into Roane County.  The combined labor on the Buck Creek plantation was now posed for a profit-making venture, ready to produce its bulging bales of white cotton and bushel baskets of corn and wheat along with its 75 head of cattle, hogs, and sheep.  Work was hard on the twenty-eight persons who found themselves tied to the creek.  At their disposal was one harrow, three two-horse plows, one four-horse wagon, two oxen, a set of blacksmith tools, 14 hoes, a cart, and one cotton gin.  Daniel, who sometimes could barely sleep soundly due to the night heat and the loud sound of the locusts, was assigned the duty of getting out the collars, bridles, harnesses, hames, and traces for the plow horses.  Charles saw to it that the cotton was tightly fitted in the jute bags before loaded up for market.  Jennings had worked his way up to working in the meat slaughterhouse, earning him the nickname, "Butcher Jennings."  And muscle-armed William had proven himself the qualifications of blacksmith, not wishing to be a coachman for life like his father Will and grandfather George.  Their house furnishings consisted of nine beds and bedstands: one bed for each of the nine comprised families;  one cupboard, three tables, and 14 chairs.  The one kitchen in the central slave cookhouse revealed a fireplace with tongs and andirons, two ovens, frying pans, kettles, pots, a skillet, and cooking wood of walnut and cherry plank.

Jenny was relegated to being the cook along with two younger women.  The meager meals were served right on time each morning and evening, but in no way were they filling. Constant word secretly made it to the cooks from hungry souls requesting an extra handout to be stashed away in some hidden location.  "Brisborn and Margaret's daughter in need of somethin' tonite, hunger eatin' up her tummy," or "A biscuit for Israel? Someone stole his meal."  Jenny would make certain that none of "hers" went hungry.   Jenny secretly hid food in a dugout hole lined with pieces of broken brick from the kitchen fireplace. Being one of the cooks did have its advantages.

If there was one more advantage Jenny wished could be added, it would have been to carve up ole' Massa's game turkey that proudly prounced around parading itself on the plantation with its unnatural tendency of going about knocking down the small children.

"One of these days I's goin' kill that turkey...I see how it comes up and hurts the gran'children," Jenny threatened.

"Not if I kill it 'fore you do, which I'm 'bout ready to do if that turkey knock my babies down again!" Rose cried.

"Ya'll had better not touch that there bird!" warned Rose's husband Jennings. "You'll have Massa Eskridge all over us if he find out someone carved up his bird...besides, I ain't got the potatoes and the drippings ready yet!"   All three busted out laughing.

Work started at sunrise, except for sundays, and ended at sundown.  To quench their thirst, Jenny's clan bent down to cup water in their hands from the horse hoof holes that were filled by occasional early morning downpours.  There was so much work to be performed, some feigned illness to escape one or perhaps two days.  The voice of the overseer never stopped, not unless he had left for Kingston or Nashville to sell the cotton bales or buy some commodities.  "Get up !"  "You can't sit on the bucket and draw water at the same time"..."Keep picking out there...crows and corn don't grow together !!"  But the families never had any real threats from the overseer, Mr. Casey.  Except, that is, unless someone was sold.    Then Mr. Casey had to break the news and assist in "completing" the transaction.

But for the most part, seven of the original nine families stayed intact.  Some of them even could trace their family lines all the way back to the ancestors at Sandy Point. Of course, most of the families at Buck Creek were descendants of the Africans at Sandy Point anyway, whether they could orally recite their family lines or not.  There was Margaret, whose ancestor was the African Mingo.  Brisborn, a strong healthy young man, descended from Quamino on his father's side, Daniel, and from Akey on his mother's side, Ruth. There was Julia Ann, whose great-grandfather Cumey had worked on Colonel Eskridge's plantation in Prince William County.    And, of course, old woman Jenny's parents were Frank and  Akey, and her great-uncle  Bodebe, who used to call himself Botswain.

Jenny watched as her family grew.  Barbe and Charles had four children still alive: Henry, Polk, Letha, and Savannah.  Ruth and Daniel also had children:  Brisborn, Frederick, Joseph, George, and Caroline.    William and Elizabeth's living children were William  Burgess and Lindsey.    Finally, Rose and Butcher Jennings' surviving offspring were Lucy, George, Lewis, Roberta Fanny, and China Clementine.  In time a seventh and final child was born, despite Rose being in her forty-ninth year.

*In the year 1829, in the fifth month, in the first year of Andrew Jackson, President of the twenty-three states,  the woman Rose was heavy in child, near Buck Creek by the Clinch River.  In the fifth month, on the 26th day of the month, Rose gave birth to a female child, and named her Eliza.*

In 1830 a treaty between the United States Government and the Mississippi Choctaw was signed, ceding thousands of acres of land east of the Mississippi.  Land speculators and settlers were in a frenzy during this "cotton boom" as Indian lands in Alabama had already been ceded to the Federal Government.  Massa Richard's son Taliaferro and his new bride Sophia had moved there along with other siblings.

In 1832 the Chickasaw Nation in Mississippi ceded all of their lands to the United States as part of another treaty before they were removed along with the Choctaw to Oklahoma Territory. Settlers rushed to stake their claims. "Cotton King" would not be denied as long as new lands could be conquered and fresh black slaves could be supplied. The government's land office at Chocchuma sold a steady stream of land deeds. Even Tennessee House Representative James K. Polk could not resist such an opportunity, and purchased tracts of Chickasaw land through a brother-in-law. Massa Richard and brother Massa Samuel no doubt saw another partnership opportunity presenting itself. After conferring with a land agent, Massa Richard decided he would examine a certain tract of land in former Choctaw Country (now annexed and formed into Carroll County, Mississippi).

Through land grants, three to four hundred acres were purchased in an area called by the Native Indians "Duck Hill," once the homeland of Choctaw Chief Duck. Returning to Tennessee, Massa Richard informed brother Samuel of his purchase. They sat down to consider a timetable for the move. It was agreed that Massa Richard would take besides his share of supplies and animal stock, twenty slaves from their sixty-five. Instructions were given to the overseer.

One day in the first week of March 1834 when Charles and Daniel saw the two brothers and the overseer counting the cattle and horses. They wondered why and went to report this to William and Butcher Jennings. Later when they noticed the three men now inspecting the wagons and farming tools, the rumors started to fly. When the brothers conducted a census on all sixty-five of their labor camp but "physically examined" mainly the men and boys, everyone knew something terrible was about to happen.

Charles bent down to cup some water. As he turned his head, overseer Casey was standing over him. "Stand up! Put your hands out! Show your feet!" Marking his census tally sheet, the overseer carefully examined Charles from head to toe to determine if he was still in workable fit condition. The overseer turned his attention to fifty-year old tip-top shape William and repeated the same physical routine, then in turn to Daniel, then Henry, then Polk, then George Washington, then Lindsey, Aaron, Brisborn, Solomon, Israel, Ralph, Alex, Carpenter, William Burgess, fifty-six and sharp-as-a-knife Butcher Jennings, and several other males, both men and boys, including even some hired hands that Massa Richard had purchased and brought up from Alabama. Butcher Jennings turned to William, "You ain't gawn like what I'm about to say, but I think we's fixin' to be sold!"

Later that week the two brothers gathered them all together and broke the news, reading off the names of those chosen to go. That evening under a gloomy moon, the sobs of wives, mothers, and children could be heard on Buck Creek.

All four families that were kin to old Jenny were affected. Barbe's husband Charles would go. Daniel, the husband of Ruth, would be snatched along. Rose and Elizabeth would both lose some of their own: Rose's Butcher Jennings and son George; Elizabeth's William and son Lindsey. Fourteen other persons received the same fate.

The four men Charles, Daniel, Butcher Jennings, and William tried as best they could to remain cheerful. Their reasoning at that moment was all in unison: better to go and hope to be in time reunited, than to risk escaping and being caught by the dogs. Not that they were not justified. They had full right, unalienable rights from their Creator, to walk off from the plantation with their families and never return again. However, they understood the proverbial wisdom of "A time to uproot, but a time to plant, a time to break apart, but a time to rebuild, a time to throw stones away, but a time to bring stones together." They had all come this far together. "We will never forget the way back home," was collectively said among them. Besides, if they were to run away then four more men would be taken from loved ones and put in their place.

The next morning the party was ready to depart. The women Barbe, Ruth, Rose, and Elizabeth along with the children embraced their men tightly, not wanting to let go. Butcher Jennings bent down to five year Eliza.

"Baby, you be good...papa going away for alittle while."

"Where to Papa?"

"Baby, let me put it like this here: I know where I going, jus' don't know where I headed."

"But where you going Papa?  Where at?  When you comin' home?" Eliza kept asking.  Then she started to cry when catching the grim look on Rose's face.

"Take this babychild!" Butcher Jennings yelled to Rose, his anger due only to the emotion.  "I swear I'll see that girl's wedding day, Rose!  I'll live to see it, I swears it!!" He kissed daughter Lucy and told her to take care of his mother.  William now looked at fourteen year Billy Burgess.  "Help your mama look after Grandma, son."  He added, "Always remember this son and never forget it...there ain't no difference between the big house and the cabin; You got the same mind as them, ain't that right?"

"Yes, Papa."

Finally, old Jenny went up to each of the four men and kissed them.  She stepped back and started shouting to them, repeating over and over in her old vernacular *"Sedibo Nyimeyu !"*

Soon the voice of the overseer could be heard as the four men headed to the wagons.  As they cleared the bend on the curving wagon road, the four were fighting back the tears as they still could hear the shouting of old Jenny.  Then they were gone.

# CHAPTER TEN

## The Africans at Sandy Point

As I waded through Virginia house burgess Samuel Eskridge's estate probate papers dated 1747, the most important page was the inventory list of his slaves. I hoped a child's name was recorded, a slave child born that very year of the house burgess' death. According to the estate appraisers the child at birth was named Jane. She was listed as being alive on soldier Burdett Eskridge's Edgefield County estate in 1782. If I could match Jane's name on both estates, then I could link together two whole slave generations. I couldn't believe that these documents still existed. My God! African Americans who were searching into their family roots could also locate estate probate files containing their slave generations too. As I sat eager to extract and interpret the listed slave names, I couldn't find "Jane." She wasn't listed.

Even though I didn't see a child named Jane listed with the slave names on the 1747 inventory, I still felt deep down inside that she was definitely connected to those names, and the start of a next generation. Her name was no more a coincidence then her birth being the same year as the death of her soldier master's father. Who were Jane's parents?

At least I understood where my family names of Louis, Eliza, George, Tom, Hannah, and Jennings had originated. And by examining colonial Virginia's seat for the General Assembly, Williamsburg, I could see where "William Burgess" Eskridge's name probably sprang. Where did Samuel Eskridge of Virginia get his slaves? The downtown Portland library's index for wills and administrations for Virginia showed that his father, George

Eskridge of Westmoreland County, had a recorded will in 1735. I sat down to type another inquiry, then sent it off. At the library was also a "List of tithables for Westmoreland County, 1776" in where I found the name of Samuel Eskridge's widow, Jane Eskridge, the grandmother of soldier Burdett's sons Samuel and Richard. Seven slaves were tithed:

"Jane Eskridge Tithables, 1776
           Gyles, Moses, Rachel, Prue, Mimy, Merear, Sue"

I noticed the names Prue & Mimy sounded almost Spanish, African, or West Indian. If any of them were still living when Jane Eskridge died in 1781, they also would have been divided and sent to heir sons and daughters.

The year 1997 started out as a traumatic year for my family in Portland, directly affecting my mother's side of the family. In January, Grandmother Shelton passed away. She suffered a stroke two months before, and never did regain her full strength. She was truly the anchor of the family, always there to give words of advice or comfort to any of us who needed it. When she silently went to sleep for the last time several hours after New Year's Day, I cherished even more the oral recollections she shared about her lineage, which I had preserved on a taped recording. Grandmother Shelton's stories and names might lend itself to another book someday, especially upon one researching the archives of Tibbee Creek, Mississippi and the voices of Erie, Alabama.

Actually, the last four years had been traumatic, losing one uncle and two aunts, who were my mother's sister and brother Bill McCoy, and his wife, my aunt Gladys. All of them were so special, each bringing to the family their gifts, talents, and heritage, blazing deep trails and opening wide the doors of opportunity.

My position at the bank was also put in question when a "friendly takeover" was announced, resulting in department closures and employee layoffs. Fortunately I was able to stay on. But the news was still unsettling. Of course, I still had my hands full operating my genealogy service and answering requests, which by now had expanded into locating missing persons. In August on a Saturday night, as one of my brothers rode the bus home after finishing his work at a downtown giftstore, a local street gang member pulled out a gun on the bus and shot a young man in the head, killing him instantly. My brother was only a few feet away from the victim. The shooter then shouted for the bus driver to open the rear door, then jumped out and ran. In the confusion, the busdriver somehow lost control and hit a utility pole. My brother was obviously shaken but okay. When my brother and I got together the next day to talk about it, we realized how much times had changed since we were young growing up. When we were kids, a fistfight sufficed, what we used to call "fistacuffs." And a swithblade knife was pushing it. Today, it's been replaced with a gun.

I had a similiar experience. One day a group of teenagers showed up to play basketball on a grade school playground. All of a sudden, as the teens were shooting baskets, a car spun past firing shots aimed their way, hitting one of them in the leg. Here I found myself in the middle of a gangster shootout. Inside a classroom, I immediately dropped to the floor as I heard and felt the loud reverberation of the shots, and peeking out a window I noticed the wounded teen pulling out a gun from his jacket and giving it to his buddy, who hid it behind the building I was in.

Soon the ambulance, police, and a TV news station all arrived at the playground, interviewing witnesses including myself. These shooting battles, or "drive-by's," would almost always escalate into vengeful retaliations. One of our close childhood friends was shot from a speeding car while riding his bicycle. He was treated at the hospital and released. Too bad the frequently heard shots during the night didn't end. As my brother and I talked, we agreed that the angry increase of violence across all racial lines among certain segments of today's youth was significant, a sign that society was getting worse. I'm still longing for that Bible promise of a new world, a new brotherhood, where class distinction, genocide, and fratricide will forever cease to exist. You dig?

My attention now shifted back to the old world. A copy of the last will of Colonel George Eskridge finally arrived in the mail.

According to his biographical sketch George Eskridge, Ms. C. Swanson's fifth great-grandfather, was born in Lancaster, England, and took an interest in law as a young man. One day he was taken and pressed into service upon a ship to be brought to the Colony of Virginia, where he was sold to a planter as an indentured servant for a term of eight years. During his eight year term, he was not allowed communication with friends at home and was treated very harshly, made to sleep on the fireplace hearth in the kitchen. On the day that his term expired, his master found him tearing up the stones of the hearth with a mattock. When asked what he was doing, George Eskridge replied that a guest's bed was always customarily pulled to pieces upon their departure, and so he was doing likewise, throwing down his mattock as he walked out of his former master's house. He then went back to England, completed his law studies, and returned to Virginia, residing at Cherry Neck. He later settled in Sandy Point, Westmoreland County, became an attorney, and was elected to the House of Burgesses. He also held, among many other positions, the title of Tobacco Agent for Northumberland and Westmoreland counties.

George Eskridge married Rebecca Bonum and had six children--William, George, Robert, Samuel, Margaret, and Sarah, who was born in 1708. His second marriage in 1715 was to Elizabeth Vaulx Craddock. They had a daughter, Elizabeth. Colonel George Eskridge died in November 1735, and his second wife Elizabeth Eskridge, in 1744.

His will began:

In the name of God I George Eskridge of the county of Westmoreland do make this my Last Will and Testament. Imprimis I give unto my son Samuel and his heirs forever the house and plantation where I now live containing eight Hundred Acres be the same more or less bounding upon the lands of John Crucher and Robert Ball....Item I give to my Loving wife the aforesaid house and plantation and Lands before given to my son Samuel during her natural life-also I give to my said wife all the slaves she brought to me in marriage with their increase and ten other of my slaves during her natural life...**I give unto the four**

**sons** of my son George deceased **four slaves apiece** when they respectively arrive at the age of twenty-one years. I give unto my Daughter Elizabeth and her heirs a tract of land I have at Polrick in Prince William County and all the slaves and stock upon the same. I give to my aforesaid son Samuel and his heirs five hundred acres of land part of a tract at a place called Flatlick in Prince William County... I give to my son Samuel **ten negroes**, to my son Robert **sixteen negroes**....**I give five of the ten slaves** hereinbefore given to my wife during her life unto my Daughter Elizabeth, **the other five** I give unto my son Samuel. I give to my son William and the heirs of his body **ten slaves**....It is the will that my loving wife have the use of all my household stuff during her life and also the use of half of the cattle, hogs and horses upon my several plantations in Westmoreland County during her life. All the rest of my estates after my debts paid I give to be equally divided amongst my children now living....I do hereby revoke all former wills by me made and declare this to be my last will. In witness whereof I have hereunto set my hand this 27th day of October, 1735. I do appoint my sons Samuel and Robert and my good friend Capt. George Turberville executors of this my will.

Signed   George Eskridge

In all, a reference to sixty-two slaves in mentioning. George Eskridge's son Samuel was bequeathed fifteen. Where did George Eskridge obtain his slaves? Did they come directly from Africa? I started making my travel plans to now my fifth state-- Virginia--to continue my family search at the Library of Virginia in Richmond.

 One of the things I hoped to find at the Archives in Virginia would be a record of a slave ship leaving Africa and landing in Westmoreland County showing a purchase of Africans by George Eskridge. That would be like finding gold and would make my roundtrip bus travel all worth it. I took off in October, stopping on the way to see Cousin Mrytle who was now living in a care center.

 My bus arrived in Richmond. I was at the Library of

Virginia that morning. I looked at my notes. The first thing written down was to check the years 1700-1735 for possible land deeds in "Westmoreland, Northumberland, Prince William, Elizabeth City, James City, Richmond, Hampton, and Williamsburg." I wanted to check these counties and cities because these were along the James and Rappanhanock River channels where ships would sail up from the Chesapeake Bay carrying their slave cargos for unloading. But in checking the deeds index for these areas, George Eskridge's name pointed me only to Westmoreland, where he had twenty-four deeds beginning in 1698 and ending in 1727, and only one of those involving slaves. This was a 1727 deed from Augustine and Jane Washington to George Eskridge for nine slaves:

THIS INDENTURE made the one and thirtyeth day of May in the thirteenth year of the Reign of our Sovereign Lord George by the grace of God of Great [Britain] France & Ireland, King, Defender of the faith &c; Anno Dom: one thousand seven hundred twenty and seven:
....Witnesseth that AUGUSTIN WASHINGTON and JANE his wife as well in consideration of the sum of Five shillings of lawfull money of Great Britain to them in hand paid by...GEORGE ESKRIDGE....do give sell & confirm unto said... GEORGE ESKRIDGE and their heirs all the herein mentioned Negroes....to wit, Moll, Lawrence, Frank, Bess, Bett, Nan, Guss, Priscila, and little Sarah...the Negro woman named Moll and her
increase wch: is one Negro boy named Lawrence, & one Negro girl named Frank, with all their increase to be for the use of LAWRENCE WASHINGTON, Eldest Son of AUGUSTIN WASHINGTON & JANE his wife....and for want of such heires to AUGUSTIN WASHINGTON JUNR; Son of said AUGUSTIN & JANE....And the aforementioned Negro Woman named Bess and her increase which is and Negro girl named Bett  one Negro girl named Nan  one Negro boy named Guss and Negro girl named Priscilla together with one other Negro girl named Little Sarah, with all their increase to be for the proper use of AUGUSTINE WASHINGTON JUNR....And on default of such heires to

LAWRENCE...."

Augustine and Jane Washington had made another deed to George Eskridge on February 23, 1726  conveying two parcels of land situated between Popes Creek and Bridge Creek, a two hundred acre tract of land situated in Appomattox Neck, and a one hundred seventy acre tract of land in an area called the Ridge, to be for the proper use of Augustine and Jane Washington during their life and after their decease to the use of their sons Augustine Jr. and Lawrence.  Seemingly, Augustine Washington and his wife were showing notable confidence in that their family investments were secure while in the legal hands of counsel attorney Eskridge.

I looked up at the clock.  It was 3p.m.  The library would be closing in two more hours.  I had so many things I wanted to check on my list during the two days I had planned to be here-- newspapers, baptismal records of slaves, death certificates, cemetary records, and more.  Realizing that wasn't going to happen on this day, I at least needed to try and locate George Eskridge's estate inventory and also the Virginia slave ship records, or at least get started.  Locating the microfilm reel for Westmoreland County Inventories I turned to page 159  and there, about three pages long, was his estate inventory taken on February 3, 1736, listing every possible possession from furniture and law books, to cooking utensils, farm tools, and slaves:

*Negroes*
*Quamino, Jack, Jenny, Tom, Sambo, Porter, Caesar, Sam, Pompay, Jack King, Patrick,*
*Young Jenny, Adam, Judy, Dina, Maney, Sarah, Congo Judy, Akey, Rose, Jenny & her child-Mandy, Babby 12 years old, Triss, Robin 4 years old, Samson 5 years old, Will, Beck the house-servant, Hannah the house servant, Murrea, Old Betty, Tom 5 years, Billy 2 years, Lettice 3- years, Willoby 1 year, Danl 1 year*

*Taffy, Botswain, Mingo, Tom, Willy & her child Will, Peg, Phyllis & her child Jenny, Dina, Quamino, Tom Tinker, Mogull,*

*Dick, Jenny*
*These 15 lost to Dr. Robt. Eskridge*

*Jack, Adam, Rose & her child Winny*
*The above 4 lost to Mr. Saml. Eskridge*

*At Musos Quarter Negroes*
*Frank, Will, Peg, Sarah, Ned 4 years, Tom 1 year*
*These above slaves to Mr. S Eskridge*

Another inventory was also recorded in Prince William County listing six more negro slaves:
*Negro boy named Will, Negro woman named Sue, Negro boy named Sambo, Negro woman named Binah, Negro man named Cumey, Negro man named Dick*

Sixty seven human beings! Men, women, & children, these definitely were families. All of the slaves at the Sandy Point estate had appraised values written next to their names. And only the ages of the children were listed. Samuel Eskridge already had eleven slaves picked out for himself: Murrea, Jack, Adam, Will, Peg, Sarah, four year old Ned, one year old Tom, Rose and her child Winny, and surprisingly, a slave named Frank. I noted too, that some of the names sounded African or African influenced-- Quamino, Congo Judy, Akey, Taffy, Botswain, Mingo, Sambo, Binah, Cumey.

I couldn't believe it. After eight years of searching, here I had now finally uncovered African names! I could almost taste the discovery of my African lineage. I kept staring at each name, imagining which one of them might be my ancestor, which one paved the way for my own birth. I began to realize that the deeper one went back in the documents of slavery, the more likely one would find the recording of Africans by their birth names. I had plowed deep into the 1700's. And the fact that African names were recorded on the colonel's estate told me these probably were *fresh* Africans from the motherland, because their birth names hadn't yet been anglicized. If it had taken me this long to get this far, I knew full well someone else could certainly do their search much better in half the time. And I hope others will.

What also caught my attention was the very first name listed--Quamino. Did his name being listed first indicate a position of importance among the slave group? Was he someone perhaps highly respected by the group due to his age, responsiblity, or to even some African tribal rank? I also wondered if these names could help identify their country of origin.

Next I looked up the references the librarian had referred me to regarding Virginia slave ship records--naval office shipping lists which were taken by clerks appointed by the Virginia Colony Governor to enforce England's trade laws. After taken, the shipping lists were sent to the Virginia Colony Governor, who in turn sent them to England to eventually be filed in the Public Record Office at London. From 1698 to the time of the American Revolution, Virginia had six naval districts: Lower James/Hampton, Upper James, York, Rappahannock, South Potomac, and Accomack. Here was catalogued year-by-year from 1698-1775 vital information such as the owner of the ship, when the ship was built, the date of entry into a Virginia port, name of port, name of vessel, name of the ship master, number of Africans, and where they were from. Slave ships were recorded from all over the West Coast of Africa and from the West Indies into the Virginia colony. For example, on July 9, 1772 the vessel *Nancy* brought into James Port "250 negroes" from the Windward & Gold Coasts. The brig *Bassa* sailed into Hampton Port from Guinea on July 31, 1766 with "108 negroes." On July 4, 1737 the ship *Brice* came into the Port of York with "409 negroes" from Angola.

The Gold Coast, the area which today represents Ghana, was so named because gold was found there. Here many castles were built by the Portuguese, the Spanish, and the Dutch. Next to this area was the Ivory Coast, now called Cote d' Ivoire. It became known for its elephant tusks which, like gold, was sought after. Going further west came the Grain Coast, later becoming Liberia, also called the "Pepper Coast" referring to the grains from the Meleguetta plant. During the 17th and 18th centuries merchant ships came to trade for this "guinea pepper" or "Ethiopian pepper" which during that time was very valuable as it was believed to prevent dysentery during the long voyages on board ship. Among the slave "factories" along this stretch of coastland was Trade Town, and Cape Mount, where slaves were brought in as far away as Timbuktu in Mali. In 1562 the trader John Hawkins accompanied by Francis Drake took three cargoes of slaves from the area for the West Indies. Next to the Grain Coast came the WindWard Coast, now called Sierra Leone, however, in the days of the slave trade the term "WindWard Coast" was understood to include both the Grain & Ivory Coasts as well. Guinea referred to a region extending from Senegal to the Congo, as well as the actual name of the country. Angola, also along the west coast, lies between former Zaire and Namibia. The African tribes along the coast were also involved in the slave trade.

African slaves were then brought to the West Indies and the Americas. Indentured servants were brought in too. The Westmoreland County Court on September 27, 1704 had appear before them "James Bourn" and "Wm. Graham" who both swore that they "had good right to claime lands for the importation...into this colony...and assigned them to Mr. George Eskridge." Eleven persons besides themselves were imported into Westmoreland and assigned to George Eskridge: "Ellis Burn, John Yeo, James Hambledon, Owen Brynan, Simon Letterell, Tho. Fem, Wm. Moore, Henry Kelley, Ellenor Cavano, Ann Arsley, Margrett Johnson." Whether these were all slaves with surnames, Anglo-Saxons, or a combination of both, there was no question they were being brought in as servants. It appeared that Colonel Eskridge, or his overseer, would have his hands full. Adding to this full plate was an entry notated in the court minutes one month later on October 26, 1704 as to "business relating to the outcry of the estate of Thomas Allison, deceased, be referred to the Saturday before next Court and that Mr. George Eskridge, Mr. Robert Bennett and Mr. Samuel Rust do then meet at the house of Eskridge and audit all matters and accounts relating to the outcry and estate."

As I left the building on my first day, I walked over to the city library just a few blocks away. The Richmond City Library was open until 9:30 p.m. so I spent the rest of the evening reading about the history of slavery in Virginia.   In 1650 the slave population for all of Virginia was around 300.   By 1700 it had grown to 6,000.   On March 25, 1698 an act of law was passed which required that ships coming to do any trade must first be registered.   Another act was passed October 25, 1710 which stated "No Negroes or other slaves which shall be imported into this Colony shall be landed or put on shore out of any ship or vessel importing the same before the master of the shipp or vessel hath made oath of the number of slaves imported before the duty payable for the Negroes or slaves shall be fully satisfyed and warrant had for the landing of the same and that all Negroes or other slaves landed contrary to this Act or the value thereof shall be forfeited and shall be recovered of the importers or proprietors of the same."    The laws of 1691 & 1723 made it unlawful to manumit a slave although there were exceptions.  Negro boys who were reaching the working age of twelve were required to be brought before the court to have their age "adjudged."

Westmoreland County was formed in 1653, and was noted for such famous names as Richard Henry Lee, Robert E. Lee, and George Washington. As I began reading about some of the prominent families in the county, I came across the family line of George Washington.  I read how John Washington, the first generation Washington in the County, settled there in 1657.  He married Ann Pope, the daughter of Nathaniel Pope, and purchased 150 acres which later became called Bridge Creek.  What I learned next about John's grandson Augustine came as a complete surprise. In 1715 Augustine Washington married Jane Butler and had two sons, Lawrence, in 1718, and Augustine Jr, in 1720.   I now realized that this Augustine & Jane Washington were the same two persons who had made the conveyance of land and slaves to attorney George Eskridge.

But this was not all I learned.   In 1729 Jane Washington died.   On March 6, 1731 Augustine Washington, former legal client of Eskridge, married Mary Ball, orphaned at twelve, whose legal guardian happened to be George Eskridge.  On February 22, 1732 Mary Ball Washington gave birth to a son whom she named George.  Several of the books I read made the inference that Mary had named the child after George Eskridge. The place where young George Washington was born was called Popes Creek, which later was called Wakefield. The land deed from Augustine and Jane Washington to Colonel George Eskridge actually included George Washington's birthplace, since Augustine had made a provision in the deed allowing for his family to remain living on the property. The family later moved fifty miles away to Fairfax County to live at Little Hunting Creek, which later became known as Mt. Vernon. The family finally moved to Ferry Farm on the Rappanhanock River near Fredericksburg.

The next day at the Library of Virginia I ended up spending the whole day studying the county court minutes and order books for all the same counties and cities I had looked up the day before pertaining to deeds. But this time too, Westmoreland County was the only one referring to George Eskridge involving slaves. There were five entries of interest:

July 27, 1703 "Simon Bayley, Mariner....appoint my loving Friend George Eskridge my attorney for me and in my name and company, owners of the ship Lynne of Lynne Regis...."

May 2, 1704 Will of Alexr. Spence
"....my horse Rowland to my friend George Eskridge....mulatto Tom to be manumitted after my death...My trusty friends Col. Willo. Allerton & Geo. Eskridge executors in trust or overseers."

November 29, 1704 "Returned by Mrs. Sarah Martyn, wife of Jacob Martyn mariner. Westmoreland Co. Levy to Mr. George Eskridge for monies paid and expended about negro Tom-300

August 1706 "Adam adjudged at six years a slave of George Eskridge"

Eskridge Manumission of Tom. "At a court held for this said County this 28th day of January 1712. Upon Motion of George Eskridge Gent. acknowledged to be his act and deed...manumitting a certain mulatto called Tom. Court admitted to record."

From these facts I learned that as early as 1706 George Eskridge was in possession of the boy named Adam who was listed on the 1736 inventory, and that his mother gave birth to him around 1700. Jacob Martyn, whose wife imposed a 300 pound levy, was a sea mariner whose name appeared in the list of slave ships on April 15, 1702 when he captained the ship *Little John* into the port of South Potomac carrying "negroes" from Barbados. Two years later the ship *Little John*, with mariners Thomas Mountjoy and John Jones, sailed into Westmoreland County to "appoint two attornies in Westmoreland to take possession of ship....6 negroes, Will, Jack, Jane, Nancy, Betty, and Billy." Apparently it was a custom to appoint an attorney to insure protection of a ship's cargo as well as the captain against any charge of illegal importation. My attention was drawn to a note of admiration to Colonel George Eskridge petitioning the Westmoreland Court for a slave's manumission on January 28, 1712, a slave named Tom, according to the wishes of the colonel's friend Alexander Spence.

Many of the ships recorded in the minutes of the Westmoreland County Court were on the slave ship lists. Those vessels were: *Adventure, Amity, Betty, Content, Elizabeth, Industrie, Sarah and Elizabeth, Seaflower, Speedwell,* and *Susanna.*

It was interesting and revealing to notice throughout the court minutes the dozens of judgements handed down in court cases that were awarded in payments of Tobacco. In fact, not only were slaves purchased in sterling or gold, but payment in tobacco or tobacco notes was acceptable as well. For example in a February 11, 1683 letter, William Fitzhugh, the 17th century lawyer, planter, and politician, wrote about a proposal to buy himself slaves "offering to give 3000 lbs tobacco for every negro boy or girl between 7 & 11 years old, 4000 lbs between 11 & 15, 5000 lbs for every young man or woman that shall be above 15 years & not exceed 24..."

In the County Court Minutes for Northumberland, I found

the appointment of George Eskridge as guardian for Mary Ball. According to the will of Mary Ball Hewes, probated on July 19, 1721, her daughter Mary was "to be under the tutlidge of Capt. George Eskridge during her minority."

It was now closing time again. After leaving, I stopped one last time at the public library to make a few more investigative notes, after that, devouring a pepperoni pizza on a bench. Then it was on to Raleigh, North Carolina to visit the State of North Carolina Division of Archives and History. On file was the last will of Burdett Eskridge's brother Richard who left Virginia and moved to Caswell County, North Carolina. In his 1816 will, I discovered the names of ten slaves bequeathed to seven of his children:

"girls Lucy & Moll, girl Henrietta, woman Ann, man Ben
young negroes Simon & Hale, girls Anne & Atha
boy Adam"

I noticed that one of the names was a boy named Adam. I had no doubt his name had been handed down and traced to the slave Adam who was on George Eskridge's plantation and was later inherited by his son, house burgess Samuel Eskridge. In trying to trace what became of these ten slaves, I could only locate two of them: the boy Adam, who ended up being sold in Leasburg to an Eskridge family granddaughter in February 1837 for $980; and the girl Lucy, sold on April 11, 1836 at the estate auction of Martha Eskridge Lipscomb, with her two children Goodly & Issac for $800, along with two other female slaves, Lucinda and Melinda, to a Caswell County, North Carolina neighbor named William A. Lea.

According to Alex Haley, his great-great-great-grandmother Kizzy was sold in 1805 to Tom Lea of Caswell County, North Carolina, the son of William Lea and Nancy Graves. Kizzy later gave birth to a boy in 1806. The father was slavemaster Tom Lea, who named Kizzy's child "George", later known as "Chicken George." In 1827 Chicken George mated with Matilda and soon raised 8 children. Amazing as it sounds, it is very possible that the five slaves William A. Lea purchased in 1836, descendants of the slave Adam who lived at the Sandy Point plantation, may have crossed paths with Haley's ancestors.

Kizzy, Chicken George, Matilda, their 8 children including Tom, born in 1833 and who later became the blacksmith Tom Murray, were still on Tom Lea's plantation during the same time period William A. Lea purchased Lucinda, Melinda, Lucy, and her two children Goodly and Issac.  After checking several sources, however, I could not determine the relationship of William A. Lea to Tom Lea, although the fact that they were in the same county, with their distinct surname spelling, told me they were of the same family.  Marriage records also revealed the Leas giving their signature as witnesses to several wedding ceremonies of the Caswell County Eskridges.  Futhermore, Caswell County Richard Eskridge's final will was witnessed by Leas, and Richard's land was adjacent to George Lea.  The Leas and Eskridges were close neighbors.

Later that October back home in Portland, I compared George Eskridge's  1736 estate inventory to the 1747 slave inventory of his son Samuel.  I wanted to identify any family members that Samuel  inherited to confirm a slave generational line.  There was Will, Jack, Sarah, Tom, Hannah, and Jenny; but the Africans Quamino, Congo Judy, Taffy, Botswain, Mingo, Sambo, Binah, and Cumey had disappeared.  Either Samuel's brother Dr. Robert Eskridge and his other siblings had inherited them,  or sold off to other owners,  or they had died.

Although I was disappointed that the African names could no longer be found, there was one African name that did appear on both lists of father and son.  I looked again.  My eyes blinked.  I burst out, "Samuel Eskridge inherited an African!  Samuel Eskridge inherited an African!"  Yes, there was one  name that remained, that of Akey. *The African Akey had remained.*

Because this name was listed both times next to female names, and had an appraised value of 15 pounds, I concluded that Akey was probably a young woman in her early twenties.  Could I find out what her African origin was?  Could her name have an African meaning?  Did my family descend from her?

**"The rest and residue of my property...I give and bequeath to Samuel Butler Eskridge the son of my nephew...of the State of Mississippi."**
**Last will of Samuel B. Eskridge, March 29, 1852**

## CHAPTER ELEVEN

### From Buck Creek to Duck Hill

I recall how excited I was going to visit Osage City for the first time. After arriving in Topeka, Kansas by bus, I went to Osage City by car rental to spend the entire day snapping photographs of the former homestead site of the family, and looking up their deeds and tax records at the courthouse and town library. The next day when I entered the car rental office, the staff were huddled around a radio listening. Something about the Pentagon. The front desk rep said, "Two planes hit the World Trade Center in New York." I asked, confused, "Was it an accident?" He then turned his face to me. "I don't think so." My greyhound bus connection to Jackson, Mississippi was running late that morning. When it finally did arrive the driver, speaking very emotionally because of the attacks, announced that all buses would be shutdown, and to make room for more passengers because all airline flights were grounded.

Within minutes, my bus was jammed pack with scores of people who hours ago had been literally in the air, their destinations abruptly cancelled. After almost an hour wait we got the green light, and two days later I crossed the Mississippi state line from Louisiana. I called my wife and my folks to let them know I was safe, and then headed to the state archives. As I entered Mississippi I thought about how my ancestors came to the state.

"After reaching Nashville three days later, the party now

embarked onto "Natchez Trace," the old Indian trail that once ran through the proud Choctaw and Chickasaw Nations, but now a wagon road for settlers, mail carriers, traders, and thieves. They also were on the lookout for bats, various creeping things, and poisonous creatures. Poor villagers and farmers along the Trace, holed up in their shacks and shantys in the valley interior, caught a faint glimpse of the dark human train moving through the dense forests, a long marching chain-gang, fleetly advancing through the country jungle. The dirt path they walked upon still showed the distinct foot-grooves of gang coffles that strode through months and weeks earlier, to be auctioned out in Frenchtown and Kosciusko. One of the bondsmen, walking in the group behind Butcher Jennings and William's party, became the unfortunate casualty of an army of hornets at a water spring, when he unwaringly stepped barefoot right into the hornets' nest. They were on alert constantly to protect the livestock and horses from deadly snake bite.

The first night on the Trace, Massa Eskridge decided to stop at the country hotel Grinder's Inn for his family to spend the night. The twenty others unrolled their blankets and tried to make themselves comfortable outside. Butcher Jennings, William, and the rest of the camp slept sound. It was good that they did, for little did they know it had been rumored the Governor of the Louisiana Territory, Meriweather Lewis, had been murdered at the Inn twenty-five years ago. Since then, all kinds of mysterious disapperances and killings had occurred along the trail. It had developed also a reputation of being notorious for horse thieving and slave stealing.

Sunrise introduced another long exhausting and grungy day. While Massa Richard and his family caught a bite of breakfast before resuming their trip, two men introduced themselves to him and inquired if the "negroes" outside were his. The men were John McClancey and Virgil Strom, who introduced themselves as preachers. McClancey had wanted to know if the men outside, and their female cook, were from the area.

"No, not from this area, we from East Tennessee; I'm taking them with me down to Choctaw lands in Mississippi,"

Eskridge said.

"Is that so?  Why, every time I come up and down the Trace as I do my sermons, I'm steady running into people left and right heading to the new lands of Mississippi.  Seems to me so many of 'em in such a hurry to get down there with they negroes, the Government must've put up a BIG sign saying, "FIRST COME, FIRST SERVED," McClancey remarked.

"Government's got the sign out alright, the planters just got to make sure they got the capital--money and slaves; Isn't that what the good book say, "Fill the earth and subdue it, yes, happy are they that inherit the land?"

"Well, it do say ALL MEN ARE CREATED EQUAL, don't it?  Well, I don't want to hold you, you got a long trip ahead of ya.  I bid you good day and a safe trip;  If ya'll are anywhere near Cypress Inn or Cherokee town come Sunday, we'll be holding our camp services;  The title of the sermon will be "The Truth that sets Men Free," McClancey said.

As the family headed out the door, Massa Eskridge thought to himself, "I... just might even come hear that sermon."

By Monday the party had crossed into Alabama and by nighttime they had reached the Tennessee River crossing where they settled for the evening.  The woman cook brought along named Charlotte, part African and part Indian, pulled out her skillet and pot, and mixed her bag of seasonings into something she called "Ngumbo," a combination of okra, ham, sausage, tomatoes, cayenne, and vegetables, that ignited into a mouth-watering stew.  The young boys George and Lindsey held their own so far on the long trek, keeping up with the pack fairly well, but the boys were nearly exhausted.  All the time, though, Butcher Jennings and William kept a close eye on them, making sure they didn't wander off as young ones their age had a tendency to do.  William remembered part of the story Mother Jenny would tell him of how Grandmother had been snatched by the "soldiers" when sitting under a tree, and put upon a ship with her uncle and brought to Virginia.

As they ate supper the storytellers emerged, including the cook Charlotte, who began telling her story about the "Ride and

Tie Man" from Kentucky.  "After losing most of his money gambling at Natchez he decided to split the cost of a horse with a boatman...they made a deal that when they left for Kentucky the next morning, one would ride the horse until noon while the other walked...the one riding would then tie the horse to a tree for the other and begin his share of the walking;  This they kept up till evening;  Before turning in for the night, the man from Kentucky said to the boatman: "Remember, tomorrow's  your turn to walk;" Next morning, only the boatman left out...three days later a wagon train found the Kentucky man's body in a swamp when they stopped to water the horses."  Another story, "Hard Head Man," was told by one named Jordan.  "He never listened to no one, always actin' like he knew everythang...one day he and a gang of darkies had to travel all the way to a plantation in Vicksburg...when's they stopped halfway to build a fire one night, one of 'em picked up an axe to chop some wood, but "Hardhead" grabbed it from him and boasted, "I'll do the chopping," Why, he ain't never chopped a piece of wood in his life;  He went up to bring the axe down on the log--like this here--and bro't it right down on his foot...they worked the axe free from his foot while "Hardhead" went screaming into the woods...they says at night you can hear him limpin' through the woods looking for food from someone sleeping."  As soon as that was said, everyone at the campfire started looking around in fright, especially when they heard what sounded like tree branches snapping in the distance. Still yet another storyteller, Harrison, rose up with a talltale passed down to him of, "The Rattlesnake and the Farmer's Animals." When he sat down yet another, called Keauni, couldn't wait to tell the story of, "Qua, the Prince," who was of royal descent but died a slave in Augusta, Georgia at the age of one hundred.  They finally turned in for the  night, but not before the last one of them  related a tale of the cunning rabbit, and the spider, more pieces of  folklore brought over on the slave ships.

After the morning meal of grits, biscuits, and molasses, the group resumed their trek past cypress trees, swamps, and small scattered Choctaw villages.  They reached the village of Duck Hill on the last day of March.  The next month they began clearing the

land and erecting the main house and slave quarters.  The work
was far from easy.  The backs, legs, and feet of the chain gang
were wore out from each day of clearing, their dirt fingers pricked
apart from bushes and thistles.  In time other slaveholding settlers
began moving in around the newly tilled plantation.  They were
typical southern ante-bellum names such as Benjamin Campbell of
North Carolina, T.R. Sutton of Louisiana, Sherman Bovinett of
Georgia, and a string of others, even businessmen from New York
and Vermont.

About that time, talk had been heard around the county that
a man had been arrested and brought to trial for attempting to
organize an insurrection among the slaves and planning to
massacre the white plantation owners and set up an independent
state.  It was said that the conspirators had planned to arm and train
the Mid-South slaves and lead them in an insurrection schemed to
take place on Christmas Day, 1835.  The plot had been revealed to
the authorities by one within the group who had turned traitor and
eventually led a posse to their hideout in Arkansas.  Apparently the
group of outlaws had been operating a horse-slave stealing outfit
from another hideout along Natchez Trace, where they would
ambush people, strip them of any valuables, then throw their
bodies into the deep swamp holes.  The name of the group's leader:
John McClancey.  The group member who turned him in:  Virgil
Strom.

Massa Richard's sons and daughters began establishing
themselves in the county, marrying and extending the family
property.  His daughter Rebecca and granddaughter Mary Tabitha
married town merchants James Weed and Squire Albert McNeil,
just as Massa Richard's  sons Samuel, Thomas, Taliaferro, their
wives, and their slaves all arrived from Alabama to round out the
family line and aid in the new venture.   His son Thomas had
among his slaves a family of three, comprised of a grandmother,
her granddaughter, and the granddaughter's child.  As Butcher
Jennings and William gazed at the grandmother, who was called
Polly, they both wondered if they had somehow known her before,
and if so, where.  In time she was employed as a house servant
along with cook Charlotte, while the granddaughter, who had

acquired the art of weaving, was made the plantation seamstress. Each week Butcher Jennings would see the grandmother when she came to the meat house to pick out meats to be cooked for the day. His son George Washington worked separating the cotton and wool that were to be to supply the granddaughter seamstress. Lindsey worked in the fields as a picker, while William labored in the blacksmith shed.

One evening, about the time the "Bowel Complaint" was spreading throughout the county but before the time that the heavy cotton loss onboard the boat *Gladiator* in neighboring Grenada County became widespread news, an incident occurred next door on Massa Benjamin Campbell's homestead.

A wild and frantic knocking was heard at the back door of Massa Richard's big house. The newly arrived grandmother, Polly, turned the doorknob to find a hard-breathing messenger servant boy standing before her.

"Ma'am!  My Massa Campbell tol' me to comes straight over this instant and tell Massa Eskridge he need to fetch his plantation midwife real quick!" the boy said, talking so fast and bunching up his words so much that Polly at first had a time in trying to understand him.

"Slow down, slow down!  Now what your massa say 'bout a midwife?"

"He say he need a midwife tonite!  Massa Campbell fixin' to have one a his slave gals give childbirth any second!"

"Stand right here!  I'll go get Massa Eskridge!" Polly said, as she rushed to Massa Richard's study room.  Polly excused herself for the intrusion, then informed him of his neighbor's urgent plea.  "Bring the boy here!" Massa Richard said.  Polly grabbed the boy and brought him to the study.

"What's all this commotion coming from the Campbell plantation?" Massa Richard asked the messenger boy.

"Massa Campbell asking if you can spare's one a yo' plantation midwives right now tonite, Massa Eskridge!  Massa got a young girl havin' trouble comin' alongs!  My massa say the girl likely to die if she don't get help right now!"

"Why, I ain't got but one, midwife Dorcas;  What happened

to Mr. Campbell's midwife?"

"She fell sick, massa;  Massa Campbell afraid to use her."

"Sick?  With what?  The Bowel Complaint?"

"No suh!  She got dizzy spells and fever."

"Fever!  Why, that Benjamin Campbell wants me to use one of my good gals for his sickly slaves?  That girl's probably got the bowel complaint for sure!  Where's his sick midwife at now?"

"Massa puts her by herself in a cabin way downs by Bogue Creek."

"Why, I'll be...he got her in quarantine!  Oh no!  He not goin' kill off my prized hands, no way!!"

"I'll go, massa," Polly offered.

"You'll do what?"

"I's a midwife, too, massa;  I knows all 'bout childbearing and done plenty my share."

"You say you willing to go up there and take a chance on catching what this sick slave woman's got?  Then come back here and spread that contagious disease all over my plantation?  You must be crazy!  Why in the world you'd think I'd let you do that?  Huh?"

"No, dear massa, I weren't meaning to do's that way never!  I jus' don't want massa to be in no feud with his neighborly Campbell plantation over jus' one sickly negress that stand a chance at livin'," Polly said.  Polly didn't want two deaths, the mother and her child, on her conscience, especially knowing she might prevent both.

Massa Richard sat awkwardly silent.  Polly's words had reached their target.  The servant boy began to tense up, knowing each minute that continued by might already be spelling death to the expectant mother, a girl named Mariah.  Massa Richard now spoke.

"Go...Go!  And tell Mr. Benjamin Campbell to bring you back as soon as the child is born! If you later develop a sickness due to this, I *will* sell you;  Now hurry!"

The next morning everyone headed in line to the main house for the morning meals.  As the grandmother began to serve William's portions he whispered to her. "Is your name Hannah, I mean, is your real name Hannah?" Polly shrugged him off and sharply advised him, "You better sit down and eat 'cause you ain't got all day." Later that afternoon when Polly entered the smoke house, Butcher Jennings stood blocking the door and spoke.

"Good afternoon Ms. Polly, what can I gits ya?...there you go...pardon me, ma'am, I don't mean to meddle in nobody's business, but ever since you come to this here plantation, my brother-in-law, William, been meaning to ask you somethin',...wasn't your name once "Hannah"? Now, don't be afraid, he ain't told nobody but me, and he just want to know, because if so, he just want to say thank you."

"Thank me for what?" Polly asked, bewildered.

"For helping his wife give childbirth up at that plantation in Carolina! Ma'am, he ain't seen his wife or his child in three years now, and he just want to know if you the one who brung out his boy, that's all he want to know, and me too!"

Polly said not a word and Butcher Jennings said no more either, only standing at the door and awaiting an answer to his question. Finally "Polly" gave in, saying, "Don't none of ya'll peep a word; Just have him help carry some things into the carriage house after supper for me; NOW PLEASE OPEN THE DOOR !"

After supper William carried some empty crates for "Polly" to load on the horse carriage in preparation for Massa Eskridge's trip into town the next morning. As they both entered inside the carriage shed, "Polly" began to lunge into her well-kept secret up to this time, as William lowered the empty store-supply crates into the back of the wagon carriage.

"I reckon I got somethin' to confess; My real name's not Polly--my real birthname's Hannah."

"I thought so! And you the woman who helped my 'Liza deliver my boy!"

"Me and my daughter Phyllis; She still back there in Nawth' Carolina; My massa and your massa were cousins as I understoods it, and massa decided to sell me and my grandchild to Massa Eskridge's son; But he kept my daughter."

"Have you heard from her?"

"There's no way on earth I'm goin' hear from her now, as

far apart as we is now;  Phyllis had a husband back there, too;
Then he somehow got a crazy notion in his head to try and run
off."

"A man gotta do what he think best for his family;  Did he
escape all right then come back for her?"

"He call his'self planning to come back--he ain't been heard
from since;  Even up to the time I left;  Now it's jus' me, my
grandchild Phyllis, named after my daugher, and my great-
grandboy Dallas."

"What 'bout your husband?"

"Ha!  Sold off."

"I'm sorry."

"Ain't no reason for you to be sorry;  But someone goin'
sho' be sorry when God Almighty comes!"

"Amen;  So, have you seen or heard anything 'bout my wife
and children?  It been three years since I las' seen 'em up there at
Buck Creek that run right into the Tennessee River."

"Oh William, I sho' wish I could say I seen 'em, sho' wish I
could say that."

"I tried asking massa 'bout 'em;  He keep saying he'll ask
his brother to write, but I ain't heard nothin' yet;  My people been
owned by Massa Richard's family all the way back to Virginny;
My grandparents and great-grandparents, too;   Someplace in
Virginny--I can't quite remember exactly where no more."

"My peoples been with Massa Richard's people in Virginia,
too;  I was born 1775 or 1776, during that there "Revloonchenary
War" according to my daddy Adam, and his daddy's name was
Adam;  Then, some of my people I heard got sold to my massa's
son in Caswell County, Nawth' Carolina, then, after his sons and
daughters died off, to some massa named William Lea."

"You jus' as much my family as my own flesh and blood;
You helped bring my boy into the world and for that I's forever
grateful," William said filled with emotion.

Suddenly a voice shrilled out.  "Polly!  Aren't you 'bout
done in there?"  Massa Richard yelled out from afar.

"We gotta go!  Massa callin' us!"  Hannah trembled.

"Wait!  I got one more question," as William grabbed her

arm. "Why didn't you jus' tell massa what yo' real name was?" Hannah looked straight at William and concluded in a matter-of-fact and serious-than-a-heart-attack way.

" 'Cus after the many slew of massas I done had who called me what they wanted and did what they wanted, I swore they never goin' take my birthname from me!" William nodded in affirmation.

That year in 1837 they really did become "family" when Butcher Jennings' son George married Hannah's granddaughter Phyllis. In January 1838 they had a son. They named him Frank.

The time of separation for the women Ruth, Barbe, Rose, and Elizabeth from their husbands taken to Duck Hill continued to mount. Already it was coming up on eight years now since their removal, and still no sign of ever being reunited. But over those years they were occasionally allowed to keep in touch through letters that Massa Richard and his brother Massa Samuel would write each other, as they would include a corresponding line or two from any of their slave families. The opportunity was lent to them again on this particular occasion:

September 7, 1841

Dear Bro. Samuel,

I received your letter last month; The cotton is growing good and the teams are busy as usual gathering the crop. The going rate down here is about 7 cents a pound right now. Need about 3 or 4 more hands to gather all of the rows; Send some down as soon as you can. Still waiting on the order in Memphis for a new gin--suppose your friend Governor Polk can contract his out? Talked to neighbor Benj. Campbell, his gin in full use with another team.

Still plenty hogs for meat the rest of the year. Negro clothing for this winter in need of 34 pair shoes & blankets. Weather has been very dry since August. Give greetings to family, both white & black.

R. Eskridge

The boy Jennings I now write for his wife Rose

dear Rose, how are you? how are my girls Lucy, Roberta,

China, & Eliza, hope they are growing up to be fine girls--suitable for some good fine young husbands I'm sure. how is your mother Jenny? Our boy George may be coming up for supplies just before cold winter so he can see all of you; his wife Phyllis & their toddlers Frank & Lewis are well. Please send word from your country. Charles, Daniel, & William send warm affections to all their families. Tell master Samuel and mistress Sophia we wish them good health.

     Jennings

     And as Massa Samuel always made sure of, he too, kept constant contact with his brother:
October 5, 1841
Dear brother,
     Greetings. Recd. your letter on the 20th; Our agent J. Brown has ordered supplies for winter including the clothing, but says the gin still hasn't arrived. My dear friend Governor Polk I just wrote him recently. He is coming down to his plantation in a few weeks, but seems he is awaiting a new gin himself. As you probably heard, he was defeated for reelection; Personally, I think he is considering a run for the Presidency the next time.
     You asked for more hands--I am sending Jordan, Wash, Clara, Matilda, & Edmond with nephew Taliaferro. Had five new births from the negro women, and lost woman Jenny during the last harvest. Hot and dry up here as usual. Everyone busy at work. Make sure to come on up when clearing is done.
     Saml. Eskridge
I write a few lines now from woman Rose to her Jennings
  we are all well; Ruth's boy Brisborn old enough working the fields now. Master Eskridge took some on a trip to Virginny last spring. I sewed some garments for the babies--one I sewed for you last winter but maybe you too big to wear now. Tell William Elizabeth hopes to see son Lindsey if he comes up, and I await my George, wish I could see babies Frank and Lewis, and to put my blessing upon them; tell master Richard and his children we are in good health. We loss mama about this time last year during

harvest.  Tell William

Rose

As soon as Massa Richard read his brother's letter and his
eyes came upon the reference about Jenny, he respectfully handed
the letter to his son Taliaferro, and instructed him to break the
news privately to Butcher Jennings only, which he did right after
the field hands had all turned in for the evening and readying
themselves for the serving of dinner.  Taliaferro, always seeming
to have a peculiar fondness of heart and humanness for his father's
slaves, had delicately chosen his words before Butcher Jennings, as
if he was softly setting him up so the fatal blow of words he would
have to utter next would perhaps blunt Butcher Jennings
anticipated pain, but even more so his own.  This was why
Taliaferro kept saying in advance "...got somethin' to say and don't
quite know how to say it...just received a letter from my Uncle
Samuel...he say your people doin' fine, uh, most of 'em...I sho'
wish that day would come when we all will live forever, but you
know, Butcher, some of the old ones by nature got to go at some
time."  Butcher was now starting to get a sick feeling in his
stomach.  "Your people been with my family a long, long
time...why, it's a godly blessing to be blessed with..." Taliaferro's
voice dropped.  It picked up again.  "Look at Hannah; I jus' don't
know how she keep goin', even old Jenny...I remember my papa
and uncle both telling me when they was small, how ole' Jenny
raised 'em like her own..." His voice trailed off again.

Butcher had heard that reminiscent story before from
Massa Richard, but he also knew the story told him by his wife
Rose how Massa Samuel had Jenny sold off to a relative.  It would
have stayed that way had not Jenny moved the conscience of the
highly religious relative to having Jenny returned as hired help,
and just in time before her mother, Akey, died.  "I'm afraid to say
that ole' Jenny's not with us anymore...she passed on during harvest
time last year;  I thought that by telling you this privately, you
should be the one to tell William."  Butcher Jennings' head
dropped.  "Oh Lawd have mercy."

That night Butcher Jennings didn't know how he got the strength to break the news to William, especially when William knew from house servant Hannah's talk that Massa Richard had received a letter from his brother, and assumed there must not have been any news sent along about his family, since Massa Richard hadn't mentioned any as he customarily would do.   Butcher Jennings quickly spoke up as they sat eating, that indeed news had been sent: how Rose had sewed some garments for the children, and that all were anticipating the visit of young George during his trip to Buck Creek to pick up supplies.  Butcher waited again until the evening's heat had started to cool off to tell William.  The moment of truth finally came, and soon was seen Lindsey being instructed by William to hurry and run over to Daniel's cabin and next Charles' cabin, the boy telling them to come immediately. Huddling them all together, William passed on the words that had traveled to him hundreds of miles away.

Massa Richard's son-in-law, Squire McNeil, Mary Tabitha's husband, had a cousin, Albert F. McNeal, an attorney and merchant trader, who operated as a purchasing agent for Tennessee Governor James K. Polk for his Yalobusha River plantation, ten miles north of Duck Hill.  (Squire McNeil's cousin continued his client relationship even up to Polk's Presidential election of 1844).

One Sunday, Mary Tabitha and Squire McNeil paid an afternoon visit to see "Granddaddy" Eskridge as their carriage came up the hilly driveway and to the front porch door.  Mary Tabitha knocked, expecting to see, as usual, the black face of house servant Charlotte to greet them, and go on about how "I sho' missed seeing you Ms. Mary, Massa Squire; Oh, I so glad to see both ya'll again!"  But when the door opened, it was the face of Hannah.  "Yes'um, Ma'am, Massa, how can's I do you?"  Realizing that new servant Hannah was still not familiar with Massa Richard's children, Mary Tabitha politely gave Hannah a hint: "Is "Granddaddy" here?" before pushing past the door.  Later, as Massa Eskridge sat visiting with Mary Tabitha and Squire McNeil in the living room while being served by Hannah, Mary couldn't help but ask:

"Granddaddy, just where is Charlotte?  Is she not helping in the house anymore?"

"Charlotte's still here, she just fixin' to have a child, 'bout six or seven months into it, as I've been told," Massa Eskridge said, while finishing his swallow of Southern lemonade.

"Charlotte goin' have a child?  Why, I'll be!  She never said a thing to me the last time I was here;  Who's the daddy?" Mary Tabitha asked, notably shocked.

"That's because she wasn't showing the last time you were here, my child;  Now, just because you two been knowing each other since you were little bitty girls don't mean she got to tell you all about her negra business."  Then finishing another swallow, he added, "I'm not quite sure who the daddy is, apparently Charlotte hasn't come out and said who;  But I'm sure that the father will step forward soon and take responsibility."

Squire McNeil then added, "Let's hope he do, otherwise Charlotte will have to make him!"  As the deriding joke went around the room, Hannah stood in the background, staring at Massa Eskridge, then caught herself and stepped back into the kitchen to fetch more juice.

Soon the conversation turned toward business, Massa Richard knowing the need for a cotton gin would greatly increase his field productivity, and knowing too, that none of his neighbors had one available except ten miles down at Polk's plantation, which Squire McNeil's cousin could possibly obtain.  "Yes, I could ask him to look into it," said Squire McNeil, "But even better yet, why don't I ask if your remaining bales can be carted down for process this week!"  By late the next week George along with two other field hands, Luke and Mitch, were permitted off the plantation and soon were carting down Grenada Road several cotton bales to Massa Polk's plantation alongside Yalobusha River.  As they arrived they were met by two slaves, Wilson and Harry, and an overseer named "Mairs."  For the next two weeks the last remaining bales of Massa Richard and his sons' cotton were sent with Butcher Jennings' son George to Massa Polk's plantation, run through the cotton gin, and then shipped by boat to New Orleans.

As the team consisting of George, Lindsey, Luke, and

Mitch broke company with Massa Polk's team at the end of the
assignment towards the first of November 1844, they made their
way back down Grenada Road toward Duck Hill.  The next week a
man named Armstead, born 1818 in Norfolk, Virginia and whose
passed down surname was Crockett, a slave belonging to Massa
Campbell and whose wife was Mariah who survived one
childbearing night thanks to Hannah,  was pulling his wagon
alongside Grenada Road until he reached the junction that turned
toward the county seat, Carrollton, where he was heading to pick
up lumber and supplies.  Approaching the junction, he noticed a
caravan of three carriages as well as horsemen coming toward him
and flying dust everywhere as he yielded to the right.  Some two
hours later as Armstead drew his loaded wagon back into Duck
Hill, he passed Massa Eskridge's plantation and noticed the same
three carriages parked there.  Armstead had his horse pull the
wagon over to the edge of the fields and then climbed down,
approaching one of Massa Richard's field hands to inquire what
was taking place, but got no satisfactory answer.  He next
approached a female slave hand, asking her what did the carriages
mean, but she too, wasn't certain either, except to say something
about there would be, "some fancy dinnin' tonite."  Finally he
happened upon another field hand and was told, "Oh, 'dat there the
man  'dat jus' got his'self to being President, he the new "Hickory
Jackson," Massa Eskridge's brotha' know hims real well, and
Massa Squire cousin work fo' him;  They supposed ter have some
fancy music and some eatin's soon's we git done out here;  Butcher
Jennings gawn' be cookin' it up, so you better go git yo' miss'es an'
git ready 'cause you know if DEY gittin' ready to hab some music
and dancin', then you know WE's got to hab some!"  Armstead
replied, "Let me get on back and tell my Mariah, 'cause it sho'
sound like they goin' be some corn shucking tonite, and I know
Massa Campbell goin' wanna get in on the action!"

Butcher Jennings had now been delegated to "master cook"
by Massa Richard as soon as he had one day tasted some seasoned
charbroiled ribs that Butcher Jennings had turning over a fire pit.
Ever since Massa Richard let out, "Butcher, these here the best ribs
I done ever tasted," Massa Richard had recruited him for those

special occasions when company came or when the social elite of
the community came by to dine. In fact, Butcher Jennings and his
barbeque specialities were making quite a name throughout Carroll
County. It would be no different on this early afternoon amid the
special guests, which Jennings knew would stretch into late
evening without question, as Massa Richard tried to restrain the
nervousness in his tongue as he excused himself from the presence
of President-elect Polk and his other entertained guests and went
out the back door, hoping to be reassured from Jennings that the
marinated meats were barbequing fine, and on time.

"Butcher...Butcher...where in criminy are you?" Massa
Richard cried out desperately.

"Here I am," as Jennings came around the corner of the
meat house carrying a pan full of freshly-cut chickens covered in
his secret sauce. "I got some chicken here to go along wid the beef,
I makin' sho' nobody go home hungry today!"

"Butcher, this day means a whole lot to me; You do this
dinner for me just right, why, I'm gonna have to owe you one," as
Massa Richard put his hand around Jennings' shoulder.

"Owe me one, Massa?"

"Owe you one, anything you want; Just do this dinner just
right for me; Why, I got the President of the United States right
here in my house! Why, whatever happen here today may affect
this whole country the next four years! Why, he may even go on
and "free" your people!"

"Free my people? This here man? Why you think he
would do that?"

"Why not; It's been a long time coming; Besides, he's
heard about you--why you think he come here to stop and eat?
Shucks, what you do for him today will make a lasting impression
he'll never forget; You can take that to the bank--or to the White
House in his case."

"So, if I make it so that all these here people go home filled
up, then you say you owe me one?"

"Whatever it is, just say it...you want Saturdays off? More
corn whisky? Increase your purse when hired out? Go visit..."

"My family be "free"--my wife Rose's family here and up at Buck Creek--can you do that for me, Massa Richard, can you?"

"Well, Butcher, I would first need to talk to my brother, of course...as soon as that could be done...well...I'm sure...we'll have to see about making some kinda arrangements, have to write it all out so it be legal...your family been with my family a long, long time, Butcher, way back to my great-grandfather Colonel George Eskridge...and if there ever was a family that deserved to be manumitted, I think it would be yours."

"I 'preciate what you tellin' me Massa Richard, but Sir, you ain't said what goin' happen if these people *not* end up holding an appetite to your pleasing?"

"Don't worry, they'll be, Butcher."

That night as Massa Eskridge's guests including the President-elect finally departed full and satisfied, Jennings couldn't sleep, the massa's words about being "manumitted" still ringing in his ears, worrying if he meant it, worried if something he may have done wrong that day might have cancelled out freedom's offer. As he slept on his wood pallet bed underneath a musty-smelling wornout blanket covering him and his son George in the same cramped cabin with William and son Lindsey, Jennings kept wondering if Massa Eskridge perhaps was going to free his family in his written will, or perhaps through a petition at the Carroll County Courthouse?  And would older brother Massa Samuel be agreeable to any such talk?  Could younger brother Massa Richard really be counted on to put his foot down if it came to that?   A letter later received by Massa Richard from Massa Samuel indicated that the subject had been brought up and discussed, which Jennings had found out about from Hannah, who had overheard Massa Richard discussing the letter's contents to his son Taliaferro, something about, "Samuel's not against the idea, but what about the crop? Who'll replace them?" and, "Where would they stay, where would they live," to which Massa's son Taliaferro was heard to have said, "They can stay right here, right next door to me, that way there'll be no trouble," to finally she hearing, "...need more time to think this over...from the sound of the news coming out of Texas, it may be prudent to wait." As time went on,

President Polk's expansionist policy, the northern Abolitionists anti-slavery stance vs. the southern slaveholders position intensifying, and the smell of war--the Mexican War--soon engulfed Massa Richard's thoughts, burying Butcher Jennings request for his family's freedom altogether. He didn't bother to bring it up for discussion again. It was now "business as usual." And Charles, Daniel, and William wouldn't lose sleep over it, either. If it happened, fine. If not, life went on.

One cloudly, overcast day in 1846 at Buck Creek plantation, the field hands stopped work briefly as it came time for the serving of the noontime meals. While the four women Rose, Elizabeth, Barbe, and Ruth as always never missed the chance to at least wash their hands before eating, Billy Burgess, Brisborn, and the other male slavehands didn't waste any second to devour the freshly-cooked corn-on-the-cob, diced ham, and baked beans. As Brisborn began biting into his juicy corn cob, his cabin mate, a slave named Kendall who was just then coming out of the fields to eat, suddenly came running excitably towards the grubbing workers, shouting, "Dey done brung another one! Massa brung another one!" Just then, Massa Samuel's two-horse wagon pulled into the plantation off of the junction from Kingston Road, in the back of the wagon a man in shackles who had just been purchased from Nelson County, Kentucky. The man, a twenty-year old handsome mulatto slave named Jefferson, had been purchased by both Massa Samuel and Massa Richard, who they planned to eventually hire out to neighbors near Massa Samuel's private residence in Midtown, Jefferson being a skilled carpenter.

"Where you reckon dey gonna put him?" Kendall asked Brisborn.

"Don't know; But I sho know he ain't gawn be in our cabin as full as it is; I 'magine the overseer gawn have to put him by hisself for awhile, till he git a feelin' for this here place," answered Brisborn. Sitting next to Brisborn and Billy Burgess was their cousin Hiram, who began saying sarcastically, "Dat's all dis here place needs now is another man 'round here fo' 'dese womenfolk to git all crazy 'bout." Billy Burgess then replied, "As far as I looks at it, you got two choices:  either you better hurry and get yo'self a mate, or you better plan on having some more nephew an' nieces."

After about three months on the plantation, Jefferson finally began to feel at ease, not at first used to working on a plantation with over ten workers such as back in Kentucky, as he was soon put to work on Massa Samuel's projects--repairing the slave cabin roofs, the schooner wagons for travel to Nashville or Knoxville to market, and keeping up Massa's residences at both Buck Creek and Midtown.  The single women as well as the single mothers were thrilled when handsome Jefferson was seen about, totting lumber over his shoulders or carrying his handtools, especially when he came around to working on their cabins.  One day Jefferson was building several cots for certain cabins and then placing them inside each one selected to receive the additions.  As the sunset began, the fieldhands began returning to their private huts before the serving of the dinner meals.  As Rose and her girls Roberta, China, and Eliza approached their cabin, they were startled as they entered and saw Jefferson inside setting down a bedcot.

"Excuse me ladies, I didn't know you was jus' comin' in;  I brung this here extra bedcot for whoever need it," Jefferson said, embarrassed as he quickly stood up to leave.

"Oh no, don't you mind us," Rose responded.  "You finish what you doin', we just gettin' ready to have supper;  Girls! Get the man a cold cup of water!"  Roberta, the older of the three, wasted no time in grabbing the only cup in the cabin before China and Eliza barely had a chance, and soon brought it back full from the drinking well stationed by the central slave kitchen.

"I wish I could put four beds in here fo' you ladies, and I sorry I not got to those leaks up in the roof, but I's gonna get to it real real soon," Jefferson apologized.

"We doin' 'jus fine wid what we's got;  We knows you keeps real busy 'round here;  My girls need the sunshine that come through in here," exclaimed Rose, trying to put her best foot down in promoting the three unmarried girls she still had left to a potential son-in-law, as she introduced each one.  "This here my second eldest, Roberta, and this my third daughter, China, then after her be my youngun Eliza," as the girls gave immediate curtsies on cue. Jefferson insisted he had to quickly leave, and handed the finished water cup to Eliza. His hands brushed her fingertips. Eliza's eyes looked downward and embarrassed. An unconscious attraction had begun to germinate, although neither one was aware of it. The mouths of the other two sisters dropped. They were aware of something.

By the next month, Jefferson was becoming use to his horse wagon drive on Kingston Road going back and forth between Midtown and Buck Creek doing repairs for Massa Samuel, although never would he get used to the strung identification collar clamped around his neck. Massa Samuel still had plans of hiring Jefferson out soon, and that would squarely come to an end with a successful escape. Jefferson was surely thinking about it, too. Each time he drove the main County road he became more and more familiar with the various turn-offs and country trails. And he knew which way was Nashville and which way was Virginia. He knew he didn't want to run off that way. But when on certain days he would get bold enough to even think of planning to escape, his thoughts were soon dashed when he would see the "paddyrollers" routinely passing by.

As Saturday afternoon arrived to end the field work for that week, the Saturday night festivities soon took over in the form of fiddle music, roasted pig and chicken, and dance. As all the single women and single mothers turned out--to the cheer of the few men and growing manhood boys--there Rose and her three daughters made their appearance. The young men Brisborn, Billy Burgess, Hiram, and the other young men rapidly chose their dance partners to start off the dance, then paired off again. As Eliza and China danced with their partners to the fast-paced playing of the fiddler, Roberta sat down to catch her breath while at the same time gazing about the yard for a new fresh dance mate. "May I have this pleasure?" as a voice came from behind her. Roberta turned in surprise to see Jefferson extending his arm out. After they had danced full-circle, Jefferson was then passed off to lock with the arms of sister China. As they kicked and swayed, his eyes happened upon Eliza on the opposite end, her colonial cascading hairlocks, peachy cheeks, and smooth-oiled lips, her body bouncing in perfect rhythm with the furious playing of the fiddler. As the mates came full-circle again, this time Eliza became paired with Jefferson. But as they locked arms the music stopped.

"It's sho' good to see you again, Miss 'Liza, and yo' sisters, too; Where you learn to dance so fine?" said Jefferson, before he realized he was still holding Eliza's arm and let go.

"My sisters teached me, but they dance awhole lot better than me; Seem like *you* the one that be footin' pretty good; That how they dance back in Kentucky?" asked Eliza, as she started to feel herself breathing harder and her heart beating faster, but not as a result of the fiddler's 'round and round.'

"In Kentucky we kicked up a little dust," as they walked over to the punch bowl, "but only now and then; Not like you people do out here in Tennessee EVERY SATURDAY; But back there we did least have something to go with this here punch--but I guess they don't serve that out here..."

"I know what you talkin' about!" as Eliza gave out a little giggle. "And I never tried it before neither! Mama say it make people act all crazy, and my daddy say "Whisky make you drunk as a skunk!" At least that what he used to say 'fore he got taken to Mississippi; You have family back in Kentucky?"

"They's was all sold off," as Jefferson made a deep sigh, "my brothers, sisters, and my mama; I never even seen who my daddy was; Figure now this here my family; I just got myself now--don't even got a wife or children--but I gots plenty time fo' that! I's just twenty-some years old!"

At that moment, big sister Roberta came up and grabbed Eliza, saying "little sister, don't you want to get in on this next 'round and round'? They gettin' ready to start up right now!" Then turning to Jefferson, added, "I sho' hopes to see you in this next dance, too, Mr. Jefferson."

The next two Saturday evenings resulted in the same envious eyes and jealousies among the young women and the young men, itching to mate up and start families of their own. And Roberta and China didn't letup in their striving for Jefferson's attentions, while Jefferson continued to feel at ease in the company of eighteen year old Eliza. Even Eliza's oldest sister Lucy, although twenty-four years older and a single mother, began to flirt and vie for the attention of Jefferson. Finally by the fourth Saturday social night as the fiddle and the banjo played on, the smell of barbeque scented the air, and the punch bowl spiked, the girls Roberta, China, and older sister Lucy were occupied with three men hanging onto them, concluding that if Jefferson wasn't interested by now, then he never would be. Jefferson's focus was converging on someone else among them.

As Eliza finished the fiddle dance with Jefferson along with several foot-happy fieldhands, she sat down to cool off. Jefferson flashed her a smile.

"Eliza, can I brings you a cup of that cold punch?"

"No thank you, think I had enough of that, it tasting mighty stronger than I used to drinking."

"That 'cus someone spiked it; Can I gets you a cup 'o water?"

"That'll be fine."

Jefferson hurried himself up to the water well and scooped a cup from the bucket, though in such a rush afterward he spilled it while bumping into two small children, causing him to go back and fetch another cup.

"That sho' took long; I thought you had forgotten me," Eliza said as Jefferson handed her the cup and she began sipping away.

"Alright, you got your strength back; Come here! I want's to show you somethin'," Jefferson said as he pulled giggling Eliza up by the arms, spilling the water again. Jefferson and Eliza broke from the loud party and strolled to the far outskirts of the property line over to a quiet spot by a tree stump.

"Jefferson, why you bring me way out here?"

"Look up! See all them stars!"

"They's beautiful; Jus' hundreds and hundreds of 'em."

"See how they hang loose and float so freely; Can't nobody touch 'em or tell any of 'em what to do, nobody 'cept God; Watch! We might see a shooting star!"

"Jefferson, why we come all the way out *here* to watch the

stars?"

"Keep looking;   Did you ever hear 'bout how the cow jumped over the moon?"

"No;  I want to know why we..."

"Hey diddle diddle, the cat and the fiddle..."

"Jefferson..."

"The cow jumped over the moon;  the little darkies laughed to see such sport..."

"Massa goin' think we running off!"

"And the dish ran away with the spoon!  Alright!  Don't get yourself all flustered."

"Look!  There goes a shooting star!" Eliza shouted.

"You 'member when I told you all my family was sold away?"

"Yes."

"And I said this here plantation my only family now?"

"Yes."

"And how I don't yet got a wife or children but I still has plenty time fo' that?"

"Yes, 'cus you said you only twenty-some years old," Eliza chuckled.

Eliza knew all along the purpose of his talk, and cut right through the chase. "So, when you gonna *start* this family?" as her inviting eyes looked straight at him.  Jefferson could no longer hold back and burst forth.  "Woman, I want you for my wife!" then buried his brown lips into hers.  Soon her rosewood gold lips had completely covered his.

Later as first Rose, then Massa Samuel, both approved of the union, the marriage ceremony took place on the afternoon of the fifth Saturday.  Jefferson made sure his cabin would not have any holes in the roof that weekend.  But after nine weeks had passed, Massa Samuel and his brother Massa Richard had decided to hire Jefferson out twenty miles away in Midtown to do carpentry work for the County's academy school, the overseer Mr. Casey putting him in shackles for added measure and placing him in the wagon to depart.  Massa Samuel promised Jefferson he would be allowed to come home to visit on weekends, but that soon became a rare occasion as Jefferson's employer was always too busy to write up a pass, and Massa Samuel was too busy to remind himself to send Mr. Casey.

*In the year 1847, in the fourth month, in the second year of James K. Polk, President of the twenty-nine states, a young girl named Eliza, barely in her womanhood, was heavy in child near Buck Creek by the Clinch River. In the fourth month, on the 30th day of the month, she gave birth to a child, a manchild, and named him William, according to custom, after her grandfather.*

During the early part of 1852, Massa Richard Eskridge received the painful word that his brother Massa Samuel had died, and being that he had no living issue his entire estate, including seventy-five slaves, were bequeathed in his will to Massa Richard's ten year old grandson, Samuel Butler Eskridge of Duck Hill, the son of Massa's son Taliaferro.  Now, critical judgements regarding the Buck Creek plantation needed to be resolved.  A decision was quickly made to bring some of the families that Massa Richard jointly owned at Buck Creek and have them transported to Duck Hill.

When they arrived, what pure joy were in the faces of Charles, Daniel, Butcher Jennings, and William as they were reunited with their wives.  The day of the arrival that month in June, Charles and Daniel were at that time laboring in the cotton fields and so were the first to be surprised as the horse-drawn wagon carrying the group of women entered through the wooden-fenced gate and into the yard.  Immediately upon catching sight of their wives Barbe and Ruth, the two men dropped their hoes and began running towards them while making moaning-like sounds.  When they reached the wagon and hugged their women, there were no words exchanged.  Only groanings and cries and tears.

As Butcher Jennings, now seventy-four, was butchering some fattened hogs over by the meat house, he could hear the sounds of someone shouting and wailing, making him wonder if some poor soul had gotten himself into trouble and was now feeling the consequences.  "Sound like someone fixin' to get tore up with the whip for somethin'.  I hope's they get it over quick, 'cause I jus' don't want to hear it today."  As Butcher Jennings peeked around the corner of the shed to see if he could get an eye on who the likely "victim" was, he instead caught sight of a scene he never ever expected he would see.   "That...Charles and Daniel...who that with them?  Is that...?  Is that...my Rose?  That ...my Rose!  Oh, God, THAT MY ROSE!!"  Quickly he covered up the headless hog and bloody mess, washed off his hands, and sprinted down to the momentous event, stopping only for an instant at the blacksmith shed where William was inside, and shouting, "WILLIAM, OUR WOMENS BACK!  LAWD GOD ALMIGHTY OUR WOMENS BACK!!   I ain't lying...YOUR WIFE HERE!!" then took off again.

William took only a moment to register what words had been said.  Dropping the sledge hammer upon the iron work block, sixty-eight year old William scampered his way up to the shed's entrance and looked out as he saw Jennings running furiously to the assembled group of women and children gathered in the plantation yard.  "My Elizabeth?"  William wanted to be sure this was for real.  He  remained posed and hesitant at his spot by the shed, gazing upon the features of each of the women, wanting to be certain, hoping Jennings was certain.  Suddenly, he fixed upon a woman among the crowd, whose features immediately kindled a romantic flame within him.  Her ebony bodily shape that aroused pleasure to his muscle-bound frame was proof that his eyes were not lying to him.  Even though her pony-tailed hair was somewhat now longer and turning grey, the mannerisms of her hands, how she turned her head, and her inherently strong legs finally made William begin to walk, then run down despite his old legs.  As Elizabeth spotted him, she began running halfway to meet him, shouting,  "Oh, Will; my DEAR WILLIAM!"  He put his hands around her.  "I can't believe this is true!" groaned William.  Their embrace was as hard as iron.

Sadly though, not all of the children had been brought along.   Due to legal procedure arising from the estate, the remaining human souls who were considered "property" had to remain and await their fate, since the legitimate will had now entered probate court, awaiting the appointment of appraisers to conduct an inventory of the estate.  Upon the consent of deceased

Massa Samuel's ten year old heir through his appointed guardian could only they later be released.  The children who did make it out prior to the Probate Court's intervention  included Charles and Barbe's daughter Letha, William and Elizabeth's son Billy Burgess, and Butcher Jennings and Rose's daughters Roberta, China, and Eliza along with her child.  Mother Jenny was not among the arrivals.  Allaying that bittersweet fact for William was when he realized sister Rose's daughter Eliza now had a son, named after the son's great-grandfather he never got the chance to meet,  the man who was blacksmith William's father, whom he also was named after.  Unfortunately, Jefferson had tried to runaway the year before but had been caught by the dogs.  His punishment was still ongoing, for he was unallowed to come to Mississippi with his family.

When William didn't notice his mother Jenny among the new arrivals, he didn't need to be told again the obvious reason why.  After Rose had confirmed to brother William the death of their mother that evening, he retired to his wife Elizabeth's new slave quarters for the night instead of his shared cramped cabin with Butcher Jennings, who already was planning on a long private night  with his "Eve."  As William sat admiring the sight again of his long-separated son, Elizabeth began to mention their son Billy had something he wanted to tell his father.  Now twenty-seven, the young man William Burgess began:

"Grandmama died  October 30th, eighteen hundred and forty."

"Auktober thurtith?  That what they tol' you?"

"Unh-ugh;  It was the same day as the Herald when it come off the mail route and I brought it up to Massa Samuel."  Billy wasn't finished;  Picking up a piece of wood he kneeled down on the dirt floor and began chiseling into the earth the words: **GRANDMA Jenny, OCTOBER 30 1840.**  Next, Billy pulled out a worn-out and folded-up piece of newspaper from the front page of the *Nashville Herald*.  It was dated October thirtieth, 1840. Billy carefully unfolded it and held it up to his eyes with both hands.  Then his lips began to move:  "Local News--Today at Twelve Noon at the courthouse the following auction of slaves will take place--A valuable carriage driver, 30 to 33 years old;  A likely girl seamstress about 16 years old;  Two children, one 6 years old, the other 3;  A Negro Wench about 25 years old and capable of a good days work in the field;  A very valuable Blacksmith in the prime of life and very sound, about 35 years of age.  News from Connecticut--An update concerning the testimony of Joseph Cinque, leader of the slaves onboard the schooner *Amistad*."

William was speechless. Billy Burgess was reading. "Go on!" William rang out. "What they saying 'bout this here *leader* of the slaves?"  Billy, embarrassed, brought the wrinkled piece of paper down from his face. "It don't say no more, Papa. The rest torn off." Billy Burgess had learned to read and write, attributed to a series of early Bible reading occasions in the evenings when he would sometimes sleep over at Brisborn's cabin along with his bunkmate Kendall, who had been sold to Massa Samuel from a nephew out of Hancock County, Georgia. Kendall could quote and read all kinds of verses and passages because of being allowed to possess an old Bible which the nephew's wife mistress had given him.  Billy Burgess had taken the readings a step further by catching on quickly the sounds, syllables, and numbers contained therein, eventually associating them with the objects and activities of Buck Creek plantation.  Clasping both wife and son, William uttered tearfully, "There no difference between the big house and the cabin, there a time to break apart but time to bring together, a time to be slave, but time to be free."

When Saturday night came, the families of Charles, Daniel, William, and Butcher Jennings gathered around a burning fire to welcome and celebrate their returned kin, who were weary and bruised from their travelling ordeal but definitely up for the special evening.  Several went to relating stories well into the wee hours of the night.

Rose now took the occasion to ask daughter Eliza and grandson William a question.

"Do you know "who" you come from?"  Twenty-three year old Eliza didn't know what she meant.

"You mean from Mama?" asked grandson William.

"Do you know "where" you from?"

"From Buck Creek," said daughter Eliza.

"From Nashville!" five year old  William said confidently, the only "Big" place impressed on his young mind.

Rose looked straight at her siblings Ruth, Barbe, William, and shook her head.

"I's not talkin' about them accursed places!!" seventy-three year old Rose snapped back, "I's talkin' 'bout where you *FROM*, who you "*IS.*"

It was time now for Rose to tell the story.

"Billy, you come from yer' mama here;  and 'Liza you comes from me;  Now, I comes from my mama, yer' grandmama Jenny, and froms my papa, yer' grandpapa Will;  Now, theys' was born here, in this here country, back there in Virginny;  But now, who was "my" grandpa and grandmama?  They names was Frank and Akey, but they wasn't from anyplace 'round in this here country, no, they's was born in a different country--did you know that?"  Grandson William nodded his head at the same time he shrugged his shoulders.  Everyone was at rapt attention, staring in awe at Rose.

"Ole Grandpa Frank, he was born Jamaica, West Indie;' And Grandma, she born where her family at--in AFRICA!" Rose said.  "Her father was Mennah, which mean crewman, and her father's brother was Bo'sn, a skilled boatman;  She was brung on a ship, a slave ship, and had her tied up, tied her up and sit her by the ship's jumbo;  Yes, they did!  Tied her up and made her eat peanuts, and yams, and corn so to keeps her alive so they's could work her like a mule!...at nighttime she be there looking up at the moon while the ship be going over the waters;  She look up at the moon every night while she be tied up, and the moon kept her alive, kept telling her that she was still her mama's child."

At that moment, Eliza's five year old William pointed his finger up at the night sky and exclaimed, "There the moon!  There the moon right there!  I mama's child, too."

In 1853 William Burgess finally got married to a young girl named Amanda, brought in from Alabama off an estate from one of Massa Richard's relatives.  By October the following year, Amanda had given birth to twin girls, Nancy & Eliza.  Although

William Burgess' cousin Eliza was happy for Amanda with the birth of her twins, Eliza wished that she, too, could bear another child. It had been seven years since she and Jefferson had planned to begin their family with the birth of little William, but it was now going on two years since they had become separated. A maternal craving yearned to be satisfied deep within her. After going to sleep she would soon find herself waking up in the middle of the night and then go peek out her cabin door, faintly hoping that Jefferson would miraculously by chance be tip-toeing up cabin row to meet her. She would never forget the man she used to embrace. "I want you for my wife!" Eliza finally snapped back to reality and quickly got back into bed before Butcher Jennings, Rose, Roberta, and China were awakened. They would be for sure once Amanda's twin girls started their crying in the cabin next door. Eliza wanted her man back and another child.

Already twenty-five year old Eliza's singlehood had caught the attention of a thirty-five year old slave named Drew who lived on a nearby plantation. Drew was a short man whose front teeth jolted out a bit, but he appeared well built and took pride in being in physical shape. Every now and then on Fridays, Drew would exercise his duties as coachman to carry his massa, a Massa Binford, to Massa Richard's home to gather with others about that week's county talk coupled with their pastime of card-playing. As Drew remained at his post by the carriage he would never miss an opportunity to try and figure Eliza out when she would be told to bring out a meal for him when his Massa Binford would be staying late. But Eliza couldn't stand him.

"How you doing there, Miss 'Liza?  I sho' 'preciate you bringing this here meal to me;  You a girl that got mighty fine manners!" I would say you comes from real good upbringing, am I right?" Drew asked.

"Oh, I isn't nobody special;  I just make do's to survive," Eliza answered. After Drew finished off his meal tray and Eliza had brought it up to the kitchen, her son William had noticed the coachman talking to his mother.

"Is that daddy, Mama?"

"No that's not your daddy, boy!  That man don't have

nothin' to do with us, he just here to take his massa home, that all," Eliza emphasized.

The next Friday, Drew brought Massa Binford again. Eliza was instructed again to bring out a meal, a large slice of ham, green beans, and two sweet potatos.

"Do you peoples eat this fine over here?  Why, I sho' would like to come here on your Saturdays and see what ya'll fixin' then! What ya'll do out here on Saturdays?" Drew asked, preparing an opening in case his massa chose to suddenly come for a Saturday evening visit.

"Some do alittle this, some do alittle that," Eliza remarked, defensively covering all her ground.

The next Friday Drew's tactic turned to just remaining silent while eating, hoping that Eliza would speak first and break the uncomfortable silence between them.  But Eliza didn't say a thing.  Two Fridays later Drew came again, and, after being handed the meal tray from Eliza continued his silent approach except for his greeting formalities.  But this time he handed the tray back.

"I just not quite hungry today, Miss 'Liza;  I sho' thanks you and yo' cook, but today's been a long day, got somethin' weighing on me pretty hard," Drew announced, as Eliza visibly showed signs of concern.

"What wrong Drew?  You not like that," Eliza stated.

"Oh, I be okay;  I just needs a break from all this working; My massa done got so he forgot all 'bout us people needs to have a good time, too!  At my massa's plantation my people hardly ever get a chance to even have music or dancin';  That why I feels pretty low today, Miss "Liza, 'cus I know ain't gawn be no fun when I leaves here to go back;  We hear 'bout your corn shuckings up there," said Drew, knowing that he was just feeding Eliza a few lines so she would feel something for him.

"I sorry but I got to go back now; Maybe  your massa come out here on Saturday," Eliza said, all in one quick breath then turned around and headed to the kitchen, now feeling a bit sorry for Drew and subconsciously wishing there was a way to "solve" his lonely feeling.  To her surprise, three weeks later Massa

Binford came to visit Massa Richard that month every *Saturday* evening and Drew was beaming from ear to ear, now fully committed to making the best use of his time in woeing young Eliza. Her sisters Roberta and China didn't even bother for Drew's attention and crooked front teeth.

By the fourth Saturday that month, after having achieved his goals the previous weeks of dancing with Eliza and presenting her with flowers, Drew finally had her at least to go for a walk along the outskirts of the cotton fields after he had showed off by letting her sit undetected inside Massa Binford's carriage for a few seconds. Soon Drew had led Eliza over to a certain tree. There was no uncertainty as to what he wanted to say and do on this night. As they stood under the tree looking up at the night stars, a voice suddenly could be heard "Mama, Mama! Where are you?" just at the moment Drew was about to say what was in his frustrated heart. As they both turned, there was Eliza's son William with a few other children, groping in the dark. "Let me go get this boy," Eliza sighed to herself, as Drew quickly dropped his hand and his nerve.

"Boy, what you doin' out here with these children? Come on, it time for us to get to bed!" Eliza yawned.

"Mama, who that man?" William asked, barely able to see Drew in the dark as he slowly followed behind his mother.

"This man just here to take his massa home, that all son," Eliza said, as she whispered in William's ears.

Massa Binford didn't show up for about eight weeks to Massa Richard's home. Finally when he did resume his visits, he was no longer driven over by Drew, but rather by a new black coachman. As the house servants Charlotte and Old Hannah could overhear Massa Richard's conversations with his guests, they soon quietly repeated it to the other women: Drew had escaped and made it safely all the way up to Canada.

Three years later in 1857, about the time the late Massa Samuel's widow passed away, Overseer Casey brought the final supplies down to the plantation in Duck Hill from Buck Creek according to Massa Richard's orders to close out his Tennessee accounts. Since receiving the news that his late brother's wife

Sophia was now deceased, Richard had turned weary over the prospect he would have to manage the demands of Buck Creek as an absentee surviving partner miles away in Mississippi. Besides, Sophia before her death took liberty to deed the estate and her remaining slaves to Samuel and Richard's nephew in Hancock County, Georgia, complicating further Massa Richard's claim to his brother's property. The chances of a heated legal contest in court against a nephew seemed to kill Massa Richard's desirability to any rightful claim altogether. Along with Overseer Casey was Jefferson, who finally had ceased being hired out by Massa Richard due to the increase of white carpenters being employed. But that meant nothing to Jefferson in comparison to what it now meant for him and Eliza, now reunited again.

Eliza had also hoped to be reunited with her oldest sister Lucy, but due now to the death of widow Sophia, with the subsequent legal probate proceedings to follow, it would surely stretch her waiting period even longer. And if any debts were to be charged the estate, it was certain that slaves would have to be sold to satisfy any creditors, let alone any inheritance rights.

It was not her fault society had placed these barriers upon her. Eliza now looked to the future. As her uncle William the blacksmith would many times remind her, "A time be slave, but a time be free." Each year Eliza would look for the fulfillment of that proverb. But that prophecy would not come to realization soon. The sign she received indicating this was the arrival of the new overseer in 1858. Marion Hanks, a distant relative of Massa Richard's mother, had now been hired on. The overseer had arrived in Mississippi from Pickens County, Alabama around 1846 along with his brother Taliaferro. Marion in time soon developed a partnership with a local blacksmith, Chesley Holloway, with dreams of running their own plantation outfit together. His real ambition, however, was to one day become a wealthy planter and have a plantation all his own. However, after the death of partner Holloway, Marion felt now the time had come to make his move and begin learning the world of slaveholding. He was given a salary of $2,500 for the year and quickly bought himself a pleasure carriage, which he kept at the overseer quarters.

By the summer of 1858 he had made his presence felt.  One hot summer day as Jefferson and Eliza awoke to begin their day of work, Eliza felt terribly sick and told Jefferson, "go on ahead of me and tell ober'seer I be there if he ask, but if he don't ask and don't mind me, then I plan on restin' a spell." The overseer, six feet high, grey hair, dark complexion, and his Massachusetts-made pocket watch, made his way around to Eliza's cabin after hearing the news, to verify her condition. It was later determined that Eliza was pregnant."

# CHAPTER TWELVE

## He Who Eats the Ishin Knows How to Remove the Deadly Part

Heading back to the public library and to Portland State University to look up books on African names, I was amazed to learn how much anthropologists and onomatologists could gather about a people or culture by the study of them. I learned, for example, that the names Quamino and Cumey were anglicized versions of the Akan West African language names Kwami, or Kwame, which meant "Born on Saturday," and Kumi, or Kumiwa, which was translated "forceful" or "a brave warrior."

This language was mentioned in Dorothy Spruill Redford's book *Somerset Homecoming,* describing her genealogy search and reconstructing the lives of her slave ancestors at a plantation in Tyrrell County, North Carolina. Just as I, she too, had discovered slave records containing African names, whose proper pronunciations were still clearly discernible despite having undergone anglicized spellings.

Akan was a language spoken over a wide area in Ghana and extending into Cote d'-Ivoire. Akan was also referred to as the African peoples who speak the language, although they are known mainly by their tribal names: Ashanti, Fanti, Ewe, Akim, Akwapim, and others. Akan and other African tribes had the custom of naming their children corresponding to the day, time, or season of their birth. I thought back to Great-uncle Murt's nickname "Moon" who was born in the month of June and fourteen days before the start of summer, making me wonder if my great-grandparents were practicing that very African-naming custom. I also appreciated the fact that  West Africans  lived in extended families, made up of parents, unmarried children, married sons and their families, and sometimes grandparents, aunts, uncles, and cousins.  The name Sambo meant "Uncle" in the Fulah, or Foulah language.  If his name was originally spelled "Samba," then it would become a Wolof name.  The Fulah and Wolof peoples today inhabit several countries along the West Coast region, which region those engaged in the Slave Trade once referred to as "Guinea."    However, I could not find the name "Akey" or any possible meaning of that name in the books on African names.  Neither could I find any  meanings to the other African-sounding names.  The woman "Congo Judy" more than likely came from the region of the Congo, whereas "Botswain" sounded similiar to Botswana in southern Africa.  In the country of Botswana, in which the predominant language is Setswana, tribal groups are denoted by the addition of the prefix "Ba" at the beginning of their tribal name.  Hence, the Tswana tribe are known as the "Batswana." But Botswana seemed a long way off from the West Coast of Africa where most of the slave trade during the 15th to 18th centuries took place.

   During that time arose many African Kingdoms such as Mali, Songhai, the powerful states of Hausa, Dagomba, & Gonja, and the Akan states of Bono & Banda.  In 1482 the Portuguese built Elmina Castle and the European slave trade began.  Some forty more castles were built along the West Coast over the years.  Then the Dutch came, followed by the English.  Competition & rivalries began to develop as to who would control the slave market.  As the Europeans became more and more increasing in their demands for more slaves, this led to rivalries spilling over into the African kingdoms, such as the Ghanian States of Akwamu & Denkyira, pitted against one another for monopoly control of the slave routes that led to the coast ranges.  The end result for the losers in battle was vassalage, with prisoners of war becoming the sold goods.   Other Africans sold to the Europeans included criminals, the mentally or physically handicapped, those in debt, or other types of outcasts from their society.   Some were even kidnapped simply by travelling through the wrong village.  By the end of the 17th century a powerful military kingdom emerged known as the Asante, or Ashanti. The wars that resulted with the rise of this Akan power led to the migration of many Akan tribes into the forest country of the Ivory Coast.

The African Quamino could have come from either Ghana or the Ivory Coast. But I didn't know how old he was or what year he had come to the Colony of Virginia. The ages of the children were certain, all born between 1723-1734, and appraised the English currency value starting at three to sixteen pounds. Also certain was the age of the slave named Adam, born in 1700, and appraised at twenty-five pounds. Quamino was valued at twenty pounds, almost the equivalent of twenty-one gold guineas, so he possibly was between 20-30 years of age. Akey was appraised at fifteen pounds in 1735, the equivalent of Colonel Eskridge's fifteen heifers. But could anything be learned about her name?

During that third week in October 1997 during a lunchbreak, I decided to stop by a large downtown book store, needing a welcomed breather from correcting that morning's error-filled reject report of inaccurate name & address bank accounts. I remembered seeing a copy of Webster's Third New International Dictionary on a previous visit and wondered if it might be able to help me. I turned to the "A" section and scanned the pages for the name "Akey." There was nothing. But then I thought, "Maybe the name was spelled in an anglicized form, and so would not be listed under its anglicized spelling." So I looked again. This time I came across a word spelled "Akee." As I read the definition, I thought I was dreaming:

**Akee or Ackee,  a tree(Blighia Sapida) of the family Sapindaceae, native to tropical West Africa and grown throughout the tropics for the white or yellowish spongy flesh of the aril which is attached to black seeds....which fruit is edible when cooked...**

A tree in West Africa where the slave trade took place. I spent my whole lunch in the book store, causing me to literally run back to work! I was in a daze all day long, not able to concentrate on my work. I was just too excited. That word "Akee" just kept echoing through my mind. I kept peering at the clock to see if it was time yet to logout and go home. I couldn't wait to begin seeking the meaning of that strange word. Maybe I could find out the facts about my lineage that day, the answers I'd been seeking for eight years. That truth which had eluded me my entire life. When I had first started hiking down this road, my initial purpose was to simply find out who were my living relatives on my father's side of the family. But the more I kept digging, the more names I kept connecting together--Hugh, William, Eliza, Jefferson, Rose, Tom, Hannah, Jane--and the more pivotal years and pinnacle dates that kept charting my course and progress--1870, 1852, 1781, 1747, 1736--the more I came to terms that my journey had begun experiencing a transformation.

Now my odyssey had taken on a greater, more urgent meaning, as my heart began to burn over the reality that I could possibly go all the way to the motherland. And if I succeeded in doing so, I vowed to glady share my baby steps with as many others, so they too, could acquire the hunger for such an experiment.

For the next several days I went around trying to get my hands on anything having to do with the Akee Tree. I found the word in a 1953 edition of the Encyclopedia Americana:

**"fruit tree...It is a native of tropical Africa, reaches a height of 25 feet or more with numerous branches. Its leaves resemble those of the ash. The fruit is about the size of a goose's egg, contains round, black and glistening seeds. With sugar and cinnamon it is used as a remedy for diarrhea. The distilled water of the flowers is sometimes used as a cosmetic..."**

And the 1995 New Enclodedia Britiannica said:

**"...of the soapberry family...indigenous to West tropical Africa and naturalized in the West Indies since the close of the 17th century...brought to the Caribbean area with slaves from**

**Africa...was introduced to science by William Bligh, famous as Captain of the ill-fated "Bounty," hence, its botanical name..."**

The Akee fruit was not onboard the *Bounty* with Captain Bligh during his infamous voyage in 1788, but rather he later introduced it to the Kew Royal Gardens of Britain in 1793. On Tuesday morning, October 28, I decided to call Mrytle from work during my morning break to see how she was doing and to tell her about my trip to Virginia and also about the African Akee fruit tree. But the receptionist at the nursing home told me that Mrytle had checked out of the home and had gone back into the hospital several days ago. The receptionist gave me the phone number of the hospital and also to Mrytle's next-door neighbor designated to act in her behalf in case of emergency. Immediately I called the neighbors to get in touch with Mrytle. A woman answered the phone. "They just buried Mrytle this morning; We just came in the door from the funeral." My voice shot up. "You're kidding me, Mrytle died?" I asked, in a state of shock. "She died last Thursday," the woman said, as she went on to explain a relative had taken care of the arrangements and staying at Mrytle's house. I felt in a stupor that whole day. That night a call to the relative confirmed what had happened. I had only seen Mrytle just some three weeks prior. But even then in my heart I knew she would not last much longer. She would have been ninety-nine the next February. There was something that daughter of Africa once told me:

*"It used to be if somebody died at your house, they'd put a crape on the door, a big black bulb, with a ribbon hanging down, and they'd call that a crape on the door; Well, you knew somebody was dead at that house; And if someone close in your family had died, you wore a crape on your arm for six months, and you changed it from coat to coat."*

That long awaited sleep she wanted to take so bad the day I was there had now come upon her. The day she wakes up again will be Resurrection Day.

"The Akee Tree...indigenous to West Tropical Africa."

Would this tree prove to be the key to where one of my ancestors came from? The Akee had been brought along with slaves to the West Indies, particularly Jamaica. In Jamaica, Akee is today the national dish, the popular phrase being "akee and saltfish," a meal of akees, onions, and codfish.

The first slaves to Jamaica were brought in 1513 by the Spanish, whom they purchased from Portuguese and Dutch traders. In 1655 Jamaica was surrendered to England, later leading to full control by 1660. Thousands more slaves were brought by the English, many from the Gold Coast. In 1663 began what was called the "Maroon Wars," the word Maroon meaning "wild, untamed," referring to runaway slaves who had escaped into the thickly wooded areas of the island. There they formed isolated communities or societies and survived by defending themselves from recapture by the English. Many of these Maroons were also called "Coromantees" because many of the Africans had been purchased from the slave port called Cormantine along the Gold Coast. These "Maroon Wars" lasted for 76 years until the Treaty at Cudjoe's Tree in 1738:

Articles of pacification with the Maroons of Trelawney Town, concluded March the first, 1738
IN the name of God, Amen. Whereas Captain Cudjoe, Captain Accompong, Captain Johnny, Captain Cuffee, Captain Quaco, and several other Negroes, their dependents and adherents, have been in a state of war and hostility, for several years past, against our sovereign lord the King, and the inhabitants of this island...and whereas his Majesty, King George the Second, King of Great Britain, France, and Ireland, of Jamaica Lord, Defender of the Faith, &c. has by his letters patent, dated February the twenty-fourth, one thousand seven hundred and thirty-eight, in the twelfth year of his reign...to negociate and finally conclude a treaty of peace and friendship with the aforesaid...

Another treaty followed in 1739. Some of the leaders of the Maroons are noted in Jamaican history, such as Cudjoe, Three-Fingered Jack, Quaco, Quashie, and Nanny Crue. Many of the "Coromantees" were later transported to Nova Scotia and Sierra Leone, West Africa.

Quashie may have spoken one of the dialects of the Akan language, his name coming from the Akan child-names which correspond to the day of one's birth.  In their anglicized form they are for boys:  Cudjoe(Monday),  Cubbenah(Tuesday), Quaco(Wednesday),  Quao(Thursday),  Cuffee(Friday), Quamin(Saturday), & Quashie(Sunday);  for girls in the same order: Juba, Beneba, Couba, Abba, Phibba, Mimba, & Quasheba. Thus, place-names in use today in Jamaica are traced to African origin, such as Quaco Bay, Quashie's River, and Quao Hill.

In 1775 with the outbreak of the American Revolution, the American colonies would refuse to deliver goods and supplies to British ports in the West Indies.  As a result, the British encouraged the cultivation and importing of foods and plants.  In Jamaica a botanical garden collection owned by Jamaica's Receiver-General and Treasurer, Hinton East, was being maintained holding various types of plants.  The catalogue of exotic plants in the garden of Hinton East contained all types of various species such as Guinea Pepper, African Garlic, Egyptian Pea-Tree, and The Pale Flowered Crotalaria.  An entry concerning the Mango Tree read:  "This plant was found on board a French ship(bound from Mauritius for Hispaniola) taken by Captain Marshall on his Majesty's ship *Flora* on of Lord Rodney's sqaudron on June 1782."  The entry in the catalogue that I was greatly interested in was:

**Nov. Gen.\_\_\_\_\_The Akee   Africa   Dr. Tho. Clarke 1778 "This plant was brought here in a slave ship from the coast of Africa, and now grows very Luxuriant, and producing every year large quantities of fruit.   Several Gentlemen are encouraging the propagation of it."**

Where in Africa did this slave ship come from?  I tried to search for more information about this ship or where in Africa it had picked up the Akee slips but could not find out anything more except that the tree grew largely in the tropical forests of the Ivory Coast, Liberia,  and in parts of Ghana.  So back I went to Webster's International Dictionary to see if there was anything else I could

learn about my original word.  To my amazement, the dictionary
noted that the word Akee was   from a language called "Kru,"
which the definition for this word was given as:


**1a. An indigenous Negro people of Liberia skilled as boatsmen;
b. Member of Kru people.  2. A Kwa Language of Kru people;
3. A Language group containing Kru, Bassa, and Grebo.**


So the "Kru" were a coastal people of the country of
Liberia, formerly the "Grain Coast," and the language being
included in the  branch of the Niger-Congo Language Family
called "Kwa," which contained other Akan languages as well.  As I
read about the Kru I learned that they were a fishing people and
also skilled boatsmen.  Their knowledge in the art of deep water-
fishing may have come from the Fanti people centuries ago when
they migrated into the Grain Coast region from Central Africa.
The Kru of Liberia belong also to the same ethnic group as the Kru
forest people of the Ivory Coast, and are divided into patrilineage
social units in their villages, tracing descent through males to a
common male ancestor for both the men and women.
The Kru word akee was closely related to the Akan word
"ankye" meaning "wild cashew tree" in the Twi dialect of Ghana.
In the Ashanti language of Ghana the akee was called "achin."  In
the Yoruba language of Nigeria it was called "ishin."  The danger
of eating poisonous unripe akee by not removing the aril of the
seed is well known throughout West Africa.  Hence, the Yoruba
proverb: "He who knows how to eat the ishin knows to remove the
deadly part."  An old African saying is that "even the Parrot knows
this."  The Akee tree in Liberia is found along the River Cavalla,
which forms the boundary with the Ivory Coast.  "Cavalla" was a
Portuguese word meaning "Mackerell," referring to the Mackerell
fish found abundantly in the river by the Portuguese when they
arrived and began their exploration in the 15th century.
The Kru are mentioned in an old folktale of the Grebo,
another coastal tribe in Liberia.  According to the tale, one day
while searching for prey, a hunter named Pudi Nimle cited an
unexplored piece of land off in the distance.  Pudi quickly reports

this to his tribe, and persuades them into going by canoe to explore the land. The canoes earnestly head out, but some in their number capsize. The rest of the tribe continue on. When they finally reach the new land they discover the land already inhabited by the Kru, whom the Grebo described as the "people who lived on the coast as fishermen."

The Kru originated east along the gulf of Guinea, then made a westward migration toward the Grain Coast as a result of Mande-Mali traders. During the 16th century European merchants made contact with the coastal Kru. Soon they were invited onto the European vessels to serve as seamen due to their seafaring skills. Many were taken all the way to Liverpool, London, and other European cities during the slave trade and allowed to return to their homes in Africa, bringing with them European attire and other articles. It had even been suggested that the English word "Crew" may have possibly been a corruption of the word "Kru", which derived from the occupation the Krumen or "crewmen" had in common on the English ships in the 16th & 17th centuries.

Because of the inability of the 17th century English men to correctly pronounce kru names, nicknames were given to them. That seaman nickname custom was still being practiced in the 20th century, as I came across a 1922 issue of *National Geographic* on the Kru, where in its October issue mentioned how the purser, in signing the Kru boys on ship, gives them sailor names which he can spell and pronounce, which names the Kru boys held proudly. The Kru would take charge in loading and unloading a ship's cargo, including "slave cargo." Because of the absence of natural harbors along the Grain Coast, a ship's approach would prove dangerous due to hidden underwater rocks. Adding to this the great tropical heat which caused sickness and death among the crews, the English and others soon saw the advantage and necessity to hire the Kru to canoe their slave cargo to awaiting ships out at sea. According to his *"A Slaver's Log Book, or 20 Years Residence In Africa,"* slave trader Captain Theophilus Conneau, born 1808 in Italy and raised in Massachusetts, wrote in 1836 of being sent by his employer to the Grain Coast to establish a slave factory. Noting the Kru, Conneau wrote that the men of war, merchantmen, and slavers landing on the Grain Coast were at the mercy of hiring the Kru's skills and labor. Captain Conneau described in his log book how on one occasion he hired the Kru to fill a brig with slaves four hours before nightfall. Burdened with the almost impossibility of the task, the Kru collapsed onto the beach, completely exhausted. Realizing that darkness would soon fall upon his unloaded "cargo," Conneau described how he then began bribing the Kru women: mothers, sisters, lovers, with mock coral venetian beads, into raising the men to renewed efforts to finish the loading.

The Kru were involved in slave-trade bargaining as the "middlemen," or as they themselves would put it, "o nina nye to koa," that is, "people-buying work." Although loyally vowing never to sell another Kru as a slave, they were themselves sold into slavery. The Europeans held the belief the Kru had the reputation that if held captive onboard vessels they would either commit suicide by drowning or by starving themselves to death. Conneau also mentioned of the tribal wars that took place for the purpose of selling captives to the slave factories, as well as his recorded details of his "factory" operations and illegal slave-trading activities. In his slaver's log of November 1839, Theophilus Conneau recalled an incident while on board the *Crawford* which was to take him from London back to Africa. As the ship stopped in Havana, Cuba two black free women boarded. One of the women was 40 years old and returning home to the Grain Coast region called Galinas, an area dwelling of the Vai people, after an absence of twenty-four years. When she was 14 she had been sold into slavery and sent to Havana where she was purchased by her owner who employed her in selling cakes and pies. She was soon able to hire herself out and eventually saved up money to pay for her freedom.

The Republic of Liberia traces its beginnings to December 1816 when the American Colonization Society was founded in Washington, D.C. Bushrod Washington, nephew of George Washington and Associate Justice of the Supreme Court, was the Society's first President. The Society expressed the belief that blacks, who had been held in slavery for two hundred years in

America, could best achieve their full potential in Africa. In 1818 two agents were sent by the ACS to West Africa, Samuel J. Mills & Ebenezer Burgess, to find a suitable place for settlement. In March 1819 the U.S. Congress passed legislation authorizing the government to transport slaves removed from American ships engaged in the slave trade and appropriated $100,000 for the project. Later President James Madison directed that the money be used for a future settlement in Africa.

On December 12, 1821 Lieutenant Robert Field Stockton and Dr. Eli Ayres landed at Cape Mesurado, territory of Bassa tribe King Peter, which the British at Freetown, Sierra Leone had strongly recommended as suitable area to purchase. After King Peter reluntantly agreed to sell a piece of land, then later changed his mind and refused to do so, Stockton and Ayres marched to King Peter's camp, with pistols drawn, and ordered the King to sign a treaty of cession. King Peter and five chieftains ended up reluctantly deeding Cape Mesurado to the American Colonization Society three days later on December 15th. By April 1822 the settlement was established. In 1824 a town was named Monrovia, in honor of former President James Monroe, and the colony was named "Liberia," meaning liberty. By 1825 King Peter surrendered control of Cape Mount, an area above Monrovia. Over time, other tribes ceded to the colony other areas of sought after land. Between 1820-1843 according to an 1843 U.S. Congress report, 4,771 blacks in the United States, freeborn and emancipated, had agreed to be transported to the colony. In addition, many recaptured Africans taken off of captured slave ships also became part of the Liberian population. The descendants of those recaptured Africans became to be called "Congos."

The origin of the word "Akee" led me to the Kru tribe along the coasts of Liberia and the Ivory Coast. But could I really be sure that my African Akey really had a Kru name? Who were her father and mother? Did they name her, or did someone else just happen to name her as she stepped off the ship that brought her, if she did indeed come off such a ship? Perhaps she was born in Virginia, or even Jamaica?  I began summarizing my notes into ten points: **1.** Akee was brought to West Indies from West African Coast since the close of the 17th century.  **2.** Whoever named her was someone who had knowledge of the word or of the Kru people. **3.** The Kru served on merchant & slaver ships during 16th & 17th centuries.  **4.** Merchant/Slaver ships operated along Grain Coast.  **5.** If someone other than a family member named Akey, why did they select a name of African origin?  **6.** Why did Akey, who had an African name in 1736, still have that same African name in 1747 whereas the other slaves listed had only Anglo names?  **7.**Several African Maroons in Jamaica preserved their Akan birth names. **8.** If Geo. Eskridge allowed African Quamino to retain his name, it seems reasonable he would have allowed Akey, too.  **9.** The word "Akee" is pronounced differently in the Akan, Ashanti, and Yoruba languages than in the Kru language.  **10.** Akee fruit grows along Cavella River that borders Liberia and Ivory Coast where the Kru have resided for centuries.

I began to wonder if there were any other slaves at the Sandy Point plantation besides Akey that could have come from the Grain Coast, or may also have belonged to the Kru tribe.  I kept looking for clues, but the more I looked, the less I found. Strangely enough, while coming home from the office one day in early 1998 on the city transit and immersing myself in a book about missionary work in Liberia, I came upon a page  describing a charter ship.  The large vessel had arrived at the coastal town of Cape Palmas, where the Grain & Ivory Coasts meet, to pick up delegates ready to return home from  a Christian convention.  In order to get onboard the ship, each person had to be hoisted by means of a "boatswain's chair."  "That word sure looks familiar."  I pulled out the slave inventory of George Eskridge.  That was the name of one of his slaves, except it was spelled "Botswain."  I then grabbed the dictionary and looked up the definition:

**Boatswain, (bo sn, or as a literary word, botswan) n,  On a war vessel, a warrant officer in charge of the riggings, anchors, cables, etc.   On some merchant ships, a superior seaman having similiar duties."**

I realized that I had just possibly found another Kru!  Who else would be in charge of a vessel's mast, and have the duties of a superior seaman?  I recalled the article in *National Geographic* which mentioned how the Kru boys would be given nicknames. Apparently the man Botswain had been dubbed a similiar one. That fact brought back to mind the nicknames "Jumbo" and "Gub" for Great-uncles Clifford and Granison Hanks, both nicknames having reference to the sailing of a shipping vessel--the forestaysail of a ship, and the food plantains for slaves that were loaded onto a ship.  Later I  learned there was a ruler in Liberia during the early 19th century named Sao Boso, a king of the Kondo Confederacy, who was also called "Boatswain" by the Afro-American settlers.

This king was also known as Chief Tom Boatswain, called "Boatswain" because of having served in that capacity on British ships, and known as "Chief," not by descent or inheritance, but for being an astute trader.   Some suggest he may have been Mandinko.   King Boatswain or his father had established a Mandinko colony centered at Boporo, situated 90 miles west of Monrovia, where King Boatswain organized a mixed confederacy of Kondo, Mandingo, Kissi, Vai, De, Kpelle, Bandi, and other tribes, which became known as the Kondo Confederacy.

An agent for the American Colonization Society, Dr. Richard Randall, described travelling through "King Boatswain's Country" in a December 1828 report:  "Several of the colonists have, for the purpose of Trade, visited King Boatswain's town, situated, by the present route, about 150 miles in the interior , which is represented as containing 1,000 houses, & 8,000 armed men to its defense.  The Country beyond abounds in Gold and is believed to be the only one intervening between Boatswain's and Foota Jallou (Territory of the Foolahs)."   The report was part of a committee on commerce  to the U.S. House of Representatives on the African Slave Trade.  Ironically, while studying this history about Liberia inside Brandford Price Miller Library at Portland State University, I came across an old advertisement posted in the newspaper *"South Carolina Gazette and County Journal"* of

November 10, 1767 for a runaway slave:

> "...a Negro man named
> **BOATSWAIN;**
> **of the Grain Coast Country,**
> he is a likely, stout young
> fellow about 27 years of age,
> five feet eleven inches high,
> and had a spur on when he went away..."

From the evidence learned about the African names and origins of Akey, Botswain, and Quamino, there was no way I could pass up a more favorable time than now of going back to Virginia and seeing the place where those Africans set foot:  Sandy Point, the colonial plantation home of Colonel George Eskridge.

Was the site still there?   Was the home still standing? Were his personal papers and plantation records still in existence? Soon I would have the answers to those questions.

I arrived in Richmond on Labor Day, September 7, 1998 and began my drive to my reserved lodging at the Best Western Hotel in Warsaw.  As I neared Warsaw, a bridge took me over the Rappahannock River, the river where many slaves were brought in by ship to Leedstown, an old trading town of its day.  Finally I arrived at the hotel and settling down for the evening, prepared my notes for the next day.

Tuesday morning I headed to the Westmoreland County Museum in Montross.  Entering the museum I came upon several historical items such as ancient Indian artifacts, colonial pieces, and other local history.  As I gazed about, two portraits caught my interest.  The Museum Guide informed me that they were portraits of Colonel George Eskridge and his first wife, Rebecca.

After explaining the purpose of my trip the Museum Guide, Darlene, said she would be happy to help me, as the museum held a research room and family files on the second floor.  I had brought my camera along but a photograph of the portraits were not allowed since too much light would pose a danger to the pictures. However, copies of the paintings were available from the Virginia

Historical Society, who held the originals.

Darlene asked what exactly was I looking for.  Without hesitation, I mentioned wanting to see the location of Sandy Point and any personal papers of Colonel Eskridge relating to his slaves. Darlene showed me the cabinets of family files and told me to please help myself.  The Eskridge family file was the largest one in the cabinets.

For the next six hours I traced through pages of files. Although there was much information concerning the white Eskridge families, there were no slave records.  I did learn, though, that the Colonel had obtained over 12,000 acres of land grants in his lifetime.

There was, however, one file that was significant, relating directly to my family.  It was entitled "The Colored Eskridges" and submitted by a woman who obtained the information from relatives of her  black maid Lorraine, on the day of Lorraine's funeral in Louisville, Kentucky:

"Both Eskridges were 78 years old.  He very big & black & shiny, she lighter.  They were both from Duck Hill, Mississippi, between Grenada & Winona in Montgomery, Miss.   On the Railroad between Winona and Duck Hill is a station called Eskridge.  Before the Civil War all the land about was a great plantation belonging to the Eskridge family who owned many slaves.  **The owner had a child by his Indian slave, a cook in the family.  This child, Indian & White (no negro blood) married Frank Eskridge, another negro slave of the family.**  Their child married a Creek Indian woman & was the father of the man in Louisville.  The colored children & the slaves were named for the white owners, & the names William, George, Sam, Burdette, and Harrison come in.  The father & 2 uncles of this black Eskridge lived on small farms that had been a part of the original Eskridge plantation, which farms were given them when the slaves were freed."

Frank Eskridge was one of the sons of George and Phyllis Eskridge, and the grandfather of Tommy Hanks in Chicago.

According to this account, the plantation owner had a child by his Indian slave cook. I doubted, however, part of the story that their child had "no negro blood," since the law of that era defining a "slave" meant you were African descended, no matter if your skin was black, brown, or light-skinned. In all reality, the child was more than likely Mulatto/Creole/Mestizo. This child was Eliza McDaniel. Frank Eskridge married Eliza McDaniel who was part African, part Indian, and whose mother was a woman named Charlotte who married Sam McDaniel, according to Cousin Carleen McBride who had related this story to me four years earlier. Who was Eliza McDaniel's father? The plantation owner had to have been Richard Eskridge. The story was believable, especially since it was interpreted and then written down by a relative of Richard Eskridge as she heard it from her maid's relatives. Frank and Eliza went on to have ten children including Jennings, who later married Florence Hanks, the daughter of Tom Hanks Sr. by a previous marriage. So the 78 year old man in Louisville, who was born around 1888, was evidently one of Frank Eskridge's grandsons. It was exciting to have come across this file and have it confirm some of the names, places, and events that I had documented previously.

By this time Darlene had now come over with a couple of books in her hand. "According to this, the Eskridge house at Sandy Point burned down in 1887." My heart sank! How I had wanted to see that house so bad. Yet, I still had to go see the original area where my ancient ancestors were shipped. The books went on to describe what the plantation home looked like. Col. George Eskridge settled at Sandy Point around 1700. The house stood in the middle of a green lawn surrounded by trees, flower plots, and gardens. The wooden structure was one and a half stories high, with a Dutch roof and dormer windows. There were four large rooms, the Parlour Chamber, the Chamber Closet, the Hall Chamber, and "the Little Room." Two rooms were downstairs and two upstairs. A large hallroom encompassed the main floor. A long veranda ran the back of the house with two small rooms on each end. The only original part of the site mentioned to be still standing was a small smoke house, no doubt used by the Colonel's slaves in his plantation operation. Colonel George Eskridge later died in November 1735 at Horn Point, another of his estates located along the northwest channel of the Yeocomico River.

Darlene continued: "There is a house on the original foundation which was built by the lawyer John R. Dos Passos," the father of the famed writer John Dos Passos. There was a picture of the present Sandy Point House in one of the books, and Darlene provided me with a map as to how to get there. I thanked her for her assistance, and Darlene made it a point to let her know if I came up with any more questions later on.

Now it was time to take my journey. The night before there had been a lightning storm, but today was sunny and warm as I drove through the Virginia countryside. Every once and awhile I would pass by  historic plaques describing the events of the area. At one point I noticed a highway sign named "Yeocomico" which according to my map meant I was nearing an old 17th century church called Yeocomico where  the Eskridge family attended including Mary Ball, who it was said would ride her horse into the courtyard. I pulled up to take a look. As I got out of the car a man who was working in the yard approached me. The Caretaker of the grounds, Samuel Gaskins, began explaining the history of the building;  built in 1655, destroyed by a fire, then rebuilt in 1706 out of brick made from a kiln which he showed me in the courtyard. Before I left, Mr. Gaskins directed me to George Eskridge's tombstone.

After driving a few more miles, I approached a plaque just ahead on the road.  It said:

## SANDY POINT

**Here at Sandy Point, Mary Ball, George Washington's Mother,
Spent Her Youth in the Home of Her Guardian,
Colonel George Eskridge.  Here She Married
Augustine Washington in March 1731.
She is Supposed to Have Named Her
Eldest Son, George, For Colonel Eskridge.**

I proceeded up the road past the tobacco and corn fields on both sides of me, and, seeing a lady looking out her screen door, stopped to ask about my destination. "I'm looking for an old home called the Sandy Point House;  do you happen to know where it is?" I asked. "This is Sandy Point House here," the lady replied as she came outside to meet me. "This home was once owned by John Dos Passos but was built on the original site of Mr. George Eskridge's home." She continued, "Mr. Eskridge owned most of the land around here...there used to be a bridge there heading north...Mr. Eskridge would jump in his horsecarriage and take off to his other plantations."

She then showed the old smokehouse that was still standing. We chatted a little more as she allowed me to take pictures and look around. I stood amazed and imagined just what was seen by those who lived here:  entering the house and seeing the four large paintings on the wall and the floor cloth of painted canvas in the entry;  the leather chairs;  the spinning wheel;  the clock in the hallway with the backgammon table;  the maps;  the portraits of Colonel Eskridge and his wife;  the 81 book library including "The Laws of Virginia," "Speeches and Passages of Parliament, 1640,"  "The History of All the Religions of the World," and "The Origins of Nations;"  the Colonel's Escritoire; The Parlour Chamber, where Augustine Washington and Mary Ball were married;  the punch bowl;  a casket of cider brandy.

Outside I could see where  the slave cabins were once scattered about, some by the mules quarters, some by the dairy, and some more by the tobacco house;  Yes, here was where tobacco was grown, the money crop for a profitable minority, but the crop of death for the black majority.

Here the forty plus adult slaves would sow the seed beds in March or April, then transplant them to the fields in June. Then the skilled servants would come around to top the tobacco plants with the use of their sharp thumbnails. By hot August the Africans and Virginia-bred harvesters would go out and cut the mature plants down to hang in the tobacco house and undergo the curing process for the desired Oronoco or Sweet-scented variety. Finally after being thoroughly dried, the leaves were bound together in small bundles called "hands" to be put into casks called "hogsheads." The slave carpenter would construct the hogsheads, others would bind the hands, while another slave would climb inside the casks barefoot to lay the hands until the hogheads were full, after which they were weighed, marked with the owner's initials, then rolled or transported by sloop to the tobacco ships waiting to be loaded.

I marveled at how Africans and their second & third generation borne descendants were able to hang onto survival amidst this life of misery, wondering even how "Kwame," Taffy, Sambo, or the other blood Africans on George Eskridge's plantation reacted on days when the eternal social rank of slavery were just too much to bear. How did Botswain, Mingo, whose name in Hausa means "defiant, rebellious," or even "Kumi," whose name meant "forceful" respond? The colonial Virginia *Gazette* was full of runaway advertisements, including those submitted from Sandy Point masters. The Virginia *Gazette* of November 21, 1745 announced a runaway "from the Plantation of the Hon. Philip Lightfoot, Esq; at Sandy-Point...a light-complexion'd Mulatto Man, aged 25 Years, nam'd Ben; he is about 5 Feet 3 Inches high, has a down Look, a low Forehead, talks good English, and has been well whipped. Whoever brings him to me, or to my Overseer at Sandy-Point, shall have Two Pistoles Reward." The *Gazette* of October 17, 1771 advertised the runaway of "a Negro Fellow named Sampson...tall black Fellow, of a serious Look, is in the Habit of common Plantation Negroes...Also a Mulatto Fellow named Harry, rather tall, has a very wild Look, a wide Mouth, generally wears his Beard very long, has a flattering Tongue, is clothed as is usual...Whoever will deliver either of the said Slaves to me, at Sandy Point, shall have a Reward of TWENTY SHILLINGS, besides what the Law allows." On August 31, 1699 the Westmoreland Court summoned attorney George Eskridge "To answer James Orchard of a plea of Trespass on the case wherefore he by Force and arms two boy servants to James From the seventh day of August last past did detain and keep...George Eskridge saith that true it is he did detaine and keep the two boys but said it was by the order and for the use of Peter Ouchterloney." The wives of James Orchard and George Eskridge were related by distant marriage, and so both men were already acquainted with each other, if not openly. The Court proceeding continued to present the facts of the case relating to the stolen servants "upon the plantation of James did enter and two boys, servants to James, the one named Wm. Rosse and the other William Crookshanks, unlawfully did seize and carry away." The Court later ordered that the two boy servants be returned by Ouchterlony and to pay James Orchard 500 pounds of Tobacco. Sadly, I recalled the response Master Eskridge gave out to a captured runaway of Mary Ball Washington's mother described in the court records of Northumberland County July 19, 1721--the same day her mother's written will was entered into probate:

"Ralph Smithherst, servant of Ms. Mary Hughes, declared having run away from his service, ordered that he have 20 lashes on his bare back and that Captain George Eskridge, executor of the said deed to have liberty put on the said servant  irons."

Reading that document brought back to mind a passage from the King James Bible, written the same century George Eskridge was born, that not even a lowly beast in the field would have been rendered treatment such as  this. As the passage read: "Thou shalt not see thy brother's ass or his ox fall down by the way, and hide thyself from them:  thou shalt surely help him to lift them up again...Thou shalt not deliver unto his master the servant which is escaped from his master unto thee." Albeit white men during those days received lashings too--for crimes such as stealing or fornication. But contrary to black male slaves, white males could be released upon serving their time. Not so for black males--they were property--valuable property--especially during the harvest time.

Other field hands were no doubt busy in the corn & wheat fields, picking in the apple orchard and the grape vines, to be put into the press and ground to produce powerful cider brandy or red wine, the Colonel's wine bottle seals some of which were later excavated at Augustine Washington's estate, or hanging meat or fish in the smokehouse over the hardwood fire. The plantation straddled alongside the Potomoc River.    There oysters    were roasted on the sandy shore.

But did any slave ships come into Virginia from the Grain Coast during George Eskridge's lifetime before his death in 1735? There were only three known ships into Virginia between 1698 to 1735 that came from the Windward Coast, which included the Grain Coast, and all three ships landed at the port of York. Two of them were--the *John and Mary* on June 11, 1724 with 135 slaves; and the 80 ton, 4 gun, 20 man *Molly Galley* pulled in with 163 slaves on October 4, 1726.    Incidently,   the ship *John and Mary*--which just seven days before its entry was attacked by a Spanish pirate ship and plundered of thirty-eight of its choicest slaves--was at the time of arrival captained by  John Jones, who in 1704 co-captained the ship *Little John* into Westmoreland County and soon thereafter sought an attorney to take possession of the ship with its six slaves. He soon became the owner of the *Molly Galley*--registered and bonded in London.

The third ship, however, caught my attention even more. It was a 40 ton, 10 gun Brig built in 1721 and insurance bonded on October 13, 1724 at London named *Providence*, carrying 174 slaves on June 7, 1725, and again on July 15, 1726  carrying 141 slaves.    The *Providence* sailed again into the port of York on September 22, 1727 with 125 slaves, this time only reporting that it had come from "Africa."

The 10 gun brig *Providence* was captained by Egerton Cutler and owned by Cole & Dudley Digges. Cole Digges and his father, Sir Dudley Digges, were both members of the House of Burgesses in Williamsburg, Cole Digges serving as President of the King's Council in the House.    Could Colonel Eskridge have purchased Akey off one of these ships? There was no way I could tell.    However, he may   very well have purchased her off of *Providence* because he, too, was a member of the House of Burgesses attending the House sessions held in Williamsburg, only some twenty kilometers from Yorktown, which provided him plenty of favorable seasons to purchase at the slave auctions taking place or even directly from a fellow House member, just as prominent members  William Byrd,  Robert Carter,  Thomas

Newton, Jr. and others were known to have done, ordering slave consignments and then selling them upon arrival. *Providence* was also registered in Williamsburg--April 13, 1724.

  Although I could not pinpoint exactly when or where Akey and the other slaves were purchased, I had a strong suspicion that they had, in fact, been purchased in Yorktown because of another reason. There were two names familiar to Westmoreland County that appeared on the slave ship records, whose ships also chose to enter at the port of York. On June 1, 1752 the ship *Alice*, captained by Richard Jackson, entered Yorktown with 260 slaves, the ship having been reported bound for the Windward and Gold Coast. And on June 20, 1727 the ship *Margaret*, owned by a Samuel Bonham, entered the port of York with 244 slaves from Angola. On August 25, 1727 the vessel *Sarah Galley*, again owned by Samuel Bonham, arrived at the port of York with 400 slaves from "Africa." George Eskridge's father-in-law was a Samuel Bonum, the family surname sometimes spelled Bonham, and George Eskridge's first wife Rebecca also had a nephew by the same name, who had married Mary Ball's half sister Elizabeth Johnson. It struck me that Yorktown was chosen as the port of entry, as if that were a more favorable and preferable landing dock for slave-selling. The famous planter and politician William Fitzhugh, according to the book *William Fitzhugh and His Chesapeake World, 1676-1701*, "often had to send to York or Gloucester to ask a friend to buy him some likely Negroes before they were all picked over, as they surely would be before the ships arrived in his neighborhood, if they ever did arrive."

  Many thoughts were going through my mind as I snapped the last photograph of Sandy Point, walked over to the rental car, and slowly began my leave. I started to wonder what ever happened to all of the Eskridge slaves? Whatever happened to those who were inherited by Dr. Robert Eskridge? Part of that answer may have been found in an advertisement in the Virginia *Gazette* of April 7, 1738:

To Be Sold For Ready Money

A tract of valuable land lying on Potowmack River, in Westmoreland County,...containing about five hundred Acres with an overseer's house, Quarters, and three large Tobacco Houses, a good orchard,...also several fine Slaves to be sold with the land or separate...Whoever has a mind to purchase the said land, Negroes, etc. may repair
to the Subscriber, at his house in Northumberland County
Robert Eskridge

Shortly later according to the Westmoreland County Order book Dr. Robert Eskridge conveyed to Richard Jackson a tract of land called "Gerrard's Neck" on June 5, 1738.  That year Robert and his wife were said to have left Virginia and went to England.   But to give the honest truth, I didn't know what happened to Botswain, Quamino, or any of the other men, women, and children whom were brought to this place;  brought here to grow tobacco.

I knew what happened to those who were inherited by Samuel Eskridge, for they became my lineage, beginning at the Grain Coast of Africa.  There was no doubt that his son Burdett inherited a portion of his slaves and brought them to South Carolina.  And after Burdett's death his two sons Samuel and Richard brought the descendants of those slaves with them, eventually ending at Duck Hill.  The 1747 inventory listed Akey and seven other slaves on the colonel's former Fairfax County estate.  Fairfax County was formed from Prince William County in 1742.  Recalling George Eskridge's will again, it stated:  "...I give to my aforesaid son Samuel and his heirs five hundred acres of land part of a tract at a place called Flatlick *in Prince William County* to be chosen by him in any One place out the said tract."  Whatever beliefs, customs, and other information Akey heard and learned among her new family clan, she would have passed on to the next generation of Eskridge kin.

I couldn't help but wonder if any of my ancestors had seen George Washington as a boy?  Perhaps they may have seen him at three years of age when surely Mary Ball Washington would have attended the funeral of her legal guardian Colonel Eskridge in 1735.  Perhaps my ancestors may have met the future President again in November 1744 if he and his mother paid their respects at the Eskridge home when Colonel Eskridge's second wife Elizabeth passed away.  Quamino may have greeted them at the front gate. House servants Hannah and Beck would surely have seen them inside the home while tending to their hospitality duties and making guests comfortable.  Akey might also have been assigned chores in the big house.

Ironically, two slaves from Sandy Point, William and Jane with their three daughters Ruth, Barbe, and Rose may have very likely seen Washington as President, when, on Saturday May 21, 1791 he left Augusta, Georgia six o'clock that morning on his way to Columbia, South Carolina during his Southern States tour that Spring.  According to his diary on that date, Washington said he stopped and "dined at a house about 20 miles from Augusta."  This house, a log tavern called the "Piney Woods House," belonged to Captain Van Swearingen of Edgefield County, South Carolina whose property was adjacent to Burdett Eskridge.  The main wagon road in the area which Washington and his party rode, stretching from Augusta to Charleston, went right through Burdett Eskridge's land, which by then was inherited by his sons Richard and Samuel.  If the Eskridge slaves were out in the fields that Spring morning they may very well have witnessed the entourage go through, and seen the man of  whom they might have recalled hearing stories about, as well as of his mother Mary Ball, from their slave parents and grandparents back at Sandy Point.

Did the shackled Africans and Virginian-born black slaves that George Washington dealt  and conversed with in his life have any impact on his conscience regarding slavery? Possibly.  Who knows?  The President's dispatch during his stay in Augusta didn't seem to show any overly concern about the Georgia Governor's complaints regarding the fugitive slave problem and Spanish Florida, who were granting freedom to any American slave who crossed into their jurisdiction.  And one can only guess over the well known fact as to why he stipulated that his slaves be freed upon his death;  Or why the ACS presided by his nephew Bushrod Washington chose the Grain Coast of Africa to transport African-descended Blacks from slavery to freedom.

As I later walked along the shores north of Sandy Point, I peered across over the Potomac River, and visualized 300 years ago Akey and Botswain being captured and sold to the slave traders. They now were shackled away from their motherland, never to see it again. They now were headed to a land where their mothers would be naught.

I could see the slaver finally coming into Virginia's ports from its monstrous voyage, carrying human cargo now half dead. On slave buying day, people are coming from all over to pick out their finest choices. "STEP RIGHT UP, STEP RIGHT UP! Just ARRIVED TODAY-- from AFRICA a CARGO of CHOICE HEALTHY WINDWARD COAST SLAVES...the SALE will BEGIN TODAY UNTIL ALL ARE SOLD!"

I can picture seeing the newcomers, Akey and Botswain, arriving at the plantation on their first day. There they are led away to the slave quarters to receive their "breaking in" sessions on the rules of slave life, at the feet of an old-time Virginian-born slave prisoner himself. I can see the frustration on that old slave hand's face as he tries in vain to communicate. There off to the side another slave observes, an African slave named Quamino. There he stands and listens to the language of these newcomers and, seeming to recognize some of the words sounding familiar to his own dialect, goes over to speak to them. To his amazement, they understand words in his tongue. The old slave hand smiles for a second, then quickly brings his finger to his lips, "Shhhh..."

I can also see Lady Eskridge and the two girls Elizabeth and Mary, preparing themselves for the arrival of husband and father, who having been in session at the House, now is coming home. Perhaps that night, with all his sons and daughters present, they hold a banquet in their father's honor with food, merriment, friends, and enjoy the melodies of Handel and Purcell.

Perhaps that night, too, in the slave quarters, a celebration is held in Akey and Botswain's honor, to welcome them as new members of their extended family. But their celebration is to the sounds of an African beat.

October 30, 1998. Lying down on the bed this lazy late

Friday afternoon, my wife and I snacked in front of the TV set, not really paying attention to it, but rather, to our potential weekend plans.  We had just recently attended the concert of Herbie Hancock and the Headhunters when they rolled into town a few weeks ago at the Crystal Ballroom in downtown Portland, so the musical notes of fusion jazz was very still warmly flowing through our veins.  As we sat viewing in our bedroom Oprah Winfrey's segment in which she invited guests to review her movie *Beloved* and the topic of slavery, I soon sprung to attention when one of the guests introduced herself as a descendant of Colonel George Eskridge.  Quickly turning up the sound, I listened as Oprah showed a picture of Colonel Eskridge, while the woman went on to briefly mention of two family documents involving the Colonel and his slaves: one showing how many slaves he was taxed, the other describing how he whipped a runaway slave.  The woman concluded by saying how the physical whipping she watched in the movie had now painfully touched her in a profound personal way because of what she knew had also occured in her own family's past toward the family slaves.  Those family slaves were my ancestors.

**"To any Person Lawfully Authorized...You are hereby Licensed to celebrate the RITES OF MATRIMONY between Mr. *William Wilkins* and Miss *Rosetta Campbell*." The Carroll County Freedmen Marriage Register.**

## CHAPTER THIRTEEN

### "Maybe They Need to Be Free!"

A visit to my parents on the first day of winter found my two brothers and I all sitting at the dinner table together for the first time in I don't know how long. Since we had all grown older, we had also grown apart, always seeming too busy to sit down together at the old dining room table that used to serve our meals when we were growing up. But on this Sunday winter night we all joined together with our parents to enjoy fresh-cooked salmon, baked potatoes, and hot-buttered rolls.

After the hearty meal, we watched a football game while discussing a half different topics from religion to world news. But before the night was out, I brought up to Laurence and Michael the story of our ancestors and a printout of the family tree. I talked with my mother and father about the history of Duck Hill and of the South, my visit with C Swanson, the lynchings in Segregation, the abuses during Reconstruction, and the pre-civil war judicial courtcases involving slaves. The litigations and legal battles over human rights continue on today, as my visit to the Civil Rights Museum during the family reunion in Memphis clearly demonstrated. I remember a trolley car had brought us from our hotel to the museum, housed inside the old Lorraine Motel where Dr. King stayed when he was cut down, and it was a trolley again that took us back to our lodging. The sound of the wheels on top of those tracks took me back to the family story.

"Two years earlier before Overseer Hanks arrived, the State of Mississippi had issued a charter for the Mississippi and Tennessee Railroad line, from Jackson to Memphis. When the railway was finally built through Duck Hill, Eliza's son William, along with the other boys, would run towards the end of the fields to watch the train roar past.    The children on the adjoining Campbell plantation would be seen doing likewise when they too heard the blowing of the whistle.    During the summertime when Massa Eskridge and Massa Campbell's families came together at times for socializing, the slave families from both sides of the fence were allowed passes to hold corn shuckings.    Throughout each year everyone was fed just enough to stay on the slim line of healthy, although during winter months the whooping cough would affect the children, which required the administering of the black cohosh drink, also used on those suffering from asthma or those with violent convulsions, which in their case the herbs of black cohosh and skullcap were mixed together.    When the fury of winter or other times of coldness proved too harsh, the seasonal workhands and those assigned to carry for the livestock would sprinkle cayenne pepper on their feet or inside their wornout brogans during chilly days and before retiring to bed.    By October 1858, William Burgess and Amanda had a boy, William Henry.

As December 31 passed and New Year's Day came, Eliza continued to keep on the watch for hope of deliverance from the heavy yoke placed on her people.    Overseer Hanks was hoping as well, his heart centering heavily on owning slaves and his eyes were now upon Eliza and her soon to be twelve year old son William.    The question that kept hounding him each day was, did he have enough nerve to make an offer to Massa Eskridge to purchase some of his slaves in preparation for his own future dream?    When Overseer Hanks came around everyday  to inspect the cabins, he would take note of who he might make good on.    His salary was increased to $3,000 for the new year, making him feel very pleased about his performance.    The overseer was learning his "respectable trade" well and receiving praise from his boss; perhaps from even some among the forty-eight he lived among day in and day out.    The last thing Overseer Hanks wanted was "unmanageable slaves" which, he would never fail to remind them, would force Massa Eskridge to "have to put someone in his pocket."

By the end of January, Eliza gave birth to her second son, she and Jefferson naming him Thomas. Oddly though, this birth did not feel right with Eliza. She had yearned so long for another child to nurture and raise with the help of Mama Rose, now pushing eighty, along with showing Amanda that Eliza was no longer barren, but this time the planting nature of Eliza's conception was done without she or Jefferson's consent.

Old Mama Rose gripped Eliza's hand as she lay on her back on the cushioned pallet, while Amanda stayed focused to the childbirth at hand, holding the baby's head as it began to emerge and pushing out of the wet womb.

"Keep pushing! Keep pushing! It's coming!" cried Amanda's encouraging and coaching. Now the child was nearly running out, first the head, then chest, then it's arms, legs, and finally feet. "It's a boy!" Rose cried out. But as Amanda wiped the baby then placed it in Eliza's arms, she quickly noticed the strange color of the boy, fielding Rose a perplexed look.

"This child be named Jefferson also, Thomas Jefferson," Eliza exerted out in a soft low tone. "Look at him Mama, he my boy...my sweet new baby boy."

"Yes, daughter, he sho' is," Rose said, then fielded back a shocked look to Amanda.

The baby was light-skinned, almost yellow.

"Daddy Jefferson gawn' be a new pappy," Rose said gently to Eliza, almost as if she were trying to elicit a true confirmation, or else a true confession. Eliza became silent. "I say Jefferson gawn' be happy to be a new daddy," Rose repeated again, but Eliza remained silent while continuing to hold her child. All at once, Eliza's eyes became flooded with tears, soon which were rolling down her cheeks.

"The baby yellar," Amanda said, as her arm wiped from her forehead the laborious sweat of a mid-wife. The statement pierced Rose's heart, which until that moment was merely serving as a protective buffer from the reality.

"Is this Jefferson's child?" Rose asked contritely, forcing the words out of her mouth.

"Nooooooooo," Eliza mumbled painfully while at the same

time shaking her head, the tears streaming even more.

"Did a white man force this on you?" Old Mama Rose now had to ask.  Eliza nodded her head yes.  "Oh Lawd!  Dear God, my baby!" Rose shouted out, almost losing her balance and falling, had not Amanda caught her.  "Why did you stay silent!"

"Please, Mama..."

"Who was the bastard!  Who?"

Mama, please, I don't want no trouble..."

"I said 'Who was he?' How could you not say something?"

"Mama, please!  I can't do nuthin' 'bout it now, 'cept raise this baby--my baby--and give him all the love in the world!"

"Baby, you gawn' tell me who the daddy of this mulatto child is before we leave here...!!"

"Quit Mama Rose!" Amanda now jumped in.  "Stop!  Ya daughter don't need no ill-feeling sermon or confession from her mother rites now!  She jus' needs yo tender lovin' care rites now!"

Rose instantly stopped her words in mid-sentence, and looking as though she had been hit by a ton of bricks.  Soon both women had dropped to their knees in front of Eliza, giving her loads of reassurance hugs.  "I's sorry baby, I's sorry," Rose said.  Then Eliza pleaded with them.

"Please promise me you both won't tell Jefferson!  I don't want nuthin' to happen to him or this baby!  Promise me!"

After both giving their bound oath, Amanda stood up to go get more hot cleaning water.  As Amanda stepped outside the cabin door, there was Jefferson awaiting word.  "How is she, Manda? And, how's the baby?" Jefferson asked.  "You a brand new pappa; Go on inside and see yo new boy!  Yo wife alreadys got a new name fo him," Amanda answered.

As Amanda went to fetch more water, Jefferson made his steps up to the cabin, opened the door, and went inside.  He and Eliza stayed inside the cabin all that day.

As later snow fell then melted, and winter soon turned to spring, new settlers began  moving into the Mississippi Delta while old deed holders moved out.  Even Mistress Sarah Polk, widow of the late President, had put their Yalobusha River plantation up for sale, while at the same time some of Massa Richard's relatives from North Carolina began moving West into neighboring Choctaw and Chickasaw Counties along the old Natchez Trace before the following winter.

One day, Eliza's cousin William Burgess had stumbled upon parts of the town newspaper, Carrollton *Advocate,* crumbled up in the henhouse. William Burgess balled up the paper and stuck it into his cotton jean pocket. Later on at night, after it was assured Massa Richard and Overseer Hanks had fallen out, assembled the family relations of just men and women who could safely come, to his father's cabin upon realizing the seriousness of what he had read. As George's son, Frank, stayed behind and kept a close watchout on Overseer Hanks' cabin, William Burgess began to read under candle light.

"It dated, October 18, 1859;  Some of the words are torn off, but THIS is what I reads:  ".......should not...in any way...interfere...with States' rights.  It is the right of...citizens to...determine their own destiny and not the abo...abolitionists...Breckenridge and Lane say they are for States' rights,...secession,...and slavery;  Yet, the newly formed State called "Oregon" which Lane is a senator, voted 7 thousand...7 hundred 27... to... 2 thousand... 6 hundred 45...rejecting slavery; Who knows what will become of...Kansas...Territory?  Lincoln crys the...slogan "No More Slave States" and is...determined not to bend his knee to...appease...sec...secessionists...nor accept any compromise policy;  Our only ray of hope is Stephen A. Douglas, who is a man of full nerve, will, and rich...heritage, who will not back away from his belief in...popular...sovereignty for...determining whether a territory should be slave or not."

Just then, Jefferson soon interrupted. "Burgess, that sound all good and fine, but just what do it mean?"

"Just hold on, I ain't got to the most serious part yet, I'm gonna explain the whole thing!" William Burgess answered back, resuming his deliberate slow reading.

"The...recent...events at Harpers Ferry...underscore the need for either true leadership in Washington for...protecting...proslavers, or the call to a new pro-slavery...government;  It is the weak...Presidency of...Buchanan that...fosters the likes of John Brown, who with his band of white and colored,...seized upon the United States...Armory yesterday in Virginia to carry out his plan of... overthrowing the Government and setting up a Free State;  Already the United States Army have... marched down to take the armory back."

William Burgess held the paper down and began to explain the meaning of all the strange, fancy-sounding  words.  "Some white man named "John Brown" fightin' fo' the black man, he attacked some kinda building owned by the President that got all kinda guns and rifles;  Sound like the whites worried a whole lot 'bout this man 'cause he fightin' fo' freedom;  They worried 'cause the Union now got a new free State, somethin' they call "Oregon," and they 'fraid this man John Brown gonna start up a whole string of free states if he win this here war he in the middle of."

"They gonna kill him," groaned Jefferson, shaking his head sadly, "'fore you ever see a free negro in this country."

"That's not true, Jefferson," Eliza replied. "I heard of free negroes living right here in Carroll County;  House servant Hannah even told me herself Massa Eskridge's son Taliaferro used to have a free negro family living with him and his Ms' right here in Duck Hill!"

George's wife Phyllis echoed her sentiment.  "My grandmama sho' did say that, said they name was "Waters," that family that be walkin' past here everyday headin' to Carrollton!"

George, now feeling the need to stick up for Jefferson, calmly uttered, "I don't doubt what Mama Hannah done tol' you, but we not talkin' 'bout a few handful o' free colored, we talkin' 'bout every black man, woman, or child stand a slim chance, if any, of being free on account o' one white man."

William the blacksmith now stood up for his son. "Did anyone hear what he just read you?  Do you not read the sign? Times a'changing!  If this white man can understand the evil, how many more out there thinkin' the same way?"

"Das rite," chimed in Butcher Jennings. "At least he doin' more than what Massa Eskridge done for me."  Suddenly, on the other end of cabin row, lookout Frank noticed a movement in Overseer Hanks' quarters, causing him to run up and warn the assembled meeting.  The large family gathering of only men and women quickly scattered out the door and through the backyards to each one's home.

Little did William Burgess realize until two weeks later that the newspaper he had read from was already two months old, when first he heard Massa Richard say everyone would have the whole week off because, "this Saturday is December, New Year's Eve," then later when he overheard Squire McNeil say to Overseer Hanks that John Brown, "was hung three weeks ago."

As 1860 came, Marion Hanks was still the overseer, and Massa Richard was still the estate owner.  In March the widowed landowner turned eighty-five, just about the time his grandson Samuel Butler Eskridge was sent off to continue his schooling in Rockwood, Tennessee where he soon would be receiving ownership of his great-uncle Massa Samuel's former estate.  This was now the start of Overseer Hanks' third year on Massa Richard's plantation, and yet not one purchase of slaves to call his own.  If he was ever going to  make a bid, it needed to be now.  A few days after Massa Richard reached his eighty-fifth year, Overseer Hanks came up to the main house to pay him a visit one Friday morning after all forty-eight of the workers had finished the morning meal.  Charlotte opened the door to let the overseer in.  Overseer Marion Hanks walked in, finding Massa Richard reading the daily Carrollton *Advocate* in the front leisure room.  The overseer approached him as Massa Richard now noticed his presence.

"Good morning Mr. Hanks;  How is everything?"

"Fine;   real fine, Mr. Eskridge;   The field hands just finished up eating and heading out to work;...ah, I came over, ah, to discuss,...to discuss  something with you...ah...I want to, I mean...I would like to make you an offer;  I'd like to have the pleasure of purchasing one of your likely young negro bucks, just as a way of preparing for my own future plans."

Massa Eskridge put his hand to his chin, then turned toward the window to look out at his laborers.

"You want to have title to one of those fieldhands out there?  You have one in mind?"

"How 'bout that boy Billy, Eliza's boy;  He'd make a mighty fine working buck."

"How much you thinking of paying for his worth?"

"I'm ready to give you three-hundred right now for the boy, I been settin' a little aside from my salary each year," as the overseer reached inside his vest to pull out his notes of legal tender. "Three-hundred?"  as Massa Eskridge began musing it over.  "Well, let's go back in the office study so's I can write it up...my account ledgers are in there."

Massa Eskridge sat down, opened up his slaves ledger, and upon going down the column with his ink pen finally located the entry line, "Eliza's William," noting next to it, "Sold to Overseer." Next, he began writing up the bill of sale, "Richard Eskridge of the County of Carroll and State of Mississippi for and in Consideration of the Sum of...," interrupting his hand at the point of inscribing the final transaction amount so to be certain of the closing dollar figure before he set his hand and seal.

"Is it just *one* negra' you want, or would you like  to pick out a gal too, to go along with your strong buck?  You ain't been foolin' 'round with any of my gals, have ya Hanks?"

"No sir!  The boy will suit me fine for now...but if that offer stands open, I may very well  consider it in due time."

"Alright then;  You jus' let me know when;  Let's see now..."the Sum of Three hundred dollars in hand paid by Marion Hanks of the County & State aforesaid the Receipt whereof is hereby acknowledged hath Bargained, Sold, & Delivered unto the said Marion Hanks negro boy named viz:  Billy, about thirteen years of age;  I hereby fix my hand & seal this 9th day of March, Eighteen hundred & Sixty."                                          R. Eskridge

Overseer Hanks finally made an offer which payed off. Now he had his first slave:  a thirteen year male--Eliza's son William.    In time he purchased Eliza and her son Tom, later adding more increasing value to his investment when Eliza gave birth to a daughter, Bettie Amanda.  Overseer Hanks may not have been the wealthiest planter, but he was shrewd:  the owner of the mother  always owns the offspring.  However, the owner of Rose and Butcher Jennings would no longer be the same either.  An incident would soon occur in 1861 that would shatter their lives together forever.

On December 19, 1860 Massa Eskridge passed on.  The very next day, December 20, the state of South Carolina seceded from the Union.  Three weeks later the state of Mississippi became the second state to secede.  News of the secession quickly reached the towns of Duck Hill and Carrollton.  About that time, Butcher Jennings, now eighty-three, had been requested by his new owner Booker T. Eskridge to be hired out to a relative the following week so to cook at a formal dinner engagement being held.  Although slowed by age, Butcher was still sought after by leading families in Carroll County, and still being paid for service just as he had been for the past seventeen years, and turning portions of each earning over to Rose to store away.

The guests on the following week's evening felt special to have the old man Butcher cook for them, viewing him as "the faithful servant of the late Richard Eskridge," while watching him at work, his white curls and hairline, glowing next to the cooking flames in the dark, under an old railroad conductor cap, catching the drippings off the fiery-marinated meats into a cup to be poured back over.

But as the company of overeating and overdrinking guests retired for the evening, it was at that time reported that the kitchen pantry had been broken into, and a group of seven or eight prized slavehands had escaped off their master's place during the night. Knowing that Butcher Jennings was entrusted with locking up the pantry and meathouse, the housemaster and his overseer stormed into Butcher's overnight cabin reserved for him and, raising him from a sound sleep, began barking in Butcher's face like  violent wild dogs:

"Did you leave the pantry and meathouse open!? Someone's broken into the food pantry, and eight of my nigger slaves are nowhere to be found!!"

"No sah! I made sho' to lock up the meathouse, an' I ain't even been in the pantry tonite,"  Butcher Jennings shot back, sounding sure of himself.

"You had better tell us what happened boy, real fast!"

yelled the overseer.

"I don't know anything," Butcher Jennings said firmly.

"You listen real good;  I don't care if you someone else' slave or not...if I find out you were involved in helping my slaves escape...," warned the housemaster.

"Like I says Massa, I don't know a thing 'bout any runaways," Butcher Jennings repeated, but this time in a slight irritated way, disappointed that they would even think of accusing an old man close to seeing his grave of being in on such a plot.

"THEN WHERE ARE THEY?!  Tell us what you *do* know!!" the overseer shouted.

"I TOLD'S YOU I don't know nothin' 'bout your slaves!! Maybe they *NEEDS* to be free!!"  Butcher fired back, losing his temper and letting out his pent up resentments and frustrations all at once, a result of old Massa Richard's broken promises and dreams to him years ago.  Butcher Jennings actually felt joy inside him that the slaves had broken free.

"Don't you RAISE your tone!  Why, you sassy black...!" the housemaster and overseer both charging Butcher, grabbing his frail body by his shirt collar and, with Butcher putting up a useless struggle, flayed him across the room, slamming him head first into the wall next to the brick fireplace.

"Get up!" commanded the housemaster, staring across the room at Butcher Jennings' twisted-up body.  He didn't move.

"I said get up!"  Butcher didn't move.

When Rose finally heard what had happened, she let out a terrifying scream that sickened everyone who heard it that day, followed by uncontrollable sobs, begging that the news broken to her wasn't true.  When Booker T. was told that Butcher Jennings had assisted eight runaways and was himself caught trying to escape which led to the accident, he refused to believe it and filed suit at the Carrollton courthouse.  Word spread of the upcoming trial like wildfire through Massa Booker's slave row, as his fieldhands could hardly believe Massa Booker was actually going to sue his own cousin over Butcher Jennings' death.  Old Hannah put it this way: "It's some bad blood 'tween 'em;  But they say-- *blood thicker than water!*  And it don't take nobody with a brain to figure out who the *water* and who now the *blood!*" The day the trial was to begin, local citizens from Duck Hill and Carrollton had the courtroom packed out. But it was no surprise that Rose wasn't allowed to attend. A slave was still a slave regardless of the fact the trial involved the loss of her own loved one. Rose wasn't expecting to show up anyhow. The grief of her loss was still too great, as daughter Eliza could attest to, while giving all her might to console her mother. However, Eliza's boy, William, so broken up over Butcher Jennings' death, somehow stole away off the plantation in the confusion on the morning of the trial, and, without anyone looking, walked the entire 5-mile road over the hill to the courthouse. Carrying his cotton tote bag to make him appear as merely on an early-morning errand, William miraculously reached the back part of the courthouse and, crouching behind a bush, popped his eyes through a side window.

"All Rise! The Honorable Judge Sebastian A. Parsons!"

"You may be seated. I, Sebastian Parsons, prescribed court Judge for the County of Carroll and State of Mississippi, do now preside over the case involving, Booker T. Eskridge, the plaintiff, and Chesterfield Eskridge, formerly of Alabama, the defendant; I understand that the plaintiff, Mr. Booker T. Eskridge, is being represented by prosecuting attorney James Williamson?"

"Yes I am, your Honor."

"And the defendant Chesterfield Eskridge, cousin of the plaintiff, is being represented by defense attorney Micijah Leddell?'

"Yes your Honor."

"Very well then; Mr. Williamson, you may begin your opening statement."

"Thank-you, your Honor; Gentlemen of the Jury, you will hear in this court today the facts of this case, that my client, Booker T. Eskridge, an honorable citizen in this county following the tradition and good character of his grandfather, the late Richard Eskridge, had in good faith sent his faithful negro slave, one called Jennings, a well-known servant and cook in this county, and as I understand in surrounding areas as well, to his cousin Chesterfield Eskridge, for the expressed purpose of hire, and by so doing entered into a binding contract for payment of services rendered, and in addition, to be promptly returned the property rendering that service;  Gentlemen, as we sit here today while our leaders in Jackson and South Carolina are boldly taking their stand to preserve every man's right to bear property--you don't need me to remind you what was once written and today faithfully honored in southern tradition--"eye for an eye, tooth for tooth, soul for soul, beast for beast;"  The day any honorable man suffers loss of property and fails to be fully compensated, will be a day when all of us suffer loss;  BECAUSE it will be proven by all the facts presented today in this court that the defendant, Chesterfield Eskridge, deliberately and with gross negligence inflicted permanent injury to his cousin's property and is so fully liable to provide FULL COMPENSATION and LOSS OF SKILLED LABOR to Booker Eskridge!"

"Mr. Micijah Leddell, you may now proceed and present your opening statement and defense."

"Your Honor, Gentlemen of the Jury, and Honorable citizens present...I too, agree with my well-respected colleague that every man, and woman, shall forever hold the right to bear property, and to be fully compensated for destruction thereof;  But the issue in this case is not about that;  The ISSUE, as the facts will bear out, is connected to the same reason why our countrymen in Mississippi, South Carolina, and as I now hear this minute, the states of Alabama and Florida, are standing up for--to preserve our traditional institution of being FREE LANDHOLDERS, and PROTECTING and GUARDING OUR PRIVILEGES under the law against northern abolitionists who foster and foment our slaves into unlawful runaways and violent gangs of open REBELLION and INSURRECTION!"  The last statement drew loud murmurs from the audience.  Micijah Leddell continued his client's defense.

"For this I applaude my client Chesterfield Eskridge for not being cowardly or timid to stand up to acts of open rebellion when a slave, to wit, one called Jennings and property of my client's cousin, was openly caught and confronted during the act of leading eight desperate slaves to escape right at the same time you and your loved ones sleep snug and unguarded in the darkness of night!"  Many in the audience nodded in loyal agreement.

"For this I implore you to render a verdict of NOT GUILTY, when a man attempts to protect not only his family and livelihood, but those of his neighbors!  Do not penalize him for asserting his right of self-defense, nor force him to dish out his hard earned money for a mere slave, no matter how old that slave may have been, when that very one emulates the very spirit that could bring our most cherished way of life crumbling down!!  Just like the slave in this case, there was another in our recent memory thirty years ago who also appeared innocent, harmless, and well-spoken of---until August 22, 1831;  That slave's name was Nat Turner!"

Nearly the whole courtroom exploded into a roar.  Judge Parsons immediately demanded order in the court.

Then the trial began, starting with the defense, who quickly called on witnesses to paint the good character of the defendant, and other witnesses, actual guests that night, who swore they saw Butcher Jennings by the meathouse upon leaving.  One such witness called to the stand by Micijah Leddell was Mr. Kyle Jensen:

"Please tell the court what you noticed as you left that night?"

"I come out the door to get in my carriage and I saw the cook servant right there over by Mr. Eskridge's meathouse, and he was carrying a sack when he left!"

And a Bernard Bennett also testified:

"I was escorting Miss Monica Turner to her horse carriage as we were leaving that night, my watch I believe read 11pm, and I distinctly recall seein' the cook standin' at the meathouse, and waving his hands like he was calling for someone!"

Following this, Attorney Leddell presented two male slaves to be sworn in as witnesses, Linus and Romaine, whom neither one had a choice in being forced to bear evidence against a dead comrade.  "Your Honor, I wish to call up for testimony two negro slaves at this time, not to testify against any party in this suit, since that would be inadmissible.  Rather, they are here only to give weight to indirect evidence, facts of evidence that were found at

the kitchen pantry and at the extra sleeping quarters."  Attorney
Leddell had Linus take the stand first:

"Please state your name and who you belong to."

"My name's Linus, an' I belongs to massa Chesterfield
Eskridge, same massa dat my papa Caesar and my mammy Venus
belong to!"

"Tell us what you saw on the night of the dinner party as
you walked past the meat pantry."

"Well sah, I's walkin' pas' the pantryhouse that night, I
wasn't supposed ter be out that late, so I knows massa Eskridge
gawn be mighty mad at me..."

"Oh no--you fine, boy;  You not in any trouble today so
long's you tell the truth;  Go on--continue."

"Well, I was hungry, real hungry, so's I went out to see if I
could git somethin' out the pantry to eat;  But when I gets to the
pantry, I seen the door broken out, like someone broke in to steal
somethin'!"

"Like what YOU were planning to do?"

"No sah! I wasn't gawn steal nuthin';  I jus' wanted to see if
somethin' was jus' laying 'round 'cause I was powerfully hungry!
Anyways, I got scared when I seen the door all broke out the way
it was so's I ran!  An' when I was runnin' I come up to a cabin an'
seen pieces of bread an' an' meat, look like someone dropped 'em."

"These pieces of bread and meat were found in front of
whose cabin?"

"Wasn't nobody's cabin, sah;  It was in front of the
sleepover cabin dat the slave cook was found dead at!  And right
when I seen the food on the ground like dat, I seen the overseer--he
come up to me an' ask me..."

"That'll be all boy;  You can go on and take your seat now."

After Micijah abruptly stopped the testimony of Linus for
some unclear reason, he soon called Romaine for his observations
that night, as Romaine hesitantly took the stand:

"My name Romaine."

"State who you belong to boy;  I SAID, STATE WHO
YOU BELONG TO!"

"Massa Eskridge, sah."

"I can't hear you, boy;  Speak up!"

"MASSA ESKRIDGE."

"Very well then;  Now tell the court what you saw that night."

"Jus' as the sun went down an' I finished eatin', I seen all dem peoples over by massa's house still eatin' and playin' the music;  Jus' 'bout dat time I heared some noises in the bushes over behind the fence but I didn't see no one;  'Bout right after dat I come past the pantry and seen the door all busted out!  Somebody broke in there!  So right aways I went and tol' the overseer to come quick!"

"And do you know who broke into the kitchen pantry?"

"No's sah!"

"Do you know who worked in the pantry that night?"

"It was dat cook dey found dead up in the sleep cabin."

"Did you know that eight slaves escaped that night?"

"Yes sah;  I's heard it from massa Eskridge the next day."

"What were their names?  Come on, Romaine, you know the names of every single one of them runaway niggers, don't ya?"

"NO SAH, I...I don't know NUTHIN' 'bout dem runaways, not a thing;  DON'T KNOW NUTHIN' 'BOUT DAT!!"

Finally, the defendant's overseer was called in, Overseer Foxworth, who described the fight that took place, and quoting Butcher Jennings' words, *"they need to be free."*

Now well past noon, William's stomach was growling as he kept peering through the side window of the courtroom.  He knew he was in trouble for having done what he did.  William wanted so bad to stay and listen longer.  He knew he was in for a whipping once he got back to the plantation, either from the overseer or from his mama Eliza.  William figured he'd take his punishment one way or the other, because on this day he was going to show his respect for his fallen grandfather.  William stood and listened a little while longer, then soon peeled down the road to Duck Hill.  William was fortunate Overseer Hanks hadn't missed him after all.  And neither Eliza nor Jefferson did a thing, except to tell William to not let it happen again.

The prosecutor James Williamson now began his cross-examination of the defense witnesses, raising the question of how certain ones who exited through the front where their pleasure carriages were tied could have even seen the meathouse which sat in the back of the residence, or how they could have seen anything at all as drunk as some reportably were. He started first with Mr. Jensen:

"So you say you come out the door to get into your carriage and that's when you saw cook servant Jennings standing right there by the meathouse, is that correct?"

"That's exactly right."

"And what door did you come out of?"

"Let's see..it had to have been the front door...that's right, I left out the front door, and Mr. Bennett and Miss Turner were right ahead of me."

"I see; And from your vantage point at the front of Mr. Chesterfield Eskridge's home where your pleasure carriage was tied, can you describe what side of the meathouse the cook servant was standing--behind, on the side, or right straight in front of you?"

"What kind of question is that? He was right there in front facing the road! I seen him with my own eyes!"

"Mr. Jensen, did you have anything to drink that night?"

"I had a couple drinks."

"Just a couple?"

"I wasn't drunk if that's what you asking!!"

"After you came out to the front of the house, what was the first thing you immediately did next?"

"Helping Miss Turner up into her horse carriage."

"I thought Mr. Bennett had escorted her."

"Well I did too; Then afterwards he helped me...I mean...I then went to my coach."

"I see; I guess that's all for now Mr. Jensen--except for one thing--can you please explain why the cook servant would be standing by the meathouse in "front" of you facing the road which is north, but the door entry to the meathouse is facing south?"

"Uh, hum..."

"Or can you please explain why only a "couple drinks"

would so cloud your memory, when it is a proven fact that it is practically impossible to even see the meathouse from where the pleasure carriages are kept tied up?"

"I...uh..."

"No more questions, Mr. Jensen."

Following him was Miss Monica Turner's testimony:

"...I got ready to leave, Mr. Bennett walked me out, and my driver took me home;  So as far as seeing who was by the meathouse, I really couldn't tell you, I don't recall being preoccupied with looking in that direction."

"But Mr. Bennett and Mr. Jensen both helped you into your carriage that evening?"

"Mr. Bennett did;  Mr. Jensen kinda jus' "came over."

"Please explain what you mean by that."

"I guess there was some confusion on his part as to which carriage was his;  Mr. Bennett kindly helped the gentleman to his coach."

"Was this confusion due to any heavy drinking that night?"

"I couldn't answer that sir, certainly not on my part;  You would have to ask those two gentlemen about that."

Linus was next to be cross-examined:

"You said earlier Linus, that when you noticed the bread and a ham bone on the ground in front of the sleep-over cabin, you noticed the overseer just coming, is that right?"

"Yes sah;  He come right then;  I 'spect that 'cause Romaine had seen it 'fore I did, an' went telling Overseer Foxworth right away."

"You said something else earlier--that when you saw Overseer Foxworth he asked you something?"

"He ask me did I see dem runaways!"

"And when was that when he asked you this--during or after the dinner party?"

"Let me see...he ask me when massa's guests was still there--they still eatin'!"

"Who was over there cooking the food for those guests at the time Overseer Foxworth saw that the kitchen pantry was broken into?"

"Dey called him "Butcher," he the cook servant who died dat night."

Next, the hiring record of Butcher Jennings was established, as three employers spanning some seventeen years as could be found were subpoenad--Mr. Lott the postmaster, Mr. Purnell the merchant banker of Duck Hill bank, and Major Bigbee--and testifying they never encountered a single problem during his services.  The most damaging blow, however, came from the overseer's own mouth, who had earlier failed to mention that the eight escaped slaves had left long before the dinner had ended, reluctantly admitting he had spent considerable time searching for them elsewhere before reporting to his housemaster.  Overseer Foxworth now took the stand:

"...I went into the servant cabin along with my employer and confronted the cook servant as to whether he had properly locked up the meathouse and pantry;  The servant got smart, denying he knew anything about helping them eight runaways, but he stood up right in front of us, raised his voice saying "They need to be FREE," then grabbed Mr. Eskridge's shirt, trying to assault him!  They got into a struggle and unfortunately the slave couldn't finish what he started."

"Let's go back to when you encountered the two slaves Linus and Romaine;  Did not in fact one of them tell you--I believe it was Romaine--that he heard noises in the bushes?  How did you react when you heard those words, coupled with the damaged pantry door he brought to your attention?"

"Naturally my first thought right then was that I probably got some runaways on my hands;  I then did a head count and discovered eight were missing;  Didn't take me no more than 10 or 15 minutes to get a head count."

"At that point?  Before the dinner party was over?  What time was it when you saw the kicked in door?"

"It was coming up on 9:30 pm according to my watch."

"But according to all the testimony so far given in this case, you didn't approach the cook servant Butcher Jennings until after the guests left around 11pm;  Why was that?"

"That was because Mr. Eskridge wanted me to come with

him and ask that slave what he knew!"

"That's fine, Mr. Foxworth;  All of us can understand that; But what we don't understand and what now seems to become the real question is--when did your *employer* know?  *WHEN* did you tell Mr. Eskridge that you knew eight slaves of his had escaped--at 9:30 or at 11:00?"

"I don't remem..."

"How could Butcher Jennings have aided eight escaped slaves around 9:30 when he was busy tending to his course meals at that same time?"

"He...uh... must have...uh..."

"No further questions Overseer Foxworth!"

Impartial witnesses then swore Butcher Jennings never left his post throughout the whole dinner--always too busy taking pride in what he did--and finally from circumstantial evidence of the kicked-in broken wood door of the pantry, which reasoned to be unnecessary had it been deliberately left unlocked.

The second round of testimony started again with defense attorney Leddell, who continued to fan the flames of prejudice and sway sympathy in the minds of slaveholders present on the jury, while never missing the chance to emphasize his client's reputation as a leading member of the county community and his charitable actions, even how he came to the aid of eight orphaned children, slaves of his whose parents had died.  Attorney Leddell went on, describing how Mr. Chesterfield Eskridge was moved by the orphans plight, hugging them, and providing clothing, food, and shelter right in his own home during a cold winter month, much to the joy of his very own playmate children.  Attorney Leddell's client, he maintained, had no alleged mean streak in him, no deliberate bent to maim or strike without provocation.  "He is no monster" was echoed throughout the courtroom.

But no sooner had that been said, then the skill of prosecutor Williamson went to work, questioning and probing for any past pattern of relevant misbehavior or abuse.  None could be found, and everyone recalled seemed to plea amnesia--until Booker T. informed him of what occurred in Marengo County, Alabama seven years ago, and also of what happened to a free man of color just last year in Carroll County.  A recess was called, while a pair from Williamson's legal team rushed out, one to find a certain person of color, the other to board a train and retrieve a certain trial case in the state of Alabama before the next day's resumption of court.

"All rise!  The Honorable Judge Sebastian A. Parsons now presiding!"

"This court is now in session;  Before this court adjourned yesterday, it was brought to my attention that new evidence is to be presented in this case by the prosecution.  And what is it that the prosecution intends to prove with this material Mr. Williamson?"

"Your Honor, we have discovered some new information regarding the defendant that upon examination will seek to contradict what has so far been presented to this court regarding the character of Chesterfield Eskridge, and by admitting these new facts regarding the past behavior of the defendant will establish clearly without question that the defendant is subject and prone to fits of uncontrollable anger when no provocation existed, and which fits of anger we feel, your Honor, drove the defendant towards the fatal actions he took in this case."

After the objections by Micijah Leddell to release the material was overruled, the newly discovered facts began to be presented.  In the *State vs. Eskridge, Marengo County, Alabama,* attorney Williamson read directly from the summary of facts, stating how Chesterfield Eskridge on the 30th day of June 1854 "was indicted for disabling the leg of slave Maria by shooting, as testified to by the physicians who amputated the limb...the defendant was much intoxicated when he attempted to chastise the slave...loaded his gun and called to her to stop...the slave moved off and told him not to come near her...and thereupon he shot her...the owner of the slave was compensated."

Next, a "free man of color" was called to the stand, Buck Bladock, who testified that on the fourth of July 1860 was accused by Chesterfield Eskridge to having stolen two hogs from him and proceeded to severely beat him, then searched Mr. Bladock's home that very hour but found no hogs anywhere.  Still yet, Mr. Bladock was warned not to pass his plantation again, or else "I'll put you where they'll never find you!"

Each side then rested their case.  Attorney Williamson presented his closing statement to the jury, summarizing the points of his brief.  Then Attorney Leddell began his closing statement:

"Dear prudent and respectable citizens of this honorable Jury; I now solemnly ask you to give great forbearance to my final words.  Yet, my final words to you come not from me, but from the rule of law that continues to govern this great State as part of the Confederacy.  The law does not hold a master responsible for killing a negro slave when the master is in defense of his life...the laws of this State have consistantly absolved a master in cases when a slave died under *moderate chastisement.*  Although the taking of a person's life attempting to commit a crime is considered second degree manslaughter, a negro slave does not enjoy the rights of a citizen...according to the 1857 ruling of the U.S. Supreme Court, they are inferior and are not protected even under the American Constitution...a dead man is not a legal person.  Each of us have what is called antecedent rights or legal rights...antecedent private rights in *rem*, meaning, to the entire civilized world, include the right to personal safety AND THE RIGHT TO CONTROL ONE'S FAMILY...these rights are always under the protection of the State through its power to police...for example, the State does not simply punish stealing, it prevents it...so also with slave insurrections, the State does not only punish runaways, it seeks to prevent them for the protection of EVERYONE...neither can a remedy for compensatory damages be argued under the "Cruelty to Chattels Law" since the law is clear that willful or malicious conduct to animals is not a criminal offense, nor was the chattels law enacted to blueprint *humane* ethical standards.  Liability, therefore, does not exist because no person suffered bodily harm or injury...the contract for hire was cancelled out, since BOTH PARTIES SUFFERED A MONETARY LOSS!  Furthermore, it cannot be proven the exact cause of death...due to the great age of the hired servant, it is highly possible that he collapsed from over-exertion as a result of attacking his employer, thus inflicting fatal injury himself! Respected men, I hold you to handle your charge judiciously and discreetly. Mr. Chesterfield Eskridge cannot be liable for acting as an arm of the State in protecting your community!"

Attorney Williamson stood up, slowly looked around the entire packed courtroom, then approached the jury in rebuttal.

"I can remember as a child when I would go in the barn and watch our family's old hen brood her eggs. I'm sure most children have entertained themselves likewise. Perhaps even most of you. I remember this one time, why, I stayed in that barn all night. Slept overnight in it, waiting for those chicks to hatch. The next morning I was so excited. I wanted to count how many chicks that hen had. You know how many eggs hatched? Only one out of fourteen. ONLY ONE. But that one defenseless little chick grew up and stayed in our family until she died. And that was even after she produced her own babies. You're probably wondering why I'm telling you this. Well, I could probably stand here all day and refute all of my opponent's arguments. I could address antecedent rights verses remedial rights *personam*. Or I could argue *injuria absque damno* verses gross negligence. I could even try pleading my case on the charge of murder without malice, and *manbote* as a redressive remedy. But since in this case a dead man is not a legal person, nor the killing of a slave admissable under manslaughter unless the lack of self-defense is proven, it seems my client's cry for justice has been stripped down. His faint hope for compensation under our common law seems to hinge only if the defendant can be found guilty on cruelty to a *domestic animal*! Yet, my highly educated opponent Mr. Leddell wishes that I not even try this case under that animal law. DRED SCOTT! What am I left to try this case under? If Butcher Jennings' life cannot even find relief in a law written for beasts, then what was he? Who was he? A man? But the U.S. Supreme Court ruled that he wasn't. So there we have it. DRED SCOTT! Dear friends of the jury, I ask you to consider *all the facts* in this case. Consider, not only the laws in our statute books on justice, but even a higher law. Is it not somewhere written: "What man is there of you, whom if his son ask bread, will he giveth him a stone? Or if he ask a fish, will giveth him a serpent? What man shall there be that shall have one sheep, and if it falleth into a pit on thy sabbath, will he not lay

hold to lift it out?  How much then is a man better than a sheep?"
Mr. Leddell mentioned to you about the right we all have "to
control our family."  The word "family" is something that I can
agree with him on.  Because a servant IS FELT TO BE PART OF
YOUR FAMILY!  Is that not true?  With that right to control your
family, *all* your family and servants, comes also the right *to protect
them*."

"Dear servant brethern, whether you uphold slavery with all
your might, whether you hate it with all your heart, or whether
your conscience sometimes pricks you on certain days because
you're just plain confused about collateral issues, consider this one
word:  "Companionship."  If a man can go hunting and not feel
lonely due to his faithful hound, that's companionship.  If a man
can feel the loss of his old horse that has been there since the day it
was born, that's companionship.  When your son or daughter who
plays with the little negro child says to you: "He's my best, best,
friend!", then cries when you explain the little boy or girl just got
sold away, that is called companionship, too.  From the mammy
that held and weaned each one of you, to the servant who saved
your life when you either cut your hand, fell down, or got bit--tell
me that you don't like the way you turned out?  Tell me they didn't
play a part in you sitting in those chairs today?  What I'm saying is
true, true of all of us!  You might be able to put a price on how
many warm meals were cooked you, how many winter fires were
made to warm you, or how many other times your servant catered
your everyday needs, BUT YOU CAN'T PUT A PRICE on when
they made you laugh, made you cry, or just plain made you feel
good.  The amazing thing is, they were doing all those things *to
survive*.  Did Butcher Jennings get a chance to survive?  He and
my client had a close companionship, a warmhearted bond my
client was entitled to have.  Did Mr. Booker T. Eskridge's entitled
friendship survive?  You can't put a cost on friendship, but the
price is heavy when someone takes it away.  Gentleman of the
jury, if a child can stay up all night watching an old hen brood just
one chick, and the next morning jump for joy when he sees that
defenseless little fellow crack out of his shell, then can't a man
who's lost his defenseless companion stay up all night until justice

is born?"

The following morning the jury's verdict came:    Full compensation.    Later Booker T. Eskridge turned in Butcher Jennings' earnings that night, and extra on top of it, over to Rose, along with his railroad conductor's cap, which she gave to grandson Frank, while the money she placed in a tied up cloth kept hidden under the floor boards of their cabin.  Butcher Jennings was buried in Massa Richard's family cemetary.

Rose succumbed that year also--the last to go of the three sisters.  Daughter Eliza and grandson William  had begged her not to go out to work the rows that hot August day, but to stay inside and stay cool.  The overseer would have understood.  He would hardly put up a fuss when an older one said they couldn't work on a certain day.  But not Rose.  She didn't care if she was eighty-two years old or not, she was not going to stay home and watch while others were busy sweating to make up her lost time.  No, Rose pulled her own.  That's what she had learned from her family and that's what she taught her family.  By three o'clock p.m. that August day the fieldhands were raising Rose's stricken body from the cotton rows and out of the merciless hot sun.  She was later buried in the slave section of the Eskridge family cemetary, next to her husband.

The pain that William carried inside himself over the cold-blooded death of Butcher Jennings never really healed up, like a finger-cut from sawing wood usually did when the wound first becomes puffy and tender, then after seven or fourteen days the outer edges of the cut begin to dry and crust, turning hard and feeling itchy.  Then new skin appears, then finally the scab to pick at and peel away.  It wasn't that Grandmother Rose's death was less painful, for William felt her passing too.  But his grandmother's death was due to old age coupled with over-exertion in the cotton fields.   That was enough to be considered a natural death for anyone born a slave and planning on leaving this here world.  But Butcher Jennings' death was in no way due to old-age or over-exertion.  Being beaten down until dead by a hired boss and his overseer would never be accepted as "natural" even though

Southern law said it was and had it spelled out in writing.  Not even a twelve-man jury who couragously voted their consciences was going to change that.

Sixteen year old William's pain, the same sharp pain when he first heard the news and the same lingering pain when he peered into the courtroom's sidewindow from the bushes, was the kind that made him reel with anger each time he observed one of his kind being undeservedly mistreated by the ones who were "always in charge."  Through William's eyes, the world had now changed.  When he was a youngling at five, everyone's position looked natural and normal.  The community Massas and their sons, the gents, were noble and wise, praised and honored.  The Madams and their daughters, the belles, were worshipped and glorified.  And not to be touched by anyone not white.  On the other hand, the poor and wretched black, whether male or female, husband, wife, or child, were considered the off-scouring of the land and forever inferior.  Yet, how amazingly great in servitude.  And the strong-willed women who kept William's race alive were allowed to be touched and fouled by any "free" man.  This was the world William's innocent mind had earlier accepted and embraced.  But the death of Butcher Jennings altered his world's view.

On this fourth day in January 1863, William had overheard Overseer Hanks and the neighbor, Massa Campbell, ranting with a group of men on horseback about two slaves who escaped from the plantation once owned by former President James K. Polk, now owned by J. Avant in Yalobusha County.

William, who was picking up a meal from Charlotte at the slave kitchen for his mother Eliza, purposely slowed down as he crossed the side yard of the big house, intently trying to pick up what he could of the report about the two runaways, the horseback party looking dead serious and conversing rather loudly, from which William learned they were the slave patrollers his mother had warned him about.  William acted like he accidently dropped pieces off the warm cornbread that rested inside the pie-tin along with the slices of bacon fat, his ears picking up snatches of the story regarding the manhunt.  The two runaways had somehow obtained a forged pass and had stolen their massa's stagecoach, showing the pass to the road patrol on duty near there and allowed to proceed. The fake note had stated the two were permitted a journey to Memphis to pickup supplies their massa had "put on order."

They had left the plantation early that morning while their massa was sick in bed. By the time he had awoke and reported the escapees and stolen stagecoach, the two slaves whom William called "freedom riders" had already gained a four-hour lead. One of the slavecatchers seemed to question if the two runaways were truly heading to Memphis or if that was only a ruse, thinking Cairo, Illinois was the intended destination, the first town north after crossing the spot where the Mississippi and Ohio rivers intersect. William hadn't ever heard of Cairo before. He focused sharply on that exotic-sounding place when he heard the slavecatcher say Cairo was in "Yankee territory." William did know what "Yankee" meant, the *Union Army* that was fighting the Confederacy in Mississippi and he thought also Virginia and South Carolina in one big wrestling match.

William handed the cornbread pie and the slices of bacon fat to his mother. That day, a Saturday morning, William all of a sudden didn't feel hungry. Even though the food on his platter stared him in the face, the alarm caused by the two runaways dominated his entire thoughts. At that very moment, William wondered where the two slaves had gone. Would they make it successfully to Cairo? Could they? Were they scared? Had they left behind their families? Or were they trying to reach them? When his father gave the prayer over the family meal, William prayed too: that the two men would make it safely to freedom.

Throughout the afternoon William slowly strode past the side yard near the big house, peering over his shoulder to see whether another gathering of the slave patrol was taking place over by the fence posts. He was eager to learn of any new developments on the two runaways. But no gatherings occurred. Even news that usually traveled through slave row from errand-bound slaves passing by on the road with their legitimate passes didn't carry any update either.

By Sunday evening, when it was time for his father

Jefferson to leave the warmth of his wife Eliza and return to his hired massa before Monday's sunrise, fresh news about the runaways still had not reached the area.  But by the following week's Wednesday, a gathering of a different nature began to occur among the fieldhands bent along every cotton row on the Eskridge plantation.  Not a physical gathering, but a convening of great emotion, a summons of kindred spirit.  William could tell something was in the air.

He noticed there was something different in the sway and swagger of the fieldhands around him as he filled his cotton sack. Apart from the usual working efforts put forth by each worker and the regular hymns that drove the teams in united rhythm, every adult worker throughout the day seemed to look up at the other with eyes wide, as if each one knew something that the other knew. Their stares of confirmation seemed to grow more profound everytime the overseer on his horse rode away from the field and left them by themselves.  Each time, after the overseer was out of sight, the fieldhands, including William's mother Eliza, would suddenly stop working completely, as if confused about their roles and just what were they supposed to do next.

By the evening of Wednesday's end, each tired family marched to each one's respective cabin home in such a dignified and solemn way than ever before.  The overseer scratched his head, sensing that either a sacred religious observance was planning to be privately performed, or else something powerfully important had spread through slave row's gossip grapevine.  Even the massa noted that the hands didn't mingle about in the yard during the evening meals like most customarily did.  The children weren't outside playing about either.  William's mother had even asked him to come inside on this historic night.  It wasn't until the time when the moon had clearly rose in the sky that Eliza gathered her children William, Tommy, and Betty Amanda and told them the news they were not to repeat or mention in the presence of whites: "We been freed!  The Union dun' freed us!  We slaves no mo'!!!"

However, by the time all the working fieldhands reached the cotton fields the next morning, Massa and the overseer rode out hastily to them to make an announcement: they too had heard about President Lincoln's Emancipation Proclamation, but the massa gave a warning to ignore it. "All you negras are *my* property, and that no account Yankee Doodle President bafoon isn't gaw'n change that!" the massa growled. "Any one of you all try to escape from off here and you'll see what I mean!"

William raged inside at the words spewing out of the massa's mouth. Then William's next thought went straight to whether the two men running for their lives had also heard of the Emancipation. Better yet, William now thought, could he himself perform a successful escape and reach this new world called Cairo?

William kept quiet about his escape plan, not wishing to distress his mother about his decision, nor yet ready to hear her and his father both tell him that he must be half-crazy to have even concocted the idea in the first place. William was, of course, going to inform them eventually but only at the right time, if there ever came one.

After several days of perfecting his planned escape route, William was ready. Tonight was the night he would go. He felt highly confident for a young man of sixteen. Being that he didn't have a forged pass at his disposal, William fully understood that his youth and physical energy would now become his only asset. He had told his mother and father of his risky ambitious calling the previous Saturday, as he knew his father Jefferson would be coming that day to spend the weekend. Jefferson was furious and Eliza was delirious. Both tried talking William out of his most certain suicidal mission, but William would hear nothing of it. Ranting and raving, William protested that he was now a man (male slaves turning sixteen years of age became prime investments on the auction block, as was the same with young breeding-age girls), and if he didn't stand up for his freedom now, then he might as well never be free.

Jefferson tried other convincing arguments, such as the real threat of being whipped or lynched when caught, feeling the tearing teeth of blood hounds, or being tortured then shot by the Confederate soldiers if they got ahold of him. But William wouldn't be persuaded otherwise, reminding his parents that the Union had declared them free, yet how Massa had vowed he would never release them. And if the tide of the current war shifted towards a total Union collapse, the massa would be laughing in their faces. Eliza then tried next by using emotion, sentiment, and a mother's enduring bond to her baby to try and keep her son from "breaking up the family." William's fury slightly cooled, his emotions becoming confused, but clenching both his fists to his side while tightening his stomach muscles, William held firm his unwavering determination with the last remaining threads of willpower he had left. Almost close to sobbing, he reaffirmed to his mother the source of his inspiration, derived from her own father's defiant words the night he was killed: "They need to be Free!"

Realizing now there was nothing else that could be said, Jefferson and Eliza finally pitched in their support, and prayed to God the family would be reunited soon. If Cairo really was a safe haven, they faithfully hoped that William might prepare a place for them there. Although they didn't tell William, Jefferson and Eliza also prayed that their son, if he was caught, be reunited to them alive. They didn't put the Lord to the test by praying William be returned unscathed, just that he be kept alive. That enough would be a miracle.

About the time when the moon tilted further to a right-degree angle and a certain distance away from the line where the sun always set, William sprang up from his pallet quite wide awake and, after long and gripping family hugs, stepped out and then down from the lobsided cabin porch. Crouching low, William's eyes bulged wide to carefully examine every inch of ground between slave row and the distance to the first road. His left hand gripped tight to his folded bed-blanket and the right hand to his napsack containing cornbread cakes and biscuits, some of which William calculated might have to be given up to feed any barking dogs he encountered. William's eyes squinted through the night's darkness at Overseer Hanks' cabin. Everything appeared quiet over there. His heart beating, William raced across the soft grassy yard behind the east end of slave cabins, past the blacksmith shed, climbed through the fence that boxed the plantation, and finally ended up: facing the open woods!

William's heart fluttered with overwhelmed joy that he was running open and free through the untamed woodlands. At the same time, fear pulled at him whether he could get past the major first test: the road patrol at the main intersection. William knew that Campbell Road, running in the same parallel direction as William was taking, was patrolled by D.D. Wilkins. The intersecting road, Grenada-Middleton Road, was patrolled by B.R. Eskridge. Both men were the type that would check out even the mere snap of a twig. Fortunately both men sat slumbered on their horse carriages in a deep sleep, which was a good thing for William, as his foot had snapped at least three fallen twigs. Clearing the railroad tracks which marked the limits of Duck Hill Village, William continued his dash by way of unpaved trails in the midst of forest brush. The warm rush felt in his body from the pumping adrenalin had made William not even feel how chilly the night air was. The cold misty vapors that lifted from the ground covered William as his streaking black limbs cut through the white fog.

William had reserved his energy well the week leading up to his planned escape, not exerting himself as much in the fields nor lifting too many heavy loads so to avoid any physical injury. Having gone about who knows how many miles in about who knew how much time, William stopped briefly to catch his breath. Leaning against a tree and his chest heaving, William hoped to reach the Mississippi at least well before the time that the fieldhands' morning workbells usually rang. By reaching river William figured there could be an abandoned floating device, a boat, a bugeye, a makeshift raft, anything he could take to increase his speed and distance. He had no idea how much darkness yet remained before daylight, nor how many miles he had run. So far, the only part of his body that felt the cold was his feet. But his feet was the crucial ingredient needed to propel his success. At least his beatup leather brogans were holding up and his sockless feet weren't blistered.

William was now stopping more frequently, and spitting, as

the burning sensation in his throat now had reached his chest. Quickly William opened his napsack to inspect that all his food had not slipped out.  The biscuits were still intact, but the cornbread cakes had practically crumbled apart.  William pinched a few crumbled pieces and threw them into his mouth.  The crumbs stopped the burning in his chest and throat momentarily.  William looked concerned.  He glanced up and studied the moon's position. What he saw frightened him, as the moon had shifted closer to the sunset's line.  Immediately William shot out with a burst of speed across the opened meadow field and reached another thick patch of woodland, frantically looking for any sign of the great Mississippi. William finally spotted a flowing stream and followed it on down.

Clearly, William was getting winded, leaning against trees, coughing up spit, while bent over, but he could now *hear* the river up ahead.  Then there it was:  the Mighty Mississippi!  The sound of its roar rejuvenated William's tired frame.  William strode up towards the riverbank to celebrate the second phase of his freedom journey.  Suddenly a hand reached out at him from behind a bush, followed by another hand.  William found himself being tackled to the dirt ground before the attacker realized his mistake and released his hold.  The man, whose name was Vassar, was also a runaway.

Vassar and William were both shocked out of their wits that each had taken the other's escape route along the dark and dangerous countryside.  Vassar was about twenty-seven, and had escaped from his massa much further away, having been on foot for three nights from the Winfrey plantation at Poplar Creek, owned by one Absalom Winfrey of Choctaw County.  Vassar been sold to Massa Winfrey by his former owner in Roane County, Tennessee.  Vassar's wife and babychild had been sold off to a fur-trading businessman in St. Louis, Missouri.  Vassar had vowed to fetch his wife and daughter, then hideaway to a free state, Michigan, Ohio, Wisconsin, it didn't matter as long as it was free. William respectfully listened to his new comrade's plight, but inside himself he thought Vassar was on a suicidal mission for sure.

With no floating device in sight, both of them agreed there

was no sense in traveling on foot now, as daylight any minute was ready to overtake them. Their most urgent need now was to find shelter and concealment. After concealing themselves all day in a thicket of shrubs surrounded by tall grass, William and Vassar resumed their navigation to freedom once night arrived. Amazed they were that not a single Confederate guard was in sight along the river, nor were Union soldiers spotted either, whom William had chosen as a second option of rescue in case he came upon the Federal Army's camp.

During their third day of concealment, which now had become a collapsed shack long ago abandoned in the forests by its owner and tilting on its side, William and Vassar noticed the large steamboats, showboats, and riverferrys crossing up and down the Mississippi, which William and Vassar took as a good sign they might be on the outskirts of a big town, hopefully inside Memphis, Tennessee and outside the Confederate state of Mississippi. Vassar got excited at the thought of perhaps nearing Memphis, explaining toWilliam that he had heard Memphis was the best hiding place for runaways, since the town was practically one hundred per cent made up of slaves allowed to hire themselves out and setup their own independent shops and stations. Runaways, Vassar gleefully told William, blended easily within the city.

Since Vassar was empty-handed as to foodstuffs, William had been the one keeping him alive by sharing his remaining few fragments. As they sat down to another snack of breaking bread with William's blanket draped warmly across both of them, a noise was heard outside the shack. Both men sprung to their feet and strained to peer out the loose wood panels in the wall. The noise of footsteps kept inching closer and louder, but William and Vassar still couldn't see who or what it was.

And no wonder! Two small white boys who had ventured and explored that shack well over a hundred times were the source of the noisy clamor. William and Vassar had unknowningly picked as their hiding place the boys' playhouse! William and Vassar still couldn't see who it was nor that the boys were preparing to enter. The boys surely didn't expect anyone to be inside. They ran right in.

Seeing two black men, the boys screamed and immediately ran out. William and Vassar stood frozen. The next second, Vassar ran out after them. His intent was to kill them. William shouted for Vassar to let them go. Vassar continued after them anyway, intent on never allowing the boys to reach home and divulge their whereabouts, but the frightened lads' quick headstart on Vassar was what ultimately saved them.

Soon a raging Vassar returned to the shack, scolding William unceasingly as to why he hadn't assisted in the capture of the two white boys. William threw a strong rebuke against Vassar's obvious lack of judgement, telling him that his impulsiveness was foolhardy. What would taking the lives of the boys have accomplished? A *thousand* slavecatchers on pursuit instead of perhaps three. Either way, it was now time to move out quickly to find another hole. William was looking at the confident side, calming the storm of Vassar's unrest with the thought that perhaps it would be their fortune the two scared-to-death boys wouldn't utter a word of their sighting.

Trailing completely away from their former area, the scuffed-up weary men camped further down the snake of the Mississippi and stayed low. William hadn't planned on carrying a second runaway with him. At some point he and Vassar would soon have to separate and reach their own destinations. William began to wonder if that time was drawing near. He certainly didn't want Vassar, whose temperment was unpredictable, to spoil his dreams altogether by doing something rash and giving them away. William felt taxed by having to watch Vassar's every actions in addition to keeping a steady lookout. Staring at his napsack, William heaved a sigh when thinking how he had planned so carefully to ration his food between long stretches of fasting, yet now he was down to four biscuits left out of the original nineteen, due to feeding Vassar. The cornbread crumbs were long gone, some of it lost the night Vassar had tackled William to the ground.

This day had been a long one. The sunset would begin shortly, giving William and Vassar their fourth night to roam. Both of them began formulating their next strategy of how they would ease into the streets of Memphis, relishing the thought of being in the company of blacks who could help shelter and feed them. They also came to grips with the likelihood they would then go their separate ways and would probably never see each other's faces again. William extended his hand to Vassar, promising with a handshake that their next reunion would be on free ground. Then Vassar flinched. "Did you hear that?" William glanced around from their camouflage of broken tree branches, but didn't detect any sound. "Listen; There it is again!" Vassar cried out. The faint sound of hound dogs broke the tranquil peace of sunset. William and Vassar crouched hidden under the piled branches that had no leaves. The barking disturbance came from the direction of the collapsed cabin shack.

The hounding barks became louder and louder. Soon the wildgame-deprived canines were within fifty feet. The next second, one of the animals followed a stronger scent and the others tore off after it. William and Vassar instantly found themselves surrounded, and holding the bloodhounds at bay with tree branches. The ten slavecatchers were following closely behind and soon arrived at the scene on horseback. William and Vassar attempted one last vain burst of escape, opening up the napsack and throwing the biscuits into the hunting pack, then darted towards the river to dive in. But the horsemen and hounds cut them off and rounded them up.

Tied to a tree, William crumbled as the whip slashed across his young back over and over. Vassar got the same. William, slumped unconscious, was taken back to Duck Hill. Arriving at the Eskridge plantation, Overseer Hanks was furious at the slavecatchers for marking up William's back so badly. As William fell into his mother's arms and brought to the family cabin, Eliza knew that Jefferson's worry for his son would be unburdened during his next stay: It appeared the Lord had heard their prayers.

Mississippi had plunged deep into the Nation's civil war. As the battles of the war reached the Capitol at Jackson, Overseer Hanks enlisted in the Confederate Army at Grenada in August 1863. The railroad lines going into Grenada and Duck Hill had been destroyed by Sherman's forces eight months earlier. While Union troops occupied Jackson, Eliza and her family cautiously awaited the final outcome. Too many years past she had waited for freedom to step forward from its shadow, but each time refused to come into the light. True, the overseer was gone for now, but the fighting had not ceased. True, she had heard about the Emancipation and saw black men riding on horses in soldier uniform, but the war was not over. The course of the war had even reached Buck Creek plantation, as infantry deserters came upon the plantation one night and stole a freshly cooked meal right out of a slave woman's skillet.

Near Canton, Mississippi, a Confederate army camp garrison pitched their tents. As private Marion Hanks and his comrades retreated from the flames at Jackson, his battalion, Culberton's Battery, were reduced from full frontal assaults down to splinter raid attacks on unsuspecting Union outposts.

On this marked evening, a skirmish broke out as private Marion and his company were spotted by Union soldiers, their bullets and cannon balls in hot pursuit. "Maintain your positions! Keep firing!" barked the battery's Confederate captain, as private Marion stood among those holding the left flank of the firing formation. A man standing next to him suddenly was hit and fell. Private Marion dropped to his knees and keeled over him, frantically asking the man withering in pain, "Jasper...Jasper...can you hear me? It's goin' be alright! We goin' get you outta here, just hang on!" An officer spotted private Marion holding his rifle but not standing, and yelled, "Stand up! Hold your position!" But just as six-foot private Marion began to rise, the other soldier positioned on the other side of him then dropped to the ground, his face gone, as more bullets began flaying wildly in every direction. For some reason, the loud explosive sounds of battle and sheer fearfulness of the moment caused private Marion's hearing to strangely deafen, resulting in not even hearing the orders to retreat, only noticing his retreating comrades running wildly and crawling over bodies. "Move!" as a company soldier grabbed private Hanks by his uniform and pulled him along. Certainly private Hanks knew his ear affliction was already getting worse even before he had enlisted, stemming from an infection contracted on Massa Eskridge's plantation. Here he had only enlisted to serve two years, yet was losing his hearing instead of his limbs, and that was at risk of being lost in due time, too, amid the nightmarish carnage on the battlefield. That night private Marion questioned the "peculiar price" many had paid that day to preserve a "peculiar institution."

Toward the end of October 1863, private Hanks' two year enlistment abruptly came to an end twenty-one months premature when he was called into consultation with the company captain, Captain James T. Smith, who with one look could tell private Hanks was finished, his grey hair having now turned white, and his hearing was barely left.

"I just read the report from the army surgeon; Seems he has tried everything to improve your hearing--doesn't sound too good."

"Yep, I know; But I still got my hands, my feet, an' my head; Until them Yankees take that, I'll be here for the duration," Hanks quickly answered.

The captain paused, trying to grasp the right words of what he was about to say, to somehow soften the blow he was about to deliver.

"Private Hanks, what happened in Canton when I gave the command to retreat? What happened five days ago when your flank was ordered to backup McClung's men at Kosciusko? It was reported even last night, that a Union army sniper came within one hundred yards of blasting my men's brains out on your nightwatch?" Before private Hanks could answer, the captain concluded: "Based upon the frequency of these incidents, I have no choice but to recommend that you be discharged as unfit for the duties of a soldier."

When Marion Hanks was seen by a field hand, riding his horse up Eskridge Road and into the yard, the field hand quickly went around spreading word of his citing to the others in the field, "Overseer Hank come back! Overseer Hank come back!" But a new overseer, Colonel John Binford, was now in charge, having been appointed by the probate court to take charge until Massa Richard's heirs returned from the war. Watching Hanks retire to his shack still standing on the land he had purchased from the late Massa Richard's estate, Eliza hoped that he had all forgotten about her family still being "his slaves," especially now that she would soon be expecting by May of next year.  Jefferson's presence was still absent.

"You knew I was comin' back home, didn't ya?  Boy, we sho' goin' have to warm up this place a little bit tonite, if you know what I mean," as he hinted and made his advance.

"Oh, no, please Massa Hank! I already four months along, Massa, please no!  Let me brings you a jug o' corn whisky for you, Massa, 'cus I knows' you powerfully thirsty!" Eliza begged, hoping to buy herself time.

"Fetch me some," smiled Marion as he loosened his hold, knowing he hadn't tasted a drink in three months.  But instead of herself bringing the corn liquor, Eliza had her son William bring it to him.  Soon Marion was sleeping like a baby.

But by May 1864 Massa Hanks' sleep had become less and less than that of a baby, his health worsening and his hearing had practically left him unless someone spoke loud.  One evening that month as round-belly Eliza finished cooking Massa Hanks' meal, while young William tended to the hot coals underneath the cooking stove, noticeably thin Marion Hanks sat at his dinner table, an eating-bibb tucked under his shirt collar, wearing a soiled Confederate uniform, and began reflecting.

"You know Liza, you been real good to me over the years, you and your boy William;  Sometimes I get to thinkin' where would I be right now if you hadn't been here helping me the way you have;  Why, ever since my wife died 'bout fifteen years ago when I first come out here from Alabamy, I feels like you and yo' children is jus' like family to me;  Don't reckon I done ever said that before, but that's the honest truth," as he sunk his teeth into a hot meal of crispy fried chicken and began devouring it.

"Thanks you Massa Hank, I sho' 'nuff will 'member that."

"Where your two younguns at?  They still growing strong?"

"My two younguns doin' fine;  They stay's at my cabin; Both little Tommie and my little missy Bettie growing real fine, real fine massa."

"I suspect they is, them little pickanannys, on account they come from this here strong stock!  I got my eye on 'em, you can be sure of that;  Soon as they get fieldhand age, I'm goin' have plenty work for 'em, too!  And when they get's 'bout mating age, they sho' goin' bring me a fortune, by golly!  Even that there little one you carrying 'round right now, why, I got some real big plans for that there child!"

"Yes, massa."

"Now look at your boy William here;  Look how big he done got!  Why, I remember when he could barely fill up the cotton in his jute bag;  Now look at him, he lifting all them heavy cotton bags right onto the wagon!  William--I here you been working hard since I been away."

"Yes sah, I been helping Oberseer Bin..."

"Shhh, boy!!  He mean he been working steady till the real oberseer of Massa Eskridge plantation hurry up and gets back here, o' massa!  An' see!  What a surprise you done brung him."

"You think I don't know what that boy was fixin' to say, Eliza?  Don't matter no how anyway;  I'm gonna get my old job back in due time, soon as Captain Eskridge get back from the war;  Then William, when I get old, I goin' make you the overseer of my own plantation!  How that sound?  A cat got your tongue, boy?"

"No sah."

"Then what you got to say about becoming a "big man" on the plantation?"

"I...reckon so,"  as William's voice trailed off to the unappealing prospect, knowing in the back of his mind he had been told that slavery had ended, although still not quite understanding why, then, they were still slaves.

"I'll even pay you then William;  You jus' keep your head on straight, don't sass nobody, and stay in your place."  William and Eliza looked up at each other, then William lowered his head.  The former overseer's remarks stung William's scarred back.  Marion continued.  "Soon as this here soldier fighting dies down, I'm aiming to move all you on my new land, down by the train depot;  Purchased it right from "Overseer" Binford 'bout four years ago!  Now how's that sound?"

Eliza fell cautiously silent. Hearing the word "move" brought a fear inside her, a dreadful fear that she and Jefferson could once again be separated. With survival instinct, Eliza immediately killed the conversation by setting a jug of corn whisky on the table in front of Marion. Just as soon as he had uncorked the vessel and started his swigs of the whisky jug, quickly Eliza and William made their exit. Soon again, Marion Hanks was sleeping like a baby.

The next morning, Colonel Binford rang the workbell. William, waking up and wiping the drooling from his mouth, noticed that his mother Eliza hardly budged. Her young ones Tommy and Bettie were huddled up to her body under the sleeping blanket. The overseer continued ringing the bell. William called out to his mother to wake up, but Eliza remained still. That wasn't normal. Now William was concerned. Throwing off his blanket, William rolled off the pallet and stretched his half-awake frame over to his mother's bed to help arouse her.

If they didn't get up in time for Hannah's breakfast serving, they'd go hungry until midday, even maybe until sundown. "Mama, wake up!  Wake up!!" William kept repeating while nudging his mother's shoulders, but Eliza wouldn't move. Tommy and Bettie had already been awake from hearing the bell's first ring, and simply just didn't desire to rise until Eliza herself did.

But she didn't. She looked like a life-less rag doll. William then became frantic, shaking his mother's shoulders and shouting. Just as he began to try pulling his mother from off the pallet, Eliza finally awoke, having been in one of her deep dreams. She explained that she hadn't been able to sleep all night. Eliza's unborn was due any time, and she hardly had the strength to work the fields. She longed to sleep in. But at the same time, Eliza didn't want to lay up alone in her cabin all day if former overseer Hanks was also going to hang about and start poking his nose around.

Eliza told William to take the two children to the morning meal, and then to hurry and slip off carefully to peek whether if Hanks' pleasure carriage was gone or not. William took Tommy and Bettie and placed them in the serving line, but as soon as he went to spy on his former owner, Colonel Binford grabbed William to take out the colonel's slopbox.  Missing breakfast, William slipped around the corner of the chicken coop and grabbed a handful of goobers from the peanut barrel.  From that vantage he saw Marion Hanks' carriage still parked in front of his cabin.

"GO FETCH HIM for me," as William heard Colonel Binford assign Amanda, telling her to inform Marion Hanks that the colonel needed him for something that moment.  Amanda rapped on the former overseer's door.  The colonel was surprised the near-deaf man, who was usually one of the first persons up before sunrise, hadn't yet shown his presence.  After finishing off his goobers, William tended to the slopbox, returned it, then headed late to the cotton field.  But all of a sudden he saw Amanda running wildly and wailing.  Colonel Binford's first thought was that Amanda had spotted some Union Army soldiers.  "Massa! Massa Binford!!" Amanda cried out.  "Marion Hanks' stone dead!"

Two weeks later, May 26, 1864, Eliza gave birth to a girl and named her Rosie, after her mother.

On April 9, 1865 the black residents of Carroll County finally received news of the surrender, thousands of blacks throughout the South now free, but also homeless, as many were driven off the very homes they had for years supported.  And when the "Great Emancipator" was gunned down in Washington, D.C. only six days after the wars' end and seven months later the "Black Codes" were cleverly invented, freed Blacks  realized that their recent emancipation from one evil institution did not shield them from another waiting in the wings.  Persons without work were subject to arrest for vagrancy, resulting in forced labor contracts to become  hired hands to their former slavebosses.  Children were taken from their parents and apprenticed out  to work for  former slaveholders.  The immediate plight of freed Blacks soon after  the war caused the U.S. Congress to act, and an agency was created called the Freedmen's Bureau, one of the offices of the Bureau being stationed ten miles away at Grenada.

By 1868, life for the freedmen in Carroll and  other surrounding counties had worsened.  Threats, intimidation, and harassment were daily directed toward those desperately trying to provide for their own. Although Butcher Jennings, Rose, and most of their generation were no longer alive, their children were now taking their place, picking up the legacy that was left for them. Some of them still lived in the same cabins they were born in on the Eskridge plantation, now being administered by heir Burdett Eskridge and his wife Mollie. After the war, Burdett Eskridge had given Jefferson and Eliza and their kin family portions of farm land to live on that they had slaved under his grandfather Richard. Even old Hannah was still there at the age of ninety-two. Although she wasn't serving the food anymore at mealtimes, Hannah was still, in her mind, directing the orderly flow of the eating, and getting on anyone who left any food on their platter. Too many times the children, and some grownups as well, had heard her tell them the story of why the dog said to the rat, "No rice gets past me."

But it was a blessing to hear old Hannah's story than to be without food altogether. With farmers disputing the terms of their earlier agreed contracts, freedmen and freedwomen were being denied their wages and share of crops. Pressure was so great that some families fell apart under the mental and emotional toll. Due to the upcoming elections, several were beaten or whipped, others murdered, for having voted. That year the Freedmen's Bureau were flooded with complaints and reports of abuses such as:

April 13 1868

Alexander Harris, Freedman, reports that Jeff Davis of Duck Hill, Miss. is retaining certain property belonging to him. Also states that Wm. Collins of Winona refuses to settle with him for service rendered during the year 1867

April 25 1868

Lee Johnson, freedman, reports that after working three months for Jas. S. Simmons at Duck Hill for $6 he was driven off with two months wages due him.

May 1

Lewis Barnes  States that there is due him for Labor on the Miss & Tenn R.R. and that he can't get his time card from -----Sanders--

Coldwater, Miss.--who refused to give it to him.  He worked 2 mo.s fr. 1 Jany 1867--1 Mch. at $27.50 per Mo.  has recd $20.00 in all, from -----Livermore.

Jun 9 1868

Billy McChristian says that his wife Harriet...left him and that she is now with Dr. Stratham    that about the 20 May Stratham sent & took harriet's clothes from his house.  Dr. Stratham says that the boy has been maltreating his wife and that she will not live with him.

Jun 20 1868

Ephraim Wesley says that his wife Alice Wesley has left and has gone to work for Ed Fultz at Duck Hill.

July 16, 68

Reddick King was killed by KKK last Monday.

Sept. 21/68

Jas Gates states that he labored for James Collins who lives near Winona, during 1867 (about 7 months) Terms:  $200.00 for self & family, for the year,    <u>cause</u> of leaving before finishing contract: Gates caught James Collins son Aleck in the act with his wife, and his wife and family moved into Choctaw.

Oct 10/68

Laura Jeans
Dan Williams
and others
Ku Klux

Laura Jeans whose husband is not able to report in person--states that Dan Williams (colored) and others (whites) came to her house on the night of the 7th Oct 1868, put a rope around her husband's neck, (George Jeans) and took him into the woods and nearly whipped him to death--She expects to find him dead on her return home.  All because he voted the Radical ticket.  George Jeans lives with Culpepper Jeans 7 miles from Graysport, and if living can tell the names of the white men, also.

Oct. 14, 1868

Henry Ruigstaff...Choctaw Co...Tom Armstrong told Ruigstaff that the "Ku Klux" in that neighborhood are all his Friends...

Nov 17/68

Levi Nalty states that Darril Green of Carrollton engaged him to split 7000 rails, that he has split 3000 rails, and that Green has turned him off without pay.

Nov 20 1868

Parris Ferguson states that Jim Ferguson of Attala Co. shot him through the hip for voting the Radical ticket. that he left that county and is afraid to return. His wife, Jenny Ferguson, he left on the place to finish the crop, but that Ferguson will not give her anything. He put in 23 acres of corn and 11 acres of cotton--New Ground, which he was to have for 2 years as payment for clearing it.

Eliza and Thomas Jefferson's affections climaxed in the summer heat of that year with the birth of a light brown infant girl. Jefferson asked Eliza, "What name you like to give her?" Eliza had to think. All throughout her life she was proud of the fact that Mama Rose's family had chosen names in memory of some relative, one who could not continue the journey of life with them. She began recalling back some of those names. Looking up at Jefferson she said, "I have a name; I just had to think about it awhile." She was thinking about her sister Lucy who never made it off Buck Creek plantation.

Eliza's son William, now twenty-one, soon became employed under D.D. Wilkins, a large landowner and husband to one of Massa Taliaferro's daughters, who ran a mercantile store. William would work in the back, loading and unloading the stacks of goods and supplies that the merchant traders would drop off which the local farmers and county residents would pick up. Ever since the February 17, 1867 passage of the State agriculture legislation, the store had become steadily filled with persons presenting their supply contracts and shopping lists. By the end of each day William would be wornout from the constant loading and lifting.

At this time, too, freedmen and freedwomen became engaged in choosing individual surnames for themselves and their families, a need for individual and social identity. Many families chose the surnames of their former owners, not out of a sense of fondness for them after having experienced their lives ordeal-- although fondness may have been a factor for a few fortunate enough to have been kindly manumitted--but rather as a way of timemarking their own family origins. In the case of families who lived under one large slaveholder, many chose the same surname, although that surname sometimes meant something different to different families.   One family might have chosen the surname because it reminded them of some important event; another family may have because an ancestor had it before them; yet another family or person might have chosen it out of convenience because it was the name that associated them while growing up on the plantation. William chose the surname *"Wilkins"* even though his mother Eliza and her husband Thomas Jefferson chose the name *"Eskridge."*

In 1869 William became attracted to a pleasing young eighteen year old part Creek Indian freedgirl by the name of Rosetta Crockett, she and her parents living nearby from having formerly worked on the Benjamin Campbell plantation. William and Rosetta were married that year, upon securing permission from Rosetta's father, Armstead Crockett, a hardworking family man from the old school, "I was born in Ole' Virginny, raised in North Carolina, but a slave in Mississippi;  I reckon I been working all my natural life...that's the only way you ever gonna succeed in this here world;  Now, you take my here Rosetta;  BUT, you better just make good & sure you KEEP ON working, ya here?"   The ceremony was conducted right on Eskridge plantation while his mother, half brother Tommy, half sisters Bettie, Rosie, Babie Lucy, cousin William Burgess, and all his other relatives & cousins looked on. After the marriage was consummated, it was officially recorded in the Freedmen Marriage Register of Carroll County.

After Mr. D.D. Wilkins and his family left Duck Hill temporarily for Tennessee in August 1870, William went back to farming. He then changed his surname to *"Hanks,"* the name he identified himself with when he was purchased at thirteen. As William put it, " 'cause that's when I left Mama and started working on my own." True, he had left his father too, back there at Buck Creek, but he was too young to remember Jefferson. No, William was not seeking his own social identity at that point in time.

All William was trying to do now was just "fit in society." And picking a surname would help him a bundle to that effect. It didn't matter if the surname belonged to the overseer. As far as William was concerned, that name didn't belong to the overseer anymore now that he was dead. Choosing his surname was simply an act of utilizing his independence.

To William, although he wouldn't have admitted it anyhow, the overseer was the powerful male figure in his life during the early childhood years when his real father Jefferson was being held in bondage hundreds of miles away in Tennessee. William couldn't deny that it had pained him to watch the overseer shrivel up in his last dying days. William couldn't disclaim that he actually felt pity for the man when he ended up turning deaf as a bat. But feeling pity for someone didn't excuse their monstrous actions and sins. Yet William knew not all whites were the same. William would often remind himself that Mr. D.D. Wilkins gave him a fair shake. In a short time, William had somehow picked up the philosophy that "hard work will improve the status of the colored race" and "be an example to the negro race by law-abiding obedience." The trouble with William, then, was that he had not come to realize "being obedient" was not taken from the amendments of freedom and equality, but rather, from the law of "Jim Crow." Mentally, William had given up the fight he used to clothe himself in his younger days. He didn't want the old wounds on his back reopened.

Soon the branches of the Eskridge family were blossoming. On the second day of winter in 1871, William and Rosetta celebrated their first child, a daughter born in freedom, who they named Susan. Three years later a son was born free, James, and the next year another son, Clifford Jumbo. By June 1879 they

would have daughter Maria.   George and Phyllis' son Frank
Eskridge married Liza McDaniel who was the daughter of cook
Charlotte, and had Matt, Mollie, Ward, Booker T., Mable,
Amanda, Harrison, Milton, Jennings, and Nathaniel.   George and
Phyllis' son Louis Eskridge married a girl down the hill near
Carrollton, who he brought home riding on a mule. William
Burgess and Amanda's twin daughter Nancy Eskridge married
George and Phyllis' third son William Harrison Eskridge, and their
children were Eugene, Frankie, Virginia, Sidney, Henry, Hettie,
Maud, Stanford, and Augustus.   William and Amanda's other twin
daughter Eliza married Rosetta Hanks' brother Harris Crockett,
whose children were Lloyd, Dell, George, Evans, Clarence, Rosie,
Wheeler, Carrie, Lona, Will, and Lindsey.   The branches of the
family tree were now growing in all directions.

William Burgess Eskridge's seventeen year old son Henry
was fascinated that one of his father's old slave ancestors had come
from Africa.   Although his father could not recall or recite the
details of this story, Henry was amazed even at just hearing the
word "Africa."   The fact that his father had learned to read and
write  even while a slave fueled his interest even more. Few black
families  could trace back to a known ancestor of that continent.
The passage of "grandfather time" and the unwelcomeness of death
had either dulled the memories or killed the souls of many who at
one time could have recited the sproutings of their family trees.
One Duck Hill neighbor, Dave Binford, claimed that both of his
parents were born in Africa.   Liza, the wife of Frank Eskridge,
stated that her mother, woman cook Charlotte, was born of African
parentage in the West Indies.

Henry would talk to these ones and listen intently to their
answers.  His questions directed at the teacher from the Freedmen's
Bureau over at Camp New Fountain were constant each week.
There was another world outside Duck Hill, outside Mississippi,
and Henry was curiously eager to explore it.  If he could have done
so, Henry would have left right then, taken a steamboat or railtrain
down to the Gulf of Mexico, and went out to sea into the Great
Atlantic.   His parents had emphasized to him the goods of
education and the evils of ignorance.   Henry's brother-in-law,

Frankie Eskridge, and his nephew, Milton Eskridge, had just so happened to have become hired hands on the Mississippi-Tennessee Railroad line.  That was their at-present route out of Carroll County, albeit until time for the returning route and ending of their shift.  After becoming thus empowered first, perhaps then one day Henry might take such a trip, too.

Such an exploration would prove a relief from the fear and abuse African descended citizens were being subjected on the sidewalks of the Delta counties.  Intimidation, violence, teachers flogged, school-houses burned down, and men and women murdered in the night was the order of the day in the South throughout the time which was so-called "Reconstruction."  The statesman and civil rights activist Frederick Douglass along with other Black suffrage leaders arrived in New Orleans by train to address these abuses in April 1872.  Frankie and Milton rumored that they saw him on board their train when it was bound for St. Louis from New Orleans.  After having finished his lecture in New Orleans, Douglass departed to the train station to make his connection, accompanied by a military escort of two companies of black soldiers.  As it happened to turn out, Frankie and Milton had been assigned to work that very train.  While Frankie was providing service to his assigned compartments, there was one distinguished door he knocked upon:

"Come in," answered the six foot, fifty-five year old Mr. Douglass.

"Is there anything I can get you, Sir?"

"A Gin on the rocks for now, and perhaps something later from your 'Orleans French menu before we get into Memphis;  By the way...how you being treated on these trains?  Are the conditions for the porters tolerable?  Excuse me, what is your name?"

"Frankie, Sir;  Frankie Eskridge.  Everything is fine, Sir;  Of course, some days are better than others, Sir...most times the people are pleasant, then sometimes..."

"That's okay, young man;  I know exactly what you mean...the same goes with my job, too;  Say, there's something else I just thought of you can get me--how 'bout one train ticket to

Canada."

"Sir...?"

"Oh, I'm sorry, I thought this was the "*Underground Railroad*";  Guess I'm not conducting that train anymore," Douglass joked in his heavy baritone voice.

"I'll get your drink, Sir,"  Porter Frankie replied with a grin.

By evening of the following day the Illinois Central pulled into Duck Hill Depot from St. Louis.  Unbeknownest to Frankie and Milton, a relative stood awaiting them at the depot as the train came to a final halt.  Eager to return home with hearty appetites, the two cousins Frankie and Milton climbed down from their porter car after changing out of their official uniforms.

There stood William ready to greet them, who had been asked by his wife Rosetta to go see if the two young men would accept an invitation to eat a fine prepared meal at William and Rosetta's cabin that evening, this being Rosetta's pleasure not only because Frankie's mother and Rosetta were sisters-in-law, but also because it had become Rosetta's custom and privilege of cooking meals for the freedmen porters.  It was no secret that black porters could practically starve to death while working the trains if were it not for the generosity and kindnesses of the women found willing.

"Hey there William!  What brings you up here?" asked a surprised Milton.

"Say William, guess who famous rode our train?" Frankie quizzed.

"Who?  The President?  The Jubilee Singers?  Or you talking 'bout the singing of porter Burrell Campbell?" joked William, referring to one of Frankie and Milton's porter comrades from Duck Hill.

"Man, you not even close;  We had Frederick Douglass on here yesterday!  And I got to serve him all the way to St. Louis!" Frankie said proudly.

"Shucks!  Well I'll be darn;  You rascals putting me on?"

"This the honest truth;  Or else I be hit by lightning!"

"Okay now, jus' tell me when the lightning come a calling so I don't be standing next to ya;  Say, Rosetta got a meal waiting for us down at the house;  She wanted me to come up and fetch you two hungry porters;  y'all some of the darkest looking porters I done ever seen!"

"Ha-ha William, you plum crazy;  Come on then!  Let's get some grub Milton!"

"You the one behind me, mister."

The April air was warm this early evening.  It was still light, as the unloading dock was full of disembarking passengers crowding to carry away their luggage.  The three youthful men in their early twenties led themselves away from the unloading dock and began their exit down to the small town's boardwalk.

"Man, I can't wait to tell everyone who we seen," exclaimed Frankie.  "I heard all about him;  Did you know he been all over to London Town and the West Indies, and a whole bunch of other places."

"And to Canada," William added.

"And to Canada, yes!  He still trying to free our people, not from the massas no more but from the Ku Klux Klan!"

"Shhh, Frankie!  You talking too loud!" William cautioned.

"Don't worry;  No one can hear me;  The Klan trying to pass this here "Jim Crow" but Douglass telling people everywhere we ain't gonna put up with it, they not gonna push us down no more!"

"Something needs to be done right here in this county;  You heard what been happening near Elliot Station and Greenwood? Women and baby sisters getting raped right in front of they men!" Milton said.

"I couldn't take that;  Man, they'd have to kill me if I saw them do that;  I'd have to jump in and save my woman!" Frankie groaned.

"We still got the Colored Troops stationed at Grenada; And the Freedmen's Bureau take reports then go and make arrests," William said.

"They ain't doin' enough, and them Colored Troops, they under the white general's command!" Milton said.

"It ain't gonna be like this forever, that I can say for sure," William replied.  "Man, I'm getting hungry."

As William, Frankie, and Milton continued their youthful man stride, there appeared two white men in their thirties walking on the same boardwalk toward them.

"Look!  Now here come these two;  They expect us to jus' turn aside, while they continue right on through?" Frankie barked under his breath.

"It sho' 'nuff not the law, but we don't want any trouble neither," William warned, the tone in his voice showing his hesitancy and dread in challenging "Southern custom" on this evening.

"Trouble?  How can there be any trouble?" Frankie asked. "Don't we got jus' as much right to walk on this here sidewalk as they?  They don't have any gun holsters either;  Come on!  Let's show them we know what our rights is!"

But William and Milton strayed off the boardwalk to the left and into the dusty, dirt street.

"Frankie!  Come on off there before something get started!" Milton urged.

"This what Douglass' talking about!   Watch this!" as Frankie strutted on toward the two men.

Quickly the two men caught onto the challenge from Frankie and readied themselves to make sport.  One of the men began purposely straddling more of the boardwalk than necessary, taking up almost half of Frankie's space.  Each step moved the three men closer and closer.  Then finally they all converged. Frankie refused to budge from his pathway as one of the cocky men's shoulders violently slammed into Frankie's, nearly causing both men to lose their balance.

"What's wrong with you boy!   Don't you know you supposed to step off when you see people coming!" said the man who tauntingly hit Frankie's shoulder.

"I'm a citizen of this state and don't nobody have to move aside for any man, unless he a  blindman," Frankie said calmly.

"Well then boy, you must be, 'cause you seen me coming way ahead of time, yet you tried to block me!   Pete here's my witness!"

"The way I see it, you bumped into me;  They's plenty room on this sidewalk for both of us."

"You should have done like your obedient boys and stepped aside;  Now I want you to say you sorry!" the man snapped back.

"No need for that;  I don't feel bad 'bout nothing;  Should have stayed on your side," Frankie said in unapologetic terms.

"What's your name boy, your face look familiar," asked the second man.

"I hasn't been a boy since I was little;  I'm Frankie Eskridge and I work right here at the train station," responded Frankie again calmly, excusing the man's error about his "age" and also not fearing a thing about giving out a brief character profile.

"I thought he looked familiar," said the second man to the first.  Now the first man returned his verbal jabs.

"Eskridge?  You hear that Pete?  Why, that was the name of that wealthy planter Chesterfield Eskridge who got sold down the river in that big courtcase 'bout ten years ago--sold down the river by the testimony of some lying nit-wit slaves!  Boy, I want an apology from you right now, and you had better hurry up before I have to make ya!"

"Like I said, I got a right to walk down this road like anyone else--so you ain't getting no apology from me!"

"I warned you boy!" as the first man's rage exploded and lunged for Frankie's throat with both hands.

Frankie swung and hit the man on the side of his face, dazing him for a second, while at the same time the second man jumped from behind and put Frankie in a headlock, holding Frankie steady as the first one rested a blow to Frankie's stomach.  Immediately William and Milton flew to Frankie's rescue, William tackling the first man just as he prepared to deliver another punch, and Milton coming behind the second one with punches to his kidneys, bringing a release to his headlock.

As now a magnet of a crowd and older men began to rush upon the fight, William, Frankie, and Milton peeled off running into the woods toward home, while the two instigators kept shouting, "Catch 'em!  Catch them niggas!  We gonna get ya!  We gonna get you niggas!!"

Finally the three reached home an hour late for the serving of Rosetta's meal, normally a thirty minute walk from the depot but which on this night required a series of backtracking. Rosetta was upset when hearing the initial story, yet relieved as details of the incident unfolded before the dinner table.

"You still could've gotten yourself killed William; Me and little Susie was worried something happened, and something sho' did happen!" Rosetta sighed.

"It wasn't no big deal; Jus' some couple of white boys trying to test us, that's all; They probably been drinking," William explained.

"Well, you all better not tell Frankie's mama and papa 'bout this; They be mighty angry!"

"Mama might be; I not too sure 'bout Papa; Remember he the one used to go around telling all us children 'bout 'Old man Butcher Jennings tol' the massa: The Colored needs to be Free!' Then the massa killed him," Frankie said.

"Even my papa I can remember telling my big brothers about what happened to Butcher Jennings," Rosetta added.

"Later Marse Booker T. went and took his own cousin to court and won himself hundreds of dollars!" William said.

"Sold him down the river; This what that boy was saying to me at the depot, saying we lied to the judge and got Marse Booker's cousin guilty; No-no-no! It was the law got that man guilty; This what Frederick Douglass been talking about all over this country; The law's on our side so long as both sides are fair; I believe that! If I had to go to the judge tonite over our little tussle, the law would prove me right!" Frankie proclaimed.

"You know, maybe we should tell Marse Booker what happened tonite, in case them two fools try and start something tomorrow when you go back to work," William offered.

"That may be a good idea; Might be better for him to hear the story from us than from the wrong people," Milton echoed.

"I don't care what story they say to make us look bad; We know what happened!" Frankie bellowed, still in a stressed state as he and Milton finished their plates and prepared to retire home about fourteen cabins down.

The twelve o'clock hour soon struck that night which signalled the birth of a new day, as the half round moon shone brightly to one side amid the grayish clouds enveloping.  The midnight air was still warm while the dark country insects, rodents, and carnivorous took cue that this time be their special watch, as it was now the cabin people's turn to sleep sound--men, women, and yes, children--that generation which had been born free.

While the families along cabin row at Duck Hill cuddled gently during the first few seconds begotten in that twelve o'clock hour, a flickering of burning torches and images appearing to be as if twenty white phantoms on four legs began marching forward in the direction of cabin row, and, finally reaching the breath of their destination, stealthly rode down the middle of the small community, then stopped towards the center.

William and Rosetta laid together sound upon their blanketed pallet, while their only child at this time, four month old Susie, slept silent incredibly well in her crib.  Then there was a loud noise.

"BANG!"

William's whole body jolted as he fell out of the bed.  The sound of rifle fire now had William's full attention as he whispered to Rosetta to stay quiet.

"We want the boy that calls hisself 'Frankie Eskridge' who work at the train depot to come out here right now!" yelled out over and over one of the white sheeted men on horseback.

William carefully peeked out the cabin door.  "What is it William?   What they shouting out there?" Rosetta whispered intensely.  William's head dropped.

"It's the Ku Klux Klan!"

The white-hooded spokesman commanded again.

"Frankie Eskridge better come out here now!  We here in this county don't tolerate any person of color who thinks they above law and order!  Tonite we goin' make it plain and clear what we mean!  Come on out boy!  We know you here!  We goin' make a lesson outta you!"

Then the hoodman gave an ultimatum: "If you--Frankie Eskridge--don't come out here like a man then we goin' take one of your colored gals in exchange! And we goin' keep comin' back here each time for a new one until you turn yourself in! Now, how you like that!"

At that moment horror shone in William's eyes. What if this rape gang flooded into his cabin and grabbed his Rosetta? Their cabin was not more than thirty yards away. William now was starting to fill up with anger, which kept overpowering his other emotion of panic. Why didn't Frankie just listen to he and Milton to step around the two troublemakers? He wondered what in the world Frankie himself was thinking at this moment. Some of the cabins had backdoors. William tried to remember if Frankie's family had one. The horse stable was also out back. Frankie's family kept their horses tied up right beside their cabin. Would Frankie have snuck out back, jumped on a horse and taken off? But then this would have meant that someone's wife, daughter, or sister was set to be taken. William's two sisters of ten and eight years were just eight cabins away. On the other hand, would Frankie choose to step out and face this posse? But that would spell certain death.

"We giving you ten seconds to come out your cabin, or we taking someone!"

William peeked out again, noticing now that others were peeking out carefully too. Frankie's door was facing across the second row of cabins, but no one there appeared to be coming out. Suddenly William's backdoor swung open. It was Rosetta's father Armstead Crockett.

"Rosetta! William! Get little Susie and follow me to our place next door!" Quickly Rosetta grabbed the child while they all rushed out. However, as soon as William came out he told Rosetta, "I'll be right back! Stay with your family!" then he ran off in the opposite direction.

"Nine, eight, seven, six, five, four, three, two...one! Alright boy! This your last chance!"

Frankie was nowhere.

Then a voice came from around the corner at the cabins' road entrance.

"I'm the one you looking for, and I'm right here if you want me!"

It was William, who had decided that if the Klan did indeed attempt to carry out their threats, which all indications showed they would, then he would sacrifice himself in hopes of appeasing the insane mob.

"We gonna get ya alright!" barked another of the masked men.

Before the cat-calling and hooting hoodlums could yet take even four steps toward William, two separate voices shouted out in unison from the rear end of the house rows.

"Which one of us did you want?"  It was Frankie and Milton on two horses, barely visible in a blanket of night darkness.

Frankie and Milton bolted.  William sprang towards the road entrance and jumped on a waiting horse.  The white-sheeted mob party went mad and split in two directions.  William made a good head start on the faction that chose to pursue him.  Finally cutting away from the main road, William surged his horse through forest paths only he was familiar and visible only by the luminary's light, as twigs and tree branches snapped like crushed reeds. William continued to increase his distance from the Klan but could still hear their rustling and shouting.  Suddenly William heard three large guns blasts deep in the distance.  William began to pray that Frankie and Milton hadn't been shot.  Soon practically an hour went by without detection, which gave William a good feeling he had found an obscure path.

Starting to tire, William led himself to a huge fallen maple tree so he and the horse could hide and rest at the same time.  His eyelids starting to flutter, William kept trying to fight off the craving of sleep that the body was overriding the mind.  Wishing this were merely a dream, William was at a loss inside himself as to how he had been propelled into this nightmare.  If only Frankie had listened!  But then William recanted, realizing it was only a matter of time before the terrors of the Ku Kluxing that hit Greenwood and Elliot Station would have reached Duck Hill.  He next started thinking about Frankie and Milton's whereabouts, and how they truly did come through valiantly at the last second. Frankie was right. People of color could no longer cowtow to the likes of "Jim Crow" without a struggle. Even a mere mule could only take so much before even it refused to budge. Actually, the people of color had been training for these moments all their natural lives, including William's own family. He began to reminiscence about the stories he used to hear Grandma Rose tell about her African grandmother who was rundown and kidnapped along with her uncle; How his grandfather Butcher Jennings stood up and died in the old system; How Father Jefferson was bound out as hired help and kept away from Mother Eliza during William's childhood bonding years. Here now William didn't even get the chance to tell his parents goodbye, before his body would be found rotted away. "Goodbye Mama; Goodbye Papa," William whispered softly. Then his head dropped as sleep overtook him.

Come early dawn, the folks at the colored community between "Eskridge Road" and "Campbell Place Road" had stayed up the night. No harm had come upon them, thanks to the courageous efforts of three young men who took a gambling bet that a lynching mob would chase them and in the process lure danger away from the village. But this explanation of their actions did not answer as to their whereabouts. However, just before the hour when the roosters would start crowing, a battered black figure stumbled out of the woods. It was Milton who had come in first, having lost his horse. Milton explained that both he and Frankie got separated at a critical moment and that both of their horses buckled from gun shots, but how Milton managed to swing free and keep running. He also reported that William and his horse burst in another direction, then pointed to the route he took.

After the roosters started crowing and some people started preparing breakfast and black coffee then next William entered, trotting in on his horse. Just as a wave of consolation as well as praise had met Milton from his family kin, so now William became surrounded by his loved ones with solace mingled with admiration.

"I know I raised you good Billy, but I never dreamed you'd go out there and try to fight the whole Klan! I'm proud of you child," said mother Eliza.

"You done something real fine son;  You showed yo'self a man!  Thank God Almighty dey didn't let the dogs out on ya like dey did me a time back when I's growin' up!" said father Jefferson.

"How many times you gonna keep me frettin' 'bout you William?  I thought I lost you las' time at the depot;  How many mo' times you gonna keep killing me, Sweetie?" cried Rosetta as she and William caressed each other tightly.

William was fortunate to be back.  He was thankful to still be alive.  That was a given.  So why all this fuss of being extolled a hero?  He didn't believe he had performed something special or acclaimed anything.  He simply made response to what grave events gave reaction the moment of the klan attack.  William knew he couldn't take any special merit, for just the day before he had showed his lack of courage and loyalty to 'Jim Crow' by stepping off the boardwalk and leaving Frankie to fend for himself. William was smart enough to admit that if he had made time to think, he would not have thrown his life into the jaws of diseased wolves.  What William didn't come to realize was what father-in-law Armstead brought home to him:  "What you, Milton, and Frankie did wasn't from your head, it was from inside your heart."

Soon it dawned on William that Frankie was not present, and was quickly told he still hadn't returned from the woods. Fearing the worst, William vowed, whether or not he would ever see Frankie again, that he would some day remove his family to lands far away from these hostile intolerant conditions if it ever came in the power of his hand.

After some considerable time waiting for Frankie's emergence, a consensus was reached among the freedmen to send someone immediately to the Freedmen's Bureau headquarters in Grenada to file complaint against the Klan's activities and a missing person report on Frankie.

For the rest of the day a search party went out for Frankie until evening, when two white Federal soldiers arrived to patrol the area.  The following four days the daylight search party were joined by two Colored Troops as only could be assigned, who extended the perimeter of the lookout.  Two dead horses with gunshot wounds were discovered. Towards the end of their fourth day's effort one of the soldiers yelled out from a remote open field. Soon the rest of the tired team reached the soldier's location, and, while the other troop soldier steadied his horse, a knife was pulled out to cut the rope. Then Milton and William were called up to the front of the scene. Holding hankerchiefs to their faces while batting away flies, William and Milton could not make an identification. But in their hearts they knew.

The passing of nearly three weeks seemed to slowly rekindle the spirit of Duck Hill village since its tragedy, as staying industrious to the fieldwork at hand kept the community moving forward. Although no arrests were made on any suspected of being the Klan, the attempted siege and lynching drew the attention of federal soldiers to make random patrols around Carroll and Montgomery counties.

William's brother-in-law, Granison Crockett, heard about some long-term and short-term labor contracts seeking ditch-diggers for a water canal project. Even though the job was thirty miles away at Coffeyville it provided a good opportunity to gain some much needed money for his family, since his regular sharecrop earnings had been severely affected the previous year due to a poor crop season. A short-term assignment was all Granison needed, as he really didn't plan on staying long at such a faraway distance from his family, and the pay would still be good, nearly enough to recoup most of his losses from last year. Besides that, one of Ole' George and Ole' Phyllis great-grandsons worked in Coffeyville as a house servant for a well off white family, and very much needed a ride back into Duck Hill for a well overdue visit.

Granison was immediately hired for a term of thirty days with Sundays off and was quickly put to work. On his first day there he noticed a man who looked familiar serving fruit and drinking water at breaktime. He walked with a noticeable limp. Granison yelled out to the man since they were both a good distance apart. "Joe Starks!" The man didn't respond. Granison came a little closer this time and went up to fetch a watercup. The man's back was turned but started to pivot around as Granison inquired about his name again.

"I can't believe it!"

"Granison!  Oh, thanks the Lawd!  I been blessed to finally see someone from Duck Hill!" said the fruit and water server.  It was Frankie.

"Everybody thinks you dead Frankie!"

"Dead?  I'll be darn...well, I guess I can't blame 'em on account I ain't been able to get back home."

"Man, we was looking all over for you...even the Union Colored Troops went out looking for you...we found a lynched man up in a tree and thought for sure it was you!!"

"Oh no!  May God have mercy on that poor man's soul; What about Milton and William...?"

"They fine!  Both came back the next day after the Klan went after ya'all;  So what happened to you?"

"Them hooded crackers shot up my horse, shot me in the leg real bad...Milton took off another way and I didn't know if he was dead or alive either...somehow I made it up and over a hill and crawled down to a sharecropper's shack who lent me his horse...I rode all night with my leg nearly shot off!"

"So why didn't you come back?"

"Fell on some hard times;  The Klan chased me through two counties clear up to the Yalobusha county line;  I kept on till I got here to get my leg mended;  Then the horse lent me got stolen...been workin' here 'bout a week now trying to earn enough to get back home!"

"They gonna go cotton-pickin' crazy when they see you; I'll take you back this Sunday!!"

"Thanks you Lawd Almighty!  I would've sent ya'all some mail, really, but you know I can't trust nobody out here to write for me;  Shucks, someone might been liable to turn me in!"

That Sunday when Granison finally brought Frankie by horseback into Duck Hill, that cabin row community hidden between Eskridge Road and Campbell Place Road simply went wild.

By 1878 though, talk had been heard of movements to send those willing to emigrate to Africa, or to Kansas or Texas. Some families chose to leave the South rather than allow their sons and daughters to grow up in a climate where their manhood was being threatened and their womanhood was being raped. The Eskridge, Hanks, and Crockett families discussed among themselves the possibility of making such a move. Many of them had become comfortable living on the land they were now on, the land where some of them had been born. Besides, they were now FREE, free to live wherever they wanted, whether that meant leaving, or the freedom to choose to stay. Some of the young men and women had now started new families of their own, attaching themselves to new in-laws and kin. Others also were presented with the added responsibilities of caring for aging relatives, who very likely would not endure a long strenuous journey. Yes, there were many factors to consider.

But something else that year would also seize the attention of the Freedmen of Duck Hill just as importantly as a decision to migrate. For during that year a mysterious plague, called Yellow Fever, hit the area, having spread from neighboring Grenada. Many abandoned their homes in Grenada and fled into the country or to homes in Carroll County seeking help, spreading the disease right into Duck Hill. Much looting was reported, as victims fleeing their homes left them unlocked, causing unscrupulous ones to take advantage of the crisis. So terrifying was this disease, whose cause and source was still baffling to the medical and scientific world, that a news reporter arrived from *The New York Times.*

The town's sewer drain, which collected drainage from privies and stables, was believed to be the source of the plague, especially when it became known that the stench was caused by the festering carcasses of hogs which had gotten trapped inside. The mayor of Grenada, Mayor Milton, put out an order for the drain to be cleaned out. But while that project went forth, the first victim dying from the plague had been recorded.

Doctors and nurses were called out to stop the epidemic, but their efforts were futile. Even the number of caskets gave out for the grave diggers, while the voice of the wagon driver could be heard calling out at each house "Is anyone dead?" as he made his patrol.   By the time the disease had finally ceased, over three hundred people had succumbed to it.   Included was Eliza and Jefferson.  He was the first to go between them.

Eliza lay on her bed while William Burgess' wife Amanda would come make her rounds to try and keep Eliza's fever down. Eliza lingered in and out of a coma for several days, her oldest child William seeing her each morning before he would proceed to the cotton field.  Early before picking time began, William came into her cabin to check on her that morning just as he had the last nine days.   Seeing her soundly sleeping, he whispered in his mother's ear. "Sleep good Mama, you tired out thang, sleep on...will help ya' harness your strength."  Then, fearing her fragile body could give out any time before he even reached back home, William made a point to utter another thought, his voice this time quivering.  "You wore yo'self out trying to raise me, Mama...you did yo' best...I never forget that, Mama."  William headed to the cabin door, then turned around and back to Eliza's bed.  "I love you Mama...the next daughter Rosetta bears I swears I name for you." Then he gingerly kissed her forehead and headed off to work. Later that morning Tommy, Bettie, and Rosie came into the cabin. Eliza, now awake, and being happy to see them, called them over to her bedside.

"How my babies doing today?" inquired Eliza, her cracked voice dry from a need for water.  "I's glad ya'll here together, 'cause today I got something to tell ya; Something I should've told ya'll a long time ago;  But I'm not gone yet, so it's best to tell all you now."

By now the three were anxiously awaiting what their mother could possibly tell them that she hadn't told them already. In the background the sound of the Mississippi-Tennessee rail train could be heard coming down the tracks.  Eliza continued. "There's something I need to tell ya about your daddy;  Your *real* father...,"

The train's loud whistle blew at the same moment she spoke, while muttering a devasting revelation, causing the children to stay with her all day and not wanting to leave her side.  But by the sweltering heat of late afternoon young Tommie had ran up to the cotton fields to fetch William and telling him to hurry at once to their mother's cabin. William dropped his jute sack and took off running, the cotton spilling out, while the other fieldworkers stood back and watched him hurdle the fence, losing one of his fall-apart shoes for Tommie to pickup, as his feet raced at a desperate pace toward cabin row.   As William entered the cabin door there was Rosetta, Amanda, William Burgess, and several other family kin all in prayer and huddled around Eliza's bed.  The children were kept out of the small dividing bedroom and told to stay in the front room.  A sheet was over Eliza's head.  "Cousin William, I'm 'fraid she's gone," William Burgess said as he pulled the sheet away so William could view her again.  That night after a memorial service Eliza Eskridge was buried at forty-nine years of age.

March 1879.  That spring, word spread that large numbers of persons were leaving the South and heading to the land called Kansas, where "someone" had rumored free acres of untouched land awaited any who chose to come.   Others had heard that several had left Vicksburg area and had written back to friends saying land wasn't free but was cheap and affordable.   Already at that moment thousands were leaving Kentucky, Tennessee, Alabama, Mississippi, and Louisiana either by steamboats along the banks of the Mississippi or by cramped railcars.  When word reached Duck Hill, about five families immediately made plans to depart, while others were not so sure.  Was free or affordable land really waiting for those who would come?  Or was it just a wild rumor?  But then, why were hundreds instantly willing to abandon ties and take that gamble?  Those joining the exodus were truly caught up in the emotion of the moment.  That emotion soon caught up with William *Hanks'* family, as he and Rosetta discussed among their kin their firm decision to join the "Exodus of 1879" and whether any others were coming aboard.  Rosetta's two older brothers Granison and Harrison themselves voted to stay in Duck Hill, whereas her aged parents and younger siblings voted to go.  As for William's siblings of twenty year old Tommy, seventeen year old Bettie, fifteen year old Rosie, and eleven year old baby sister Lucy, they, too, voted to stay, choosing to remain among well-known established family kin of their dead mammy, rather than venture onto the unknown, fearful, and unestablished path belonging to older brother William. Besides, growing man Tommy and William hadn't quite seen eye-to-eye soon after mother Eliza just before her passing revealed that Overseer Hanks was Tommy, Bettie, and Rosie's real father, adding more fuel to Tommy's inner anger just as much as William's efforts in trying to look after them.

Tommy's vote was solidified soon later when family head Frank Eskridge, Phyllis' son, held out to cousin Tommy the invitation to sharecrop his land, some forty acres, which Mr. D.D. Wilkins had felt moved to sell Frank, as a way to compensate for the wrongs done in slavery times.

"That settles it then, Tommy," William said. "If you and your sisters wants to stay here, that's fine; Just look after 'em and I hopes you all be happy out here; Me--I gots to give my childrens a fresh start; They goin' need that after what we both done seen; You goin' see me off tomorrow mornin'?"

"Of course I'm goin' see you off! Ain't you my big brother?!" Tommy said as they both gave each other a hug and pat on the back.

On the morning of their leave in hot July to join the thousand others pouring out of the South, William and Rosetta made their rounds to say their goodbyes to one and all. As they headed out to catch up with the other five families already heading down the dirt road leading to the tracks to catch the next nine dollar per head railcar ticket to Kansas City via St. Louis, 103 year old Hannah was heard uttering to them "Now, don't any of ya forget where ya from," as she added her farewells. William *Hanks* turned around to her. "Don't worry Hannah; We never goin' forget the way back home!" "

Soon it *was* time for everyone to head back home, as the 7th Bi-Annual Crockett family reunion now came to an end in August 2000 until all would be called together again.

But on that heat-rising Memphis Sunday afternoon, I wasn't

yet ready to return home.  Instead, I was now on my way down Interstate 40 toward Roane County, Tennessee to meet who I believed was another branch of my family, a branch that didn't come into Mississippi like my family did, but had stayed in Tennessee.  This branch had no idea mine existed due to a family split that took place almost 150 years ago.  A split that occured from slavery.

Molding influences and driving forces were urging me to continue searching, sifting, and repiecing.  In the beginning, I had no idea how long this project would last or where my journey would take me in trying to reassemble my ancestors' lives.  I was like a moving ship coasting from one harbor to the next for directions toward my ultimate goal--seeing if I could discover *evidence* of my family's African lineage.  I needed navigation.  My relatives had come to my aid at several crucial junctures.  But the success of this trip would take more than just family.  It would also take friends.  Even unlikely ones--descendants of the family that once had bargained and herded my ancestors as human chattel.  Yes, that family was just as much bound to me as those at the reunion whom I had just extended goodbyes.  Like I said before, if I had not decided to contact also those descendants, then, I know for a fact, this whole story could not have been told.

# CHAPTER FOURTEEN

## A Griot in Tennessee

I had never been to Africa. Could I travel to West Africa, specifically that part of the continent once called the "Windward Coast" of Africa, and try to meet my distant tribal kin? That question had long been answered with a resounding *yes*. The only unanswered question now was: "When could I go?" William Henry Eskridge, the son and grandson of slaves William Burgess and William Eskridge of Virginia, had gone. But *where* in Africa did he go? Did he possess knowledge of the family origin? Did he possibly go to the Grain Coast, the Ivory Coast, or even perhaps to the Gold Coast?

I suspicioned he may have gone to Liberia, since historically Liberia had always been looked up to by black folks from the 1860's through the 1930's as the Motherland and symbol of Freedom for their oppressed people, as was demonstrated, for example, with the "Back-to-Africa" movement conducted by national rights leader Marcus Garvey, a native of Jamaica and son of an Akan Maroon, whose American delegation landed at Cape Palmas, Liberia near the Ivory Coast border in July 1924 to begin setting up preparations for a mass migration expected that October. The exodus almost succeeded had not it been for certain U.S. diplomats who pressured the Liberian government to reject their earlier endorsement.

So, for some reason, I had an instinctive feeling that Henry went to Liberia. Now that instinctive feeling was telling me where to go. I don't know what knowledge Henry had, but I knew I had an ancestor's name, a linguistic meaning of that name, and a tribe connected to that name.

I paid a visit to a West African who lived in the neighborhood not far from my home. He and his family had moved to Portland from his birthplace of Sierra Leone, one of the countries that bordered Liberia. He wished me well on my planned trip but said to be cautious as Liberia was just coming out of a seven year civil war, and his own home country was presently experiencing battles between the government and rebel forces.

Later I conferred with a friend serving as a missionary in Sierra Leone who happened to be in the United States visiting her parents. As we spoke on the phone, I soon learned that the fighting in the Sierra Leone capitol Freetown had turned worse, resulting in she and her missionary companions having to be evacuated. Describing Liberia, she mentioned that the country was still unstable and without electricity throughout most of the country including the capitol, Monrovia. She then gave me two telephone numbers of friends in West Africa to contact.

During the late fall of 1998, an effort was made again to try and contact persons in Duck Hill in hopes of meeting other branches of the Eskridge family, and also to learn anything more about Henry's trip to Africa. After several telephone inquiries, I soon made contact with a lady named Ms. Malisso, a former Head Start Teacher and the mother of thirteen children. "I was born in 1927...I remember Henry Eskridge, he was my school teacher," Ms. Malisso said. I then asked if she knew or heard anything about Henry's trip, but she said she never heard about it, and wasn't related to that branch of the family. "I just can't remember too much of back then," Ms. Malisso politely stated. I then asked if she knew my cousins the Crocketts and she said she knew who Leon Crockett was. She also remembered Madie Jones, too.

Before concluding, I now wanted to find out about her family, to at least try to salvage something from our quickly ending conversation. "My father was George Washington Eskridge, he died in 1975 and was 82 years old...my grandfather was Willis

Eskridge...I remember my father mention he had a brother named Marshall, and my Aunt was Aunt Evabelle, she married a Townes, and another was Aunt Hester who married a Davis." That was as far as she could take me back, but oh, how valuable! Her father was named George Washington Eskridge. Where did her family branch come from?

Next, I got in contact with Adine Brown of California, whose family had moved there from Duck Hill in the early 1950's. Adine also was born in 1927. I asked about Henry. "He was my school teacher in third grade, at the old school called "Wilkens Chapel," a one room school house in the country...he had Indian in him, 'cause he looked reddish, and his hair was straight...he would ride the school bus, the school bus would come pick him up, and his dog, a german shepherd, and he would ride in the school bus with the white kids while we had to walk," recalled Adine humorously.

As we warmed up to each other, I then asked if she knew about the trip. "I remember my parents saying, "Professor Henry Eskridge went to Africa!", they were very excited about it...he taught my father, too...both the whites and the blacks had respect for him." This was something new. Adine said that Henry even taught her father, and that both her parents recalled hearing about his trip, not Adine, who was born *after* this event occured. I now asked, "Who was your father?" Adine said, "They called him Louis Eskridge, but his real name was Lou George Washington Eskridge...my brother's name was George, too...father died in 1973...my grandfather was Morris Eskridge, and my grandmother was Clara."

At this point I was about to fall out on the floor. Her father, too, had that old familiar name, and her grandfather was Morris, which meant that two of her uncles were Hugh and John Eskridge, the latter living to 100 years of age and had stated that Morris was "born in Jamaica." It also meant that Adine's great-grandfather was Louis Eskridge, her great-great-grandparents were George & Phyllis Eskridge, and her great-uncle was Frank Eskridge, the one who was said came from Africa.

Before we said goodbye, Adine asked if I would promise to

call back when she found out I was tracing the Eskridge family tree, as she wanted to find out more herself. "I definitely will be calling back," I said. Adine then told me to call her 92 year old second cousin in Duck Hill.

Anderson Elliot, born on July 14, 1917, lived on Martin Luther King Road across from the Duck Hill elementary school. Did farming all his life. Anderson's mother, Annie, was first cousin to Morris Eskridge's wife Clara. Anderson's sister-in-law who lived just down the street and next door to cousin Leon Crockett was Ella Mae Elliot, a great-great-granddaughter of Frank Eskridge. By now my lead in questions were becoming routine. "Old man Henry Eskridge taught me one session, first grade...we'd go in the morning till evening; boys had to go in the field, after laying the crop then they'd go [to school]...you carry lunch with you, meat & molasses." I now knew Anderson was taking me back, back to Henry's earlier school sessions.                    But Anderson didn't recall anything about a trip to Africa. Now I was really wondering. William Henry was born October 1858. If Mr. Elliot didn't remember hearing anything about the trip, but Adine Brown's parents did, that would put Henry's trip somewhere close to the late 1920's. Henry would have turned 62 years old by the fall of 1920. Just how long did he live? Mr. Elliot concluded, "He had a red horse, would feed it apples, and just about anything else he ate...his wife Esther taught school for awhile there, too." I then asked if he remembered where they lived. "They lived on "Back Lane" they called it...Rosie Jones lived back there, her husband was Pete Harper...Madie Jones lived there...Rosie was her mother."

Finally I spoke with Ella Mae Elliot. She couldn't recall anything about the school teacher Henry. Some of Ella Mae's branch of the family moved to Louisville, Kentucky during the 1950's. But she did share a recollection she had with her grandfather Harrison Eskridge, born September 16, 1871 and the son of Frank Eskridge. When Harrison was about ten years old he was working as a house servant in the home of slaveowner Richard Eskridge's grandson James L. Eskridge of Coffeyville, Mississippi in Yalobusha County, who was the son of Taliaferro Eskridge.

"I remember my grandfather Harrison telling me back then

they'd go to school for four months then work in the fields...my grandfather told me he was born after slavery, said they wouldn't beat 'em and take their food like they did to 'em in slavery times...said he got enough to eat,"  related Ella Mae.  That comment truly made me wonder what was life really like on the Eskridge plantations during slavery.  I recalled the many slave narratives I had read from those who had lived the nightmare. Many of the narratives spoke of beatings because of being caught stealing food.  Now I understood Harrison's comment: "...beat 'em and take their food."  It's one thing to be a thief.  It's another thing to watch your family go hungry night after night from not being *given* enough to eat.

One Saturday morning during the summer of 1999, as I headed out the front door of my apartment building, the mailman happened to approach and handed me a large box.  It was from my cousin Billie's husband Robert, who had sent a large binder.  Later the telephone rang.  Robert was calling to make sure I'd received it. "Stephen, an Eskridge relative sent me alot of research...mentions about the slaves...how some were even brought to Mississippi...you're going to enjoy reading all of it!"  As we kept talking I soon gathered from Robert's excited voice that the relative who answered Robert's Internet e-mail request for any family records pertaining to slavery in Carroll County was a descendant of Duck Hill landholder Richard Eskridge, and lived right in the same city of Dallas, Texas.  This descendant's name was a familiar one-- Jack Grantham--the man who had sent C Swanson notes about the Eskridge family, several of which she had sent me.  But was family historian Jack Grantham really someone that open in providing access to information on one's slaveholding ancestors?  Would his collection of documents really include something substantial to me as a black genealogist, or just simply biographies of proud Southern families listing off a high order of society accomplishments while at the same time mentioning their blacks as mere property tax figures?  Could his personal papers offer to me anything of solid and weighty value pertaining to my search and family kin, or just plain ordinary aggregate slave data?  That day I would find out, and later would receive a phone call that would mark a turning point during now the tenth year of my search.

Robert, the ole' family historian griot on Great-grandmother Rosetta's family the Crocketts, also shed more light about Henry Eskridge, who was the brother-in-law to Rosetta's brother Harrison Crockett who had married Henry's twin sister Eliza. "Henry died in December 1944;  Maybe his obituary might say something about his trip to Africa, but I can't find it in the newspapers;  Three years ago I talked to a Thornton Smith of East Chicago, Indiana, born in 1910...he was raised by Grant Crockett's family when they lived in Carrollton before Grant died in 1926;  Thornton told me: "Eliza Crockett's brother was the school teacher, Henry Eskridge;  When I was a teenager during the 1920's I moved to Duck Hill for six months and remembered hearing Henry bragging that he had gone to Africa, telling the school class how dumb they were and how smart the Africans were." Every teacher has there own motivational style. "Professor Eskridge" apparently had his reasons for the classroom comparison that day.

The personal family papers Jack Grantham had e-mailed Cousin Robert contained additional court document citations and oral histories regarding not only Richard Eskridge's lineage, but also about their family slaves.  But Jack didn't just "brush off" or "delete" references to named slaves in his thesis of documents as is so often done in published journals for Southern and Colonial America genealogies.  He made a point of including a slave's name on his circulation of findings among his fellow family cousin historians, quoting slave names just as they appeared in the original texts.  Clearly what stood out in Jack's research was the painstaking way in which he recorded numerous courthouse entries from at least six Southern States whenever black slaves involved his family.  I plopped the large box beside me on the couch.  This was too good to be true.  I opened up the box feeling like I held the greatest gift in the world.  I pulled out the bulging round-ring binder, perusing it most of the afternoon, took a break, then resumed that evening until clear past one in the morning, and for the next several days.

I now had two powerful books in my home, the binder and the Bible.  And so help me, I made sure to give each one its rightful due and proper place. What made this partial family collection even more authentic was that the owner, Jack Grantham, was a genealogist, too. For me to have decided to contact the descendants of slaveowner Richard Eskridge and to now learn that one of them was into genealogy like I was--why, that was like hitting paydirt. At least I hoped so.

Some of his findings corroborated the research I had uncovered. But there also was new information. Off I went again to the State archives in Jackson to verify the new information pulled from the Carroll County courthouse.

On Wednesday, January 4, 1837 Richard Eskridge "...of Carroll County, in the State of Ms;...in consideration of the sum of one dollar to me in hand paid by my said son, Taliaferro Eskridge...do give, grant, bargain and sell unto my said son...the following Negro slave...about fourteen years old...In witness whereof I have hereunto set my hand and seal this the 4 day of Jan. 1837." The slave was a woman born around 1823. Her name was Phyllis. As the facts would later bear out, she would soon bear a son in 1838 and name him Frank, with the help of her husband George.

Another deed dated February 9, 1837 from Richard Eskridge to his son Thomas Livingston Eskridge, conveyed "one negro girl named Winny, about seventeen years old, Dolly about fifteen years, & Ruth about five years old." Reading the name Ruth immediately brought back to mind the daughter of Will and Jane who also was named Ruth, born 1773, and living on Burdett Eskridge's Edgefield County plantation in 1782. I had no doubt five year old Ruth was named after her.

But that was not all. On Thursday, September 22, 1842 Richard Eskridge conveyed four slaves among his twenty grandchildren. The names of two of those slaves were very familiar. One of them was, "the following Negro, to wit, Mary Jane, a girl about fifteen years old." In due time her life and that of her children would soon be bartered back and forth between three of the grandchildren until one of them, William Chiles Eskridge, would finally settle upon keeping one of the children, Wesley Ann, and driving her mother Mary Jane off the plantation with threat of violence in 1867.  However, these new court documents revealed that daughter Wesley Ann, along with eight other minor children, had actually been held since 1865:  "It further appearing to the Court from the proof, that Wesley Ann is a minor aged five years and having no putative father, and that she was abandoned by her mother in June last.  It is therefore ordered and decreed that the said Wesley Ann be apprenticed to the said Wm. C. Eskridge for the period of thirteen years, that is until the 20 Dec 1878."  But just as Mary Jane had explained her actions to the Freedmen's Bureau, so too, I myself would have "left" upon threats of being whipped. In 1878 William C. Eskridge later lost his life along with hundreds of others as a victim of the deadly yellow fever epidemic that spread through Carroll County that year.

The other familiar name conveyed that day in 1842 was the man Jordan, born about 1823 in Alabama whose future daughter Francis would later marry freedman Henry Hanks in 1868. Realizing that Jordan was mentioned in this conveyance, I pulled out the 1853-55 court records obtained in 1992 that dealt with Richard Eskridge's deceased son, Samuel Burdette Eskridge, and began comparing the names of the slaves that were divided out to Samuel's three children who had become minor wards of the court. Jordan's name was among them.

As for Eliza Binford, the wife of David Binford, mother of Willis Eskridge, and freedwoman who had listed her parents birthplace as Africa, another court document provided a possible explanation as to why her son's surname was *Eskridge*, as well as what plantation she may have lived on.  The Carroll County Probate Court Minutes for 1862 read as follows:  Richard Eskridge Estate   "Whereas it appears to the Satisfaction of the Court from proof filed that the Executor of the last will of Richard Eskridge deceased is engaged in the present war and that said Estate is exposed and liable to go to waste from the absence of said Executor or some one else to look after the same,   It is therefore ordered that *Jno. A. Binford Sr. be appointed to take charge of the plantation* of the decedent until the further order of this Court." Freedwoman Binford may have lived on the Eskridge plantation during the period of time when John A. Binford was appointed by

the court to temporarily oversee the plantation until the executor of
the estate, Richard Eskridge's grandson Burdett Eskridge, returned
from the civil war.  Perhaps that explained why her son's surname
became Eskridge, but who really knew?

Cousin Robert also sent me a deed that he himself had
uncovered during one of his trips to Duck Hill, dated "the 30th day
of May A.D. 1905" from "D.D. Wilkins to Frank Eskridge," a land
conveyance from a 71 year old man to a 67 year old one.  The deed
read: "I deed, convey, and warrant to Frank Eskridge, his heirs and
assigners the following described land  SE 1/4 of NE 1/4 Sec. 13
Township 20 Range 5 East, the interest purpose of this deed is to
convey to Frank Eskridge *the 40 acres of land he now lives on."*  It
seems that Drury D. Wilkins had made good on the Civil war end's
promise of "40 acres and a mule."   This deed apparently
demonstrated that C Swanson's grandfather wanted to ensure it
stay that way by putting it in writing.

Other documents showed also that during the 1851
December term, the court had ordered John A. Binford and
Benjamin Campbell be appointed to divide the slaves belonging to
the three children of their deceased father, Samuel Burdette
Eskridge.  During the next term of the court, "Robert Neal, Sr.
Guardian of Thomas Eskridge, this day made a report of the sale of
the slaves belonging to his ward.  Made on this 7th Feb 1853
amounting to the sum of fifteen hundred and sixty three dollars
which was examined, confirmed and ordered to be recorded."  This
was the same exact day that the estate appraisal for Richard
Eskridge's deceased brother Samuel Eskridge of Roane County
was presented to the Tennessee Court and recorded, including the
75 name slave inventory.

Four of those 75 slaves--Maria, Edmond, Lewis, Jordan--
were the same names as those alloted to the three Eskridge wards
of the court in Carroll County.  I could not accept this as being
mere coincidence.  These four slaves were either the same persons
listed on the inventory and were being sold or hired out, or they
may have been  children belonging to families among the seventy-
five.   In December 1853 the Roane County Court assigned
proceeds to be set aside for the widow Sophia Eskridge, including

$150 to buy clothing and $150 to buy shoes & mending for the families & individuals comprising the seventy-five person workforce.

What became of those families and their descendants almost one hundred fifty years later?  What became of the young ones, whose blistered feet fitted into those purchased shoes?  Or the babies of the mothers, who happily clutched onto new outfits to replace their filth-infested, torn-tattered, wornout garments?

Encouraged with the success in contacting the descendants of Richard Eskridge's former slaves of Duck Hill, I decided to put forth a similiar effort to try to contact, if possible, any of the descendants of Samuel Eskridge's slaves who once existed on the Buck Creek plantation near the Clinch River in Roane County, Tennessee.

My growing desire to make contact with those descendants in Tennessee was obviously clear since Great-Great-grandmother Eliza and Great-grandfather William were born there, but also because of another reason stemming from what I later discovered regarding the family branch of Ms. Malisso.

Her father George Eskridge, who was known as "Washington" in the family, was born August 4, 1893 on the family farm in Duck Hill to Willis and Julie Eskridge.  In turn, Willis was born March 1853 on the Duck Hill plantation and was the second of thirteen children to Wash and Susan Eskridge.  Wash and Susan had six sons.  The oldest, Marshall, later in 1886 named one of his daughters Susan after his mother.  Marshall's brother Willis, in turn, named one of his sons "George Washington" after his father Wash, and named another son after his brother Marshall.

The significance of slave-naming patterns had become all too familiar to me since  learning of it when I first began doing name comparisons within my own family eleven summers ago.  But even more significant was the birthplace of Wash, Ms. Malisso's great-grandfather.  Wash Eskridge was born 1815 in Tennessee.

"What city"?  "What listing"?  The voice response system when dialing directory assistance I had probably heard over a hundred times now since having begun this journey. On this particular Sunday evening it was no different. "Kingston." "Eskridge."

Kingston, Tennessee. I had chosen this location to initiate this new search because Kingston was the nearest city on the road pike just down from the head of Buck Creek--Kingston Road--the same road that troops under civil war leaders Major General Ambrose E. Burnside of the Union and Lieutenant General James Longstreet of the Confederacy headed down in the siege of Knoxville in 1863.

The need for jobs and employment would have attracted the descendants of Buck Creek to nearby towns in order to rebuild their futures and that of their families. But when I asked the operator for the listings to all Eskridges in Kingston, I was told there were none.

"But what about the surrounding areas?"

"There's listings in Rockwood and Harrimann."

"Can you give me all of them?"

"There's too many; I can only give you two."

"Just give me the "names" of all of them, I'll call back for the numbers one-by-one."

I ended up getting six for Rockwood and four to Harrimann. As I dialed down the list, there were those who answered, those that didn't, and those whom messages were left with. Those I did talk to kept telling me I needed to talk to a certain senior man who resided in Rockwood. When they mentioned his name I looked down at my list and could see there was one more phone number before him, which I decided to call so to make sure I wasn't skipping over anyone that might possibly help me.

I proceeded to call the next number on the list and a man named Jerry answered, close to my age, a few years more. He began by telling me there were many Eskridges in the area, many that were family. After explaining to him that there was "a white man born in Duck Hill, Mississippi who inherited a plantation with slaves in Roane County from his great-uncle," I asked him if he had ever heard of Samuel Eskridge. "I heard about a man name

Sam Eskridge who owned a plantation near Kingston. There's a monument of him in Roane County Park." He then went on to mention of a church built in 1857 that had a plaque on it citing black persons named Eskridge who helped build it.

I asked Jerry what names were mentioned. "There was Tyler, Hiram, and Bris." Why, Hiram and Bris were two of the 75 slaves on Buck Creek. Hiram was born in 1835 and Bris, referred to in the Roane court records as Brisborn, was born about 1810 in Virginia and buried in the old Rockwood City cemetary. His slave wife was Margaret, born about 1807 in Tennessee.

I next asked Jerry who was his grandfather and great-grandfather. "My grandfather was Gerald Eskridge who worked on the railroad, my great-grandfather was Calvin and my great-grandmother was Etta; She lived to be 107 years old, she died in 1976." Before we concluded our conversation, Jerry told me there would be a family reunion in August 2000 and would let me know the date. He also mentioned to me about that person I needed to talk to. "His name is Rue and will be 84 next year. He's my great-uncle."

After several attempts I finally got ahold of Rue Eskridge. Once he started to relate the oral history of his family passed down to him through his father, I could hardly keep up with him. Mr. Rue Eskridge began:

"I'm 83, born February 16, 1916. My father was Calvin, born September 18, 1857 and died February 1943. My mother was Etta Love, she lived to be 107 years old, she died October 8, 1976. When my father died, she married a Roddy. My mother's mother was Sadie Love, she married Alfred Love, he played a fiddle while they danced in the barnyard. My grandfather's name on my father's side was Marion, and my grandmother's name was Mary. She was a cook for the slaveholders. My daddy's father, he stayed not far from her. She was out a little distance. They lived at a place called "Caney Ford" 'round there, the "'slaves" place during the civil war."

Things were starting to get interesting, real interesting. Here this highly respected family pedigree narrator--a modern day griot--was taking me back to a time that I had only read about. I recalled the papers I received in 1992 from the genealogist in Kingston, and how I first came across the name Marion Eskridge who was born in 1835 Tennessee and buried in the Roane County cemetary called Hickory Flats, listing his parents' birthplace as Virginia, and his wife Mary Frances, born January 1841 in Tennessee and buried next to her husband, who listed her parents' birthplace as Mississippi. And Rue's reference to "Caney Ford" was the name of a shallow river crossing where the East Tennessee and Clinch rivers meet, just near a town on Kingston road called Midtown. Brother Rue continued:

"There was a Sam and a George Eskridge. A slave house was up there by Midtown, between Kingston and Rockwood, my daddy's mother worked for those slaveholders up there. My daddy's father, he would go at night to meet her when she got off; She was cooking in the kitchen oven, putting on the coals, and had steak & cornbread in the skillet when the stragglers came, them soldiers who deserted the army, came in and took the food, ate it all then left out of there. So they had to meet in the henhouse and dig a hole and put the meat in to hide it."

The stragglers. There were many during the civil war, on both sides. I couldn't tell which side these soldiers were on during the incident Rue was describing, but the way his voice described the event as told to him by his father indicated to me that it had occured one night, one night on the plantation. Soldiers were definitely in the area at that time, such as what happened when Confederate soldiers under Lieutenant General James Longstreet left Chattanooga on November 4, 1863 coming up the East Tennessee River until they arrived in front of the Little Tennessee River near Loudon. On the night of November 14, the armies were spotted by a Union outpost as they crossed the river which sparked a race between both sides as to who would first reach the intersection on Kingston Road near a junction called Campbell's Station. Union soldiers under Major General Ambrose E. Burnside reached the intersection 15 minutes before Lieutenant Longstreet and retreated into Knoxville, where the city was later besieged by Longstreet's armies until December 4.

"One time the slaveholders had a big turkey. My father

went out there to it, had on a red flannel apron, he was a little fellow, and the turkey just knocked him down.  My father had kept those bullet moulders the soldiers used.  I used to have 'em, then the old house we lived in burned down.  When the slaves were thirsty, they bent down and drank the water on the ground that filled up in the horse holes.  Lot of 'em came by wagon from Virginia on daddy's side and on my mother's side.  My uncles were Sam, Joe, Tyler, and Melton.  My aunt was named Luberry, used to have pictures of them until the old house burned down.  Daddy talked about Hiram.  Alot of the oldtimers came to daddy's house.  My mother ran a boarding house 3 miles from Rockwood.  Tramps & hobo's who needed a place would ask where to stay and were told to go there.  Daddy would light a lantern so to see who was coming, "Who is it"?  "Come down here so I can see ya"!  They couldn't see the way how to get down there."

I recognized the names Tyler and Melton from the cemetary records, buried in Citizens Cemetary on Black Jack Road along with Calvin, their Aunt Aggy, and Hiram's son Hiram Jr.  Many more were also buried in Rockwood whose marked graves had long since faded and now covered with overgrown weeds.  Who knows how many were buried at Buck Creek?  By 1802 Samuel Eskridge had arrived in Roane County from Edgefield County, South Carolina.  In 1817 he was listed with nine slaves, who were more than likely the parents of Marion, Aggy, Hiram, Wash, Eliza, and any others who were brought "by wagon."  I then asked Rue if he knew Marion's father's name:

"My grandfather Marion, his father's name was Bris, Brisborn.  He wasn't born here.  He *immigrated* here.  They said he preached the first sermon in the church here, said he couldn't read or write but could preach 'cause that's all he knew was the Bible.  They came in wagons, they all's up from Virginia, that's what my daddy said.  I got relatives all down in there.  Some in South Carolina and North Carolina, too, but I don't know where, I never met 'em."

Apparently he never met the slave inheritor of his father and grandfather, Samuel Eskridge's great-nephew Samuel Butler Eskridge, either.  He and his wife Mary had left Rockwood sometime after 1900 and moved to Grand Junction, Tennessee in Hardeman County, just near Memphis and the Mississippi border, some two hours from Duck Hill. Before saying goodbye to Rue and asking him to let me know about the reunion, he told me the story about a strange letter he received one day:

"A lady who was sick in a rest home in Knoxville say my name and called me. She wrote me a letter, said she was born in Rockwood. Her name was Eliza Eskridge, and was trying to find out about her family. I couldn't find out anything, even asked around to the people in Rockwood, but nobody ever heard about her. She was older than me, so her people must've already gone, since nobody 'round here remembered her. I don't quite remember how she got my name, I got the letter around here somewhere...two or three years ago they sent me a clipping she had died, gotten senile, had her leg amputated. Got so her mind was going. They tried to find out where she was from, but she got so she wouldn't even talk after awhile. I wrote her a letter about a month or two before she died... said she was born in Rockwood."

As we concluded our one hour exchange, Rue mentioned that he was the last one left of four brothers and one sister. He had lost his 92 year old brother just last week. I later drove up after the family reunion in Memphis to meet Rue, in his humble country home with his three large bulls grazing around the yard, and listened in person to the family stories that had been passed down from his father and grandfather.

Rue insisted on taking me into town and treating my wife and I to lunch at the local buffet restaurant. On the way, he took me first to the spot where his father's house once stood, now buried by decades of grownup woods. Next, we followed him as he drove to the former location of Samuel Eskridge's residential home in Midtown, some fifteen miles by car from his plantation near Buck Creek. Rue pointed to an open field, hidden off from the main road by high weeds and tree limbs, where a tall-standing gravestone could barely be seen. "Go down and take a look, if you can get through there," Rue said. Juggling three or four of my steps off the road and down to the open field, I made my way over to this lonely tombstone. The grave-marker read: *"Samuel B.*

*Eskridge, November 3, 1763 Loudon Co. VA--April 19, 1852; Life
is How Short, Eternity is how Long."*

I pulled out the old census records that listed the families
Rue had mentioned.  I noticed that very familiar slave-naming
custom and pattern among them, such as with the children
belonging to Brisborn and Margaret's sons Marion, Solomon, and
Frederick.   Solomon and his wife Aggy had two sons named
Joseph and Samuel by 1880.  His brother Marion and wife Mary
also had two sons Joseph and Samuel that same year.   A
connection seemed to emerge in Richmond County, Virginia that
same year of 1880, where another freedman named Frederick
Eskridge was listed by the census taker, eighty years old and born
in 1800.  Ten years earlier in 1870, freedman Frederick was living
in Cople Parish, Virginia, located in Westmoreland County,
residing near three other recently freed families with the surname
Eskridge, headed by Henry, George, and Joseph.

These freedmen still would have held at this time the fresh
memory of slavery, especially if they witnessed the trauma of
having a sibling sold off.  Families were forbidden to have
meetings, even religious meetings at night, unless in the company
of a white person.  Slaves in Westmoreland County would recall
the secret religious meetings they held at night in barns or in the
woods.  To keep the sound down from travelling, the custom was
to turn a cooking pot upside down at the cabin door.  One slave in
Sandy Point recalled hearing slaves screaming at night from a
nearby plantation as they were being whipped.  It was rumored that
some had been beaten to death.  I wondered if those brought to
Tennessee "by wagon" was for better or for worse?

Brisborn, whose name meant "Circumcised birth" and
listing his age to indicate he had been born in Virginia about 1810,
named one of his sons "Frederick" at Buck Creek.  The names of
the freedmen families in Cople Parish, Virginia in 1870 was strong
evidence that they very well may have been Brisborn's family.

Almost every day I would find myself staring at the names
on the 1853 estate inventory of Samuel Eskridge which listed his
seventy-five slaves, hoping that the more I kept staring some clue
would jump out at me and provide that missing link from Great-

great-grandmother Eliza to the other members of her family line. Her name and Great-grandfather William's name were both on that list. But I had no explanation with which to connect them to those other names except by a profound gut feeling. Here I had tried to follow the paths of practically all of the 75 enslaved at Buck Creek, but could not produce the crucial link of *how* they related to my family.

Now I was starting to feel the frustration and anger of how slavery had virtually destroyed the lines of descent to the generations of the past. When Great-great-grandmother Eliza and her son William were uprooted and sent to Mississippi, they themselves lost that link they had to the families in Tennessee. My frustration felt even more apparent during my interviews with Eskridge family members when they would eventually ask me how I was related and which branch of the family was I related to: "Well, Eliza's surname was Eskridge, but her son William changed his surname to Hanks, which name he borrowed from  the plantation overseer, who in turn took Eliza and her children...," it was a complicated explanation to say the least.

That's the legacy slavery gave to her victims. Disruption of generational family lines which virtually destroyed linkage to African ancestral lines of Black Americans. What made linkage more difficult was the custom most families held, including mine, of avoiding discussion about "slavery days" to their children. To further disrupt learning about my past generational lines were the premature deaths of five of my great-grandparents' ten children: James, Clifford, Margaret, Granison, Murt. Now the other five were all long gone. *"Don't give up now, you've come this far,"* I reminded myself.

I stared again at the list of names. Polk. Carpenter. Alex & Jane, whose name was also spelled Jinny. Brisborn. Margaret. The names of their children followed. Several of the names on the inventory were biblical: Israel, Delilah, Hiram, Joshua, Issac, Jordan. Two names of Brisborn's children were also, Solomon and Marion. Marion's name on the inventory was oddly spelled Mariah, a pet form of Marion which in Latin lands were given to boys. I recalled that even Duck Hill overseer Hanks' first name was sometimes spelled "Marah," which in the Bible meant "bitterness." The account found in the book of Exodus mentions that soon after Moses led the Israelites out of Pharaoh's Egypt and through the Red Sea, the Israelites gave way to complaining that they were unable to drink from a certain body of water because it was bitter. As the account went on, Moses was directed by God to an unidentified tree. Moses cast the tree into the water and the water became sweet. Afterwards, the place became called "Marah" in rememberance.

The name Hiram also caused my wonderment whether he was another of Brisborn's sons, since a biblical story connected the two names "Solomon" and "Hiram" together. Found in the books of 1 Kings and 1 Chronicles, King Solomon of Israel had asked the half Jewish, half gentile Hiram, King of Tyre, to provide him building materials to help build Israel's temple. Interestingly enough, on the 1853 slave inventory the name "Will" was written one name over from "Hiram." Rue Eskridge recalled that his father Calvin talked about Hiram and that alot of "the oldtimers" came to his father's house. Chances were that Hiram was related. Great-grandpa William would have been about five or six years old at the time. I gazed again at the names listed next to Brisborn's family--"Elizabeth, Eliza...Rosa Ann, Eliza." There had to be a connection. There had to be. For some reason, my mind kept going back to the ancient story of Solomon and Hiram. As I did, I found myself pulling out a short article written by Rue Eskridge, a copy which he had given me, describing the history of his black congregation that supposedly was built in 1857. According to the article, during a union meeting in May 1894, Brisborn Eskridge, then seventy-four, was asked to preach a sermon that snowfall weekend, and wood was cut and split to provide as firewood. According to those present, Brisborn chose the text from the Book of Revelation, chapter 14, verse 13, then concluded by saying, "This the first time I had the opportunity to worship in a church I could call my own." The next month, June 1894, Brisborn was buried. Prior to this, a committee had been established that year to organize the project of building a black church in Rockwood, the committee being made up of six men, including Rue's father

Calvin Eskridge, Rue's uncle Solomon Eskridge as chairman, *and Hiram Eskridge*. This told me a family project was involved. Later when Hiram's son died in 1920, he was buried at Citizen's Cemetary on Black Jack Road, the same cemetary in the year 1919 that laid to rest four of Brisborn's family: his son Solomon's wife Aggy in April, the cause of death being eighty-year old fractured ribs due to an accidental fall;  a granddaughter in July, his son Tyler in August, his son Melton in October.

My hypothesis was soon confirmed true when I telephoned Rue again and asked him about former slave, soldier, and sojourner Hiram Eskridge.  Rue replied, "He was related; I don't recall just how he was related, but that's what I gathered from the way my father explained it all to me."  Later, I let out a gasp when I realized Hiram had a son whom his wife Louisa bore in 1858 during slavery.  Ironically, the son was named William.  Was he named in memory of a separated family member?  I believe he was, my great-grandfather.   My fond visit to Rue's Rockwood home now took on greater meaning to me.  He was of my family line.

The name patterns repeated in several of the families at Buck Creek, including Brisborn's, also started to take another meaning.  It was done not only out of love, honor, and affection, but also because the horror of a family member being separated due to a profitable slave sale was a realistic concern and a constant fear.  The memory of a separated or deceased family member could thus be kept alive in the naming of the newborn.  By the time of Emancipation, this child-naming custom borne out of slavery was now already deeply rooted in the children of former slaves.

As my heart celebrated that night over the circumstantial inferences between Brisborn's family and my great-grandfather William, my mind was already speeding ahead to the next phase of the search:  who were Eliza's parents, and would their identities point to the Africans at Sandy Point, particularly to the Kru woman Akey?

Samuel and Richard Eskridge's father Captain Burdett Eskridge held  five slaves on his South Carolina plantation at his death in 1781.  They were Will, his wife Jane who was born in

1747, and their three children Ruth, Barbe, and Rose.  By 1802, Samuel had already moved to Tennessee to begin establishing his land holdings in Roane County.  Without question this was with the help of slaves, which must have included the  parents of Lucy, the first name that headed the 1853 slave inventory, for she was born around 1804.   In 1810 Richard had five slaves when he purchased his Tennessee property on Buck Creek.  Tax records for 1817 reported Samuel with nine slaves.  What happened to Will? What became of his wife Jane, who was born the same year that Burdett's father died, House Burgess member Samuel Eskridge of Sandy Point?  Where did their daughters Ruth, Barbe, and Rose end up?

# CHAPTER FIFTEEN

## Jenny and the Final Connection

The decade of the 1990's was quickly coming to an end. 1999 had started a chaotic year with the impeachment of the President of the United States, who eventually was acquitted on obstruction of justice charges involving a sexual affair. The year then accelerated to the much publicized war in Kosovo that finally ended in June, and the slim media covered rebel atrocities in Sierra Leone. Unusual earthquakes also occured worldwide--causing the second highest year of quake fatalities in the decade. There were also positive images. In March 1998 President Clinton made an historic official visit to Africa--the first time a U.S. president made an official trip--and toured several countries, even acknowledging the moral wrongness of America's role in the slave trade at the site of Goree Island in Dakar, Senegal, a former slave port. This was followed by a weeklong visit by U.S. Secretary of State Madeleine Albright in October 1999 pledging aid for food, education, health, and an end to civil war. As the end of the year approached, talk of "Y2K" and computer preparedness didn't fail to be heard in every country, city, and neighborhood.

The year of 1999 also brought notable events involving Portland. Amid the heightened alert to detect Y2K terrorism, on December 14, U.S. Customs arrested an Algerian at the U.S.-Canada border at Port Angeles, Washington named Ahmed Ressam, for having bomb materials and timing devices in the trunk of his car and reservations at a Seattle hotel. A map of Portland was also found in the car. Homocide killings in Portland, including gang-related shootings, were at twenty-five by mid-August. Black inner city North East Portland was experiencing a period of revitalization within the community. Growth of businesses and housing was being stimulated through public, private, and non-profit networks. There was also another occurrence worthy of note that year--my scheduled goal and set calender date to arrive in West Africa for two weeks, which was aimed towards the last week of the old millennium and the first week of the new.

For some reason also that year, once the dust would settle at the end of each month among my growing collection pile of papers stacked in a corner next to my home computer, I kept having an occuring notional feeling every now and then about one particular piece of paper: a copy of the 1793 South Carolina bill of sale to that 47 year old slave woman named Jenny, sold by Samuel Eskridge's brother-in-law Joseph Thomas to Joseph's father, Captain John Thomas of Green County, Georgia. I don't know why my mind locked onto that woman's fate, but I grew curious more and more as to what became of her. My constant turning of pages through Jack Grantham's notes that Cousin Robert had sent did not include any mention of this court deed. Nor did his report files notate the estate inventories of Richard Eskridge and his son Taliaferro.

I decided to write Jack Grantham a letter and ask him my perplexing questions. Would he respond with a reply? I had no idea. He didn't know me and I didn't know him. From the tone in his lettered reports to his studious family association, he and his many kin were intensely compiling up into one official volume their genealogical beginnings, their dedication to that goal shown by a commendable torrent of note-sharing, comparing, drafting, and redrafting. To put it more bluntly, I had my reservations that this busy and knowledgeable man in his field of history would find time responding to me. He had already freely sent Cousin Robert a voluminous bucket of material dealing directly with slavery and his family. That was a milestone in my book. What more could one ask? Besides, the last time I wrote a letter to their family association a year or two earlier, asking for references to slaves among family records, I never received a reply at all. But being that I was taught to give people the benefit of the doubt, perhaps my query was incorrectly addressed. I even posted e-mail queries to a genealogy website heavily used by hundreds of Eskridge surname researchers, asking anyone to volunteer any anecdote or small nugget of information they possessed in their research pertaining to any slaves. I hardly got a response back. That Tuesday my request fluttered to the bottom of a downtown mailbox, heading this time to Texas.

Five days later the phone rang on Sunday evening. Jack Grantham, a 79 year old former surety underwriter now family historian, and the third great-grandson of Richard Eskridge, was responding to the letter I had sent him, asking if he knew what happened to Richard Eskridge's estate inventory, as well as anything he knew about the identity of the 47 year old slave woman named Jenny who was sold away in 1793. Jack thanked me for having written and happy to hear that I was researching my family ancestors. He also knew that studying my ancestral line inevitably would mean studying his. But Jack was not resentful or offended by that. On the contrary, he was very open, helpful, and encouraging, just as much as C Swanson had been in 1994, and said he would be more than happy to help answer any questions I had. I started with the question of what happened to the inventories of Richard Eskridge and his son Taliaferro, as I had never been able to locate them in the Carroll County court records. "I never have seen the inventories of Taliaferro or Richard Eskridge," Jack said. "They were kept at the courthouse during the civil war, but a document I came across at the courthouse said that the inventories were moved to another place "for safe keeping," apparently the records were eventually lost."

I knew that Jack had been researching his families close to twenty years, travelling to courthouses all across the southeast states, copying verbatim the hundreds of court entries pertaining to his forefathers, and supplying the research to his family reunions and to county libraries, including the one I had visited at Montross,

Virginia. After graduating from the class of '42 at Texas A & M and later from his enlistment in the Marines, Jack became interested in tracing his ancestral lines following the death of his mother in 1983. Subsequently, Jack entered a college course on family history and genealogy. Jack and the course were a perfect match. So I knew that when Jack said the inventories of Richard and Taliafero Eskridge were lost, then they were lost.

I was curious if he knew anything about some of the free blacks that lived in Carroll County prior to the Civil War. On October 25, 1850 there was a free black family headed by a 53 year old mulatto woman named Polly Waters who lived next door to the widower Richard Eskridge. He had lost his wife Mary in 1821. There also was a 24 year old free black named Jane Waters, born 1826 in Alabama and probably Polly's daughter, and Jane's three year old son Moses, living with Richard's son Taliaferro and his wife that same year. Ten years later on the census of 1860, another free family of color from Alabama was living with both Polly and a white family named Sullivan. This other free family was Willis and Susan Waters, and their young children Nancy, Marshall, Willis, Mary, and Jim, along with a free man named Grisby Waters. Polly Waters told the census taker that she was born in 1797 in "South Carolina." How, then, did she end up in Duck Hill next door to Richard Eskridge?

Although it was impossible to reassemble all the events and lives of history's past, oftentimes my studying the various family branches of the Eskridge family would almost always lead to a trail of slaves. In Polly's case, with the aid of Jack Grantham's manuscripts, I was led again to the Grigsby family. Nathaniel Grigsby, the maternal grandfather of Richard Eskridge, had a brother, Enoch Grigsby, who migrated out to South Carolina with Captain Burdett Eskridge and his family around 1770. Settling near Mount Willing in Edgefield County, Enoch Grigsby, who later would help settle Burdett's estate following his tragic murder in 1781, had a son, Colonel Rhyden Grigsby, who before dying of "Consumption" fathered two daughters. They eventually moved to Alabama and married two brothers belonging to a family named Waters. This small lineal timeline gave me a scrap of a clue as to who likely Polly obtained her surname and freedom from. I asked Jack Grantham if he knew anything about Polly.

"Oh, Polly? Her real name was Mary; And the woman Jane and her son were more than just living with them--THEY WERE FAMILY."

If I understood Jack correctly, he was saying that Polly and her freed family were considered part of his family, although if he meant blood related I wasn't sure. I recalled a Carroll County court entry of July 1839 involving free black John Waters, no doubt a son of Polly:

"A free negro man named John Waters came this day into court and proved by the oaths of Samuel B. Eskridge and James C. Weed, citizens of this county that the said John Waters is of good character and honest deportment. The said free negro is twenty three years of age, five feet seven inches high, tolerable well made and a little round shouldered and of a yellow complexion, though apparently a full blood negro. Whereupon this court orders in that a copy of their testimony be issued to the said John Waters agreeable to then act of the Legislature of this State in such cases made and provided."

Those minutes of the court showing Samuel Burdette Eskridge, Taliaferro's brother, coming before the court and taking an oath, to give a truthful testimony to the good character of free man of color John Waters, said something about Samuel's character. To stand up in a courtroom for a black man in 1839 Mississippi had to take courage. And for brother Taliaferro to put up one of Polly's family members in his own house also said something about his inner soul. I thought to myself how sad those days of slavery must have been if people's consciences began admitting the wrongness of that system, yet at the same time received benefits derived from the system. There was no doubt some in Duck Hill wanted to change the status quo but felt powerless. It must have been a daily wrestling match between the flesh and the spirit. What would *I* have done?

Jack went on: "Did you hear the story about Red Bamberg? According to the story, this negro slave named Red *just happened* to be roaming in the woods, supposedly abandoned by his parents or master, and the Bambergs found him and brought him into their home?  HE WAS FAMILY;  That's how they had to do back then."

The story of Red Bamberg, who lived with the family of one of Richard Eskridge's daughters, was recorded in the WPA Slave Narratives for Mississippi.  Julia Ann Eskridge, the daughter of Richard Eskridge and who married George Bamberg of South Carolina, was mentioned in her father's last will to be bequeathed the slaves Luke, his wife Amanda, and their three sons Nelson, Elias, and Abram after the death of Richard's other daughter Mary Ann Love-Smith.  He later revoked this bequest in favor of his grandson Burdett R. Eskridge.  In 1870, 14 year old Red was listed with Julia's household.  The WPA narrative read:

"Red Bamburg never knew his parents, so says tradition. When a small child, being a weakling, his parents or owner carried him into the woods and left him;  he found his way to the home of a white man by the name of Bamburg, and ever afterwards bore that as his surname;...Being a first-class cook, Red was always in demand in the kitchens of the white citizens of the town...Red was somewhat of an exhorter among the people of his own color, his theme being community spirit and cooperation with the white people.  He died at the age of nearly eighty years at the home of his granddaughter, Tooger Hackman, in North Carrollton in November 1927."

Jack had me spellbound on the phone by now.  He continued:  "Did Robert tell you about a man named William Johnston?  He had a will written and in his will he wished for all his slaves to be freed;  My great-great-granduncle Samuel B. Eskridge was one of two people who were called in by William Johnston to witness the will.  Samuel must have been a highly trusted man at that time to be called in to witness the request of something like that--to have slaves freed."

Robert did, in fact, send me the copy of William Johnston's will, dated August 12, 1834:

"...to my beloved wife Martha Johnston first all my negroes as long as she lives.  At her death, my negroes all to be emancipated and set free.  My negro woman Winny to have all the cattle and furniture that belongs to her...to each growing negro, one axe and mattock and to be settled on and the right made to them of eighty acres of land...I particular charge my executors to have my slaves attended to have their freedom and settled on the land left to them, except they should wish to go to some other state.  In that case sell their land and see them removed and settled...

Witness:  SAMUEL B. ESKRIDGE
    TALIAFERRO ESKRIDGE

N.B.  I again charge my executor to be particular and see that my slaves is taken care of if they should wish to remove...My conscience tells me they ought not to be slaves any longer."

  My questions now turned to Samuel Eskridge of Roane County, Tennessee.  "Samuel Eskridge ran a tavern...he must have given the responsibility of running the plantation to a black overseer, since Samuel didn't spend much time there...Samuel left his estate to one of the sons of Taliaferro Eskridge of Duck Hill.  That's how some of the slaves from his plantations in Tennessee came to Mississippi...SLAVES WERE KEPT IN THE FAMILY...if slaves had to be sold to settle an estate or for some other reason, they were most often sold to a family relative."

  This confirmed my conclusion as to how Great-great-grandmother Eliza and Great-grandfather William ended up in Duck Hill.  To my surprise, Jack wasn't finished with Samuel yet.  "Samuel Eskridge of Roane County was born in Virginia and was an infant in Pittsylvania County, Virginia in 1770 when Bob Chandler came by."  Who was he?  Bob Chandler along with dozens of other families, the majority related to Samuel's parents Burdett and Nancy Ann Eskridge, were heading from Virginia to South Carolina by wagon train in 1770 just before the American Revolution.  Young Samuel must have been only six or seven years old.  As the migratory wagon train reached Pittsylvania County they all decided to pitch camp there for several months before resuming.  By so residing there temporarily, a tithable list was conducted by family head Bob Chandler in order to determine which families had to pay the county tax.  The importance of this list was the fact that family slaves who were brought along over the age of 15 were listed by name, and many of them were recorded with African sounding names. The list was also important for another very special reason, one I had never dreamed could be found.

"Have you ever heard of the writer Joel Chandler Harris?" Jack asked. The answer was no, as my curiousity grew. "He was a descendant of Bob Chandler who reported that tithable list and was a relative of Burdett's wife Nancy. Joel Chandler Harris was the one who started publishing the stories about Brer' Rabbit, Tar Baby, and Uncle Remus...where do you think he got those stories? Those stories came from Africa...Joel never went to Africa...he got those stories from the slaves he lived around, many of them descendants of those Africans who were listed on Bob Chandler's list."

I honestly never heard of Joel Chandler Harris, and I vaguely heard of the tales of Uncle Remus, Tar Baby, and Brer' Rabbit, but never had read them. Subconsciously I shunned them, fearing that they stereotyped blacks and their language. But I was totally ignorant to the fact that these stories had their origin in Africa. In African folklore found among many regions are stories involving a trickster, characterized by a hare, tortoiste, deer, or a spider, who oftentimes outwits his more powerful adverseries and delivers a moral lesson at the end. Sometimes the trickster himself displayed the bad example which provided the moral lesson. As Africans were brought over as slaves, they adapted the stories they remembered from their motherland to their localized environment on the plantations. The rabbit became the slave himself, outwitting his slave masters Mr. Fox, Mr. Bear, and Mr. Wolf.

Joel Chandler Harris was born December 9, 1848 in Putnam County, Georgia and lived with his mother and grandmother on a slave plantation owned by a man named Andrew Reid. Later Joel worked on a slave plantation in Newton County. Through stories the plantation slaves would tell Joel coupled with the stories his mother would share of her experiences in the pioneer days, Joel began to publish these stories as a writer starting in 1876. Interestingly, in February 1900 Harris was reported to have said that he was working on a new story entitled: "Qua; A Romance of the Revolution," in which Qua was an African prince who had been brought to America about 1760 and had died in Augusta, Georgia some fifty years later at the age of one hundred, with two eagles tattooed on his chest, revealing that he had been either the ruler of his tribe or the heir apparent before he was kidnapped and brought as a slave to Georgia. Harris also said that both his grandmother and great-grandmother had actually known Qua, and he remembered their telling stories about Qua when Harris was a young boy.

All of a sudden, Jack Grantham said something that hit me like a thunderbolt: "The 1770 tithable list shows that Burdett had a slave named Jenny...the slave Jenny was with Samuel's father Burdett along with other slaves when they migrated from Virginia to South Carolina. Jenny was listed on Burdett Eskridge's inventory as Jane, sometime spelled Jine, you get the papers out next time and take a look, her name is spelled two different ways on the inventory. Jenny helped raise little Samuel when he was young...she later was sold to a man named John Thomas, who was from Georgia. Young Samuel was raised by the Thomas family as an orphan. His sisters married John Thomas' two sons, Joseph and Frederick."

The woman Jane who was born in 1747 was the same woman Jenny who was sold away in 1793? Jack Grantham then concluded our two hour conversation by mentioning that Burdett Eskridge was born at Sandy Point and that when he was killed at Cloud Creek in 1781 the Tories came and burned his house down. "His will would have gone up in flames, too, had it not been still at his attorney's home...the slaves helped bury the dead at Cloud Creek." Before we hung up, I asked if he knew where Colonel George Eskridge purchased his slaves. "I don't know where George bought his slaves...his son Dr. Robert Eskridge burned to death on a Guinea slave ship, the ship caught fire...they say he died on a "merchant" ship, they don't like to say it was a *slave* ship, but that's what it was." I recalled the incident that Jack had notated in his material. Dr. Robert Eskridge was the ship's surgeon on board the guinea ship *Duke of Queensborough* when he died in 1747. Dr. Eskridge had probably boarded the ship in England, since he was said to have moved there to live in 1738. The guinea ship *Duke of*

*Queensborough* was also not listed among the slave ships that entered Virginia.

As we ended our conversation for the evening, I pulled out my papers on the 1782 estate of Burdett Eskridge. Sure enough, Jane's name was spelled one way, and "Jine" another. Later I checked a reference on names at the library; "Polly" was a varient of Mary. Jane's daughter "Barbe" was a French varient name for Barbara. "Rue" was a varient of Ruth. "Fed," one of Brisborn's sons, was Spanish for Frederick. And "Jinny" or "Jenny" was a pet form of Jane.

This proved that Jenny and Jane were one and the same person. This realization I took at first as an exciting revelation, a crucial clue to my mystery jigsaw family tree, a key turning point. But later my emotions hit me. One night while looking out my kitchen window I began reflecting upon what had occurred to Jenny and started crying. She was sold! My God! My fifth-great-grandmother! Jack had said that Jenny helped raise his great-uncle Samuel, who was motherless when his own mother had died around 1779. Jenny helped raise him. But when she was sold off to a Georgia minister in May 1793, whose name was signed as a witness to the sale? Samuel's. There he watched his surrogate mother bargained and bought. I began wondering what were the moments leading up to Jenny being sold that day? Perhaps there was nothing Samuel could have done anyway to prevent the horrendous and emotional ordeal, that was the system then. Each time I thought about Jenny that night, I grew melancholy. I really can't give justice to describing the feeling I had. But if you've ever held and read the actual document or heard the oral story describing the sale of one of your ancestors, it's a sadness you'll never forget.

So this meant that Jane's name all this time *was* on the 1747 inventory of Samuel Eskridge of Westmoreland County and was a young baby at the time of his death. The young baby Jenny, valued at six pounds and equaled in worth no more than the gray horse, Ranter, and one yoke of oxen, yet only one pound more than Master Samuel's silver watch, was listed before a woman's name, more than likely her mother. That woman's name was Akey, appraised at the same value she was twelve years earlier at fifteen pounds. Jenny was Akey's child!

And thanks to Jack Grantham, who later over a four month period soon sent me packets of material from his collection, including a letter permitting me to quote him and enclosing his photo to be added to my project. His interview opened my eyes that "Jenny" and "Jane" were one and the same person, and invincibly patched the gaping hole in a long weaved tapestry of generations. But still and yet, a great thanks also went to C Swanson, who unknowingly provided a ladder to Madie Jones' tree branch, bridging the tapestry gap closer . What better example could I ask for in stressing again the importance for African-American genealogists to initiate contact with descendants of the slaveholder of interest, and build to establish communicative dialogues. The majority of people today really do want to break the silence of race and slavery that exists in their families, in their clans, in themselves.

I'm not just talking about white families either. Some of us black folk brought silence onto our children. And now those children are grown. Don't know a thing about their family heritage and don't care. Haven't a clue as to who paved the way for their birth generations ago. Let's not forget also about those who silently "passed" and never came back. Black genealogists help break the silence when they make that pilgrimage to the plantation site of where their ancestors lived. Where they celebrated birth and marriage. Where they worked. Where they died. Some may say, "That's fine, but don't ask me to contact the descendants of the person who whipped my great-grandparents." There's no question that contacting may be painful. But telling an alcoholic you're not going to remain silent about the problem anymore and that help is needed for recovery is painful, too. But is not acknowledgement the first step to healing? And so, too, for genealogists.

Sharing buried family slave records with African-Americans is crucial for many to even have a chance at searching their family trees, and initiating contact to descendants of "ole massa" will help heal many by breaking the silence and dispel the fear about discussing race and slavery, that painful topic that bounds all our families. Pain that is unmasked leads to healing and reconciliation. Does not a loving mother allow her child to undergo a painful medical operation in order to ensure the long-term health of the child? Athletes say it best with the phrase: 'No pain--no gain.' I have a better phrase: 'Love thy neighbor.'

Sometime between 1747 and 1752, Akey somehow became separated from her child Jenny, either by death or assignment to another owner. The Westmoreland County Court documents shed some light. On November 29, 1752 a distribution of Samuel Eskridge's slaves were made to his five minor children Charles, Richard, Burdett, John, and Rebecca. The minor Burdett, who would later when grown settle in Edgefield County, South Carolina, was awarded a man named George, a woman named Bess, or Betty, and the young Jenny, who although not Betty's child, was apparently being placed in her care, adopting Jenny and raising her as her own. One could only pray that the African Akey was still alive to watch her grow up. But if her fate was acted out to return to the burial dust of the earth, it was not, to be sure, without drawing out a sworn oath from the woman Betty to raise Jenny as if she were her own.

The fate of Jenny's husband Will was unknown. After Jenny was sold, Will perhaps found another mate to have other children by, perhaps sons whom one of them likely would have been named after himself. Jenny also may have borne him sons before their separation. William Burgess Eskridge of Duck Hill stated he had a father named William who was born in Virginia, very likely a son of William and Jenny. Frank Eskridge and his siblings stated their father's name was George Eskridge and born in South Carolina, very likely another son.

On the 1736 Sandy Point, Virginia plantation inventory list, Akey's name was written next to *"Congo Judy...Rose, Jenny, and her child Mandy."* Eleven years later the names Congo Judy, Rose, Jenny and child Mandy had disappeared from the 1747 inventory, but Akey's name was still listed, recorded below her infant daughter Jenny. On the 1782 Edgefield County, South Carolina inventory list, Will and Jenny named one of their daughters *Rose*.

Although I could not pinpoint or isolate what was the name of Eliza's father, a recurring maternal name kept repeating itself and crying out to me from my family documents--*ROSE*.

Was there evidence that Rose, the third child of Will and Jenny, was Eliza's mother and still alive on Samuel Eskridge's Buck Creek, Tennessee plantation when he died in 1852? Yes, there was. On his slave inventory was a name written next to Eliza's:

> **"*Rosa Ann*, Eliza..."**

Great-great-grandmother Eliza later named one of her daughters *Rosie*. Another daughter was named Betty. Jennings Eskridge of Duck Hill--a son of Frank Eskridge--his name most certainly pointed to the woman Jenny. And the other names belonging to the slaves at Duck Hill and Buck Creek had already existed before in the family line years in advance, counting back to 1736 Sandy Point: William, Frank, Phyllis, Hannah, Tom, Amanda, Richard, Samuel, George. What eventually became of Jenny after she was sold I could not determine. Her name appeared nowhere on the estate inventory of her last known master, Captain John Thomas of Hancock County, Georgia at his death in 1807. But her daughters Ruth, Barbe, Rose, and any others who may have been born before her separation, went with Richard Eskridge and his brother Samuel to Buck Creek and Duck Hill.

Recalling the family story "Henry Eskridge went to Africa during the 1920's" signaled me to try a passport/application search through the State Department and National Archives in hopes of locating any documented proof revealing a visitation to an African country. No record turned up. However, although Executive Order 2285 of December 15, 1915 stated that all persons leaving the United States should have passports and an act of Congress of May 2, 1918 made it unlawful for U.S. citizens to travel abroad without a valid passport, the law lapsed with the formal termination of World War I. Thus, after 1921 there was no statutory *requirement* that American citizens have a passport for travel abroad until 1941. Therefore, I had no proof on paper to back up Henry's story. The paper trail ended for now.

But concerning the family sayings "Frank Eskridge was

from Africa" and "Morris Eskridge was born in Jamaica," I refused to cast aside common logic that there had to have been certain events that took place in the family past which triggered these oral sayings.  For all anyone knew, the memory of that statement "Frank Eskridge was from Africa" was more likely all this time in reference to--not the one in Duck Hill who was born in 1838, but rather--the one listed as  "Frank" on the 1736 inventory who ended up inherited by Samuel Eskridge of Westmoreland County.  And the mention of the geographical island in the West Indies  quickly brought to mind the Yoruba proverb:  *"He who knows how to eat the ishin knows how to remove the deadly part."*   Now I understood.  I now understood how the stories originated.  The shackles fell off.  The poison had been extracted.  My journey was revealing that the scars of slavery and racism had not destroyed my family.  And it would never destroy me as long as I didn't allow hate to grow.  Even the parrot knew this.

The repetition of all these names were definitely the marks of identification pointing to an enduring family line.  I needed no further convincing of this long-line connection.

It was time now to make the final connection.

Each week during the summer I could feel the growing urgency of making definite travel arrangements to Liberia and the Ivory Coast soon, as by August regional confrontations within West Africa were beginning to escalate, causing me to fear that some dreaded conflict would trigger a domino effect and thus completely kill my goal of arriving there.  At first I had wanted to take off that summer, until I heard the news on August 11, 1999 of the fighting situation in Liberia, causing me to call my travel agent that same day to cancel my ticket until further notice.

Practically each day I would scan the newspaper for the latest developments, hoping I wouldn't see some breaking bad news before my new set date in December.  Even the arrival in October of my purchased travel insurance didn't help to calm my anxiety either, especially when I read my travel delay coverage provided benefits in the event I was "being delayed by, but not directly involved in, a traffic accident while en route to a departure."  My worried nerves really hit when I read what was *not* covered:  "war(whether declared or undeclared), acts of war...civil disorder or unrest...expected or foreseeable events."

Finally my passport arrived.  Then it was on to get my "shots" at Good Samaritan Hospital's travel clinic.  The doctor couldn't help to ask me why was I heading to West Africa.  "To write a book about my family; you see, I've traced it to a tribe whom I wish to meet."  The doctor was happily surprised, saying she would love to read it when it became available.  She then went on to explain how she and a group of doctors went to Rwanda soon after the genocide, and how frightened she was when a loaded rifle was aimed at her through the window of her hut as she and her team lay in their beds, an apparent attempt to frighten and intimidate them.  She had no idea, but that was the last thing I needed to hear.  At least she waited to tell me after she stuck the vaccination needle in my arm.

As I boarded the aircraft I couldn't help but think of all the unfinished business I had wanted to pursue and complete before this trip.  My brain was sending a message to my legs: "Get on the plane."  But my thoughts were still on: visiting the Buck Creek plantation site, exploring Osage City, interviewing an African American Eskridge family in Louisville, Kentucky who descended from a branch who moved out of Mississippi to Harrisburg, Arkansas.

Or..."Get on the plane"...to pursue the lead regarding the 1770 Tithable list of Pittsylvania County, Virginia listing Burdett Eskridge and relatives of his wife Nancy, indicating that Burdett Eskridge and his family had stopped and camped there while on their migration to Edgefield, South Carolina.  My letter to the Virginia Archives requesting a copy of the complete original list had already been on its way.

"Get on the plane."  I did.  Maybe I was just going through a nervous realization that I would soon be leaving home soil for the first time in my life.  Really, though, I was actually *heading* home.  I swallowed a malaria pill and fastened my seat belt.

Flight 540 landed at Port Bouet International Airport in

Abidjan, the capital of Cote d' Ivoire, after a brief stopover in Dakar, Senegal.  It was while flying into Dakar that my eyes finally witnessed seeing the West African coastline in all of its beautiful color that warm afternoon.  Here was where the ship *Providence* had combed its waters almost 300 years ago.

Our Air France jetliner landed at 4:30 pm, two hours late due to a two-hour delay at JFK International Airport because moments before takeoff, someone's passport didn't match the name on their luggage.  The whole luggage cargo had to be rechecked for security.

From Abidjan I had planned to transfer flights and head to Monrovia, Liberia, but due to security reasons those plans changed, as the Liberian Government had declared a state of emergency on August 11 as Liberian soldiers battled Sierra Leone rebel insurgents near the Guinea border when U.N. aid workers were attacked and six workers were abducted.  Just one week before on August 4 the rebel soldiers kidnapped over two dozen hostages made up of U.N. military observers, aid workers, regional intervention force members and journalists outside the city of Freetown.  These attacks came as a shock to several countries within the region, as it seemed that peace was slowly coming back to Liberia and Sierra Leone due to a Sierra Leone peace accord signed July 7 in Togo and a ceremony attended by regional leaders held in Monrovia July 26, celebrating an end to civil war since 1989 in Liberia and Sierra Leone since 1991, which resulted in more than 180,000 people killed and more than two million homeless refugees.

So on this trip, my chances of meeting the ethnic Kru in Liberia had slipped away, unless I wanted to risk my life.  Better to wait and go there another year when things were more stable, and Y2K had come and gone as well.  Besides, airline tickets were doubling for bookings between mid-December and January 1.  The borrowed money I received for the flight dictated that I cancel my intentions of leaving December 24, my travel agent instead booking me for a discount special in November.

The funds brought along on this trip would last only one week.  That was my window of opportunity.  But would that give me enough time to locate anyone of the Kru tribe in Cote d' Ivoire?

But before I started worrying about that, I only wanted now to just enjoy the realization that I was now finally here in Africa. I wanted my wife to enjoy this moment with me so I invited her to accompany me.  Our arrival coincided with the country's local cocoa and coffee harvests, a leader in world production.  The 85 degree heat hit us as we came off the plane.  Here in the capital could be seen the rural countrymen who, having left their respective villages, had come to Abidjan looking for jobs, and dreams.

There were over sixty different ethnic groups living in Cote d' Ivoire, all of them being divided into four major groups: Akan, Mande, Voltaic, Kru.  The official language was French. Many spoke English.  With the collapse of the kingdom Mali in the 16th century, waves of migrants headed southward, founding new kingdoms in the forest belt. The famous kingdom Kong, built in the 12th century, became the capital of trade with the arrival of Mande merchants in the late 17th century, the empire stretching north to the Niger River and southeast to the Akan-speaking farmers in the hills.  During the slave trade, the Portuguese were the first Europeans to arrive, the French were the last.  Around 1730 a French settlement was established at the 1472 Portuguese slave site called Sao Andrea, today called Sassandra, along the Atlantic Ocean.

Inside the arrival section of Port Bouet International Airport were dozens of African faces standing behind a string and awaiting to greet their individual parties.  Little did we know that scam artists were among the crowds as well.  We began looking for our contact person among the sea of faces, although not knowing who he looked like, nor did he of us, except that we would be wearing lapel badges with our names written, according to the sign of identification agreed upon by telephone.  But no one stepped forward.  Feeling a tinge of nervousness, we made our way to have our bags checked then walked back to see if our host had now arrived.  Still no one stepped forward.

We concluded that perhaps he was waiting outside in front of the building and so exited out the airport doors whereupon an airport security guard dressed in army fatigues standing at the checkpoint asked for passports. "Do you speak French?" the guard asked while holding our passports in hand. "No," I respectfully answered, in anticipation of our passports being routinely handed back. The guard, appearing taken aback from my answer, turned aside and took council with his partner in French, then said to me, "You come with me," then to my wife, "You can stay here."

Sensing that perhaps we were being purposely separated, my wife to her credit had the good sense of insisting on staying beside me, whereupon we were led and shown our simple mistake of not having our passports endorsed with the country's official visa stamp. That was not a problem, but I also was fully aware of the scams I had read and heard about that were run down on unsuspecting Americans in paying so-called "additional fees" due to insufficient identification papers. The fact that we were separated from ours didn't go over too good either. Honestly, I was a nervous wreck on the inside, and desperately trying to hold it together on the outside in front of this guard and my wife. I could feel sweat trickling down my back, for this guard was indeed "sweating" me. I didn't want the guard to sense my fear. To make things worse, two con men came up to us, one asking what was the problem and the other flashing a business card stating he was a lawyer and could help litigate this whole mess-up.

Although we weren't charged a fee after our passports received the customary stamp, the security guard still held onto them, causing me to request making a phone call to my host, who still had not shown up. Of course, our plane had been delayed two hours in New York, causing our arrival to be late. Yet, something was in the air. Something was making this policeman tense. We were taken to a lady who ran a booth at the airport charging use of her cell phones, charging us $5 of which I feared would have to be paid with the divulgence of a fifty dollar French traveller cheque. It just so happened I had four American $1 dollar bills which I handed him and finally after making the call, got our passports back.

Learning that our host had already left to meet us, we now left the airport building to face round two--waiting outside with the con artists on the sidewalks.  I kept my right hand on my wallet in my front pants pocket and our two carry-on shoulder bags and camcorder near my feet, while a crowd of four men surrounded us to give "greetings" under the watchful eye of the same security police guard.  As we crossed the street to stand with other passengers waiting, the four men continued to stick to us like glue, even offering us a taxi ride.  But just before we crossed the street the lady who ran the cell phone booth came outside and began talking sharply to the policeman who had dealt with us, as he sheepishly pulled out from his pocket the four dollars and handed them over to her.  The lady had the last laugh.

Approaching now two hours, I truly began wondering if our escort would be here before sunset.  What if it became dark?  What if he was in an accident or some other delay?  The pressure was getting so great on us, a culture shock to say the least.  Finally just as I was about ready to jump in a cab and take our chances, an African came up to me and said, "Stephen, hello!  It's good to meet you!  Follow me!" as we headed back into the crowd of the airport.  But before we could even keep up with him with our bags, he had vanished into the crowd.  "This is just another scam to get us back in here!  He probably read my name off my lapel badge...let's get out!" I suddenly said to my wife as we rushed back outside.  Moments later, the African returned with his wife.  It was our HOST!

Our host, of the Baoule tribe, an Akan-speaking people that separated from the Ashanti in Ghana generations ago, had finally arrived at the airport with his wife by taxi.  We loaded up our bags and headed northeast to our hotel, past the hot, humid urban districts of Marcony, Treichville, Le Plateau, and Cocody, towards the tropical suburb called Deux Plateau.  The hotel was situated one building over from the Angola embassy.  By the end of the day I was ready for a good night's sleep, my body working overtime from a yellow fever shot, and also from having been in an airplane all this time since leaving New York.  Since the room was well air-conditioned, we ended up not needing to use the mosquito net we had brought along after all.

The next day we toured the area around our hotel--a woman

in dress working in her garden with her children;  A child skipping
to his home being covered with dust as a result from playing in it;
Two old men sitting at their fruit stand, conversing about the news
of the day while watching the carpenters ontop of the hotel
balcony.  Here I saw the rich and the poor existing side-by-side:
the impressive landscaped villas with hired security guards sitting
at the reception gates, next door to the patched up homes of cement
and wood, with food stands in front selling eggs, butchered meat,
or chickens.  About five blocks from the hotel was a kingdom hall
missionary home.  By afternoon our clothes were soaked with
sweat as we retreated for an afternoon siesta.  A thunder &
lightning rainstorm soon followed as we got inside our room.

The main thoroughfares were jammed with bustling traffic,
as each and everyone headed to their next destination--young
couples to the clubs, schoolchildren heading home, the buyers to
the cash malls & supermarkets.  The neighborhood backroads
revealed the bush taxis honking for service on every other corner,
occasionally driving dangerously close to us foot pedestrians at
night, as chickens and goats unwaringly ventured out into the street
path.  At the same time the skink lizards made their way over the
curbs and onto the grassy lawn.

Later I took a moment to ask the missionary home tour
guide, a woman of Chinese descent who lived in Africa for many
years, if she knew anything about the Akee fruit tree.  "Akee?" she
said curiously as she turned to ask the young female African cook,
who was preparing a noon dish in the dining hall for the residency
guests and workers.  "How do you spell it?" the tour guide asked as
she made her way over to the convenient bookcase library located
to the side of the dining hall, holding a French encyclopedia set.
The tour guide thought hard for about a minute, then asked, "Does
it have something to do with Jamaica?"  Immediately I responded
back, "Why, yes! It's a popular dish in Jamaica!"   The African
cook now began to speak in French, which my guide kindly
translated for me.  "She says the Akee fruit grows in the interior,
up towards the north." The guide continued:  "The Akee tree
originated in West Africa...the first plants reached Jamaica when
they were purchased from the captain of a slave ship in the 18th

century."

This agreed with the research I had found in the States, pinpointing 1778 as the year when that slave ship captain sold some akee slips to Botanist Dr. Thos. Clarke of Jamaica. I then grabbed the French encyclopedia for the letter "K" and showed the guide the entry describing the Kru, explaining to her that the word akee came from their ancient language according to several books including Webster's International Dictionary, the word origin first appearing in its 1936 edition.

The fact that I now had confirmation from two of the locals that the Akee did indeed grow here in the country told me that my trip was starting out amazingly well.

Little did I realize how better it would get when during the fourth day of our stay we were discussing something with the woman cook. It was a quiet and warm Sunday morning as we sauntered outside her residence while waiting for a taxi. The topic was about what I had learned two days earlier while conversing with two locals, one whom wore profound tribal knife markings on his cheek and forehead, that the "Bete" and "Dida" peoples along the coastal lagoons in the southwest region of Ivory Coast were descendants of the Kru. I asked the cook if she could tell us anything more about them. She smiled, then answered in her soft-spoken English, "*I am Bete.*" At that moment, hearing those words in person and seeing the person who spoke them slowly marked the awakening of a ten-year dream to one day meet an ancestral member of my family's progenitor.

But my surprises were not to end just yet. One evening at the missionary home we met another Kru, a young man formerly from Liberia who worked right at the hotel we were staying. The man was deep brown, robust, with a prognathous face and broad nose. Immediately his appearance reminded me of both a close friend in Sweetwater, Texas and the shipworker Jack Abul who I had met onboard the *Spetsai* in 1976. We exchanged business cards.

I explained to both the Kruwoman cook and the hotel Kruman about my African ancestor and that she was the reason why I was so drawn to the origin of the fruit tree. The Kruman asked me to spell the fruit in English so he could write it down. I don't know if he just didn't hear me say "a-k-e-e" or if he was just trying to sound the word out, but he spelled it " AKEY." A Kru girl belongs to the mother's family but takes her father's family name, while a boy belongs to the father's family but takes his mother's family name (the family name for both coming first, then their given name). If this custom held true in the village of my great-great-great-great-great-grandmother at the time she was born, that meant she took her father's family name. However, I was still unsure whether I had her first name, her family name, or perhaps only her nickname.

When the Kru migrated into Liberia from the interior they organized themselves into dako communities as the Jloh, Kabor, Gbeta, Sasstown, Grand Cess, and Five Tribes, which composed of five towns: Settra Kru, King William's Town, Krubah, Little Kru, and Nana Kru, said to be a corruption of "London Kru." My ancestor Akey belonged to one of those original family communities. As the Kru migrated across the "Cavally River" and into the Ivory Coast they divided into further panton societies as the Bete, Dida, and other smaller groups. The Kruman mentioned there were several Kru villages in Cote d' Ivoire, all in the coastal towns west of Sassandra called San Pedro, Grand Berebe, and Tabou, 27 kilometers from the "Cavally River" as the local Ivoirians called it, and from the unstable Liberian border. These villages were about 260 kilometers from Abidjan, a day's trip one way if the buses and bush taxis were running on time and the roads were dry. Surprisingly we heard that five buses had been burned due to several political demonstrations the week before our arrival.

Another time at the mission home, we were introduced to a Krumother and her beautiful daughters. All of us were beaming, happy that thousands of miles of ocean water couldn't prevent us from meeting. That joyful moment reminded me of several others we had, such as later that Sunday when we and the cook were waiting for the taxi. We were on our way to meet a group of her friends. Walking with her on the road past mango trees above our heads, the Kruwoman cook motioned a taxi over and we all hopped in and headed to another part of town for a fare of CFA F125.

Soon we arrived at our rendezvous point and were greeted by the group who had come to assemble, a mixture of ethnicity made up of a few native-born Ghanains, Nigerians, Cameroons, and Ivoirians.   One woman approached me and extended her handshake.  The cook leaned over to me. "She Bete."

At the same time, a young man came up to me with a grin and extended his hand, too, saying, "I Bete! I Bete!"  Everyone broke out laughing as they explained he loved to always joke around  and  was just teasing me from having heard about my great interest.  Also among the group was a young high school girl soon to graduate, with whom we spent quite a bit of time getting acquainted.  As a graduation present, her parents were going to fly her to visit the United States the following summer.  Having heard about our plight at the airport, the young teen told us, "I know a friend of the family that works at the airport;  I will tell that person when you are leaving so you can get assistance to your plane."

Another day we ran into the Krumother again, this time at the supermarket across from the hotel.  She recognized me right off.  But then, who couldn't recognize this light-skinned American Congo standing out in the crowd?   Entering the market I was surprised to hear the music of Earth, Wind, & Fire playing in the background, a song called "Fantasy."

Here was where the pulse of a town could be read--at the market--where all colors & classes of society are forced to come together and face each other no matter what their belief and prejudices are, as they stand in the checkout line.   Being a foreigner I thought I was immune, just stand back in the aisles and quietly observe the pulse of the town thru the faces and interactions of the bargaining Ivoirians.  I thought, that is, until I got in line.  Attempting to save our last French franc travelers cheque and conserve our last remaining CFA's, I flashed an *American* Visa traveler cheque in hopes of procuring some extra local currency.   "We no take Visa, we take this! [CFA]," the exasperated African clerk said with a smirk on her face while another clerk shook her head.  This Congo got a strong pulse reading.

The mother's smile met us as we came out of the market.  I

saw her face for the last time as she departed one way and we went the other, returning to our kitchen-furnished room to enjoy a meal of hot chili, corn, baguettes, apricots, pound cake, and bottled water.

Sadly, the end of our week had now arrived. On the last full day of our stay, we were entertained to a soul-filling dish of seasoned beef and noodles prepared by the Kruwoman cook before a number of friends, including one who "stopped in" to eat while on his way back home to Krutown, Monrovia in Liberia, sharing his stories of life there as well as when he lived in Freetown, Sierra Leone during the war. He also did not fail to inform me that the Akee grew all over in Krutown, too. I met also at the meal a native of Ghana, who announced to us his engagement to his future "nyeno," a Krugirl. The wedding would take place in ten weeks. "You can come back again and come to my wedding," he said invitingly. If there was any way possible, I would have just stayed right here for the next ten weeks. Everyone we had met the last six days had been so loving and hospitable, truly making me feel "at home" and part of an extended family. But now it was time to take a voyage and go back across the great ocean.

Just as we departed from our meal and stepped out into the street back to the hotel to begin packing, a man came up to us, a Kruman from Tabou Village who was staying in Abidjan temporarily to work on a construction project. He had heard about the purpose of my trip, too. Through my host, who translated in French, I explained to the Kruman from Tabou that my ancestor was taken from this West Coast and ended up a slave in Virginia on the plantation of U.S. President George Washington's mother's guardian. What a delight it was when I shared with him some words in Kru that I had learned over the last year, such as "Bi" for father, "Di" for mother, and "Mu" for hurry, and how surprised he was to hear a Black American speaking words in his language. And I'll never forget that moment when it was time to say goodbye, and we shared the most important word for last: "Dieju," Brother.

On Wednesday we were awakened by the song of a bird at 5:00 a.m., the same songbird we had been hearing at that same time every morning. Jumping out of bed, I walked outside while still dark to catch one last look at the African night sky and its glowing stars, curiously wondering what those stars that I would soon be gazing at again back home looked like from this side of the world. Beautiful is the only word to describe it.

Later that morning I said goodbye to the hotel Kruman and told him we would keep in touch. Fortunately we had already exchanged addresses the first day we met, as we now were in quite a "Mu" to meet our escort who would take us to the airport three hours before departure. I didn't want to take a chance of being "bumped off" due to any overbookings or late arrivals. I had already eyewitnessed what can happen in that case when we first stopped in Senegal and watched through our airplane window a man, dressed in full traditional garb, refused entry onto the plane for having arrived five minutes after the plane door closed. And I certainly didn't want to go through what we experienced when we first arrived. This time an escort would be with us right up to the ticket gate. To our shock, when we got there, the guards wouldn't let our escort enter the terminal because of strict rules of not allowing anyone to proceed without a flight ticket. All he could do now was watch us through the large clear glass windows from the front entrance sidewalk. Soon it was our turn in line to approach the two burly security guards in their army uniforms to declare any currency and yes, present our passports.

"Do you speak French?" the guard asked me, just as the policeman had done before.

This time, though, I said, "A little."

"Go through," he told us.

After picking up our bags off the security scanner conveyer belt, we entered the departure seating lobby. Five minutes after being seated the P.A. system could be heard announcing in accented English, "Mr. and Mrs. Hank, please come to the reception desk." For one horrible moment, I had the terrible feeling that somehow we were about to miss our Air Afrique plane while dealing with whatever awaited up now. The female receptionist led us to the bar inside the first class seating lobby, turned, and asked us, "What would you like to drink?" To our relief, the receptionist was actually carrying out orders from her boss to ensure we boarded our scheduled flight. Our young high school friend had indeed kept her word! By 11:30 a.m. our plane was heading for takeoff down the runway and soon we were in the air. I took one last look down at the former slave port Abidjan and the majestic West African Coast, the "Windward Coast."

Before the plane flew over the Liberian border, I peered down from our window to see the lush rainforests and Kru huts between San Pedro and Tabou. "Bonjour, here is your Kru cousin from America, a descendant of daughter Dju Akey; *"Nenyo kani, namu nedye nyene bi, I gave gold, now I bring my father's name;* `A bientot, au revoir." Word will reach the Kru villages in due time. The new brothers and sisters we met will see to that.

Next I saw "Niwa Duyu", the Cavella River as it curved and weaved its way up to the distant Nimba mountains. Along the river were the two main border crossings into Liberia, Tabou and Danane. From either town the city of Monrovia can be reached in three days time. The main road leading to Monrovia goes thru a village town near the River Cavella. The name of this town is called Zwedru.

# CHAPTER SIXTEEN
## Reaching Out

One can learn much about dreams while flying for hours in the air. There are two sets of them, one a series of mental images, thoughts, and emotions occurring in certain stages of sleep. Another is a hope or aspiration. Clouds. Wings. Altitude. Sky. Soaring. Rainbow. Covenant. Dedication. Propellers. Sun. Faces. Some people have the wildest dreams, some rich ones, some broken ones. People can reach high out of a dream plane. Planes can reach high as people dream. But a person can reach their dream on the highest plain. The faces I saw were those seen in Africa, yet they reminded me of people I knew in the United States. The noted physiognomy of Africa that varied from one tribal face to the other, seemed to mirror and resemble those of my hometown friends or relatives. I saw my mother. My aunt Gladys and my cousin McCoys seemed to resemble Congolese. I could have sworn I saw one of my friends as an Igbo, another an Ethiopian, and several others in my community whose cheeks, noses, and headshapes gave me a hint as to their ancestry, and of faces on my travels, and not just black faces either.

Some say dreams die and end upon completion. Those who perceive that others have reached their dreams often ask: 'Who did it?' 'What did they do?' 'When did they do it?' 'Why did they do it?' 'How did they do it?' We often overlook that the word "did" is past tense. Which word carries more weight: "Did" or "Doing?" It doesn't matter what we *did* in our lives. What matters is what we're *doing.* I did go on one of the greatest trips of my life. But now, I'm living every minute of life while I have it. I'm living, loving, and reaching out each day. An old African proverb goes like this: "I Will Do It Later On" is a brother to "I Didn't Do It."

We arrived back in the states at JFK International Airport

on November 10, 1999.  The following evening we flew into Portland, where my parents welcomed us at the airport.  After my father drove our exhausted bodies to our humble home, I grabbed the mail stuffed inside the mail box for the past week and set it aside along with the camera film rolls and camcorder a friend let us borrow.   I then finished my cup of fresh ground French vanilla coffee, fell onto the bed, and closed my eyes.

In time I would be sending letters and making telephone calls to several cousins, including Cousins Patty Sue, Ernest Jr., Murt III, and Cousin Billie, saying to her over the telephone, "You a Kru!  You from the Kru tribe!"  Over the course of the next several days I slowly began to catch up on the unfinished business at hand, as well as old news.  As I read last week's  newspaper, I noticed a report coming out of Abidjan:   "IVORY COAST POLICE FIRE ON PROTESTERS."   Apparently an anti-government rally  turned violent on October 27--one week before our arrival--resulting in riot police using tear gas and rubber bullets to disperse thousands of supporters for an opposition leader in next year's presidential elections.   Five buses were also set on fire.  Maybe that explained why the military policeman at Port Bouet Airport who checked our passports was so tense.

On December 24, 1999 a military coup overthrew the Ivory Coast Government.   Had not my travel agent mentioned that special offer in November, we would have arrived December 25 right in the wake of the takeover (Every once and awhile I pull out my then department manager's approval letter for time-off during "12/24/99  thru  1/10/00"  just  to  remind  myself  how  life circumstances could change at any time).

We would later in May 2000 receive a letter from the cook Kruwoman ensuring us that she and her family & friends were all fine, but that the threat of a war uprising might break out.  True enough, during October 23-27, 2000, bloody political and ethnic clashes erupted in Abidjan and other parts of the country following the  country's  presidential  election,  as  tens  of  thousands  of protesters,  including  military  troops,  ousted  the  self-declared winner, the December coup's leader.  This resulted in a state of emergency and sadly 200 deaths.  We later received a letter from the bridegroom Ghanian in February 2001 who, now married to his Kru "nyeno," delivered another reassurance that "everything is OK."

However, that assurance was short-lived. Another coup attempt in September 2002 split the country into civil war between rebel Muslims in the north and the Christian-minority government of President Laurent Gbagbo. A cease-fire peace deal brokered by other West African leaders and France was signed in January 2003. It didn't last long. In November 2004, about the same time the couple who had hosted us in Abidjan were planning to fly out of Ivory Coast to visit us in Portland, the government violated the cease-fire by launching an offensive against the rebels. The offensive went array when the Ivory Coast's airforce accidently bombed a French military post, killing nine French peacekeepers and one U.S. aid worker, triggering violent anti-French demonstrations and deploying 4,000 French troops to airlift over 5000 Westerners out of the country. Needless to say, our friends were denied a visa to come to the States that year.

While going through my mail that week after returning home from our trip in 1999, I noticed an envelope from the Library of Virginia. The complete 1770 tithable name list of Pittsylvania County, Virginia had arrived. Now I could see the names of the slaves that travelled with Burdett Eskridge and his wife's relatives on their way enroute to South Carolina, and also to chronicle that event along with an estate inventory dated 1764 that I had discovered three months earlier.

This estate inventory was of "Captain Richard Jackson, Gentleman," who had purchased a tract of land called "Gerrard's Neck" and slaves in June 1738 from Dr. Robert Eskridge, the son of Colonel George Eskridge. According to his father's will and inventory, Robert Eskridge inherited fifteen slaves, which included the Akan African Quamino, the Kru Botswain, as well as Taffy, Jenny, Mingo, Tom, Willy & her child Will, Peg, Dina, Dick, and four others. This tract was adjacent to his father's estate, which came to be inherited by Colonel Eskridge's son Samuel Eskridge, with his all familiar by now slave inheritance, spread out between the Sandy Point plantation and his Fairfax County plantation, which included the slaves Frank, Will, Tom, Hannah, Betty, George, Prero, Akey, her daughter Jenny, and thirteen others.

But Robert Eskridge sold his share of land and slaves to Captain Richard Jackson. All this time since learning about this transaction, I had constantly wondered if the estate inventory of Richard Jackson would show if any of the slaves that Robert Eskridge sold him might still be on the estate. The inventory was dated March 27, 1764 and Willoughby Newton, the son-in-law of Colonel George Eskridge through his daughter Sarah, appeared before the court to return the appraisment. Twenty-two slaves were named, seven of them having the same identical names as those formerly owned by Robert Eskridge. *Botswain's name was among them.* Although I didn't pursue any further research, I couldn't help but wonder if the descendents of Botswain and the others later took the surname Jackson or Eskridge?

Now I turned my attention to the four page 1770 Pittsylvania County tithables, listing forty-nine slaves, many with African names. Mimi, Nipper, Munding, Primer, Sukey, Dinir, Junare, Dop, Jiberley, Waping.

One slave with a familiar name was recorded on the tithable list among Burdett and his wife's relatives on this wagon train: Frank. Burdett Eskridge was listed with three slaves over sixteen years of age. Two of their names were George and Bet, short for Betty, the couple he had inherited in 1752. Who knows how many more were present who were under sixteen. The third slave tithed was named Jenny. Why wasn't her husband Will listed on the 1770 tithable list? Because he was under sixteen years of age in 1770, as was shown to be the case according to his age recorded in 1782 showing he had been born about 1757. So actually, Will was George and Betty's son, and surely after he mated with Akey's daughter Jenny and had sons, or sons with another mate after she was sold, he would have named the sons after himself and his father George, becoming the forebearers to the other family branches in Duck Hill.

One evening that same week of trying to brush off jet-lag, brothers Laurence and Michael stopped by for a moment after finishing work with one of our cousins. Michael had come to pick up some tools to work on his car. I was glad to see them. Very rarely did a moment ever catch the three of us getting together apart from a special occasion, and even more rare that both of them would be coming to see me--getting out of the car, walking to the front door in pouring rain, and climbing up a flight of apartment stairs. Our lives were just too busy these last ten years. Plenty of times at least two of us could find occasion to do something together, but never the three of us. But now here we all were. It must have been a special occasion.  "How was the trip? Let's see the pictures," queried Michael. I pointed to the stack of photos lying on the table. "Did you videotape?" asked Laurence. "As soon as I edit it, I'll bring it by Mom and Dad's this Sunday," I replied. Later we had a humorous time as I shared with them my *nervous* moments of the trip.

On Sunday, just before going over to see the family, I had a strong desire to stop at the park up the corner from my parent's place, Houghton Park, where as kids we went to pick blackberries. I stood under the old big tree with the huge trunk, the same tree that was then a challenge for me to climb. For some strange reason, I thought about Cousin Mrytle's childhood story about Armstead Crockett's apple tree, wondering if it was even still standing. If Cousin Mrytle and Grandpa Hugh were here today, they would know.

There I stood, thinking back through all my memories of the neighborhood the past forty years, the good, the bad, and the friends and families that had come and gone, and those still there. Friends and families. Thinking back on my decennial decathlon journey, there were many families who came onboard my ship, some who now are gone. Friends, too. Even unlikely ones. But in my book, all of us, regardless of our race or place, nation or station, are related, distant cousins. I believe we all came from Shem, Ham, and Japheth, the three sons of Noah, builder of the ark.

*Akee Tree* has tremendous meaning not just to me, but to millions of persons in this country. On a personal note, the book is a partially recorded history of my family, a document that can be shared and consulted at future reunions so not to forget our story but remember the forces our ancestors were under.  It was an exhilirating and enriching experience for me, as I came away with a greater appreciation of who I am, and insights into some of my peculiar traits and characteristics.

But for millions of others, *Akee Tree* symbolizes all of their family struggles, too.  Each of our families may have trodden down different paths, yet we share common events, undergoings, and hold the same universal desires, namely love, life, happiness, freedom, and peace.  To the latter desire, *Akee Tree* extends to millions of blacks, whites, and Native Americans the encouragement to break the silence on the topic of slavery which still bounds us together from America's ugly past, offer hope to other groups of racial, cultural, and social conflicts, and bring swift reconciliation to the praise of our Creator.

A new week was making its debut on a Monday in July. The weatherman was predicting ninety degree temperatures in Portland for the next seven days.  My hope was to escape at least one hot frying-pan day with my planned drive-up route to Seattle. But I wasn't going to bet on it.  I was heading to the National Archives again, this time with a request to try and determine the birthplace of a person's grandfather.  This grandfather, an ex-slave, after enlisting with the Buffalo Soldiers was discharged at Fort Scott, Kansas and allegedly later settled in Miles City.  But his descendants never knew where he was born.

The night before, my wife and I spent part of our afternoon visiting her parents, and in so doing, we came across several old family letters dated between 1876-1895, some addressed to her grandmother who was born in Ontario, Canada, a child belonging to a family named Mott.  I stayed up past midnight reading them, especially when I realized that Ontario was the final leg of the Underground Railroad for millions seeking freedom, conducted or funded by such courages agents as Sojourner Truth, Josiah Henson, and Lucretia Mott, among hundreds of others.

On this July Monday morning I was again awaiting my mail, this time for a death certificate from Cache, Illinois near Cairo, recording a family friend's grandmother.  Our friend had never known her father's side of the family because he had never discussed them up to the day he died, taking his names and places to the memorial tomb.  I told the friend I would do what I could.  Finally the mail arrived.  A letter from the Illinois Vital Records had come this day, but stating the death certificate could not be found.  Oh well, back to the drawing board.  At least I had grown accustomed to such disappointment and setback.  But I also knew the exhilaration that one can bask when a thousand rejections are mere stepping stones to the desired prize.  I had been reminded of that when I located new cousins of mine in Oakland and Denver, one being my great-aunt Sue Hanks Orendorf's granddaughter, whose own mother's life was cut short by her husband.

Slowly beginning to awaken and becoming more alert, I decided to call Rue Eskridge that morning, since it had been a year since we last spoke.  It was good to hear his voice once again and more importantly that everyone in his family were well.  The temperature was hot there in Rockwood, too.  But senior Rue assured me he was staying in the shade.

C Swanson surprisingly called me one evening to give me her new address and also to get mine.  C wanted to send me a newspaper article she read about an old secret slave language called "Tut", an amalgam of native African tongues and English spoken by slaves, and being documented at Ole' Miss. University.  C still expressed interest in my personal quest, wanting very much to hear what my research had turned up.  I sent her a summary of my findings.

Unfortunately, Madie Jones, a cousin who C introduced me to by pure accident, had been lain to rest in July 1997, three months before Cousin Mrytle.  Soon I began corresponding with Madie's great-nephew.  It was also with sadness when I got word one day in March 2001 that Jack Grantham had died.  He is truly missed by me, a generous man and resourceful scholar, one who reached out, and whose friendly acquaintance I had the privilege.  I only hope that others, descendants of past slaves and of  past slaveowners, will reach out to each other, exchanging their family stories, research, folklore, and each other's time.

One day I had another experience along those lines.

During the course of my search, I had posted an internet message at a genealogy website asking anyone having information about the slaves owned by families descended from Colonel George Eskridge. I received two responses. One of them was sent to my personal e-mail address. The letter was very open and frank. It was concerning an orphan slave in Duck Hill named Red. The portion which now follows is paraphrased and by her permission: "He stayed with my great-grandmother's family who had two teenage sons by the close of the civil war...I've had questions about Red's wonderful loyalty...was there another connection?...Red's parents were born in Mississippi it was said...the question I have is how was it known where his parents were born if he were a foundling?...how could a foundling show up on the property...and no other negro family miss a child!...every person in the community knew the business of every other person, including the parentage of the Negroes...Is there more to the story?...I realize I am on delicate ground...if you would share any info if you know more to the story I would be more than grateful."

Honestly, I don't possess the answer, but it sure sounds like there's a story behind this.

As I brought the search for my African history and the ancestors in my father's family to a voluntary end for the time being, I still felt the weight of something that had dodged me the whole time: contacting bloodline descendants of overseer Marion Hanks. I still felt the desire to reach out to his descendants, both the black side of his family and the white side. Of course, I had already made contact with his black grandson Tommy Hanks, and his black granddaughter Madie Jones. Who also could I meet? And what further stories could I learn after meeting them? I was really eager to establish relationships with both sides of the family. I had posted internet messages for anyone out there in cyberspace who were related to the two Hanks brothers of Carroll County to please respond. But my electronic mailbox remained empty.

The African-American side were my half-cousins, we sharing the same great-great-grandmother, Eliza Eskridge. Although I had spoken to Tommy and Madie's families by telephone, we still hadn't met in-person.  The white relatives of Marion Hanks would had to have descended down from his siblings, a sister named Rossy who married a Thomas Lee before moving somewhere to Arkansas (their children were James Charles Lee, Sarah Ann Smith,and Mary Jane Withers), and from his brother Taliaferro, since Marion's only known posterity were his three mulatto children that Eliza bore him:  Tom, Betty, and Rosie.

As the years went by, I eventually caught my second wind to renew efforts in reaching relatives of Marion Hanks.  My wife and I finally drove down to Santa Clarita, California and met Tommy Hanks' son and his wife and daughters.  A former rhythm & blues musician, Jazz performer, and song writer now financial consultant, Cousin Len Hanks was totally enthralled with the family story leading from Duck Hill to his ancestor Akey.

I later called one of the editors to a new edition on the history and families of Carroll County after spotting a story on Taliaferro Hanks.  I had submitted a written sketch on my connection to the Delta region for the volume edition also, so my curiousity was running high when I saw this other writer's stories. The editor told me the writer lived somewhere in Washington State, but didn't have a telephone number for her.  I jumped on the internet and typed in the writer's last name for the state of Washington.  Seven phone numbers popped up.  The first number I dialed didn't answer.  The second one I dialed made a direct hit.  A woman's voice answered.

"May I speak to Dorothy Bellmer?"

"Who is this?"

"This is Stephen Hanks;  I read her stories in the Carroll County, Mississippi history book."

"Oh, I am Dorothy;  I thought you were a telemarketer."

Dorothy Bellmer of Gig Harbor was a distant relative of Marion Hanks.  Her maternal great-grandfather, John William Lott, born at Carrollton in 1845, was a first cousin to Francis Marion Hanks, the son of Taliaferro Hanks.  Francis Marion Hanks, who might have been named after his father's slave-overseeing brother, was born at Jefferson in 1849 to Taliaferro "Bud" Hanks and Mary "Levisy" Telford Lott, his first wife.

Taliaferro Hanks, in fact, had ended up with three wives due to sickness and death, giving him a total of eight children and five step-children.  After explaining how my great-grandfather William ended up choosing his surname after Emancipation, I then told Dorothy that to finally speak to a relative related to Marion Hanks was a moment I had been waiting for.  I could tell in Dorothy's voice that she was excited and happy I had called.  Her friendly voice quickly put me at ease, making me feel comfortable in telling her that some of my cousins were blood-related.

We warmed up to each other more as the conversation continued, while we both rattled off the familiar names of Taliaferro Hanks' children and wives.  Dorothy said that one of Taliaferro's sons, Albert Sidney Hanks, had died in 1942 in Jefferson.  His last living son, Herman Hernando Hanks, also died there in 1950.  So if anyone else from Taliaferro's direct line was still alive, Dorothy didn't know.

"At least I got the chance to talk to you," I said.

Dorothy asked if she could have my e-mail address, and then gave me hers in return.  She was surprised when she learned I lived in Portland.  Only a two-hour drive separated us.

"I drive up to Seattle all the time," I said.  "We'll have to keep in touch."

Yet, another discovery two hours away in Washington State also awaited me.  A startling discovery.

I drove up to Lakewood, Washington to meet another cousin of mine, another black great-grandchild of once Confederate soldier Marion Hanks.  Out of respect for his privacy I will give him the alias "Mr. Freeman."  A sixty-two year old commercial construction worker for over twenty years and a former Vietnam veteran, Mr. Freeman's grandmother was Maggie Jones, the sister of Madie Jones.  His great-grandmother was Rosie Hanks Jones Harper, the daughter of Eliza Eskridge and Marion Hanks.

As we sat around his kitchen table, Mr. Freeman reminiscenced about the time his mother took him on a trip from St. Louis, Missouri to Duck Hill the week of August 21, 1955 to visit his great-grandmother Rosie.  Mr. Freeman was fourteen.

Rosie, born in May 1864, was 91.

"I remember entering a store in Duck Hill through the front door," Mr. Freeman said. "The storeowner told me to turn back around and come in through the backdoor. I didn't know that's how blacks had to come in. I even sat down in the front seat of the bus, before the kids told me I wasn't supposed to do that. They had two different drinking fountains, too. I still remember all that."

Mr. Freeman was fortunate his friends were watching out for him, especially after what he told me next.

"I was in Duck Hill the same week as Emmett Till."

The name Emmett Till stirs up a painful memory and chapter in American history. While the demands for African-Americans' civil liberties put Jim Crow and the White House on notice during the middle of the twentieth century, on August 20, 1955 a black Chicago mother sent her 14 year old son, Emmett Till, off to visit his uncle for two weeks that summer in Money, Mississippi, near the city of Greenwood. One Saturday evening during his summer visit, August 28, Emmett and his teenage friends gathered outside a store. Emmett entered inside the store and came into the presence of the white storeowner's wife, who was operating the store by herself that evening. What happened next would unknowingly set off a deadly chain of events. Emmett, it was later reported, was claimed to have teasingly asked the young 24 year old storewife for a date, then squeezed her hand and waist before running out of the store. As he got outside, Emmett turned toward her again and whistled. The woman reportably picked up a gun, causing Emmett and his young friends to quickly take off.

Being raised up in the free-spirited streets of big-city Chicago, Emmett's mother had feared that her son wouldn't know how to act in the deep South, and therefore wouldn't know about the unwritten laws of Jim Crow. She had made sure to instruct her son regarding the "good manners" that were to be expected of him. But sadly, around 2 a.m. later that night, two white men drove up to the uncle's house where Emmett was sleeping and whisked the young boy away by gun-point and into their vehicle. Three days later, Emmett's decomposed body was found floating down the

Tallahatchie River.  He had been badly beaten and shot.

Two men were later arrested and put before a trial.  An all-white jury acquited the two men on the grounds that the body found could not be positively identified as being Emmett Till.  This was despite the fact that his mother had identified a ring found on the boy's finger as being the ring once worn by Emmett's deceased father, a soldier killed in action overseas during World War II.  The murder shocked the entire nation and the world.  A nagging fear now had become a grim fact among American citizens of color:  "Even children could be lynched."

Mr. Freeman remembered his visit that week to Duck Hill vividly.  I had become convinced he would never forget it.  His great-grandmother Rosie later died the following year in 1956.  I recalled taking the photograph of her tombstone inside Binford Cemetary while on my visit to Duck Hill in 1994.

"So you actually met and spoke to Rosie," I said.

"Oh yes!  She was as frail as could be," Mr. Freeman said.  "She was also as white as could be also.  Here's a picture of her."

Mr. Freeman carefully selected a photograph from his envelope of pictures resting on the table and handed it to me.  Rosie's photograph had been taken sometime during her last remaining years.  I was speechless.  This was the first time I had ever seen her face.

Then Mr. Freeman handed me another picture.  It was of a white man.  The photo looked to have been taken in the 1860's.

"This is Rosie's father," Mr. Freeman said.

"You have a picture of her father?" I asked in disbelief.

"That is what was written on the back of the photograph.  My mother in Los Angeles brought these pictures down with her when she came to visit.  I made these copies for you," Mr. Freeman said.

"Why, this is Marion Hanks!" I said while trying to stay reserved in my seat.  "He was born in Pickens County, Alabama and died in 1864 at the age of 37, about the same time Rosie was born!"  This was also the first time I had ever seen this face, the face of the man who was overseer on Richard Eskridge's plantation.  Apparently Rosie had this picture in her possession.

After Rosie died, her daughter Maggie ended up with it until her death. I was entirely amazed that this photograph had found its way into Mr. Freeman's family and remained there for at least fifty years and counting. Who knows when Rosie had obtained it? More importantly, though, was *how* did she acquire it? Did soldier Marion Hanks, who was gradually losing his hearing and turning deaf which caused his discharge from the Confederacy, present a picture of himself to Rosie's mother Eliza before his death? Did he acknowledge Tom, Betty, and Rosie as his children and their father? Or, did Taliaferro Hanks, who wasn't ever listed a slaveowner, give the photograph to Rosie when she became of age? Or perhaps yet, did one of Taliaferro's children turn the picture over to Rosie after their father Taliaferro passed away in December 1905?

Whichever way it occurred, it was obvious that someone on the "white" side knew about Rosie. Someone had a conscience, had heart.

"I didn't know he was from Alabama," Mr. Freeman said. "We thought all this time he was from Europe."

For several years I have tried to reach out to descendants of the old landowners who lived side-by-side my family. It seems now that someone long ago reached out to my family first.

Stephen Hanks  AKEE TREE
425

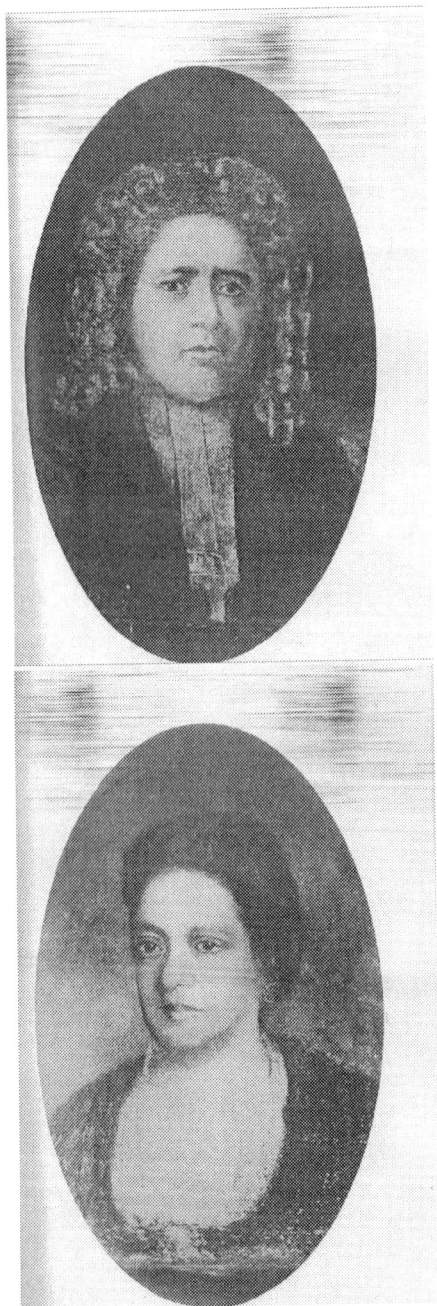

# Stephen Hanks  AKEE TREE
## 441

Stephen Hanks  AKEE TREE
443

Stephen Hanks  AKEE TREE
445

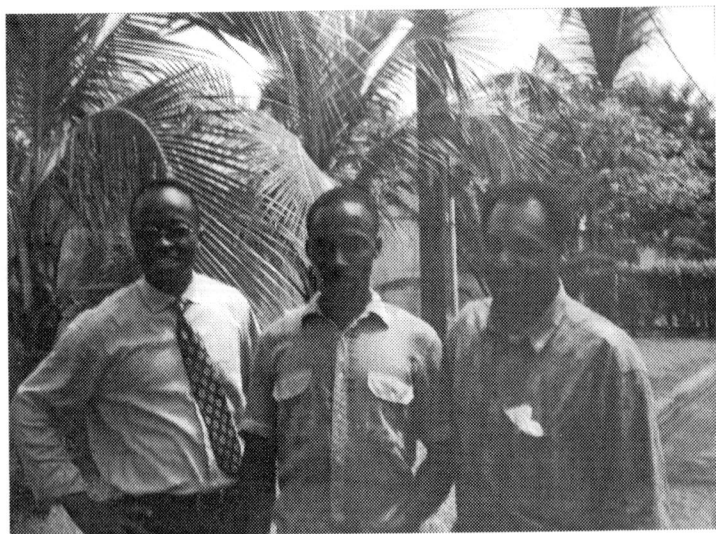

# LIST OF PHOTOS

Front cover. (top and bottom)The Akee fruit tree. (Courtesy of Sue Carolyn Bovinett)

Pg 421 Zane and Fern Hanks, the author's parents, about 1963; Zane Hanks and his aunt, Peggy Flowers, about 1979.

Pg 422 Fern Hanks and her sister-in-law Gladys McCoy, about 1957; From left to right, Michael, Stephen, and Laurence, about 2000 in the family backyard.

Pg 423 Jack Abul, on the deck of *Spetsai* in 1976 while docked in Portland.

Pg 424 James Shelton listening to his 1989 taped interview with the author and Lynn Hanks; Uncle Bill and Aunt Gladys McCoy, about 1983.

Pg 425 Billy Don Hanks, the author's uncle, about 1955; Murt Hanks Jr., the former mayor of Manhattan, Kansas.

Pg 426 Mrytle Foster, about 1940. Her father James Hanks died in the 1899 smallpox outbreak in Osage City, Kansas. Mrytle lived for a time with her grandparents William and Rosetta Hanks; Road sign on the way to Osage City. Thousands of African Americans migrated to Osage and other Kansas cities between 1879-1880.

Pg 427 Susan Orendorf in Osage City, 1930. Susan was born in Duck Hill, MS on December 22, 1871, and was the first child of William and Rosetta Hanks. (Courtesy of Velma Burrell)

Pg 428 Eliza Miller, the fifth child of William and Rosetta Hanks. (Courtesy of Helen Kanion); John Hanks, the sixth child. John left Osage City and moved to Denver, Colorado where he worked as a butler for U.S. Senator Lawrence C. Phipps. (Courtesy of Roy Hanks)

Pg 429 Murt Hanks Sr., the seventh-born. Murt's nickname was "Moon". Murt and his brother Hugh were drafted during World War I.

Pg 430 Ernest Hanks and his family, about 1924. Ernest, the eighth child, had the nickname "Teat"; Hugh and Marcella Hanks, the author's grandparents. Hugh Hanks was the tenth-born child.

Pg 431 Rosetta Crockett Hanks, who was born in slavery around August 1851 in Duck Hill, Mississippi, the daughter of Armstead and Mariah Crockett; William and Rosetta Hanks, the parents of 13 children (three were stillborn). William was born a slave c. 1847 in Roane County, Tennessee.

Pg 432 Harris and Eliza Crockett. Harris, who was the brother of Rosetta Hanks, decided to stay in Duck Hill rather than migrate to Kansas with his sister and parents. Eliza was the daughter of slaves William Burgess Eskridge and midwife Amanda. Eliza's twin sister was Nancy. Their brother William "Henry" took a trip to Africa in the 1920's. (Courtesy of Billie Rigdon)

Pg 433 Harrison Eskridge Family Reunion in Duck Hill, about 1945. (Courtesy of Ella Mae Elliot)

Pg 434 Robert and Billie Rigdon of Dallas, Texas, at the 2000 Crockett family reunion in Memphis, TN; Chauncey Eskridge Jr. was a Chicago legal attorney. Some of the clients he represented were Martin Luther King Jr., the SCLC, and Muhammed Ali. (Courtesy of Yvonne Eskridge)

Pg 435 Colonel George Eskridge of Sandy Point, Virginia in Westmoreland County. President George Washington was named after the Colonel. George Eskridge was also guardian for Mary Ball, who married Augustine Washington. (courtesy C Swanson)

Pg 436 Colonel George Eskridge was a member of the House of Burgesses that met in Williamsburg. At his death in 1735, George Eskridge owned close to 67 slaves, including the author's African ancestor. Documents show the Colonel whipped at least one slave, and petitioned the court for another slave's freedom. (permission of R.R. Bowker, publisher); Rebecca Bonum, the Colonel's first wife, the daughter of Samuel Bonum. (permission of R.R. Bowker, publisher)

Pg 437 A historic marker greets everyone as they reach Sandy Point, Virginia; Known as the "Sandy Point House" on Sandy Point Road, and replaced the original home of George Eskridge, which was destroyed by a fire. 1998 (by permission); An 18th century smokehouse, the only original structure from the Colonel's estate still standing. 1998 (by permission)

Pg 438 Rue and Catherine Eskridge, of Rockwood, Tennessee, 2000. Rue Eskridge's father, grandfather, and great-grandfather were slaves on Samuel B. Eskridge's Buck Creek plantation in Roane County, TN.

Pg 439 Samuel B. Eskridge's tombstone in Roane County. He died in 1852 and bequeathed his estate and 75 slaves, including the author's great-great-grandmother, to a great-nephew in Duck Hill; The 1860 grave-marker of Richard E. Eskridge, Samuel's brother, in the Eskridge family cemetary at Eskridge, Mississippi, just outside Duck Hill.

Pg 440 The home of Richard E. Eskridge at Duck Hill. He also owned 230 acres of land in Roane County next to his brother's property. The house was built by his slaves around 1834. There were at least thirteen slave cabins also built. At the time of his death, Richard Eskridge owned about 48 slaves. The overseer was Marion Hanks. (courtesy of C Swanson); C Swanson standing in front of the Duck Hill Bank in 1994. C Swanson, the great-great-granddaughter of Richard Eskridge, invited the author for a visit to the former plantation site.

Pg 441 C Swanson facing the spot where Richard Eskridge's house used to stand. 1994; An early picture of Madie Jones, born in 1899 and the daughter of Rosie Hanks and Labe Jones. Madie left Duck Hill and moved to live in St. Louis, before she again returned to Duck Hill in her last remaining years. C Swanson took the author to meet Madie, which became a turning point in the search. (Courtesy of Robert Rigdon)

Pg 442 Rosie (Hanks) Jones-Harper, the mother of Madie Jones and the daughter of Eliza Eskridge. Rosie's father was Marion Hanks the overseer. (1955, courtesy of Ruby Burroughs)

Pg 443 Marion Hanks, born about 1825 in Pickens County, Alabama. He and his brother Taliaferro (Tolivar) Hanks came together to Carroll County, Mississippi around 1846. He entered the Confederate Army in 1863, but was discharged three months later due to losing his hearing. He fathered three children with slave Eliza, wife of Jefferson Eskridge. (about 1860. Courtesy of Ruby Burroughs); Jefferson and Eliza Eskridge, the author's great-great-grandparents, around 1870.

Pg 444 The children of Frank Eskridge, from left to right, Jennings, Tobe, Bell, Harrison, Emma, Mack, and Nathaniel. Harrison Eskridge was the eldest at time of picture, born in September 1871. (Courtesy of Ella Mae Elliot); Frank Eskridge, born about 1838, and the son of slave couple George and Phyllis Eskridge. Frank may have been named after a slave owned by Colonel George Eskridge who was later inherited by his son Samuel

Eskridge of Westmoreland County, Virginia. (Courtesy of Carleen McBride)

Pg 445  Photos of Jack Grantham, left, and Tommy Hanks, right.  Jack Grantham, of Dallas, Texas, shared his personal collection on the Eskridge family with the author, resulting in a major turning point in a 10-year search.  Tommy Hanks of Chicago was the son of Tom Hanks and Mabel Eskridge.  His father Tom Hanks was the son of Marion Hanks;  From left to right:  Lynn Hanks, Nancy Amani, Mr. Ohinene, and Dedear Amani, in Abidjan, Ivory Coast.

Pg 446  Hotel roof's view of Deux Plateau, a suburb of Abidjan;  A worker finds a good way to cool off in the heat of Ivory Coast.

Pg 447  Friendly, smiling faces among the varying social, ethnic, and linguistic groups of people making up Ivory Coast;  The Bete-Kru cook and the author.  1999

Pg 448  The Dida woman and her daughters.  The Dida and Bete tribes are descendants of the Kru;  From left to right:  Dedear the translator, a Kruman from Tabou Village, and the author.

# SOURCES

**BOOKS/PERIODICALS**
Balmer, W.T and F.C.F. Grant. *A Grammar of the Fante-Akan Language*. London 1929
Bassett, John Spencer. *The Plantation Overseer*. New York 1925
Beveridge, Albert J. *Abraham Lincoln, 1809-1858, Vol. I*; Cambridge, MA 1928
Black, Clinton V. *The Story of Jamaica*. London 1965
Branch, Taylor. *Parting The Waters, America in the King Years 1954-63*. New York 1988
Brewington, M.V. *Chesapeake Bay Log Canoes and Bugeyes*. Cambridge, MD 1963
Brooks Jr, George E. *The Kru Mariner in the 19th Century*; Newark, DE 1972; *Landlords and Strangers, Ecology, Society, and Trade in Western Africa, 1000-1630*. Scranton, PA 1994
Coit, Margaret L. *John C. Calhoun-American Portrait*; Boston 1950
Conneau, Theophilus. *A Slaver's Log Book, or 20 Years Residence in Africa*. Englewood Cliffs, NJ 1976
Crouch, Evelyn Bell, editor. *History of Montgomery County, Mississippi*. Dallas, TX 1993
Dalgish, Gerard M. *A Dictionary of Africanisms-Contributions of Sub-Saharan Africa to the English Language*. New York 1982
Dalziel, J.M. *Useful Plants of West Tropical Africa*. London 1937
Davidson, Basil. *The African Slave Trade*. Boston 1980
Davis, Ronald W. *Ethnohistorical Studies on the Kru Coast*. Newark, DE 1976
Desmond, Ray. *Kew-The History of The Royal Botanic Gardens*. London 1995
Edwards, Bryan. *History, Civil, and Commercial, of the British West Indies, Vol. 3*. London 1819
Fraenkel, Merran. *Tribe And Class In Monrovia*. London 1964
Frost, Diane. *Work and Community among West African Migrant Workers*. Liverpool 1999
Gutman, Herbert G. *Black Family in Slavery and Freedom, 1750-1925*. New York 1976
Henderson, Archibald. *Washington's Southern Tour 1791*. Cambridge, MA 1923
Innes, Gordon. *An Introduction to Grebo*. London 1966
Jackson, Donald, and Dorothy Twottig. *The Diaries of George Washington, Vol. VI, January 1790-Dec. 1799*. Charlottesville, VA

# SOURCES

1979

Johnston, Sir Harry. *Liberia, Vol. 1, 2.* New York 1969

Madubuike, Ihechukwu. *A Handbook of African Names.* Washington 1976

Mannix, Daniel P. *Black Cargoes.* New York 1962

Minchinton, Walter, Celia King, and Peter Waite. *Virginia Slave-Trade Statistics, 1698-1775.* Richmond, VA 1984

National Geographic Magazine. *The Land of the Free in Africa,* by Harry A. McBride. October 1922.

Newman, Debra L. *Black History: A Guide to Civilian Records in the National Archives.* Washington 1984

Painter, Nell Irvin. *Exodusters.* New York 1977

Parry, J.A., Philip Sherlock and Anthony Maingot. *A Short History of the West Indies.* London 1987

Staudenraus, P.J. *The African Colonization Movement, 1816-1865.* New York 1961

Stewart, Julia. *1001 African Names.* New York 1996

Trakin, Roy. *Tom Hanks, Journey To Stardom.* New York 1995

Viola, Herman J, and Carolyn Margolis. *Seeds of Change-Five Hundred Years After Columbus.* Washington 1991

Virginia Historical Society. *William Fitzhugh and His Chesapeake World, 1676-1701.* Richmond, VA 1963

Virginia Magazine of History and Biography. *The Eskridge Family,* by Mrs. Henry L. West.Vol. VII, VIII 1900; *Genealogies of Virginia Families.* Baltimore 1981

Wells, Emma Middleton. *The History of Roane County, Tennessee 1801-1870.* Chattanooga, TN 1927

WPA--Federal Writers Project. *Mississippi--A Guide to the Magnolia State.* New York 1949, *Virginia--A Guide to the Old Dominion.* New York 1940
          Slave Narratives


PERSONAL PAPERS

Eskridge Family Records--Jack C. Grantham private collection.


FEDERAL RECORDS

National Archives  RG 29. Free Population Schedules, 1790-1920; Slave Schedules 1850-1860;  RG 105.  Freedman's Bureau Miscellanous Records.  Entry 2180,  Register of Complaints, Grenada, MS July 1866-Dec. 1868


Library of Congress. Manuscript Division, James K. Polk Papers


STATE/COUNTY/CITY RECORDS

# SOURCES

**VIRGINIA**
**Library of Virginia.**
**Westmoreland County Musuem, Eskridge Family File**
**Westmoreland County Courthouse**
**Fairfax County Courthouse**
**Richmond Public Library**

**SOUTH CAROLINA**
**Old Edgefield District Archives**
**Abbeville County Courthouse**

**NORTH CAROLINA**
**North Carolina State Archives & History**

**MISSISSIPPI**
**Mississippi Dept. of Archives & History**
**Mississippi State Vital Records**

**TENNESSEE**
**Tennessee State Archives**
**Roane County Courthouse**
**Roane County Cemetary Records**

**KANSAS**
**Kansas Historical Society**
**Kansas State Bureau of Vital Records**
**Osage County Courthouse**
**Lyndon Public Library**
**Crable Funeral Home**

**OREGON**
**Brandford Price Miller Library--Portland State University**
**Multnomah County Public Library**
**Genealogical Forum of Oregon**

**NEWSPAPERS**
> *Grenada Sentinel*
> *Manhattan Mercury*
> *New York Times*
> *The Oregonian*
> *Osage City Free Press*
> *Rockwood Times*
> *Virginia Gazette*

**REPORTS**
U. S. Congress, Senate Report and Testimony of the Select
Committee of the United States Senate to Investigate the causes of
the Removal of the Negroes from the Southern States to the
Northern States.  46th Congress; 2nd Session, Senate Report 693.
Washington, D.C 1880 Vol. 1-3

Report of Mr. Kennedy, of Maryland, from Committe on Commerce
of the House of Representatives of the United States on the African
Slave Trade.  27th Congress, 3rd Session.  Washington, D.C. 1842

U. S. Dept. of Agriculture.  Woods of Liberia, Report 2159.  1959

**REFERENCES**
Encyclopedia Americana 1953
International Maritime Dictionary 2nd Edition
              by Rene De Kerchove. New York 1961
New Encyclopedia Britiannica 1995
Webster's Third New International Dictionary 1993
Webster's 2nd Edition International Dictionary 1936

# HANKS FAMILY TREE

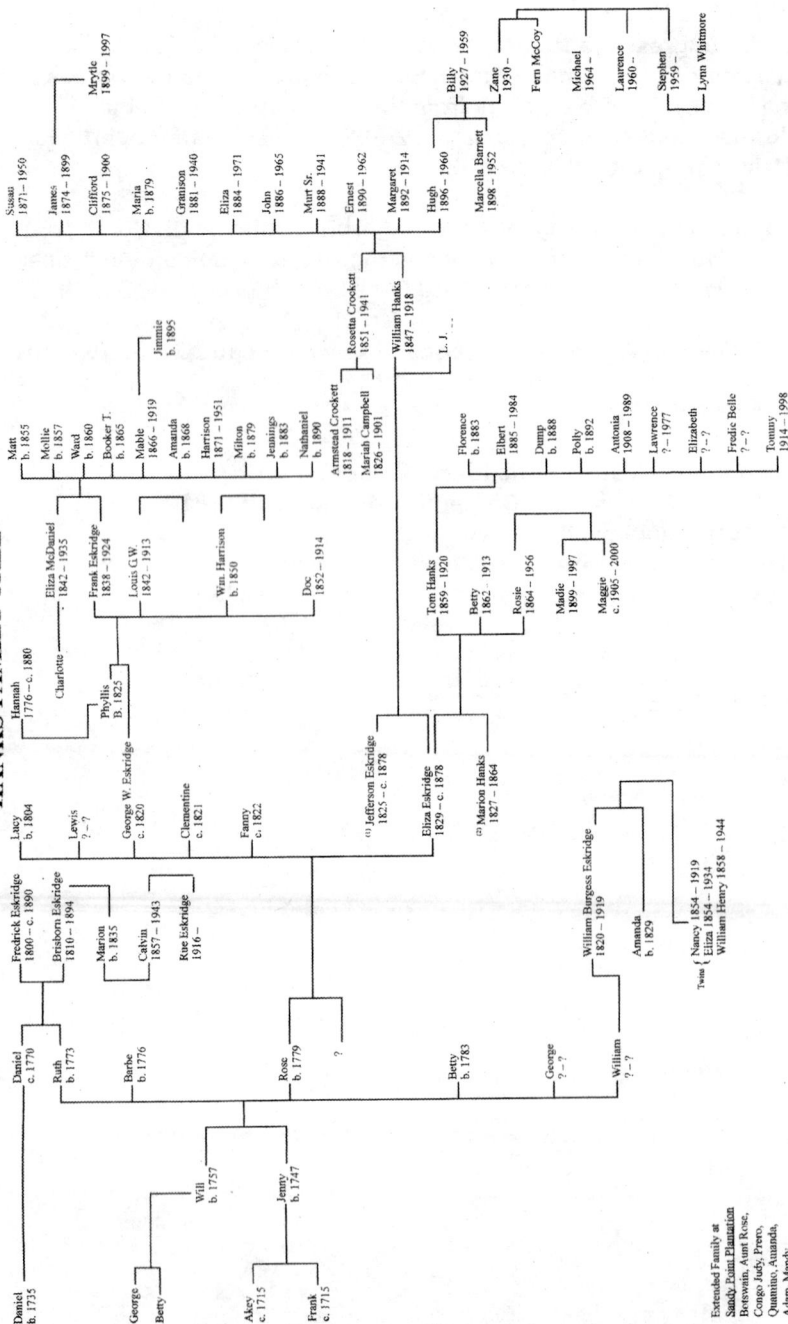

Daniel b. 1735

Daniel c. 1770

Ruth b. 1773

Fredrick Eskridge 1800 – c. 1890
Brisborn Eskridge 1810 – 1894
Marion b. 1835
Calvin 1857 – 1943
Kue Eskridge 1916 –

Barbe b. 1776
George
Betty

Will b. 1757
Jenny b. 1747
Akey c. 1715
Frank c. 1715

Rose b. 1779
?

Betty b. 1783
George ? – ?
William ? – ?

William Burgess Eskridge 1820 – 1919
Amanda b. 1829

Twins { Nancy 1854 – 1919
Eliza 1854 – 1934
William Henry 1858 – 1944

Lacy b. 1804
Lewis ? – ?
George W. Eskridge c. 1820
Clementine c. 1821
Fanny c. 1822

Hannah 1776 – c. 1880
Charlotte
Phyllis B. 1825

Eliza McDaniel 1842 – 1935
Frank Eskridge 1838 – 1924
Louis G.W. 1842 – 1913
Wm. Harrison b. 1850
Doc 1852 – 1914

Matt b. 1855
Mollie b. 1857
Ward b. 1860
Booker T. b. 1865
Mable 1866 – 1919
Amanda b. 1868
Harrison 1871 – 1951
Milton b. 1879
Jennings b. 1883
Nathaniel b. 1890
Jimmie b. 1895

Armstead Crockett 1818 – 1911
Mariah Campbell 1826 – 1901

(1) Jefferson Eskridge 1825 – c. 1878
Eliza Eskridge 1829 – c. 1878
(2) Marion Hanks 1827 – 1864

Rosetta Crockett 1851 – 1941
William Hanks 1847 – 1918
L.J. ...

Tom Hanks 1859 – 1920
Betty 1862 – 1913
Rosie 1864 – 1956
Madie 1899 – 1997
Maggie c. 1905 – 2000

Florence b. 1883
Elbert 1885 – 1984
Dump b. 1888
Polly b. 1892
Antonia 1908 – 1989
Lawrence ? – 1977
Elizabeth ? – ?
Fredic Belle ? – ?
Tommy 1914 – 1998

Susan 1871 – 1950
James 1874 – 1899
Clifford 1875 – 1900
Maria b. 1879
Granison 1881 – 1940
Eliza 1884 – 1971
John 1886 – 1965
Mart Sr. 1888 – 1941
Ernest 1890 – 1962
Margaret 1892 – 1914
Hugh 1896 – 1960

Myrtle 1899 – 1997

Marcella Barnett 1898 – 1952
Billy 1927 – 1959
Zane 1930 –
Fern McCoy
Michael 1964 –
Lawrence 1960 –
Stephen 1959 –
Lynn Whitmore

Extended Family at
Sandy Point Plantation
Botswain, Aunt Rose,
Congo Judy, Prero,
Quamino, Amanda,
Adam, Mandy

# RICHARD ESKRIDGE FAMILY TREE

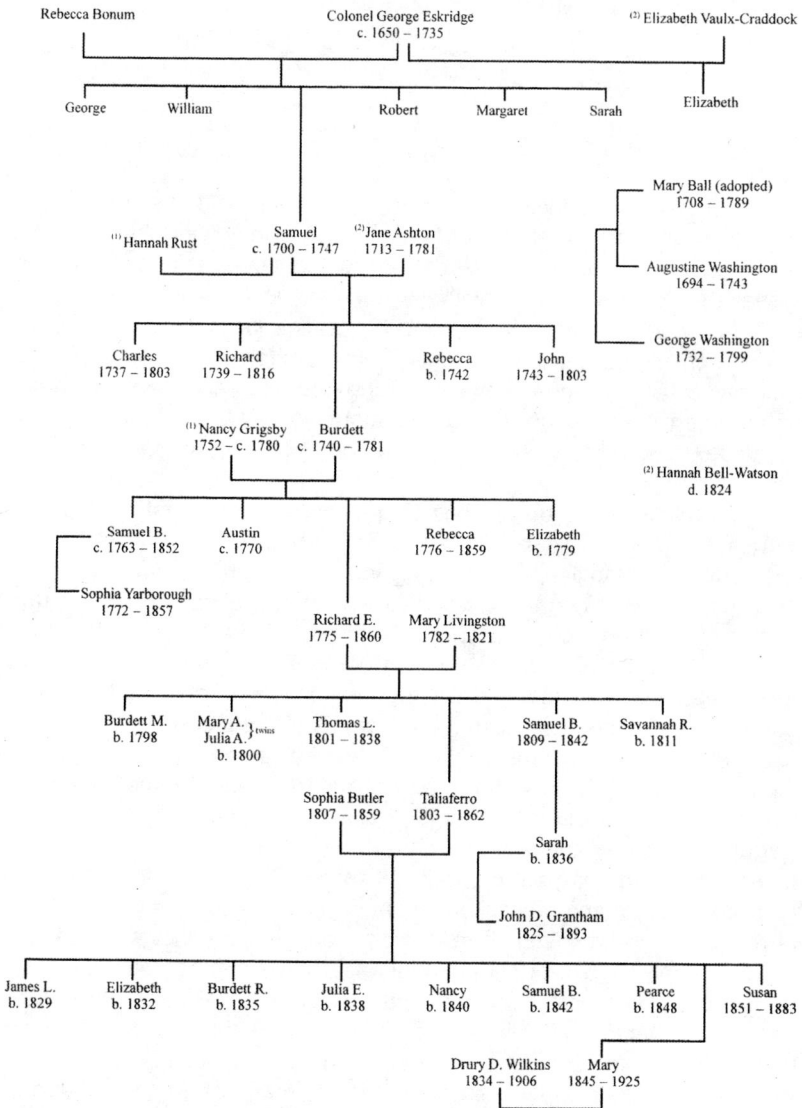

Rebecca Bonum

Colonel George Eskridge
c. 1650 – 1735

(2) Elizabeth Vaulx-Craddock

George    William    Robert    Margaret    Sarah    Elizabeth

Mary Ball (adopted)
1708 – 1789

Augustine Washington
1694 – 1743

George Washington
1732 – 1799

(1) Hannah Rust    Samuel
c. 1700 – 1747    (2) Jane Ashton
1713 – 1781

Charles
1737 – 1803    Richard
1739 – 1816    Rebecca
b. 1742    John
1743 – 1803

(1) Nancy Grigsby
1752 – c. 1780    Burdett
c. 1740 – 1781

(2) Hannah Bell-Watson
d. 1824

Samuel B.
c. 1763 – 1852    Austin
c. 1770    Rebecca
1776 – 1859    Elizabeth
b. 1779

Sophia Yarborough
1772 – 1857

Richard E.
1775 – 1860    Mary Livingston
1782 – 1821

Burdett M.
b. 1798    Mary A.
Julia A. } twins
b. 1800    Thomas L.
1801 – 1838    Samuel B.
1809 – 1842    Savannah R.
b. 1811

Sophia Butler
1807 – 1859    Taliaferro
1803 – 1862

Sarah
b. 1836

John D. Grantham
1825 – 1893

James L.
b. 1829    Elizabeth
b. 1832    Burdett R.
b. 1835    Julia E.
b. 1838    Nancy
b. 1840    Samuel B.
b. 1842    Pearce
b. 1848    Susan
1851 – 1883

Drury D. Wilkins
1834 – 1906    Mary
1845 – 1925

# AUTHOR'S NOTE

In case the reader might wonder which parts of the story are fact and which parts are purely fiction, let me answer by giving the following rule of thumb: Whatever is backed up by factual documentation, whether a legal record or by an eyewitness account, is considered as being actual fact. And whatever statement or passage lacks the same, would then be considered a product of fiction (until proven otherwise). Certain other particular passages contained in the book can also be considered factual when based upon strong circumstantial evidence that supports the context, established historical fact, or upon the weight of expert opinion.

I believe it will be obvious to the reader as to what is fact and what is fictional. This book is not only an objective and dramatic biography of my family, but is also an interpretive one. With that being said, I can say with certainty of particular scenes which sprung from my imagination and were used as conventional tools in narrative writing. For example, the courtroom scene where Booker T. Eskridge files a lawsuit against his cousin Chesterfield Eskridge is fictional drama. Both Booker Eskridge and Chesterfield Eskridge were characters I made up (although Eliza McDaniel, wife of Frank Eskridge, did bear a son named Booker T. Eskridge). The point of that scene was to focus on the fact that courtroom cases involving slaves (and slave defendants) did happen on a regular basis. Another fictional character was "Butcher" Jennings, the husband of my great-great-great-grandmother Rose. In reality, I never did discover the name of Rose's husband. But *someone* was the father of great-great-grandmother Eliza. I simply made up Jennings' character to fill that gap. (Again, Frank Eskridge also had a son named Jennings, who later married Tom Hanks' daughter Florence). I also, obviously, can't prove whether the slave ship *Providence* was the one that Colonel George Eskridge purchased slaves off of. I've already noted my evidence about that ship in the book. What I do know for sure is that my ancestor had an African name, Akee, at the time of Colonel Eskridge's death and was listed as one of his estate slaves. The book explains how Akee's lineage came down to me. I fully enjoyed this experience of researching two families, mine and Richard Eskridge's. I met new relatives and made new friends. In both families. I hope other families who are made up of more than one race will embrace the history of those cultures.  Only by understanding the wounds of the past can tomorrow be healed.

Regarding the several African words mentioned in the book, these were taken from the Kru and Akan languages.  Of special note is the Kru word "Nyeswa" and the Akan word "Onyankopan," their words for "God."  I found it very interesting that despite their belief in many gods, these two words are set aside only in relation to "a Great Supreme God," or "the God Who Alone Is the Great One," hence, a single, monotheistic Creator.  It also struck me that the Kru hold the belief, too, that God has a chief "spirit" adversary known as "the devil."

The Akee fruit in Africa and Jamaica cannot be eaten without first removing the poisonous aril.  It is said that even the parrots there know this.  This book also represents that tree's fruit in that we, too, must deeply remove all poison inside us as a people in order to move beyond trying to define race.  We should not forget that we're all related.  We're all the human race.

Let's hope we know more than the parrots.

ABOUT THE AUTHOR

Stephen Hanks is a research specialist in African-American Genealogy, and has conducted family search consultations for clients across the country since 1994.  The name of his research service is Genealogical Networking Services, which has also aided persons who were adopted to reunite with their biological family.  Stephen Hanks' research for his book took ten years.

He lives with his wife in Portland, Oregon.